RECOVERY FROM GASLIGHTING & NARCISSISTIC ABUSE, CODEPENDENCY & COMPLEX PTSD (3 IN 1)

EMOTIONAL ABUSE, PEOPLE-PLEASING AND TRAUMA VS. EMOTIONAL REGULATION, MINDFULNESS, INDEPENDENCE AND SELF-CARING

DON BARLOW

A ROADTOTRANQUILITY BOOK

CONTENTS

GASLIGHTING & NARCISSISTIC ABUSE RECOVERY

Introduction	9
1. The Narcissist's Playbook	17
2. What Is Gaslighting?	38
3. The Stages of Gaslighting	55
4. Gaslighting in Other Relationships	66
5. The Impact of Gaslighting	96
6. How to Fight Back	117
7. Recovering from Abuse	147
Final Words	171
Discussion Section	179
Sources	191

THE CODEPENDENCY RECOVERY BLUEPRINT

Introduction	199
1. Codependency, Not Clinginess	205
2. Where Does Codependency Come From?	234
3. What Does Codependency Look Like?	255
4. The Stages of Codependency	276
5. Looking for a Lifeline	283
6. Rewriting Your Life Story	310
7. The Road to Recovery	327
Final Thoughts	377
Sources	381
Suggested Recommendations	385

RECOVERY FROM COMPLEX PTSD

Introduction	389
1. What Is Complex Trauma?	397
2. Where Does C-PTSD Come From?	413
3. Symptoms of PTSD	442
4. Affect Dysregulation	470
5. Negative Self-Concept	493
6. Disturbed Interpersonal Relationships	531
7. Recovering and Reclaiming Your Identity	555
Final Words	585
Notes	589

© **Copyright 2021 - All rights reserved.**

The content contained within this book may not be reproduced, duplicated or transmitted without direct written permission from the author or the publisher.

Under no circumstances will any blame or legal responsibility be held against the publisher, or author, for any damages, reparation, or monetary loss due to the information contained within this book, either directly or indirectly.

Legal Notice:

This book is copyright protected. It is only for personal use. You cannot amend, distribute, sell, use, quote or paraphrase any part, or the content within this book, without the consent of the author or publisher.

Disclaimer Notice:

Please note the information contained within this document is for educational and entertainment purposes only. All effort has been executed to present accurate, up to date, reliable, complete information. No warranties of any kind are declared or implied. Readers acknowledge that the author is not engaged in the rendering of legal, financial, medical or professional advice. The content within this book has been derived from various sources. Please consult a licensed professional before attempting any techniques outlined in this book.

By reading this document, the reader agrees that under no circumstances is the author responsible for any losses, direct or indirect, that are incurred as a result of the use of the information contained within this document, including, but not limited to, errors, omissions, or inaccuracies.

Before we get into the book, let me offer you a free mini-book. Scan this QR code to claim your FREE People-Pleasing No More mini-book!

GASLIGHTING & NARCISSISTIC ABUSE RECOVERY

RECOVER FROM EMOTIONAL ABUSE,
RECOGNIZE NARCISSISTS & MANIPULATORS
AND BREAK FREE ONCE AND FOR ALL

INTRODUCTION

When I was four years old, I loved preschool. For the first time in my young life, I could stand up and share something about myself without my teacher or classmates rolling their eyes in response to my enthusiasm.

"This is my new truck," I told them one time. "I love it because it rolls really fast and it's a nice blue."

I stared in awe as they leaned forward, nodded in agreement. It was definitely a nice blue.

Then I went home, and everything changed. There, if I wanted to talk about myself, I had to pay the price.

Mom made sure to trip over my beloved truck, despite how I'd deliberately placed it well out of her way. I knew better than to play in the living room or kitchen.

"Why is this here!?" she'd roar. I would try to tell her it was next to the toy box—which was where I played—but my answer would always be stomped on... like so many of my other beloved toys.

"I don't want to hear your ridiculous excuses! I could have broken my neck." Then she'd stomp off to the kitchen, pour herself another cup of coffee, and talk on the phone for the rest of the day. As far as she was concerned, our minor tiff was all the parenting I required as a child.

Whenever I lived these moments, they ripped my heart out. It seemed that no matter how hard I tried to be good—to play quietly and earn praise—all I ended up doing instead was causing trouble.

My presence seemed to put my mother on edge, and rather than defend his son, my father would always side with my mother, leaning into her dramatics as if her opinion mattered far more than my development.

All of this fighting and stress made me develop ulcers at ten and acid reflux at 13, and it also inspired me to run away at 17. It wasn't until my parents stopped taking up all the space in my life that I could finally take a moment to breathe.

Their constant pressure and demands felt so normal to me at the time though that once I got away from them, it was like landing on another planet. Suddenly, I could take up space, say what I wanted, forget to wash a dish, and even express an opinion. Those first few weeks on my own gave me so much freedom that I nearly fainted from happiness.

I chose to study psychology in school. I'd always loved my classes, but after years of assurance from Mom and Dad that I wasn't "college material," it took a big mental leap to walk through the double doors of the university. However, I managed to push, and they opened to a wonderful world where people and their actions came with a science behind them.

I spent five years studying the logic behind emotional manipulation, verbal abuse, and their effects on our wellbeing and ability to have healthy relationships. I also learned the proper term for people like my mom and dad: *narcissists*.

During my studies, I met and dated several lovely young women. However, I noticed something odd—I seemed drawn to women who made me doubt what I knew to be true. All of my exes seemed to follow a script; I would meet them and feel enchanted by how they laughed or tossed their hair, their extreme intelligence, and how they had a clear passion for their chosen fields.

Then, I'd spend some time with them and hear an off-hand comment made about someone else, but only in private. One of my partners confided that she "wished that her professor had her [my partner's] brains," which I found strange. The class she referred to was a lecture packed with hundreds of undergrads; it would have been a shock if her professor knew her name at all.

It went downhill from there. Fights over what I thought were simple misunderstandings or miscommunications would escalate into accusations of "you never loved me!" or something on that level. It would be up to me to grovel and beg for forgiveness, which was doled out in the smallest pieces you can imagine.

Finally, a female friend of mine named Connie pulled me aside one day for a coffee. We got into one of those deep, hours-long conversations that is so easy to have on a college campus.

"Listen, you need to reconcile your patterns. You're dating your mother over and over again," she told me.

"What?" I countered, the blood draining from my face. "How can you say that?"

She shrugged. "Hey, it's what you know. It's how you were raised. When you see that spark of narcissism in a woman, you run right to her. Trust me, I've seen you do it." She took a long drink from her latte as I stared at her. "We all do it; we stick to what's familiar to us. When that happens, we have to break down our habits so we can leave them behind. It's the only way to move forward."

I left Connie that evening with my heart pounding. Was she right? Was I stuck in a loop of bad relationships because some sick part of me *wanted* them?

That conversation changed my life. It inspired me to write my dissertation on dating patterns and their parallels to our parents. A large group of incredible people offered to let me interview them and dig deeper into how they dated and fell in love. The experience opened my understanding up in ways I never imagined.

To me, everyone's patterns seemed crystal clear. Student X was raised by Parent Y who had a specific personality, and then Student X would go on to date others with the same traits as Parent Y. Yet, the people I interviewed disagreed with me whenever I pointed out that fact. They'd insist that their last relationship was a left turn from their norm; there were other reasons it didn't work out.

The saddest moment of my study came when I saw how few people who dated narcissists realized they were in a highly manipulative relationship. They described their partners as "really funny" or "so smart," despite how bad they felt in that person's company.

After I graduated, I kept in touch with many of those same people who helped me get my Masters. Most of them eventually got married, and many of those who were partners to hardened narcissists got divorced. It wasn't until the dust settled on their messy legal battles and screaming matches in the front yard that they finally looked themselves in the mirror and asked, "what was I thinking?"

Manipulative relationships are impossible to see from the inside, yet when we find ourselves in one, we can still sense that something is wrong. Every time we try to pin down what exactly could be the issue, we're quickly assured by our partner that we're way off. This could be thanks to a sudden rush of sweetness or a big fight in which we find ourselves apologizing, though we're not quite sure why we're the sorry ones.

That's why I decided to write this book. I wanted to help people who got lost in that bad relationship fog that makes love impossible to navigate. Healthy relationships are a constant give and take—a kind of cooperative dance. However, unhealthy relationships can disguise themselves as passion, drama, and even a state of balance. It's only with the right vocabulary and mental tools that we can escape the illusion and see the truth: that we're being used to feed our partner's ego.

I approached this book with hope for anyone feeling a low self-esteem, loss of who they are, or inability to express themselves or grow as a person from being part of a bad relationship. As someone who felt caught in the same trap many times myself, I come from a place of empathy and understanding. These situations are no one's fault, and we always have a way out. No one is trapped or obligated to stay in a destructive relationship.

To help you get away from the person claiming to love you while they slowly destroy you, I outline several ways to recognize toxic behavior and how to respond to it. I also look into the psychology behind narcissism, gaslighting tactics, and why some people feel the need to do these things, even though it doesn't benefit them in the long run. Then, we'll get into how you can care for yourself, create a safe space for yourself, and why you must prioritize your mental health.

It's my goal to get you to a mental space that feels confident and sure enough to help you walk away from a bad partner—not fix or change anyone. No one needs fixing; we all need to live a life that makes us happy and confident. I'm guessing that if you picked up this book, you're not feeling either of those things right now. Don't worry, you will, but you have to do the work.

I've worked with hundreds of people who felt tied to someone or stuck in a rut that kept them from entering a good, balanced relationship. Each of us is unique and has our own needs, but I've found that there are some fundamental things a victim of narcissism can do to better their life. I want to share these tactics with you and help you move forward. You deserve happiness and love.

This book will help you understand your partner and yourself better, identify the problem you are having, and what you need to be happy. It will also help you stand up to whoever is making you feel devalued. Are you ready to leave but can't seem to make yourself stand up and walk out the door? I'm here to help.

Spare yourself the long-term hate and negativity that can fester if you choose to ignore the problem and stay in this relationship. It won't get better and your partner will not change. You can change, but you have to decide that you're ready and willing to do something different. Maybe the narcissist in your life isn't someone you can break up with —it could be a parent, sibling, or even a boss. Maybe it's your nearest and dearest friend. Whoever is making you question your worth, it's time to turn the tables and feel amazing about your talents, your character, and what you contribute to the world.

Narcissists win when we feel small. It's time for you and your self-worth to fill up the universe.

Keep reading to learn more about how you can change your situation. Today is your day.

You deserve it.

1

THE NARCISSIST'S PLAYBOOK

Let's start off with a simple question: what is a narcissist? Narcissism is a personality. A narcissist exhibits traits that send a singular message: "I come first." This person might manipulate those around them, tell lies, deny saying or doing anything that could cause potential embarrassment, or be abusive.

It also occurs on a spectrum. That means you might recognize certain narcissistic traits in many people but only see extreme examples here and there. Self-assurance and a high confidence can help us as we go through life. We can get more jobs if we appear put together and sure of ourselves. Confident teachers can influence their students to pay closer attention in class and score higher on tests. A little narcissism can go a long way.

Traits like self-assurance and self-admiration can easily get out of control. I'm certain you've met a narcissist many times yourself and saw it right away.

Maybe someone at a party wanted to be your best friend one minute, and then seemed to forget you the moment someone who seemed "better" came along. Perhaps you've had someone offer to help you out with a project, only to conveniently forget about it the day you're scheduled to meet. You might have a coworker who takes credit for others' ideas or whom you know better than to trust.

Psychologists characterize narcissism by their grandiose sense of self-importance, a lack of caring or empathy for others, need for endless admiration, and a belief that they hold some special place in the world and should be recognized as a unique and beautiful creature.

A grandiose sense of self doesn't sound terrible on the surface, but it can manifest in ways we don't expect. I can give my own personal example—a couple friends of mine from university kept in touch with a guy named Scott they studied with in forestry class. The three of them lived in different states but kept in touch using an online group chat, all making sure to check in on each other from time to time.

Without warning, Scott dumped his two friends. He sat down and wrote them each a long, formal letter to inform them that he would no longer allow them to hold him back. They'd done enough damage, and he planned to move on. Scott asked them not to contact or attempt to make up with him. He couldn't handle them and their toxic energy anymore.

My two friends told me this story with smiles on their faces, though the circumstances disturbed me deeply. I'd known Scott in school, but we never had classes together. Instead, I'd see him at parties, pulling out his poetry and insisting everyone listen while he read one out loud. I made the mistake of listening to a piece so bad I audibly groaned. Everyone looked at me like I was insane, but hey—that poem stank.

So, Scott dumped two old school friends. Who cares? Well, I did. I saw some disturbing stuff in his decision to write those letters.

First, the three of them weren't close. They only got together for a beer a few times a year, and they jumped on a video conference even less often. This was a low-stakes relationship that no one lost sleep over.

Second, there was no need for a letter. All Scott had to do was politely turn down the next invitation he received to meet his friends. We've all done it—we find some flimsy excuse to sit at home and binge a show instead of braving the outside world. Why was Scott unable to find some excuse to sit out the next round of drinks?

Finally, the wording of the letters spoke volumes about Scott's worldview. He mentioned that his "time was valuable" and he couldn't "bend to the will of others" anymore. He seemed to think that he needed to take a stand and assert himself with two people who didn't need anything like this from him if he wanted to part ways.

Scott's behavior aligns perfectly with a test created by Robert Raskin and Calvin S. Hall back in the late seventies. It is known as the Narcissistic Personality Inventory (NPI). I can almost hear Scott saying some of the phrases present on the test.

"I find it easy to manipulate people."

"I usually get the respect that I deserve."

That letter was Scott's NPI, and he scored off the charts.

We should be able to spot a narcissist a mile away, right? Not necessarily. Narcissists never lead with the bad stuff; rather, they pull us in by lavishing us with attention and compliments. They offer a fun, edgy friendship or an opportunity to try something new. They tell us they feel connected to us more than they do to anyone else.

Narcissism can be anywhere from mild to out of control. You likely know someone who's generally a great person but does one or two things that boggle or bother you.

Connie, my truth-telling friend from the introduction, had a girlfriend who needed everyone to tell her she was intelligent. If she didn't hear it on a regular basis, she'd start quoting literature or casually dropping into casual conversation how she spoke four languages. Whenever someone was taken aback by her knowledge of ancient history and commented on how smart she was, this friend glowed.

It made her day.

Sure, it drove Connie bonkers that her friend needed so much positive reinforcement. They even fought about it a few times when Connie felt her friend crossed a line, making others feel dumb so they'd see her as mentally superior. However, for the most part, they still stayed friends.

"I know it's a narcissistic trait," she admitted to me once, "but the same narcissism makes her a fun friend. There's no one else I'd rather have on my side in a debate or hang out with at a party."

Now, Connie made sure not to bring this girl to her wedding party when she married her partner, but she was still among the guests.

I like to think of lower-level narcissists this way—be honest with yourself and don't make them a best man or maid-of-honor. But hey, you can still invite them to the wedding. They'll always jump up and dance.

That same level of fun and excitement makes narcissists easy to forgive and hard to spot, particularly when we choose them as partners. They almost completely blur our vision once we get too close. It's not until we've spent a long time by their side that our view will begin to sharpen. Sometimes that clear, unhindered view shows us that we've made a terrible mistake.

Narcissists at the high end of the spectrum can have a disorder known as Narcissistic Personality Disorder, (NPD). It is a personality disorder, meaning that it is a mentality that keeps the person from functioning normally. About one in 2000 people have it, and the majority identify as males; however, women can still have it, (I know better than anyone they absolutely can), it's just less common.

Think back to some of the coworkers you had in your current or past job. Do you remember anyone who seemed so charming and witty in a meeting, but also got completely put off when asked to do something menial like making copies? Maybe this person got disgusted if anyone interrupted them, even if it was an accident. You probably saw them get incredibly angry because they had to turn in a standard form that they forgot and railed about it for hours.

I hear tons of stories about people whom I suspect are clear cases of NPD. These people rarely get fired from their jobs. They stomp out with their heads thrown back and the doors wide open, so the whole world can see that your boss just made a big mistake.

That need for tension, drama, and attention keep those with NPD from living a normal life. Friendships become tests to see if the other party is devoted enough—can grovel hard enough—for the NPD's approval. Every job interview is a farce—everyone knows that the one with NPD is the smartest person in the building, and this company would be lucky to have them.

This obsession with themselves drives friends, family, and opportunities away regularly. Who can blame anyone for walking away from a person who finds their own reflection to be the most interesting person in the room?

The sad thing is that these people have a mental illness. NPD is one of ten personality disorders, and its nature makes those who suffer from NPD laugh at suggestions of therapy. I'm certain a high-test score could sway a few of them, but the majority simply can't imagine allowing someone else to scrutinize their life.

Narcissists have to stay in control if they want to keep the fantasy of their power and influence alive. Once that person is diagnosed, the control goes to the score—the adjudicator. To a person with NPD, that's a living nightmare.

It's a shame because those with this disorder stand to gain so much from proper treatment. Imagine if that confidence and intelligence could go toward something positive—it would be mind-boggling!

I want to break down the general traits of a narcissist. I imagine you bought this book because you already know you're living with one, but if you're uncertain, here's a quick rundown of clear giveaways.

EXPECTATIONS

More than anything, a narcissist expects you to treat them as if they're special. Don't ever assume they can manage driving through traffic. No—they must be alerted hours ahead of time, so they can make an intelligent detour and leave the gridlock to the plebians. It's your fault if they're late on that detour.

As you've probably noticed with this example, you'll find that narcissists have near-impossible standards. They'll expect everyone around them to work much harder and faster to ensure their comfort and give them a day free of friction. Anyone who lets them down will hear about it, usually at full volume.

One of my research volunteers told me about a boss she had who seethed anytime someone included the "I emailed you that already" message. He felt he shouldn't waste a moment digging through old emails, even if they were only from that morning.

"I got my butt handed to me last week because he asked for something I'd sent over and over. I resent it once, only to receive the same, 'Where's that email?' message from him again. I told him, 'You have it. I just sent it to you.' He marched over to my desk and publicly lectured me about my unprofessional behavior and unwillingness to be a team player.

"I just stared at him with my mouth open. All this because I mentioned he already had something in his inbox? I couldn't quit fast enough."

That boss' behavior reflects a narcissist's worldview perfectly. You don't tell me where something is—you bring it to me. Now. The public lecture and humiliation is another tactic we'll explore in depth later in this book.

EXAGGERATION

A narcissist looks in the mirror and sees someone special. There, in the glass, is the world's smartest, handsomest, and most influential person.

To the mind of an extreme narcissist, it's a true tragedy that they're yet to be famous and are still undiscovered. If only the world knew what it was missing!

In reality, most narcissists are smart, though not exceptional. Sure, they went to school and got a degree—the whole song and dance. But they see those accomplishments as hard proof that they're more special than you and everyone else around them.

Any narcissist confronted with the truth—that they're smart but not necessarily a *genius*—would crumble at the facts. Narcissists need their facades. They protect them from the real world and keep vulnerability at a distance.

MANIPULATION

One of the things that makes a person with NPD so dangerous is their willingness to use people. A high-scoring narcissist finds it very amusing when someone does as they command. They might talk someone out of applying for a promotion or into missing an opportunity to date their crush.

A narcissist does this because it gives them a boost of confidence. Unfortunately, it's a false confidence that will leave them feeling empty shortly after, so they have to do it again at the first opportunity.

This happens so consistently that most narcissists become professional manipulators. They can get most people to do just about anything, all while also making them believe it was their choice. It's also why someone with this personality disorder scares us—someone who can convince us to do any number of things could make us break the law or lie to a person we love. They can make us unlock the door when it should stay closed and barricaded.

Manipulation deserves to be taken seriously, and it's something we have to learn to recognize and stop in its tracks as soon as possible.

THIN-SKINNED

The trait that made me want to study NPD and those who suffer from it was their sensitivity.

At first glance, it seems out of place. After all, these are people who get others to do whatever they say, constantly tell themselves they're special, and demand compliments. With that hard work, it would seem impossible that their feelings could ever get hurt.

Oh, but they do. There is no one more sensitive or quick to injure than a true narcissist.

It makes sense once you see their confidence and self-assuredness as it is: a thin veneer draped over constant self-doubt. It's so thin that any level of criticism or attempt to stand up to them is instantly met with rage. They can lash out in a nanosecond, and their aim is precise.

The reason narcissists work so hard for special treatment—for pedestals to stand on and adoring fans—is their insecurity. They can't stand themselves without all of those props and an audience ready to jump to their feet in a standing ovation.

A narcissist alone is a person in deep self-hate and true sadness.

Don't believe me? Try calling the narcissist in your life insecure. Then, you can stand back and watch the fireworks.

WHAT MOTIVATES A NARCISSIST?

Why all this hard work to feel just a little bit special or smarter than the average person? Why do narcissists push day and night to get what they want?

A narcissist's deepest motive is never letting anyone know how insecure they feel. That's a terrible secret that they work day and night to keep hidden. So, most of what a narcissist would say or do is often geared toward hiding that side of themselves.

Narcissists also work hard to look good on every level. They might spend hours in a gym to keep a trim waistline or defined muscles. Or, they might spend far too much on clothes and accessories. Hair care is non-negotiable; they want to stand out everywhere they go.

My friend, Angie, remembers seeing her father in a department store, grabbing fancy shirts and piling them onto his arm.

"He had so many he could roll them up into a colorful log. He carried them up to pay and my mom stopped him, explaining that there was no way we could afford the massive amount of clothes he was hauling. He *lost* it! He had to have every single one of those shirts, no compromise.

"Luckily, my mom put her foot down. Us kids needed school clothes and supplies, meaning those came first. My dad stormed out and sat in the car while us kids got a few outfits each. He fumed all the way home.

"I was little, but even then, I thought, 'Wow, my dad just had a tantrum.'"

Angie's father's need to buy excessive amounts of fancy clothes is a perfect example of the narcissist's constant maintenance on his self-image. That work extends into how others perceive them. Narcissists want to be respected, even revered, whenever possible. If a narcissist is a decent guitar player, for example, they'll keep their guitar out where any visitors might see it and take every chance to play it or talk about their talent. If they're in a band, they'll want tons of solos so the audience can shriek with joy as they play.

Attention is a narcissist's bread and butter. They won't do anything if no one will see them. Why help someone if no one is looking? Why get a job with no opportunity for recognition? No, the narcissist wants to ensure that they have an audience, even a small one, before they do you a favor or put in any extra effort at the office.

Once a narcissist gets eyes and ears on their actions and words, they start to feel worthy of the praise. Without it, their guarded insecurities surface, and they'll do anything to beat it back down.

All of this affects how a narcissist relates to others. Their relationships exist to make them look good and no one else. Their thin veneer of false self-confidence can come crumbling down at any moment, and they *have* to be in complete control of their date or partner.

That means the narcissist has to assert themselves in small ways and keep anyone close to them in check. Imagine you're on a date with a narcissist and they mispronounce a word on the menu. Say they accidentally say, "monster cheese" when they meant to say "muenster." It happens, right? You politely correct them with a casual, "Actually that's 'muenster.' It's delicious. You should try it."

In your mind, you might give this all of two seconds of thought. To a narcissist, this is all part of your evil plot.

The narcissist sees the world as a place filled with landmines and enemies. Moments like the cheese incident are proof that everyone around them is dying to laugh in their face and idiocy. The whole world wants them to be wrong and wrong constantly.

Although a balanced person wouldn't give your comment much attention, a narcissist will be completely unable to let it go. They'll look for any opportunity to shoot you down through the rest of dinner. They'll silently beg you to mispronounce something, then tear your confidence to shreds. As far as they're concerned, it's all fair game. After all, you started it.

Narcissists rarely consider the long-term consequences of their actions, particularly when they have to do with others' emotions. If your date ends with you in tears, the narcissist won't give it too much thought. The important thing is that they're right and left feeling good about themselves. If you can't control your emotions, well, that's not their problem.

If a statement like this drives you away and makes you never want to spend another moment with your former date, they still won't feel bad about their actions. Rather, they'll see you as someone they managed to escape—that horrible person who tried to embarrass them in a restaurant.

Ask them for a conversation about the incident, and they'll do everything they can to avoid it. No narcissist wants to develop their introspection. That's a terrifying notion to most of them because one look inside will show them how much fear they carry inside. They're not a swaggering, good-looking superstar; they're a trembling child desperate to be loved. One glance might be all that true self needs to come out.

To keep from looking inside, narcissists will do anything they can to sidestep boredom. They want to be surrounded by people, constantly on adventures, and on the hunt for the next big thing. This can make a narcissist a lot of fun to hang out with on a Friday night, but a nightmare on Saturday morning when all you want to do is sleep, and your narcissist friend is bounding around your apartment, looking for something to do.

A narcissist can be a great friend as long as they see you as someone who will get them what they want. Most narcissists see their social group, romantic partners, or family members as special tools to unlock the life they want. And narcissists always want; they're never satisfied.

Controlling people is a 24-hour job, so they will use a set of tactics to keep everyone around them working toward the narcissist's goals.

THE NARCISSIST'S TACTICS

A narcissist works hard to make sure anyone close to them doesn't have their own interests or identity. If that happens, those people might forget to work on making them comfortable, giving them attention, and making them feel valued. Any sign that a partner or close friend has other things to do besides shower the narcissist with their attention and energy is dangerous and has to be shut down immediately.

The moment someone close to them needs to go to a special event, requires time alone, or wants to pursue a creative hobby like swing dancing or oil painting, the narcissist starts to get nervous.

They see that time and energy put into those activities or spent on your own as a threat to their delicate veneer of happiness. Thus, they'll start to make threats. These threats can be covert, disguised as something else like a request or concern, or overt, as in, you're doing this to avoid me.

I had this issue with my own girlfriends on many occasions. One partner—Jan—seemed particularly put off by my study group. She insisted that one of the girls there had a "major crush" on me, and my attending was proof that I wanted to mislead the poor girl into thinking I loved her.

"Nothing like that is happening," I explained in my calmest voice. "We have a test coming up and I need to study. That's all."

Nope, not good enough—once her original threat didn't hold, she resorted to another move straight out of the narcissist's playbook: name-calling.

"You are such a needy little prick," she hissed at me. I felt so shocked that I staggered back a bit. Needy? For wanting to study for a test? At the time, I felt genuinely confused and made the mistake of fighting back, which was exactly what she wanted.

That name-calling tactic has a goal: narcissists want the people around them to abandon their personal lives, separate identities, and sense of self-worth by arguing with them. If we're busy fighting with our partner or family member about their image of us, we're not out living our lives. The point goes to the narcissist.

Narcissists also keep us in check by making sure we never *quite* meet their standards. Every attempt we make is picked apart and held up as proof that we don't really love our partner or value our friend. No, nothing is good enough, and the narcissist will make sure you know that at every opportunity.

You'll see it when you give a narcissist a gift. Rather than a genuine, "thank you!" you'll be more likely to get a sniffed, "oh, great," or something similar. Later, you'll see the present abandoned on a table and have to hear about how you should know better than to give them something blue/antique/cheap etc. Don't you know them at all?

This constant beat down of your judgment and ability to make choices keeps your sense of self-worth low. It ensures you'll work harder to prove your love and adoration of the narcissist at every opportunity, while abandoning any other interests you had before.

Of course, all that work to prove you are on the narcissist's side will amount to nothing. Once a narcissist has someone hooked, they will keep them wriggling with blanket statements about their character.

After I skipped my study session and barely got a C on my exam, Jan made sure to let me know that I "didn't take responsibility for anything," and "could never concentrate on tests." I took that hard. School was my first joy, and it hurt terribly to hear someone whittle me down to a bad student who didn't understand that studies were important.

The comment made me evaluate my relationship with Jan. I'll take a lot from a partner, but get between me and my education, and we have a problem. The afternoon I received my test score, I mumbled some excuse about needing to get back to my place, and then avoided her calls for the next couple of days.

On day three, I got a knock on my door—it was my friend Trent from my cognitive psychology class. I was shocked to see him, since Trent and I never hung out at my place. I waved him in anyway.

"What brings you here?"

"Um," Trent blushed and looked down at the carpet. "Jan asked me to come check on you? To see if you're okay? I don't know. She made it sound like you were super depressed or something."

I assured Trent that I did not have any symptoms of depression. What I had was a girlfriend who kept me from studying and earned me a low C in a class where I desperately needed the A. Trent and I hung out at a nearby bar and talked it all over. It appeared she'd gotten a third person involved in an attempt to make me prove not just to her, but to everyone else too that I was in a healthy, happy relationship.

This move is called triangulation. Jan's claim that I was "depressed", and she was "worried" about me were meant to make me worry that perhaps I wasn't feeling quite right. Narcissists love making their partners or family members question their own sanity. It puts the narcissist right in the driver's seat and makes them look like a saint for being concerned in the first place.

Jan's attempt at getting me to run back to her backfired. Like me, Trent studied human behavior and encouraged me to end it with my girlfriend.

"It's concerning that she had no problem getting me involved," he told me over our third beer. "And your reluctance to call her and make up? That's all the proof I need that it's over between you two."

I agreed and decided to do the hard thing: go to Jan's place and break up with her. I knew she'd have a million tricks up her sleeve to keep the breakup from happening, but I also knew it had to happen.

I arrived at Jan's place the next day. She answered the door with no makeup on and her hair pulled back into a simple ponytail.

"Where have you been? I called you so many times."

I didn't answer. Instead, I laid out the breakup. Our relationship was not working, and I wanted out. Jan cried delicate, tiny tears and made little, sad sniffs.

"You're the best thing that ever happened to me," she said. "You're so handsome and smart. You're the most intelligent guy I know. And I love how you…"

She went on and on about all of my great qualities, a list I would have loved to hear during the actual relationship. At the moment, I saw her efforts to win me back as what they were: a love bomb.

Narcissists use love bombs as a way to make us feel lifted up and special in their eyes. How could you leave me? I adore you!

This happens when we first meet a narcissist who wants us in their lives, romantically or otherwise. It also happens when we take the reins and try to regain control once we see the relationship is toxic and hurting us more than helping.

Luckily for me, I was so fed up with Jan and our rollercoaster of a relationship that her love-bombing didn't work. I repeated myself, "I'm done. We're through," and walked away. She didn't call me after that, but she did make sure to parade her new boyfriend around the next day so I could see that she'd moved on.

Jan's attempt to love-bomb me during the breakup made me roll my eyes a bit. All the things she'd criticized only days before had apparently melted away, and suddenly I was the perfect man. What happened to all of my faults?

The love bomb both reaffirms and depletes the relationship. Once it detonates, it spins around the victim, leaving the poor recipient trapped in conflicting messages and dizzy with confusion. A love bomb tells you that you are loved, yet leaves you sore with injuries and makes your ears ring from all the noise. It's meant to get you back to the beginning of the relationship, so you'll bend over backwards to make the narcissist happy.

Other narcissist tactics include word salad and projection. They often blend together in an attempt to exhaust a family member or partner into throwing their hands into the air and forfeiting the fight. Instead of talking about the issue at hand, the narcissist will throw any and all topics into the fray, desperate to distract the other party into forgetting the real problem. Tossed into the mix will be phrases like "You're so mean!" or "Why are you so insecure?"

Remember that narcissists love to make others doubt their reality at every opportunity. Once your motives and actions are called into question, you'll either defend yourself or question your reality. That's a big win for a narcissist.

The tactic I want to delve into the most throughout this book is gaslighting.

Gaslighting is a common move meant to throw the spotlight on an innocent person and works to erode that individual's sanity. It's a horrible, insidious play, and if you don't know how to recognize it, you can easily fall prey to its effects.

Gaslighting happens all too often and can eat away at your self-esteem long after you've removed yourself from a dangerous situation. As a victim of razor-sharp gaslighting myself, I want to help you avoid or heal from this mental attack and become a stronger, more self-assured person.

But first, we need to investigate what gaslighting is and how it pulls us apart.

CHAPTER SUMMARY

You're on your way to a healthy understanding of narcissism and how to keep it at arm's length. Here's what we have covered so far:

- People with narcissistic traits fall on a spectrum.
- A person with narcissistic tendencies isn't necessarily dangerous.
- Narcissistic Personality Disorder (NPD) keeps a person from living a full life and functioning properly in society.

In the next chapter, we'll look closer at how a narcissist gaslights people and keeps them under their control.

2

WHAT IS GASLIGHTING?

The term "gaslighting" comes from a 1930's hit play adapted into a couple of movies, the most famous one being *Gaslight*. In it, a beautiful Ingrid Bergman falls victim to the handsome Charles Boyer, who plays a narcissist with a rather chilling precision that will make your skin crawl.

Charles' character Gregory meets and romances the beautiful opera singer Paula. He marries her after just two weeks of non-stop wooing, and then moves her into an old, abandoned house in London. However, Gregory is secretly a killer and has to ensure that Paula never finds out about his past.

To do this, he convinces her that she's going insane. A brooch disappears from her bag, and then a picture vanishes from the wall. Beyond that even, his favorite trick is to make the flames in the house's *gas lights* dim and brighten seemingly by magic.

Whenever Paula would say something, Gregory would insist he saw nothing with the lights, adding that things are disappearing thanks to her bizarre tendency to steal and hide precious objects. As a result, Paula starts to wonder if she is crazy—she can't remember taking anything and can't explain what she's seen.

I won't spoil the ending here, but I'm certain that you can see some classic narcissist moves in Gregory from that brief summary. I've seen the movie once out of curiosity, but I doubt I'll sit through it again. Although it is a stunning film and definitely worth a watch, I found it horribly triggering.

Gregory's stance, hard stare, and constant insistence that poor Paula was losing her mind all set my teeth on edge. It felt horribly familiar, particularly the gaslighting on Gregory's part. Let's get into it.

WHAT IS GASLIGHTING?

I want to clarify that gaslighting is abuse. It is an emotional and psychological beating that can leave a victim scarred and uncertain of their own reality for years to come. I don't want you to fall into or stay in the terrible cycle of gaslighting because it can do horrible things to your stress level, fear, anxiety, and sanity.

Someone who gaslights another person, such as a child, partner, or family member, wants to make that person question their sanity, memories, or perception of reality. Like Gregory playing with the lights or making objects disappear, it's a ploy to make a person feel powerless in the world and their relationship. A successful attempt at gaslighting ends with one person telling the other what's real, what their opinion should be, and what they remember. Let someone gaslight you long enough, and you'll atrophy into a kind of zombie bumping around in the world.

Plenty of people with NPD use gaslighting to keep their partners and those close to them wondering if they did in fact say or do something awful, but it's not their only move. Gaslighting is one of many ways a person with NPD will control others around them, though it is a good sign that a person is not someone you should get close to romantically.

The reason I feel so strongly about gaslighting and worked so hard in my career to help people see it is because it's a weapon. This thing causes damage, but it also violates the love and trust you've given to your partner or friend. It looks at your affection and sees a chance to twist it into a shiv that can cut you deeply and leave you bleeding for years, wondering where it all went wrong.

Gaslighting can be hard to recognize and even harder to name because it comes from someone we love. A stranger or new acquaintance doesn't know enough about us to truly get into our psyche. No, it's the ones we hold dear and stand beside who take advantage of our love.

One of my study subjects, Renee, had a boyfriend whom she'd dated since she was 16. She adored him, although she admitted he "had a temper."

"He got mad at me the other night about something," she told me. "But honestly, I completely overreacted and made a fool of myself in the restaurant." When I pressed for details, Renee seemed reluctant to tell me what her long-time boyfriend had done. Finally, after some gentle probing, I got her to admit that he'd insulted her weight, (despite her not being heavy), and made her feel ugly. The moment she got understandably upset at the insult, he informed her she was making a scene and insisted they leave. He stormed out as Renee quickly paid the bill for a meal they didn't even get a chance to eat.

"But we're fine now," she assured me. I asked a couple of questions about how they were suddenly fine. Had they discussed the argument and reached a compromise? The question made Renee look at me like I had switched from English to Latin.

"We're just, you know…" She shrugged. "Fine."

Renee's date insisting her getting emotional over something that most of us would take to heart is a common aspect of gaslighting. Any reaction, despite how nuanced or reasonable, is instantly labeled "crazy" or somehow over the line by a narcissist. The other's take on the situation, like being publicly insulted, is instantly negated.

I don't think Renee's boyfriend actually wanted her to lose any weight or rethink her diet. I think he saw her confidence growing and decided to shoot her down. I'm sorry to say he succeeded.

WHO BECOMES A GASLIGHTER?

Gaslighting tends to appear in people who have a personality disorder, and NPD in particular. However, it also appears in psychopaths, who are individuals that can't empathize with others.

We have to keep in mind that the person doing the gaslighting is hiding something. They aren't all necessarily secret criminals like

Gregory in the movie, but they each have a terrible secret. They're insecure, and some sick part of themselves believes that making someone who trusts and loves them feel terrible will build them up.

A practiced gaslighter has a public and a private face. I met Renee's boyfriend one day on my way to the library and chatted with him for a moment. He spoke with the ease and charm I found common among people with NPD. His hair had a nice wave in it, and he had pretty blue eyes. He treated me like someone he admired after a quick introduction, and I'm sure he would have kept up the facade if I'd hung out longer than I did.

However, I wasn't fooled. I knew for a fact that he treated Renee like dirt, despite her love for him. Like so many other manipulators, this guy felt the need to make sure that if Renee were ever to talk about the terrible things he did, she'd find herself faced with doubt.

To the mind of the narcissist, if they're nice to everyone else and only mean to their partner, the partner will have no one to turn to for help or support. Unfortunately, this tactic works quite often, though I find that now people tend to be more suspicious of overly charming people. We have enough evidence that the most beautiful and winning of those around us can also be the most dangerous, so attitudes are gradually shifting.

The more practiced gaslighters—the real pros—are the hardest to detect. They're extremely careful when in the company of anyone not close to them and make sure to be polite yet not lay it on too thick. They've struck a delicate balance that makes it much harder for anyone outside of their closest relationships to see their true selves.

Only their partners and families get to see the darkness they carry and often have no one to turn to for help.

WHY DO PEOPLE GASLIGHT OTHERS?

In order to understand this behavior, you have to step back and look at how gaslighting benefits that person who insists on treating others around them so terribly.

On a basic level, it helps them gain control. The person they've torn down will either question themselves, doubt something they know to be true, or leave. All scenarios are a win for the manipulator; the first two give them a willing participant whom they can continue to control, and the last gives them someone who sees their true personality out of their circle, allowing them to avoid accountability.

Over time, constant gaslighting creates codependency. Imagine every time someone asked you to do a math problem, and each time you worked it out, you got it wrong. After a while, you'd stop trying to solve math problems. Instead, you'd turn to someone else for help or guidance, certain you can't handle it on your own.

That's exactly what a gaslighter wants. They need you to see them as a guide through life, a professional to hold your hand as you stumble along. This experience makes the narcissist drunk with power. They will see themselves as a genius, able to string along partners so they will do whatever they say, whenever they give the command.

The high that comes with such an immense amount of control can be as addictive as alcohol or an opiate. Power makes people hungry for more power, even if they only wield it over one individual.

There's a radio story on the show *This American Life* called "Chip in My Brain," which fascinated me to no end. I listened to it over and over because it picked apart an instance of something called a one-on-one cult, which is an unusual occurrence. It happens when someone learns a few psychological tricks, then pulls them on an individual, convincing them that the leader is aware of a danger and happens to be the only person with the information to keep that member safe.

I won't go into the details of the story; I only mention it because the story's producer, David Kestenbaum, got the cult leader, a man in his thirties named A.J., to sit down for an interview. A.J. had recently been found guilty of intentional infliction of emotional distress in court and wasn't too happy about it. In the interview with the radio producer, A.J. gaslights like crazy.

Kestenbaum asked a direct question about A.J.'s religious beliefs, and A.J. would deflect in response. "Explain. I don't understand." Then, he redirected again. "Well, let me ask you about radios..." Over and over, A.J. refused to state what he believes or why he believes in it.

At every opportunity, A.J. would laugh out loud at a question, trying to make Kestenbaum feel stupid for even considering asking. But the producer held firm. He asked the question simply and directly. "What do you believe?" Unfortunately, he never really received an answer, but I expected A.J., a true manipulator, to refuse to state his beliefs plainly.

A.J. found young men as his easiest targets and did horrific, psychological damage to one in particular. The poor kid developed such a deep fear of demons and impending death that he missed out on a great trip to England. In college, he slept under his bed in the dorm; it made him feel safe to curl up in the tiny space.

It took years of therapy and endless love and patience from his family to bring him back to his normal self, but he still missed years of school and childhood happiness thanks to one ongoing gaslight session.

WOULD A NARCISSIST TARGET YOU?

If you're going to be on the lookout for others anxious to take advantage of your kind nature, you have to ask yourself about the qualities you have that might make you a prime target.

Consider how you talk about yourself. Do you have faith in yourself as a person, or do you put yourself down and insult yourself or your work? Do you have a hard time saying no to others, particularly if you see them as smarter, better looking, or better than you in general?

These habits can open our front door to dangerous people. When others hear us disrespecting ourselves, they see either a sad case or an opportunity to get what they want.

Other bad habits that can allow a gaslighter into your life include taking on too much or refusing to say no to someone who needs help, even if you have no time. The second action is a symptom of people-pleasing. It's a nice habit on the surface, but it's a rose-tinted view of a lack of self-respect. If you value yourself as a person, you value your time and self-care. When others see that you put yourself last, they'll follow your example.

Please don't misunderstand me—I am not blaming victims in any way. Rather, I want to alert you that some of your bad habits could attract toxic people. I want you to take care of yourself and keep yourself safe however you can.

We'll get deeper into how you can love yourself if you're in a bad situation or get out of one in a later chapter. For now, just know that you're a wonderful person and you deserve better.

Gaslighting Techniques

Withholding

Withholding references a narcissist's tendency to refuse to acknowledge another's emotions. It can also present itself as a refusal to listen.

You'll hear it in phrases like, "What do you mean?" or "You're not making any sense." These attempts to redirect the conversation get the narcissist's partner to focus on being clear rather than the actual problem.

Countering

Whenever you remember something clearly, but someone insists that thing never happened, you're experiencing a counter.

Remember the lights dimming and brightening in *Gaslight*. This move is intended to make the victim doubt her sanity and it often works. Modern versions of that move tend to focus on whether someone said or did something. A narcissist will insist you "never remember our conversations," or "it's only in your head."

I can remember constantly wishing for a stenographer or Dictaphone to have proof that what I remembered matched up with reality. If you've felt that way with anyone, you're dealing with someone who can counter masterfully.

Forgetting/Denial

A small step down from countering, the denial move helps a narcissist feel absolved of any responsibility.

This happens when a narcissist is reminded of a promise or held to their word. Suddenly, all memory of the narcissist's former commitment vanishes.

The phrase, "I never said that," will be on repeat for most narcissists.

My own mom perfected denial. One minute I was promised a day in the park, but when I asked about it, I'd be informed that I'd imagined the conversation. Worse, my mom could pretend not to hear me and refuse to address the question. As a little boy, it broke my heart.

When I was in middle school and desperately wanted to make friends, my mom would promise me an afternoon to myself. The moment I put on my shoes to meet up with other boys for a round of video games, she'd look at me and ask, "Where are you going?" I'd explain, only to be told that she'd never agreed to let me leave.

It didn't take long for me to learn to stop asking. Instead of telling my mom where I wanted to go and when, I'd avoid going home at all.

Instead, I'd go to a friend's place after school and hang out as long as they'd let me. By the time I got home, I had to face my furious mother, but at least I made friends.

Trivializing

I put this one on a higher level than many, but that's because I find it extremely dangerous. Trivializing happens any time someone minimizes how you feel.

A narcissist will tell you something like, "Oh, you got those ideas from your mom. You know she's nuts," or something along those lines.

Unlike countering, trivializing makes the recipient doubt if the narcissist is manipulating them, if maybe someone else is to blame. This kind of behavior keeps a lot of good people in terrible relationships, since they will start to see everyone who wants to help them as the true danger.

Don't underestimate this one; it can turn your life inside out.

Lying

In my book, there are two groups who can lie better than anyone: addicts and narcissists.

In both cases, the liar convinces everyone around them so well that anyone who hears them will start to question themselves and their versions of the truth.

This happens because the person telling the lie is terrified of the truth. Should they say even one honest word, they'll be ruined. Fear makes them dig their heels in and stand on the flimsy lie for years, no matter what gets proven. If they insist it's true, they'll pray and avoid rehab or facing their true, cowardly self.

Discrediting You to Others

I believe to discredit the same person you claim to love is the lowest move out there. A narcissist sees this incredibly underhanded play and thinks, "I can do that."

This is a long con. Your narcissist partner or relative will feign concern for you while dropping hints that you are "unstable" or calling you "crazy" to anyone in your personal network. This works as a defense in case you go to anyone for help.

In the narcissist's mind, your attempts at finding any support from friends, family, or other groups will be tutted away. "Oh, he told me she was crazy," they'll say while shaking their heads at you.

Real life often doesn't work this way. Some people sway easily, sure, but most of those I know don't pay too much attention when a person who should be able to function in society is written off as "crazy." Yet, it often doesn't matter. If the victim of emotional abuse already believes they have no one to turn to, they'll stay with their abuser and never seek help.

Weaponizing Compassion

It's hard, immediately after someone's hurt you, when they insist, "I would never do that on purpose!" or "That's just how I am sometimes. I was raised like this."

These are attempts to make a victim's compassion bubble up and turn anger into understanding, even when the narcissist does real harm. Most narcissists target exceptionally kind and generous people because they see an opportunity to take that kindness and sharpen it to a point. You're kind? What happens when I stab at you with your own emotion, then tell you it's not my fault? Are you still a nice person?

To have our own emotions used against us can feel terrifying. Instead of standing up for ourselves we start to see ourselves as mean, uncaring, even evil. Again, this takes the pressure off the narcissist. They can feel free to strut away from any problem, no matter how badly destroyed he's left the one he loves.

Twisting and Reframing

To take a situation and twist it around, then reframe it so someone else gets the blame, is the narcissist's bread and butter. "I didn't do it!" they'll say. "I was there, standing innocently by while all those terrible things happened. How can you accuse me?"

An example of this is physical abuse. If your partner shoves you down a couple of steps, then you confront them, their defense will be to turn everything on to you.

"No, no! I didn't push you. I saw you were about to trip, and I caught you. Your shoe caught on something, that's all."

And there goes the last of your confidence in yourself.

COMMON GASLIGHTING PHRASES

There are many tools in a gaslighter's toolbox. Here, I've compiled a set of phrases that tend to get thrown around often by these people.

- You're so sensitive!
- You know that's just because you are so insecure.
- Stop acting crazy. / You sound crazy, you know that, don't you?
- You are just paranoid.
- You just love trying to throw me off track.
- I was just joking!
- You are making that up.
- It's no big deal.
- You're imagining things.
- You're overreacting.
- You are always so dramatic.
- Don't get so worked up.
- That never happened.
- You know you don't remember things clearly.
- There's no pattern. / You are seeing a pattern that isn't there.
- You're hysterical.
- There you go again, being so ungrateful.
- Nobody believes you, so why should I?
- If you were paying attention… / If you were listening… / If you knew how to listen…
- We talked about this. Don't you remember?
- You're being irrational.

- You can't take a joke.
- Why would you say that? What does that say about you?
- Why are you upset? I was only kidding.
- I'm not arguing; I'm discussing.
- I criticize you because I like you.
- You're reading too much into this.
- You're the only person I have these problems with.
- Stop taking everything I say so seriously.
- You always jump to the wrong conclusions.

HOW TO KNOW IF YOU ARE A VICTIM OF GASLIGHTING

Imagine the narcissist in your life finds out you bought this book. Maybe they discover you reading it. What would they say?

If you immediately imagine them laughing at your silly purchase, ridiculing this text, and questioning your judgment for being suckered, you have a narcissist on your hands.

Other signs are bountiful in number, but I believe in my heart that when someone is in a bad relationship of any kind, the truth lives in their hearts. A realistic person would ask concerned questions if they saw a book you wanted to read. They might say, "You think someone is gaslighting you? Who? Can I help? Have I said something?" Those loving, helpful responses show that that person truly cares for you and knows that a relationship involves self-reflection.

On the other hand, narcissists ensure that those mature conversations never leave your imagination. I want you to read through the following checklist and see how many of these statements line up with how you feel with your partner, family member, or friend. If one person in your life makes you think or stress over any of the following, it's time to take action.

Start here:

When I'm with _____, I...

- ...ask myself whether I'm just being too sensitive.
- ...feel confused, sometimes even crazy in this relationship.
- ...am always apologizing.
- ...can't understand why I'm not happier with them.
- ...frequently make excuses for their behavior.
- ...know something's wrong, but I just can't figure out what.
- ...lie or omit facts to avoid being insulted or hearing my version twisted.
- ...have trouble making decisions.
- ...feel withdrawn; I don't want to call or see anyone.
- ...feel an impending sense of doom.
- ...wonder if I'm good enough.
- ...doubt my perceptions of a time/place/situation and personal judgments.

Any more than three agreements to the above statements should be considered as a clear red flag that you're dealing with a narcissist and it's time to start putting yourself first. You can't let someone steal your sense of self. That part of you holds your key to a happy life.

The person you thought of when taking that quiz—the one who would happily tear this book to shreds—is likely a narcissist. That narcissist is also the person you need to rid from your life.

CHAPTER SUMMARY

In this chapter, we picked apart some big topics.

- Narcissists of all kinds tend to rely on the same set of tactics.
- Gaslighting has a unique history and specific use to make the victim doubt their own mind.
- We can recognize different signs identifying when someone is gaslighting us.

In the next chapter, we'll take a closer look at how gaslighting happens from beginning to end.

3

THE STAGES OF GASLIGHTING

You might ask yourself how anyone can end up with a partner who gaslights them regularly. You may feel confident that you could never be a victim of this behavior. You might think, "thank goodness that's not me," when you read about an abusive relationship. What kind of person could possibly allow themselves to end up in this scenario, anyway?

Unfortunately, harmful relationships often feel healthy when they're clearly not, especially at the beginning.

I like to give this example; imagine you and someone close to you have to share a bed. It's gorgeous—the style you love, all your favorite colors for sheets and pillows, and the mattress feels perfect on your back. At the end of the day, you can't wait to snuggle into it and drift off to sleep.

At first, you and your partner share the mattress equally. Then, one morning, you realize your section is a tiny bit smaller than it was last night. But oh well, these things happen. However, each day, you wake up to find your section just a touch smaller than it was the night before.

Your partner, meanwhile, gets more and more of the mattress. After a few weeks, they're spread out like a starfish while you hang onto the edge, desperate to get back into that beautiful sleeping arrangement you had at the start.

The worst part of it happens when you try to bring up your shrinking section. Any time you defend your side, you have to hear about how it isn't a big deal, then how it's in your mind, and suddenly, you get called insane for mentioning a bed at all. Never mind that it's directly under you.

That's the easy breakdown of how gaslighting builds one move at a time. Let's get into the technical part of how narcissists find a partner, then pull them into a dangerous situation one step at a time.

STAGES OF THE RELATIONSHIP

The first meeting of a narcissist and their new partner almost always looks like something out of a movie. The moment explodes with love. Many partners to narcissists remember the early days as perfect. Somehow, this new person in their lives knew exactly what to say and when to say it and swore they had feelings for them beyond anything they'd ever felt. Maybe they blushed during their first early confession of love.

"I know this is crazy," they'll admit, "but I can't deny it. I'm head over heels for you."

This is love-bombing, or the **Idealization Stage.** This stage helps narcissists draw in someone who is unsure of themselves. A confident partner won't need this much attention from someone new and might find it stifling. However, someone who's recently been hurt, has low self-esteem, or feels desperate for a partner will swoon at this kind of attention.

Many people I've spoken to describe this stage as "a dream." That tells me a lot. One piece of advice I can give is when something feels too good to be true, that's because it probably is.

A man I'll call Mark remembers meeting his former partner Bee and wondering how he could have gotten so lucky.

"It was like she could read my mind. I was in the mood for a beer when we met up at a coffee shop, and she looked at me and said, 'You want to head to the bar?' Then she matched me drink for drink, something I've always liked in women. It's silly, but I think of someone unafraid to drink as a person who grabs life by the horns.

"We went out for burgers, and it was great. We talked for hours. She seemed to intuit just what I wanted to hear. I remember at one point in the evening, she sat back, took me in, and said, 'You're the kind of guy I could commit to. I mean *really* commit. And I have options, Mark. I could walk out of here and find five men who'd love to take me home. But I won't. I want to stay right here for as long as you'll have me.'

"Words can't express what that little speech did to me mentally. I grabbed her hand, pulled her out into the street, and kissed her. My whole body vibrated. My heart couldn't stop leaping up in my chest. She felt magical."

That dreamlike feeling is our subconscious alerting us to an unrealistic standard. No one feels true love on the first date. We might feel attracted or drawn to someone, but an all-out profession of love or request for a commitment in the first meeting is dangerous.

Unfortunately for people like Mark, those early seductions are carefully calculated to draw in new partners and get them hooked. And they often work. A lot of narcissists have a set of phrases or practiced speeches like Bee's that they know will get the person interested and keep them wanting more.

The moment we look at these dream encounters realistically; we start to see the cracks. Why would someone want a relationship with a person they don't know? It's because they've sensed that this is a person with whom they can build codependency. They need this person to reassure themselves that they're the soon-to-be-discovered star they want to be, while the new partner can acquiesce their own confidence to build up the narcissist's self-worth.

Of course, this doesn't start right away. After a narcissist secures a promise of love or commitment, they can start to test their boundaries.

It's hard for a narcissist's partner to say what exactly it is they did the first time. All they know is that the narcissist shifted from a deep love to a nagging discomfort. A person who started out as a dream in the

THE STAGES OF GASLIGHTING | 59

beginning may evolve into a partner with odd demands, strange claims, and an underlying need for constant attention.

They won't state anything outright. It could be a basic request for food. "I would love some scrambled eggs this morning," for example. Of course! Love to, darling. Their new partner quickly agrees and makes their version of scrambled eggs.

Several things might happen when the partner brings two plates to the table. The narcissist might take one bite and pull a face. They might blink in surprise and say, "That's how you do it?" or another comment meant to undermine the effort. Suddenly, their partner finds themselves apologizing for doing nothing wrong; they simply fulfilled a request. Instead of a thank you, they get a test.

Will they stand up for themselves or work to make the narcissist happy?

If the narcissist has chosen the correct partner—and they usually do—then they'll get the latter response. Instead of receiving a plate of eggs on their head for being a jerk, they'll get profuse promises that the next round will be better. The partner will try harder; they'll find a new recipe.

The partner will then probably rationalize the experience. Hey, they like their eggs a certain way. Some people are picky. Personal tastes are hard to punish. In the meantime, they're also trying not to tell themselves that they deserved a thank you and their eggs are delicious. They won't admit that their partner actually needs to apologize for their comments and walk out the door.

Instead, they work harder to make their partner happy. They were happy before, right? Wrong. The narcissist only presented a happy face to draw their partner in. Now, they can start the **Devaluation Phase.** After all, their first round of gaslighting their partner worked perfectly.

They've already introduced the false narrative of convincing their partner that their eggs are the problem, not the narcissist's lack of gratitude. That's a small taste of all the comments to come.

As the two of them spend more time together, the narcissist builds on that first disappointment. They'll sometimes look at their partner and ask, "Are you okay? You seem... I don't know... off." Their partner will take this to heart. Maybe they need to add an extra yoga class or therapy session to their regular regime. They wouldn't say those things if they weren't concerned, right?

The false narrative is an essential element to gaslighting. The narcissist wants their partner to feel like they fall short, no matter how hard they try. If they have a great job, the narcissist devalues the job and their role. They might pose questions like "How can you work at such a terrible place?" or "You know they underpay you, right?" no matter how much the partner likes their job.

One way a narcissist can steer a person's life into codependency is through money. If their partner leaves their job or allows them to decide how to spend their paycheck, they'll go broke and need the narcissist even more. From what I've seen in my own relationships, financial abuse is a small step away from emotional abuse. I don't mean that every narcissist uses it, only that it's an easy option.

This all feeds into the narcissist's ability to lie and exaggerate. Remember that narcissists will stand by a lie no matter what happens. To help build up a false narrative, they'll also exaggerate.

"You can't organize a closet to save your life!" they'll boom. Their partner might scramble to fix the problem, unaware that the narcissist barely even noticed their closet, and soon feel too exhausted to ask them what the fuss was about. Narcissists use this hyper focus on small matters to keep their partners emotionally worn down, too physically tired to fight back, and mentally distracted.

This second part of the relationship sees the narcissist become meaner and colder with each passing day. Nothing their victim does seems right, and they will run from one effort to another. No matter what they do, they never get home at the right time, none of their clothing looks good, and they always make the wrong jokes at parties.

All the narcissist's declarations of love are gone and replaced with criticisms and claims that their partner can't do anything, even listening to the narcissist the right way. The victim's life is now chaos. Every time they're heading home from work, they feel a gnaw in their stomach and their thoughts reel.

Will dinner be good enough? I asked them what they wanted, but what if I misheard them? Will they be happy about my progress at work or accuse me of devaluing their job again? Am I too hard on them? I must be. I don't know why I'm being so sensitive.

By the time they walk in the door, the victim doesn't know what to expect from their partner. They can almost visually see the eggshells littering the floor and the tiny spaces between them. It's up to the victim to navigate through this impossible set of obstacles without a single misstep.

The tragedy is that the victim's concentrated efforts only make the narcissist work harder to assure them that they're not good enough, mentally unstable, and no longer attractive. The gaslighting feeds off of itself and creates a whirl of chaos that swings both partners around. The victim only feels better when they get the odd kind word. The narcissist loves their constant efforts to be better but despises them for falling for their tricks.

One day, the partner finally snaps. They've caught the narcissist sexting another person while they washed all the dishes.

They hold up the phone and point to the message. What the *hell* is this?

To the victim's shock, their partner merely blinks in confusion.

"What are you talking about?" They show it to the narcissist again. Are they seriously denying what's right in front of them?

"I don't know anything about that. I'm not even sure why you're mad."

Their denial floors their partner. There, in that message, are some of the same sweet words that they got to hear once, a long time ago. Their partner could at least admit that they're flirting with someone else. Instead, they insist it never happened. They look at the evidence in their partner's hands and realize that they're in a truly bad situation.

After that fight, the narcissist's partner gets a moment of kindness. To their shock, the narcissist comes to them looking upset and apologizes.

"You're so wonderful. I hate to think I've hurt your feelings." They kiss their partner like they used to, and the partner gets a rush of that former love. The text message is forgotten, and the two go back to their evening, telling each other everything is fine.

To any outsiders, these two appear as what they are—codependent participants. Neither one is happy, yet no one wants to end the relationship. They both seem to want the rollercoaster of emotions and to get the rush of the high, despite the constant lows.

Finally, the narcissist can no longer look at the ruins of their former love. This feeling of utter disgust is called the **Discarding Phase.**

Now, the victim cannot do a single thing right. They no longer feel comfortable in their own home, which has become the lair of the person who drew them in, only to devour them like a vampire sucking out emotion.

The victim can see their partner's disinterest on their face, yet something makes them hold on to the hope that things can get better. They loved them once. What did they do to inspire so much passion and romance before? Can they recreate that same dynamic again?

The victim spends their days feeling confused, emotionally ragged, and desperate to fix whatever it is they think they broke. Our poor partner struggles to make their narcissist happy, but their last-ditch efforts to bring back the magic actually feeds the narcissist's ego, inspiring them to be worse on all fronts, continuing to wear the victim down.

There's little our victim can do, (or so they believe). Their power, respect, and safety are all in the narcissist's hands. Unless they grant their partner those things back, the partner will believe they can't have them. Now they're with someone who somehow got them to give up all their power, with no idea how to get it back.

But the victim does want it. They feel the door calling to them every day. Somehow, someday, they have to get out.

That's the moment I want you to feel. If you see yourself as powerless, in constant danger, and cringing to think of giving yourself a compliment, I want you to know there's still hope for you.

Relationships, like the ones I described, are all too easy to fall into and can seem impossible to leave, but you need to remember that nothing is impossible.

CHAPTER SUMMARY

This chapter walked us through the maze that makes up a codependent relationship. Here's what we saw:

- An unhealthy relationship can start with a love-bomb, which is an overly earnest expression of love and passion that may not really be as earnest as it seems.
- Gaslighting comes later and starts with small, easily dismissed comments.

- It isn't until deep into the narcissist's trap that their partner will realize they're actually in a toxic relationship.

In the next chapter, you will learn about different kinds of relationships in which gaslighting occurs, and what to watch out for as you open up to new people.

4

GASLIGHTING IN OTHER RELATIONSHIPS

I think most people expect or experience true narcissism from a romantic partner, but this unhealthy relationship can develop between any two people. Once two people establish a power dynamic, it's possible for one of them to exploit their relationship.

Perhaps you watched a friend couple up with someone so bad that they made you roll your eyes and wonder how much longer you'd have to put up with the jerk. You may have fallen into a bad relationship yourself and seen the sighs of relief once you left. People outside of an unhealthy relationship will find it easy to point fingers at someone else's pain, yet we all fall victim to the same tactics, particularly when they can sneak up from behind us. Do you know when to be on the defensive with a boss or one of your parents? What about a friend who seems to always get their way, even when all they want is to make a scene? Can our siblings exploit our love too?

We need to know what a narcissistic gaslighting element looks like in all relationships so we can call them what they are: toxic. Once we see the truth behind a difficult relationship, we can find ways to separate ourselves from the person causing damage in our lives.

I want to explore some of these unique relationships in our lives that can change how we live and love. It's my goal to get everyone speaking openly about these situations, so we won't laugh at or shrug off someone who's in pain. Instead, we can speak to them as an informed friend or family member and help them see the truth.

A PARENT OR CAREGIVER

Most people I know had parents who hoped to see their children leave home eventually. These kids grew up to further their studies, start businesses, fall in love, and build their own lives.

We assume that most parents want their kids to grow into healthy, functioning adults. We hope the same for anyone in a foster home or living with relatives who took the place of Mom and Dad. Parenting isn't easy; we all know it can become abusive or dangerous, but it's harder to see the gaslighting that a parent gives a child.

When gaslighting comes from a mother, father, or caregiver, it focuses on making the victim feel inadequate, but in more basic ways than a romantic partner might. Children's lives have less nuance than adults, so the abuse follows suit.

My own mother liked to nitpick my tidiness, yelling "You call this a clean room?" It didn't matter how many hours I spent organizing, scrubbing, or making my bed—none of it ever met her standards. My A's in school also missed the mark, as school was, "dumbed down to make idiots feel smart."

Unrealistic chores and academic expectations are easy ways for a parent to shoot down their children. As a kid, I had no defense. Surely my mom knew what she was talking about—she'd already graduated from college after all. Her room stayed neat as a pin. Who was I to question her?

It's that dynamic gaslighting that a narcissistic parent depends on to keep the abuse alive. These parents make themselves the hero in their child's story—as in, I'm here to tell you the truth and show you what the world is really like.

Children don't question adults. Mom and dad are physically bigger, older, and supposedly smarter. The fact that a child has no bruises or marks to prove the abuse makes it much more difficult for others to spot the damage, and a child is unlikely to report these cutting remarks. They likely don't even realize they're being abused. To a kid, the treatment becomes normal quickly, and they assume everyone else's mom and dad act the same way.

This acceptance builds over the years with several tactics. Narcissist parents make sure their child has no oasis to turn to by invading their social life. My own mother often read my AIM notes from friends out loud in ridiculous voices, hoping to make my friends' words sound idiotic. It worked, unfortunately. I stopped logging on and kept to myself, giving her the chance to point out that she had an unpopular son.

One day in the third grade, I made the mistake of inviting a friend over. I say mistake because my mother put on a show like I'd never seen before. She came out with a plate of cookies, joined us in our video game, and pelted my friend with questions about his own mom. Before I knew it, my friend was running for the door, uncomfortable with my "weird mom" who seemed to think he had come to visit her.

"We'll go to your house next time," I assured him. But I didn't see much of him after that day. Of course, my mother let me know how it was actually me who didn't know how to host a visitor.

"You could learn a lot from me," she stated, arms crossed as she looked down at me. Exhausted, I agreed.

I can remember myself wondering if my mom might apologize once she realized my friend didn't want to see me anymore. But a narcissist never says they're sorry, and certainly not to a child. It was my hope that she might say it in private where no one else could hear, and I would promise never to repeat her heartfelt apology. Even then, I understood that for mom, it felt impossible to admit a mistake.

As an adult, I met lots of people who grew up in a home similar to mine. One or both of their parents denied them friendships, made them feel idiotic, or intruded in their personal space.

Some of their stories exemplify the gaslighting dynamic perfectly. I featured them here with names changed to protect their identities.

Robert (currently an owner of an electric car repair service)

Robert grew up in a wealthy family in Stonybrook. He could remember people in grocery stores or at church stopping his parents to comment on what beautiful kids he and his siblings were. People wanted to know where they shopped, who cut the kids' hair, and if they were so well-behaved because of a special nanny.

Families in their neighborhood worked tirelessly to keep up appearances. The pressure to be the right kind of family came to a head with their kids.

"My mom used to buy me designer polo shirts when I was a kid," Robert told me. "Designer clothes! For a little boy! It was insane. The name on the label gave her an excuse to never let me play outside. I couldn't run through the mud or skateboard with the other boys. They all came home muddy with skinned knees and messy hair. But my mom made sure to have receipts of how much my outfit cost so she could wave it in my face.

"'You get this dirty and you're paying for it!' she'd scream. In hindsight, I can see this was her way of keeping me inside with her all weekend. She must have felt terrified of me making friends—she literally *paid* to keep me alone.

"But nothing felt worse than when she compared me to my older brother, Sam. Everything Sam did made her happy. Sam ate the right amount of vegetables, cleaned his room before the maid came over (hired to make her job easier), and always had a smile on his face. Sam may as well have been canonized by the church. To Mom, he was a living saint.

"'Why can't you be more like Sam?' she'd sigh, looking at me with disgust. Then, one day, I was suddenly her little golden child, and Sam was out. And this is the worst part—I bought it. When Mom threw her arms around me and said, 'You're perfect, you know that?' my head spun around at full speed.

"For a few days, Sam was the one left behind when we went out for ice cream. Mom didn't want to check his homework and hated the way he dressed. I wish I could say I eventually came around, but I was a kid. I ate it up like a scoop of Rocky Road in a waffle cone.

"You won't be surprised to hear that it didn't last. It was never meant to—Mom just liked to play us off each other so we wouldn't get close. It worked, and Sam and I have a hard time hanging out, even now. As kids, we fought constantly. Mom would come break us up, and then instantly side with one or the other, leaving the other one in the cold.

"All of her hard work decimating my self-esteem made it difficult for me to try anything new. Even a future astronaut's group in school seemed too out of reach. But I loved science and math—it was a place where all the chaos disappeared, and I could be myself. At least I had the foresight not to show my enthusiasm for the logical world to my mom.

"I grew up convinced that everyone would compare me to someone else and find me disappointing. When I left home at 18, I remember feeling relieved once my mother cut me off so I couldn't access her money. Fine, I thought, give it to your angel, Sam.

"At my first garage, I expected everyone to laugh at me and wonder how I ever managed to do anything. But that didn't happen. I remember feeling shocked. Didn't they know what a loser they'd hired? I honestly felt the job they'd given me was some kind of charity, if you can imagine that. Getting respect from my colleagues opened my eyes like nothing else had in the past. I'm eternally grateful to them."

Betty

"My dad forbade me to express my emotions.

"He didn't exactly say, 'No emotions allowed.' Rather, if I tried to tell him I felt sad or confused, he'd wave his hands in front of his face, squeeze his eyes shut, and yell, 'I don't want to hear it!' Yet, his own anger, happiness, and even his tears meant we all had to give him our full attention. He liked to give these huge, meandering speeches, and if one of us dared to yawn or look out the window, he'd scream at us.

"The message came across loud and clear to me. He could have all the feelings, no one else. In that same vein, if he did anything, it was because one of us kids 'made' him do it. The first time I saw him hit my mom, he informed me that he'd only done it 'because you kids are so impossible.'

"That confused me endlessly. I remember lying in my bed, trying to work it out. I was young at the time—only about nine years old—and I didn't think to question Dad. Instead, I tried to remember what my siblings and I did to make him so angry at Mom.

"Of course, I never found an answer. What Dad wanted was for me to stay confused. He loved it when I had no idea what he meant or what was happening. He'd give me this poor-you expression and explain everything to me like I was the world's dumbest little girl. In fact, when I got good grades in school, he always insisted that I cheated, even though I never did.

"'Be sure to thank whoever it is that lets you copy off of him,' he would say. I didn't bother responding after the first fifteen times. I only said, 'I will,' and went off by myself.

"By then, Dad had lost all interest in me. I'd learned to ignore him, and he despised my ability to switch off his voice. He loved it whenever I got upset or desperate. But indifferent? He couldn't stand it. He'd take my brothers out for pizza and 'forget' to invite me, certain I'd lose it when they got home. Instead, I used the time alone in the kitchen to make something for myself. The sight of me eating a meal I'd cooked on my own made him seethe with anger.

"The abuse didn't stop with my mom. Dad also hit us kids, though he tended to target my brothers over me. I think he saw my lack of love for him early, so hitting me didn't feel worth his time. My brothers, however, adored him. Everything he did was endlessly cool. He played the guitar and rode a motorcycle. He left my mom for a younger woman with bigger boobs who agreed with everything he said. The few days he treated them kindly made up for all the bruises and insults he liked to keep fresh and painful.

"I tried to get some counseling in high school, but Dad shut that down right away. One of my brothers told him I'd been in the counselor's office for a session, and he went straight to my mom to punish her for my actions. He forced his way into Mom's house and smacked her across the face, then pointed at me.

"'Stop making me hit your mom!'

"I never went to a counselor after that. Even now, I'm terrified of therapists or anyone who works in psychology. Dad's gone, but that memory still haunts me.

"Long after Dad died, I found out his own father used to act the same way. I'd never met my grandfather; Dad always hated him and told us we should too. That was a big deal to me. I thought, *Whatever I do, I can't act like Dad.*

"That made me hyper aware of how I treated my boyfriends and my husband, and even my kids. Instead of therapy, I read tons of books about how to communicate, be open and honest, and keep accountability. Anything to keep from falling into Dad's traps.

"It's still a struggle. It's easy to point at others and insist your pain is their fault. It's much harder to look in the mirror and ask, 'What can I do to be a better person? What needs to change?' But trust me, it's worth it once you do it."

Dana

"My mom loved rules. She loved them so much that she made up new rules all the time, and that practice caused many to contradict the ones already in place. For instance, she insisted I be up and ready early, even before she woke up. But if I did anything other than sit in the living room and wait patiently for her; if I turned on a cartoon, read a book, or went outside, she'd lose it.

"'What are you doing?' was her favorite question, and she asked it incessantly. I'd shrug and tell her nothing—which happened to be the truth—but that always seemed to be the wrong answer.

"'This isn't nothing,' she would insist. Then, she'd stare at me as if waiting for her child to magically say exactly what she wanted, though I never knew what that was. So, I'd sit quietly until she gave up and walked away, thoroughly disgusted with her daughter.

"All of my actions made her suspicious. Flip phones became available when I turned 16, and I wanted one desperately. She saw them as endlessly dangerous.

"'Who are you going to talk to? Why? When?' Her line of questioning never ended. What could I say? I wanted a phone because I was a teenage girl who hoped to talk to her friends. She used my inability to explain my desire for a phone as proof that I had ulterior motives.

"She accused me of having a secret boyfriend, drug dealer, and secret club I hoped to join. It was all so blown out of proportion that I laughed at her notion of me sneaking off to some speakeasy to score drugs with a boy. But to her, my laughter proved her suspicions of me to be true.

"To my complete shock, she surprised me with a phone one day. I remember staring at the box and not opening it, confident a poisonous snake or horrible trap hid inside. My mom was all smiles that day.

"'Go ahead, honey. Open it!'

"I stared open-mouthed at the phone inside. Mom hadn't bought some cheap, temporary phone; she'd gotten me one of the nicer models with all the bells and whistles. I remember I was one of the first kids at school to have decent games on my phone with a full-color screen.

"Despite my suspicions, I used the phone, and for a few days, it was heaven. Finally, I could talk to friends without Mom looking over my shoulder and questioning every word I said. One of my friends was called Marty in my phone contacts, (she was a huge *Back to the Future* fan), and she texted me constantly.

"One day, mom cornered me with a dark look on her face. 'Who's Marty?'

"'Huh?'

"Her question made my heart pound. I'd never mentioned Marty by her nickname to my mom. I always called her Shelly, which was her real name, to adults. How had Mom figured out her other name?

"Mom held out her hand with a hard, angry gesture. 'Give me your phone.'

"I did, but I still had no idea what the problem could be. She smirked at the screen as she scrolled through my contacts, then called the one labeled Marty.

"'Hi, I'm calling for Marty.' She said it with what was meant to be an exaggerated version of my voice. I heard Shelley on the other end, then Mom responded, 'Don't lie to me. Who's Marty?'

"Shelley didn't have time for my mom's antics, so she hung up. I'm sure she had no intention of making the situation worse, but the dial tone was all the proof Mom needed.

"'If you talk to any other boys, I'll kick you out. I'm not letting some slut have her babies in my house.'

"She stormed out and left me staring at my phone. What had Mom just done?

"Later, with the help of some tech savvy friends at school, I figured out my mother had put spyware on my phone. After that, I used it as little as possible and encouraged my friends to text me using a special code I developed. But the thing about teenagers is, if you're too hard to hang around, they drift away.

"To this day, my mom demands detailed reports of how I spend my time, what I'm doing right now, why, and with whom. It's only been after years of therapy that I've finally learned to stand up to her and maintain boundaries. But I still slip into that old exhaustion and give her what she wants when I can't push back anymore."

CHILDREN

The parent gaslighter makes me sad because our parents should be our lighthouse in a dark, confusing world. Rather than helping us navigate school, first loves, or new jobs, a narcissist parent only sees their progeny floating further away from home and finding autonomy. To a self-centered mother or father, that's a terrifying prospect.

Unfortunately, the problem can also flow the other way. As parents age and come to rely on their children for support, some sons and daughters take advantage of their parents' needs. I got lucky enough to meet Marcia, a lawyer who specializes in the rights of the elderly.

She takes on cases about elder abuse, which often include the victim's own children, the church, or those charged with keeping them safe.

"It's heartbreaking," she told me. "The true narcissists do everything they can to make their parents look demented or incapable. It doesn't matter if the mother or father in question is lucid, healthy, and fully capable. Their own kids work tirelessly to convince anyone who will listen that they can't drive, can't be left alone, or are slowly losing their marbles.

"I had one case of a son who constantly hid things from his own mother, then shook his head at her as if she were a ridiculous child when she couldn't find anything. One day, she even caught him stowing her wallet in an odd spot, but when she tried to confront him, he threatened to put her in a home. She got so scared that she ended up apologizing to him, even though he was clearly guilty.

"Another woman took her kids to court because they tried to make a big show of how incapable she'd become at their own church. Apparently, the church had a program to help take care of older parishioners, but only those who couldn't clean or cook for themselves anymore. Her kids seemed to think that if she was a recipient of the charity, then it might be easier to take over her estate before she passed.

"Of course, there are endless cases of people who start to abuse their parents physically in order to control their bank accounts, get them out of their houses, keep them dependent, and sometimes all three. It's shocking. The same people who owe these folks everything turn on them seemingly overnight, though it's clear to me that they've had narcissistic tendencies for years."

Ray talked to me about his own kids, two boys, who changed before his eyes. They went from two loving young men to conniving, middle-aged villains.

"I'll never get over it. I thought I had the best family on earth. I searched my memories for proof that the seeds of their behavior were buried somewhere, but honestly, I can't think of what made them do this.

"First, they started coming over all the time and asked about my bills often. 'You're paying your electricity, Dad? Your gas?' I told them yes, the bank automated it all for me. Why did they care? Neither of them lived in my house. A couple of times, I had to shoo them out just to get some peace.

"After their billing tactic didn't work out, they started telling me about all kinds of banking fraud. They told me story after story about people who called elderly residents and tricked them into sending money to people on false pretenses. I told them that I'd educated myself and the community center had a special course about fraud prevention. But they insisted I be very careful.

"One day, as I sat home alone, the phone rang. It was someone claiming they were calling from the bank and that they needed my account information. My money had been compromised. Now, I know better than to give personal information over the phone. So, I did what I learned in my class—I hung up and immediately called the number back. That's a good trick, by the way.

"I called back, and to my shock, someone answered. It was my son! I gave him an *earful*. I honestly thought he was scamming people like me and called me by accident. Maybe he had one of those auto-dialing doodads. He hung up on me, and I got so mad that I shook in my chair. I had to take a long walk to calm down.

"The next day, he walked in the house with his brother, a big smile on his face. I got up close to him, my finger in his face, and said, 'You have anything to say to me?'

"He shrugged and played dumb. 'Gosh, Dad, what's up? Did something happen?'

"I got so mad and torn up inside that I started to cry. That little liar had the nerve to put his arms around me like he felt sorry for me. I pushed him away, and he made this big show of falling down, but even his brother didn't buy it.

"I tried to talk to my oldest about the phone incident, but he seemed doubtful. He kind of gave me this look and said, 'Are you sure, Dad? You're not confused about anything?' Oh, that did it. I told both of them to stay away from me. Then, I called my bank and let them know that I believed my own kids were attempting to steal from me. I didn't know exactly how, but I wanted some kind of protection on my account.

"The woman at the bank made a comment, something about how they'd come to see her and asked what to do if they needed to take over my accounts. That broke my heart. I'd held out hope that it was only my younger son trying to scam me, but both? I felt everything fall down around me.

"I haven't spoken to them in months, and I don't have any intention to make up with them either. It's a terrible thing to suspect your own children. What if I get Alzheimer's? What if I fall? I can only imagine how happy they would be. It's horrible. It really kills you."

It's hard to imagine a parent so horribly abused by their children, but it happens more often than you might think. The National Care Planning Council estimates that one in ten seniors are abused at home, and about 90 percent of those cases go unreported. Older family members are often certain that if they complain about their families, they'll lose access to transportation or their finances.

In the cases of those living with narcissists, they're probably right.

A COWORKER OR BOSS

Workplaces and their predetermined power dynamics create a place ripe with opportunities to gaslight. We like to think that a good job will let us go about our business without concern for others' insecurities, personal problems, or needs to stomp on someone else's self-esteem. Yet, it happens all the time when people from different walks of life come together in an office or creative space.

As we all get hired at different levels, earn promotions, build popularity, or connect with others at work, some colleagues may see the office as a place to wield their power through lies, intimidation, and gaslighting.

Gaslighters at work can tear apart our productivity. If you have to deal with someone working to undermine you constantly or portraying you as negatively as possible, it becomes impossible to do a good job. All your focus and energy gets redirected the wrong way and responsibilities go untended until finally, you are a horrible employee. In the end, your gaslighter wins.

It can be hard to see gaslighting at work for what it is until it's too late. But I have some signs to look out for as you interact with coworkers, supervisors, or a boss.

Be aware of any false reports of missed or incomplete work reported to your boss. If someone above you gives you assignments, write them down on the day you discussed it, so you can have a clear record of what got doled out. Anytime you're accused of not doing something, check your records. Was that truly assigned to you, or is someone working hard to make you look irresponsible?

Keep track of the stuff on your desk, specifically important documents or items necessary to your job. A gaslighter will want you to doubt your own memory and might move things that belong to you. Their goal is to let everyone in the office see you searching for the missing item desperately. Then, they hope, you'll be known as a scatterbrain who can't keep track of your own stuff.

Gaslighters also love to report mistakes that never happened. Not to say everyone at work is perfect, but a gaslighter often exaggerates or lies about who made what error. This can also function as a way to hide their own mistakes from their higher-ups, making themselves feel better about their sloppiness at the office.

Or, you might hear your idea reported as that of your gaslighter's brainstorm. This happens when teams or pairs have to work creatively together and hash out an idea. Even if you have witnesses that can claim an idea came from you, many won't bother to correct the claim that it came from someone else. Rather, they'll consider it a team effort, so who cares? Your gaslighting colleague depends on this; it sets a low standard so they can continue claiming your successes for themselves.

One of the oddest stories of a gaslighter at work came from a teacher. I tend to assume that teachers are benevolent workers with students as their first concern, but my friend Christina told me the truth. Many people get into education for the chance to feel celebrated and make others look stupid.

Christina

"I taught fifth grade for ten years. I loved teaching, but I hated school politics. What disturbed me more than anything was seeing a fellow teacher not only jump into the gossip that floats around every campus, but use it to her advantage.

"One of our elementary teachers—I'll just call her X—had the principal so snowed in that it boggles the mind. She spent every spare moment in our principal's office, telling him how his style of leadership inspired her, how she hoped to be a genius like him one day, blah blah blah. She laid it on so thick that he started to believe everything she told him, even complete lies.

"First, she went after a reading coach she didn't like. The coach dared to tell X where she needed to improve some of her reading lessons, and X let her have it. She ran to the principal, claiming that she couldn't find her wedding ring after recess. We all thought, surely our principal wouldn't fall for such an immature ploy for attention, but he felt so close to X that he took the bait immediately. The ring turned up in the literacy coach's locker, and that was it. He let her go.

"After that, a lot of teachers got scared of X. Who would she attack next? I did everything I could to avoid her. One day, a member of the fifth-grade staff came into my room sobbing. She said she'd heard from X that our team leader hated her and had already posted a job ad to replace her.

"'I just got a great report from her! How could she do this?'

"I encouraged my friend to take a moment to calm down and ask our leader directly if she had plans to replace her. The two of them talked, and sure enough, this was just more lies.

"I tried to let the principal know about this infighting, but he didn't believe me. After all, I hadn't been in his office at every free period gushing over all of his decisions. But X had, and she found out that I wanted to let her principal puppet know the truth, and she lost it.

"She started harassing me every day. All of it was small stuff, designed to make me notice but not necessarily make a scene. She'd find out my class had time reserved in the school kitchen, and she would show up ten minutes earlier with her own kids, encouraging them to spill and smear ingredients around so the cleaning crew had to come and use up our time. If we headed to the garden, she photographed me and sent pictures to my team leader, asking if she wanted the parents to know how much time her teachers wasted.

"The worst part came when I tried to stand up for myself. I had no one on my side. X already had one firing under her belt, and no one wanted to be number two. I had to suck it up and work with her, despite all of her nonsense. Luckily, my team leader didn't listen to anything X said, though the principal defended her for years.

"I wish teachers like X were rare, but they're everywhere. Something about education attracts the pettiest people in the world. It's a shame, but we have to find ways to work around or stand up to these blatant narcissists."

Haddy

"I had a boss whom I'll never forget. I'll call her C. C came on to manage a design firm I'd worked with for a few months. Before she arrived, we had a really nice office culture. We let customers come in throughout the day and chat with us, check on projects, and offer ideas. I loved it.

"Suddenly, my great boss announced that he was leaving, and C arrived to take his place. C had an odd idea of how we worked in the office. One of her first assignments was to go with us to a big trade show where we got to show off our services and mingle a bit with potential clients. She disappeared for a long time, so long that we were packed up and heading out when she finally came back. She was carrying massive shopping bags—she'd gone shopping! I stared at her, openly shocked.

"'You know you were supposed to be here with us, right?'

"She snorted at my comment and made some dismissive, 'Hey, I'm the boss,' comment, then left us again. She didn't even carry out a sign.

"We tried to ignore her and focus on our work, but C wouldn't be shoved to the sidelines. She pulled clients into her office where she showed them pictures of her traveling all over the world, the gold name plate on her desk, and her framed degrees. All of them backed out, desperate to get away from her, but she made a big show of getting their numbers so she could contact them 'personally.' I'm certain she never did any such thing.

"Even her husband would come in to cause havoc. They made quite a pair, let me tell you. He would demand things like one of our light tables or a laptop, and we'd simply tell him that it was all business stuff and he couldn't borrow it. He'd come back at us with, 'My wife is your superior!' And we'd tell him, yeah, exactly. She makes more money than us, so why are you begging for free stuff?

"One day, I watched C blatantly take credit for my colleague's idea. He went to explain it to her, and she immediately assured him she'd already thought of it and started dialing the client before he'd left her office. He felt really hurt. Before C arrived, we'd always been open about giving one another credit and support. Fed up, I went to C's office.

"'C, we need to talk.' I sat down uninvited and started explaining that she couldn't steal ideas. That was not how we did business. The day she had an original idea, she was welcome to announce it. But if she wanted us to be the creative ones, she had to give credit where it was due.

"She looked at me in silence, then narrowed her eyes. 'What do you need, exactly?'

"I told her I needed her to tell that client that my colleague had the creative solution, not her.

"'I don't know what you're talking about. If your little friend out there is telling lies about me, I'll deal with him myself. And I'll remember that you took his side.'

"I called up our regional manager that afternoon, during her three-hour long lunch.

"C didn't last long. About a week after that conversation, she was gone. I found out that she'd claimed a bunch of business expenses for personal stuff while she worked for us and did take a couple of laptops home. For her husband, I guess. She also reported that she worked 45 hours a week, which was another blatant lie.

"I know I got lucky. There are plenty of people working for supposedly creative geniuses who are complete psychopaths, and they've had their bad bosses for years."

ROMANTIC PARTNER

Love can sustain and make us feel connected to others in this world, but in the wrong hands, it's a weapon.

Gaslighters like love because it opens people up and lets out their vulnerabilities. To a narcissist, a person who feels true love and trusts their partner completely is a person deserving of pity. They feel a kind of disgust at this thing they perceive as a weakness, yet they have no qualms about its exploitation.

We covered some of the typical romantic partner tactics that a gaslighter can use in chapter three, but I'll expand a bit here.

A narcissist sees no reason why they shouldn't cheat but never admits to cheating if they're confronted. Instead, they'll insist it's all in their partner's head, no matter the evidence. Cheating often gives itself away with secondary phones, hastily scribbled notes, and sexy texts, but even a clear paper trail won't make a gaslighter admit to any wrongdoing.

Remember, a gaslighter needs someone to tell them that they're worthwhile, and that takes grooming. Someone targeted by a narcissistic gaslighter requires time and effort to shape into the kind of partner they want. They need to woo their new partner with romance, promises, and declarations of love, but they also want this new partner to doubt themselves at every turn. That way, the narcissist is the source of knowledge, confidence, and even fun in the relationship.

So, the relationship itself becomes a building site to keep the victim in a state of constant doubt and confusion. This happens with the tactics we saw earlier, like word salad, denial, lies, and declarations of love paired with insults. The victim has to feel as if they're never quite right, almost on the mark but not quite. That keeps them trying in order to get back to the love they felt from their narcissist partner in the beginning.

Eventually, the relationship devolves into a bizarre cycle of:

- "I hate you and no longer desire you."
- "You can't leave because I don't want anyone else to have you."
- Repeat.

To keep that cycle at full tilt, the abuser keeps their victim away from any friends or family—anyone who might tell the victim that they're in a bad situation. They also work hard to make the victim doubt their own sanity, so that they feel like they're wasting everyone's time with their presence and instability. Who wants to hang around some loser who can't remember anything, doesn't know anything, and has no confidence? Thank goodness they have their partner—the narcissist one, of course—otherwise, they'd be completely alone.

All of this is reinforced with other tactics, like the narcissist keeping their victim broke. They might encourage their partner to quit their job, buy in excess to drain their account, or they might steal their money. Without financial independence, the victim becomes much less likely to leave and more dependent.

The gaslighter will also be sure to get rumors about their partner circulating among any mutual friends, colleagues, and even family. They want anyone who might support the victim to doubt their claims of emotional or physical abuse before they listen or help.

Many narcissists marry their victims to ensure a lifetime of someone to put down, so they can use them to build themselves up. Others stay in long, horrible relationships of endless misery, on both sides in order to keep up their confidence.

Wendy

"When I met my ex-wife, I remember feeling so happy. I was recently out and hadn't had a chance to date many women. My friends took me to a gay bar to celebrate my new life outside of the closet, and there she was, this lithe beauty. She introduced herself, Tea, and I remember thinking, *Why is she talking to me? All of my beautiful friends are here. Maybe we were meant to meet?*

"Tea and I started dating immediately. She had to see me right away, the next day. I mentioned it to a couple of lesbian friends, and no one seemed surprised. 'She wants to be your first love,' they told me. Others said, hey, enjoy it. You're finally dating within your sphere. So, I made plans with Tea immediately.

"I didn't know about love-bombing until after Tea was out of the picture, but now I know that she love-bombed me hard. She would say things like, 'You light up the room,' and 'I've never felt like this before.' Within a month, she proposed, and I said yes.

"It was then that friends started pulling me aside and telling me they'd heard bad things about Tea. One friend begged me to slow down. If Tea really wanted to marry me, she'd understand if I wanted to reschedule.

"'Live together for a while! There's no rush,' she said, eyes pleading with me. I mentioned her comment to Tea, (big mistake), and she scoffed.

"'She's so hot for you. You know that, right?'

"I wish I could say I listened to everyone, but I didn't. I married Tea, and the gaslighting started immediately. Suddenly, all the romance was gone, and she started denying every sentence she said. She'd suggest we go to the farmer's market, then turn on a movie and settle in. I'd ask what happened, and she'd tell me I was too needy, and she couldn't handle it.

"I tried to get that old romance back. God, I tried. I cleaned for her, I worked overtime to earn some extra money to buy her gifts. I hate to think about who I was in that relationship. The day Tea lost her temper and threw a plate at me, I saw her—the *real* her—for the first time. Suddenly I knew I'd dug myself an incredibly deep home. It was time to crawl out.

"I called up some friends and asked them for help. When they agreed to keep me safe, I sobbed in relief. I didn't even recognize Tea by that point. She'd gone from being my soulmate to my enemy. The women I'd cut out of my life took me back, got me into some LGBT-focused therapy, and talked over what happened with me for hours. I had to work out a lot of my internal problems, and I made sure to take all future romances nice and slow. You need to get married in a month? Keep walking."

GASLIGHTING FROM STRANGERS

I hope you have lots of people around you who love and value you at every opportunity. That's the kind of life everyone deserves. However, all that love and care can lower our guard around people whom we don't see regularly, like doctors, authority figures, even politicians.

Here's a quick list of people around us who may use gaslighting in ways we don't see coming.

Doctors

No group of impersonal gaslighters disturbs me quite like medical professionals. To be gaslit by a doctor shakes a patient so deeply that they often deny it ever happened; their brain can't fathom what just happened. No doctor would work to hurt their patients, right?

Gaslighting from a doctor can take the form of denial of your symptoms. You might be accused of exaggerating, lying in an attempt to get meds, or "imagining" the symptoms. This can make a patient wonder if they *did* imagine the situation. After all, doctors spend their entire careers studying bodies and illnesses. If a doctor tells us we're wrong, shouldn't we listen?

That's exactly what the gaslighting medical professional wants. They depend on the sight of their white lab coat and clipboard to make patients doubt their own knowledge of their bodies. The doctor could use this doubt to deny medications, encourage the patient not to waste the doctor's time by getting a second opinion, or that it's the patient's mental—not physical—health that needs treating.

Frank, an interviewee of mine, told me about a dentist who broke his tooth during a root canal.

"It hurt so terribly, I had tears running down my face. I tried to signal to the dentist to please stop. Something had gone wrong. Instead, he pushed the drill down harder into my molar and screamed at me to shut up. Panicked, I looked over at his nurse, and she smirked at me. I left that office in horrible pain.

"I called him up the next day and attempted to tell him over the phone, 'Hey, there's a problem. I need you to look at this tooth again.' He lectured me, asking, 'Who's the doctor, you or me?' I was so shocked that I hung up and started looking for a new dentistry office. I pity whoever goes in to see that guy. He's a nightmare."

Racists

We all know racism does an endless amount of damage, but a lot of racism is gaslighting. When an entire group can be maligned as "wanting attention" or written off as "uneducated," that's gaslighting on a large scale.

Much like a romantic partner wants their victim to be perceived as mentally unwell, people who maintain the narrative that certain groups should be ignored want to keep a negative lens on that group. Don't make friends with them or spend time listening to them because they're crazy!

Unfortunately, a lot of powerful people buy into these false narratives about Latino, Hispanic, Black, Asian, and other historically marginalized communities in order to write off any claims of injustice. Far too many people reinforce this gaslighting, keeping racist attitudes alive and making people internalize it, even for those who know, deep down, that it's not true.

Today, a ton of racism happens online. The use of memes, false statistics, or facts taken out of context have fanned the flames of racism like never before. I spoke to one friend who told me that his own father started posting hateful things about Muslims. Most of them were cartoons about "towel heads" and images of Arabic people armed with massive automatic weapons standing on American flags.

"Want to hear the worst part?" he asked. "We're from Afghanistan! We're the people he's making fun of."

Of course, narcissists aren't interested in facts. If they have a time and place to make a whole group of people feel small and manipulate others' fears, they'll jump. A lot of these online racists are savvy about the kinds of hashtags, photos, and phrases that get the most attention, and they have huge online followings.

It's all done in an attempt to make the narcissist feel big while hoping to make others look small. Unfortunately for the victims of this gaslighting, these gaslighters are often so desperate for that sense of importance that they'll stop at nothing to keep people afraid and angry, even if they themselves only feel hollow inside.

Politicians

I know this comes as no surprise, but we need to call manipulative politicians' lies and deceptions what they are: attempts at gaslighting.

It gets out of control when it's election time and politicians go out stumping. Many take time to make the other candidates look stupid, out of control, or dangerous or that it is only them that can save the nation, whereas the other candidates will destroy it.

CHAPTER SUMMARY

This chapter covered a ton of information. Here are the highlights:

- Gaslighting can come from many different people, including parents, children, and colleagues.
- We can run into gaslighters in the doctor's office or interactions with authority figures.
- Politicians, teachers, and other respected members of the community can twist their power into opportunities to gaslight others.

In the next chapter, we'll see how gaslighting impacts us in the short and long term, and why it's so dangerous.

5

THE IMPACT OF GASLIGHTING

Gaslighting may not strike you as severe in terms of abuse; generally, someone gets duped into a bad relationship, but they usually get out, right?

Well, we hope. The cycle of abuse between a narcissist and their victim—the fight for love, indifference and cruelty, spark of hope, then repeat—can feel impossible to break. How does one fight off the promise of love?

Of course, there are ways, but it's not easy. What's more, the damage done during that endless struggle can't be dismissed. Years of gaslighting don't fade away in a couple of weeks the way other breakups might. The mental anguish haunts us for years, sometimes the rest of our lives.

The wonderful Dr. Robin Stern wrote about the four-stage process in her book, *The Gaslight Effect*. Reading it felt horrible—I actually shook as I flipped through the pages on my Kindle. To see my past relationships laid out in such clear, clinical detail disturbed me deeply, but it had a secondary effect. It freed me. I no longer felt alone and unworthy.

Armed with my new knowledge, I felt prepared to face anything my mind, body, and emotional health needed to build up again. It took time, but more than anything, it took understanding.

Let's dive into the four stages of gaslighting's effects and what we can prepare for as we work on driving away toxic love.

DISBELIEF

If you or anyone close to you dated a narcissist, you're familiar with this phenomenon. Many people use the disbelief stage to forgive themselves for not helping a friend or loved one in a bad situation.

"I tried to tell them!" we declare, certain that was all we could do. "They wouldn't listen to a word I said."

This stage happens to anyone in an unhealthy relationship. A victim doesn't see themselves in a bad light. They're a loved adult—that's how they should be defined. If they met a beautiful or handsome new person at work or the bar who wooed them with concert tickets, walks in the park, or great dinners out. There's no logic to the sudden change in tone. A bad person doesn't take the time to demonstrate love, so how could their partner be evil?

The same happens with children of gaslighting parents. Everyone knows parents pay for things that children need and want. They take the kids to school and get things ready for Christmas morning. How could any parent be a villain?

Even in more casual settings, like between a doctor and patient, a gaslit patient won't believe they could be a victim to the doctor's narcissism. After all, a doctor heals and administers medicine. There's no way a doctor could double as an evil individual… right?

Wrong. The narcissist depends on all of these preconceived notions. They want everyone's guards down and no one to suspect their motives or techniques. It's the veneer of love or care that keeps a narcissist safe from any repercussions.

How does this look in practice?

When a narcissist tells their partner that they're a worthless idiot, the partner's brain works hard to deny the possibility that it ever happened. Instead of thinking, *"What a jerk! I need to get out of here right now!"* they get an error message in their brain. It doesn't compute. This is their love, their friend, and the one they trust more than anyone. There's no way they said that!

The victim convinces themselves that they misheard the narcissist, shaking their head at themselves. When did they get so scatterbrained?

When kids are faced with the cruelty of their parents, it's a similar reaction. Maybe a friend from school realizes a narcissist mom crossed a line when she demanded to see her child's journal. In another case, a teacher has an odd reaction when her student mentions something about not being "allowed" to spend too much time outside.

Whatever the context, the child suddenly has to reconcile the fact that other parents don't behave like their mother and there could be a reason for that.

Kids are experts at explaining things away. They might tell themselves, "Well, other kids have lazy parents. My mom cares more than theirs, that's all." Or they might insist that their mom is right to invade their personal space to keep them safe.

Rather than dealing with reality—that they and their mother have an unhealthy, damaging dynamic—they convinced themselves that they're deeply loved. To face any other reality feels too scary, and no child enjoys being afraid of their own mother.

Disbelief rarely leads to a logical conclusion. Rather, it helps maintain the very thing we need to dismantle. It opens the door and pushes victims through to the second phase.

DEFENSE

No one gets more defensive of a bad partner or out-of-line parent more than their victims. Remember that a narcissist works hard to condition and groom their victim to do what they want, and one of their greatest desires is to be defended.

I'm sure my friends recoiled anytime they heard my weak yet passionate arguments in favor of my narcissist ex-girlfriends, all of whom deserved to be left, not loved.

"You don't understand!" I'd tell them. "She has a really stressful job and has barely slept this week."

Things like that made sense to me at the time. Of course, my girlfriend got a bit short with people. She had to be lovely and charming with all her clients non-stop. That would wear down anyone!

In hindsight, I genuinely wonder if the ex in question ever managed to be sweet and charming with a single person. She could be assertive, flirty even, but to imagine anything deeper is laughable. She couldn't put anyone's needs before her own. I'm fairly certain she acted terribly with my friends as a way of training me to keep her safe from outside scrutiny.

Of course, I can't prove this in my own case. However, I can look at the hundreds of testimonies from my research subjects and see, over and over, how often victims stand up for the one hurting them.

It's sad, but we're quick to defend anyone we love, even when they don't deserve it. Often the same people who look to defend others accept the complete lack of defense for their own current state. They accept feeling alone, even when they're in a (supposedly) loving relationship.

In my case, I usually tried to get others to understand my situation. I dated the worst of my narcissists—Kay—in college, and she insisted I work tirelessly to make her happy. I had to buy expensive clothes on my limited budget so she would be proud to parade me around in front of her fellow design majors. Then, I had to change my hair and get a bizarre, asymmetrical haircut she insisted would put me miles ahead of others in terms of style.

I felt insane walking to class, yet the moment a friend of mine raised her eyebrows at my new look, I went on the defensive.

"Hey, this is the latest style," I told her. She held her hands up in surrender.

"I didn't say a word," she said. But I still caught her rolling her eyes the moment before she walked away. I felt terrible. She probably hoped to ask why the change, but I shut her down so fast she never got a chance.

The exchange made me feel even worse throughout the day. When I saw Kay later that afternoon during our usual post-class coffee, she gave me a fleeting glance as I walked up, then went back to her book. I waited for her to say something about how I wore all the clothes she picked out for me, but she had no comment.

Instead, she had something she wanted.

"You should take me out for dinner tonight," she informed me. "I need it."

"Um, I'm kind of broke..." I looked down at my ridiculous outfit again. It consisted of an artfully shredded sweater and pants so tight they pinched my legs when I sat. She sniffed at my money troubles and sighed.

"You know," she said, looking me up and down, "if you can't afford to dress that way, you can just keep it simple."

My jaw fell open. She and her demands that I work on my style were exactly why I'd bought the damn outfit in the first place! I tried to talk to her about our big fight a week before about how slovenly I dressed, but she waved it away.

"I never said that," she said, rolling her eyes the same way my friend in class had earlier that day.

After all that, I still defended Kay to the first person who had the nerve to point out how little money I had after I started dating her. I immediately launched into my usual explanation.

"Hey, she takes me to tons of events! We're always networking! Thanks to her, I'll have an amazing job and tons of high-paying clients after I graduate! I love her!" And on and on.

You can probably guess how things actually went with Kay. She got consistently worse with her demands, and none of my efforts amounted to anything. By the time I left her, my bank account was overdrawn, I had blue hair in a cut I hated, and I'd lost ten pounds from a combination of stress and an inability to afford groceries.

After the dye faded and I found a little bit of work in a lab on campus, I reflected on the whole experience. Everyone around me tried to have a civil, calm conversation with me about Kay. The only one who overreacted and got angry was me—I'd tossed aside their kindness the same way Kay tossed out any evidence that she'd hurt me.

Other victims I spoke with over the years found themselves reflecting on similar situations. One woman remembered how she'd still defended her father after he started a screaming match with another parent on her school campus.

"I told people all kinds of things. He was the victim of an out-of-control mom, had been sick all the previous week, and didn't understand the problem and thought it was over something personal. You name it, I tried it. Anything to avoid admitting I had a dad who made terrible scenes wherever we took him.

"The worst thing was how triumphant he felt after a horrible, dramatic confrontation. He lived for them! But if anyone accused him of starting them? Oh, that was the last time he'd speak to his accuser. No one who confronted him ever got his forgiveness. In his mind, he had the life of a maligned victim. Everyone around him wanted to 'take him down' or humiliate him in some way. He never considered for a second that he might be in a position to stop the nonsense. I could see in his face that he saw this way of living as non-negotiable. He had to have shouting matches constantly, or else people might see him as weak.

"One teacher offered to help me. She pulled me aside one day and asked if perhaps I needed someone to visit my house and talk to my dad about all the fighting. I shook my head no and insisted she leave me alone. I knew better than to mention the conversation to my dad. He'd have returned to my school to get that teacher fired immediately."

This constant fight to defend the people we love, despite their insistence on behaving terribly, will wear us down over the years. Worse, it works its way into our hearts and minds, leading to the next phase: depression.

DEPRESSION

The depression we will be discussing here is clinical depression that is diagnosed by a medical professional or psychologist. It is a rather tragic part of the cycle; the level of emotional imbalance makes it incredibly difficult and often physically painful for the sufferer to do basic tasks, like getting out of bed, cleaning the house, working, or accomplishing anything mentally or physically taxing.

Many people misunderstand how depression manifests in a person. An individual with depression appears pained most of the day, and I can assure they do feel deep, inescapable pain. However, they're not physically injured, so they push through the hurt to keep going, despite the mental sensation dragging their own body around, which usually comes with their own muscles and bones fighting them the whole way.

Depression occurs due to a chemical imbalance in our brains. Worse, depression presents differently in almost everyone who suffers from it. One person might spend hours and hours in bed in a shallow, unsatisfactory sleep, whereas another may feel angry and restless, unable to sleep at all.

The long-term effects of depression can make it impossible for the sufferer to make important decisions. Depression clouds our judgment like a long session of day-drinking. Our brains are no longer our own, and we become too tired and in too much pain to do anything about it.

I want to clarify all of this because depression is the brain's response to several damaging events happening in our lives combined with past problems and mental illness. All of it comes to a head for victims of a gaslighter rather terribly.

After months or years of trying to defend the narcissist, explaining away or ignoring their hateful behavior and insisting that the victim is loved, the victim can fall deep into a depressive state. The constant fight to find the love they feel certain is just under the surface is more than enough to get them deep into a chemical imbalance.

Unfortunately for our victim, that pained, listless feeling only works to keep them in a bad situation. Suffering from depression, exhaustion, and being worn out on every level, she is no longer strong enough to walk away from the person who got her into this messy state. Of course, the narcissist's disgust only increases when they see their partner this way, but what can they do? the victim at this stage is a husk of their former self. Even the strongest of people struggle to work their way out of this kind of situation, and it can take years for them to find the ability to walk out the door.

I don't write all of this to make you feel obligated to run into someone's personal life, grab them, and drag them out kicking and screaming. Rather, I want you to understand the friend who doesn't leave, even when it seems clear to you that they're deep into a horrible situation.

It's easy to look away when someone's in a bad relationship, but we shouldn't shrug off another person's struggle; we should always try to understand it, not only for their sake, but for our own. When we ignore people, we set ourselves up to be ignored in turn. When my friend Carole talked to me about facing my demons and learning to understand why I felt attracted to narcissists, it may have been hard to hear, but it saved my life.

I met a man called Dave whose ex-boyfriend was a horrific narcissist. The man even hit him a few times, only to shrug off the incidents as his way of joking. Dave worked hard to save the relationship. This was his first real boyfriend, and the thought of that relationship failing broke his heart.

"I remember standing there and letting him hit me," Dave said in an interview. "I mean, I didn't even push him away or put my hands in front of my face. He found some old picture of me with a school friend on social media and demanded to know who it was. When I told him, he threw a knife at me from across the kitchen. And I mean he *threw* it end over end like an action movie villain. By some miracle it missed me, but it still stuck right in the wall."

Dave got so scared of his own partner that he fell into an exhaustion. He lost his job as a social media director for a good company because his productivity fell so low. Then, he found he couldn't exercise anymore; it hurt terribly and required buckets of effort. His lack of enthusiasm for his usual trips to the gym was his first red flag—he had a group of workout friends who reached out and suggested that he may have depression. When he visited a doctor, he burst into tears as he spoke about all the details of his relationship.

"I didn't even have the strength to lie about my boyfriend anymore. It felt so good to tell the truth, but it also brought a whole new pain to the surface. I left that doctor's office with a diagnosis of exhaustion and depression, the name of a therapist, and the sensation of having just been hit by a car. I remember rubbing my chest and feeling a kind of deep bruise, the kind a firehose might leave on a person after they'd been blasted by the police.

"All of it felt like my body screaming at me to do something, to make changes. I got home and told my partner what happened, and he let me have it. He hit me hard across the face, but I barely felt it. I was so under the water by then. That's what pushed me out the door; a smack across the face wasn't enough to make me feel something? That sealed it—I was in trouble."

Dave required years of therapy and treatment to deal with his own self-hatred, depression, and internalized homophobia. But that's another book. I mention him because he's a good example of the underlying issues that can drive us into the arms of a gaslighter and keep us there.

SHORT-TERM EFFECTS

People like Dave fall into a group of lucky survivors. He got out before his partner could do any lasting, physical damage. However, Dave still had to deal with the fallout of that relationship for years. He went to a few therapists until he found one he clicked with, and he also went through a couple of antidepressants before he landed on one that got him back to normal. However, that doesn't mean he felt one hundred percent okay by that point.

"I felt like the ghost of the relationship haunted me for a long time," he told me. "There's no way to prepare for the damage someone can do to your psyche, especially someone you love."

Let's break down the different ways leaving a toxic relationship behind can continue to hurt, even when our ex, former friend, or narcissistic parent is out of our lives.

Mental Health

On a lower level, these relationships wound our sense of confidence deeply. It's impossible to look back on how someone treated us and not judge ourselves for putting up with the insults, mockery, pushes, and punches. Why would anyone stay?

This is a dangerous road to go down. Once we start to question our own judgment, plenty of bad thoughts can enter our minds.

"Maybe I deserve it. It could be payback for that one time…"

"I must want to be abused."

"I guess I don't know what a good relationship looks like. Maybe I never will…"

"Perhaps I'll be single forever."

All of this confusion and self-doubt seeps deep into our subconscious, and we will continue to doubt ourselves for years after our gaslighter walks out the door. That makes big decisions, like when to leave a job, where to move, or who to marry beyond our reach. We start to question everything we do, and that's no way to live.

That same life also makes it impossible to be a friend.

Social Life

All of a former victim's doubts, low self-esteem, and certainty that they deserve horrible things in their life makes it impossible for them to get themselves together in time for a social gathering.

We've all met that person—someone who wants desperately to be included, yet they're terrified of their wish being granted. They sit quietly at the edge of the party, looking down at their feet while fun music plays, people try to include them and maybe even flirt with them to make them feel desirable. But two seconds of flirting can prove to be all they can handle. After that, they're suddenly gone, leaving everyone to wonder, "Who was that odd little wallflower who didn't speak with anyone?"

When we lose our social skills, we forget how to navigate the world. The problem can go far beyond parties. We can no longer manage issues at work, as office politics or misunderstandings may be causing palpitations. Rather than face anyone trying to undermine us or who didn't get all the information, we feel like hiding under our desks. All the bad things suddenly feel deserved and unavoidable. This is now our life, no way around it.

That's all perception, of course. But perceptions are hard to shake, particularly when we can point to a former horrible partner and say, "See? I make bad choices. I like abuse. I can't be trusted in any way, shape, or form."

This attitude turns on us in unexpected ways. All of that, "I deserve this," crap running around in our minds can make us feel endlessly grateful to anyone who shows us even the tiniest bit of kindness. I'm sure you remember kindness and charm can work in a gaslighter's favor. The sudden desire to maintain someone else's happiness—but disregard our own—can leave us back where we started: ripe for the picking.

I feel certain you've met someone who lives to make others happy. This is the person who constantly apologizes or the one who can't stop picking up the bill and constantly suggests that everyone stick together. This is the boss who works endlessly to make their employees love them but not so much on their actual job.

People-pleasing can lead to all kinds of bad decisions. We spend money when we need to save, work day and night to make sure we're in so-and-so's good graces, and spend hours lying in bed and staring at the ceiling, positive we're missing out on some great get-together.

LONG-TERM EFFECTS

We covered depression and how a long relationship with a gaslighter can leave us deep in a depressive state. But what about after we leave?

Depression can get kicked off by a loss. For some, it can be a sudden death in the family or loss of a dear friend. A breakup, even one that's good for us, can have the same effect.

After a relationship ends, our lives are changed forever. Now we have ties to someone we no longer see. Our daily routine takes on a different shape. Those musicals your partner despised are suddenly fair game, and it's no big deal if you decide to spend a weekend watching your favorites.

Going out means we might run into someone who hurt us, so many of us hide in our homes for days, even weeks. We have to explain to our friends what happened and wonder if any of them might choose our ex over us. Losing a girlfriend or boyfriend is rough, but there are also often social casualties that piggyback on the breakup.

All of this can leave a narcissist's victim in the throes of depression. That means the victim won't reach out to their social network, exercise, eat well, or do anything else necessary to stay healthy and balanced. Depression requires regular help from a therapist and possibly medication, yet the people who need the most help often feel overwhelmed by the thought of leaving the house, much less walking into a therapist's office and starting to heal.

Chronic stress will haunt the former victim of a gaslighter for years after they've regained their space. Chronic stress can lead to migraines, as it keeps the muscles in our shoulders and upper back tense. It can also wear muscles out, sometimes so badly that they atrophy. That makes any kind of exercise incredibly difficult and makes it much harder to relax.

Stress can also make respiratory issues like asthma much worse. I found one article that referenced sudden asthma attacks for people experiencing the sudden death of a loved one. If a victim of abuse already has lung problems, the long-term stress can make their issues far more serious.

You may know someone with heart problems under doctor's orders to relax and maintain a healthy lifestyle. That's because high levels of stress affect the heart directly and can lead to a heart attack if they're not managed. The circulatory system also hangs onto the inflammation caused by stress, making heart health a real concern.

The list goes on and on. High levels of prolonged stress can keep us from digesting properly, impair our immune system, and even affect the bowels. Stress can sound like a minor concern at first, but high levels over a long time become major health setbacks. Their submissiveness may put them at risk to be another abuser's target.

Some people develop Post-Traumatic Stress Disorder, (PTSD), making it incredibly hard for them to get back to a normal, functioning state. PTSD occurs in anyone involved in or witnessing a traumatic event. It can even happen indirectly. If someone learns about the violent death of a family member they previously believed passed peacefully, they can experience internal trauma.

PTSD manifests differently in each person. It's an emotional memory that triggers a stress response in the body. For someone who was beaten by a parent or partner, certain smells, sounds, or sights can make their old injuries start to ache, despite having healed. Others might break out into a stress rash after smelling a cologne worn by a former, toxic partner.

It's impossible to know how PTSD will appear, but it's also impossible to ignore once it's activated. It can also maintain a presence in a person's body for years after the event itself. It takes intensive treatment and a lot of hard work on the part of the victim to manage.

Aside from PTSD, depression, anxiety, chronic stress, and everything else it brings along with it, a victim of a gaslighting narcissist can also experience a lot of complicated emotions.

Former victims find it incredibly difficult to trust anyone. How can they? Someone who swore up and down that they loved them suddenly became their worst enemy. After that, anyone who shows any interest in them or extends any kindness will suddenly be suspect. Everyone is a possible enemy in disguise.

Alongside suspicion, many former victims feel terrible guilt. One research subject told me that she honestly punished herself for not "living up to her father's expectations."

"Rather than blame him for constantly moving the standards, I blamed myself. Even when I got older and had a better understanding of the sick games he played, I still felt guilty. I felt it because I participated and kept the game going. I always blamed myself."

That guilt made her feel an incredibly low self-esteem and a high self-doubt. She felt unable to choose groceries, be alone in a room, or anything similar. She had to move in with a close friend and ask her to take care of her. Luckily for my subject, her friend agreed and coached her back to a state where she could build up a schedule, eat regularly, and trust herself to try new things. But it was still a long, arduous process because she didn't see herself as a reliable person.

She also found herself feeling endlessly paranoid. She had to get a new phone because she was certain every call was her father in disguise.

"That's exactly the sort of thing he would do—learn to spoof phone numbers and call me, letting me get excited to hear from a friend, then tear me down. I also had to change to a night job because I was certain he'd haunt all my usual places. I have no idea if he ever did these things, and I didn't let myself find out. I just ran."

Paranoia was a common vein that ran through all the experiences I recorded in my studies, but I also felt it. After Kay and I parted ways, I felt scared to shop. I thought of all the stores as her territory, even the little convenience store under the cafeteria. It didn't matter that she wasn't there—I could feel her as I picked up a bag of chips and went to pay for them. I had to keep checking over my shoulder because I was certain I'd just seen her.

I also carried a deep hopelessness for years. I've discussed that feeling with several people and many of my research volunteers. We lose hope that we know how to pick partners, doubt all of our past decisions, and wonder if we'll ever know what to do as we go through life. We believe certain things will go badly for us thanks to our lapse in judgment, not just in partners, but in everything.

Post-Betrayal Syndrome

All of this brings me to another pressing problem: Post-Betrayal Syndrome, (PBS). This is a physical manifestation of the anger, depression, and sense of loss that occurs, even after a toxic relationship comes to an end.

PBS can take many forms. It can keep a former victim from getting a good night's sleep, keep their energy low, and put their emotions on a permanent rollercoaster.

This syndrome is a distant cousin to Post-Traumatic Stress Disorder, or PTSD. What makes PBS different from PTSD is the sense of disbelief one gets from PBS. How could someone who loved me hate me so deeply? How could I stay and subject myself to all that pain despite all my education and awareness? Remember the error message—the brain can't compute bizarre behavior right away, but after some time, it can look back and parse through the details. But that's rarely a neutral process. It can create an inability to focus and a foggy mental state that keeps the victim stumbling through their day.

PBS is heartbreaking on a much deeper level. Once the victim has some distance and can see just how bad their gaslighter treated them, the pain becomes unbearable. They feel dirty; they've let someone into their psyche, where the gaslighter can stomp around and break everything the victim built for themselves. They get scared—what if they come back? What if my next love turns out to be the same kind of person? What then?

On top of this is the punched-in-the-gut feeling we all feel after an intense, negative interaction. This feeling leaves the victim irritable and with depressive thoughts, possibly even feeling abandoned. If our partner can't be there for us, are we worth anything?

Like PTSD, PBS can lead to a kind of emotional flashback, though mental and physical flashbacks also occur. Small triggers like a turn of phrase, a certain song or the sound of tire wheels on gravel can bring back all the pain for someone recovering from toxic love.

You might be wondering if there's any hope for the victims of gaslighting. It can feel hopeless, even if we leave and stand up for ourselves, but I'm here to tell you that it's far from bleak. There are ways to fight back against the gaslighting narcissists of the world.

We just need to know their weaknesses.

CHAPTER SUMMARY

This chapter delved into the deep, internal wounds caused by gaslighting:

- Serious mental illnesses, like PTSD and depression, can be triggered by gaslighters.
- Chronic stress created by a relationship with a narcissist can lead to a number of health problems.
- A unique syndrome, PBS, is caused by toxic love and relationships.

In the next chapter, we'll learn how to fight back against gaslighting and why you should defend yourself.

6

HOW TO FIGHT BACK

Before I dive into the techniques in this chapter, I want to clarify that one of the worst things we can do with a narcissist of any kind is actively battle against this person. Nothing makes a narcissist happier than the chance to be a true victim. They seem primed to fall to the floor, a dramatic hand to their foreheads, and cry out, "Why?"

I say fight back, but what I actually want you to do is confront the problem. This strategy is beneficial for everyone involved, no matter the level of narcissism involved. It gives the victim a chance to change the story; they're no longer at the mercy of someone else. Now they're in control and can stay that way for as long as they need.

There's also a miniscule chance—and I don't want you to hold out for this—that a narcissist, once confronted with their actions, might start to question themselves. Again, don't expect to see this happen. I've met very few people who have managed to fight down their insecurities and become fully realized, happy people who didn't need to berate everyone around them emotionally to feel better.

One of the saddest stories I've heard of gaslighting was also a terrifying story of domestic abuse and rape. A woman's new boyfriend attacked her in his apartment and strangled her until she passed out, then violated her. By the time she regained consciousness, she felt terrified. She grabbed a champagne bottle in order to defend herself from him attacking her again, but he filmed her with the bottle, insisting he was the victim, not her. Finally, she grabbed her coat and ran out the door.

This story stands out to me for a couple of reasons. First, this victim saw the reality of her situation right away. I'm with a dangerous person and I need to treat this person as a threat. The moment she tried to fight him off with a heavy object, he didn't run. He turned on his phone's camera and filmed her, screaming that she terrified him and already attacked him once. Finally, she got out. She saw in a moment that there would be no breaking up with this guy. It was get out or get killed.

I love that this woman survived and got herself to safety, but I love her more for facing her attacker. Granted, this is an extreme example, but it proves that no matter how toxic the situation, there's always a way to get out.

Your journey might look completely different from hers. Perhaps the person gaslighting you is a family member or parent. We can't always break up with the bad people in our lives, but there is always a way to save ourselves.

Let's take a look at how we can keep ourselves safe and even confront our gaslighter in a way that puts our sanity first and the integrity of our relationship second.

BE HONEST WITH YOURSELF

Use this book as a guide for dealing with a gaslighter in your life. It's not an easy thing to admit, but it's important all the same. I don't want you to get wrapped up in excuses or explain away someone's behavior. Rather, be honest about how you feel and why you feel that way.

Go over the common phrases I listed in chapter 2 and check off which ones you hear regularly from the person you love. No one who loves you should ever speak to you like this—you aren't crazy, and your feelings aren't unreasonable. You feel sad and confused because your love turned on you, and now your brain can't piece together how it happened.

After you come to terms with your situation, take some space for yourself. Go on a trip with some friends, move in with one of them or a neutral roommate, or head over to your parents' place. Put physical space between you and the person hurting you.

Walking away from anyone who adds stress to our lives gives us a new perception of them and ourselves. When we're physically close to someone we love but who hurts us regularly, it can be hard to remember why we got so upset. Attraction can alter our logic and make it hard to stand by our convictions, and lots of narcissists are beautiful people.

My own ex, Kay, seemed to cast a spell over me with a flick of her wavy blonde locks or a quick wink of her eye. All of my logic would vanish, and I'd feel overcome by the need to hold her. She counted on my attraction to keep me from questioning her. However, once I walked away and got some physical space to myself, I could easily see how she played me. That step back did me a world of good.

BALANCE YOUR EMOTIONAL STATE

Remember that getting upset can make it hard to present your side of a situation or make a coherent argument. Your gaslighter wants you to be an emotional wreck so they can maintain their presence as the calm, logical one in the relationship. Don't fall for it! Do whatever you need to keep yourself balanced.

If we're calm, we can face down gaslighting with a powerful, even stance of clarity. We can call it out and demand our feelings be recognized.

What do you need in order to feel calm and steady? If it's regular exercise, get it, no matter what that entails. You can go online and find a plethora of free workouts. All you need is a little space and thirty minutes to sweat and work out your stress.

If time outside helps you even out, find your natural space and visit it whenever you can. Spending time outside is immensely healing and helps us remember that our problems aren't as massive as we might believe.

Meditation brings millions of people into a peaceful state. You can do it any time of day or night. Find a quiet space and sit or lie down without crossing any limbs and focus on your breath. Notice any distracting thoughts, acknowledge them, then let them go. Return your focus to the in and out of your breathing.

That's it, that's all you need to meditate. Five minutes a day can change your life. I know it did for me, and I'm confident that meditation will help you find a healthy mental state too.

Finding our Zen does more than help us stay firm in our convictions. It also brings the truth to light and makes it impossible to deny. It helps us build faith in ourselves, which ups our confidence and maintains our conviction in our decisions. There's no reason for you to question every move you make, but you will if you don't put yourself and your health first.

IN CASE YOU CAN'T LEAVE

If your gaslighter is someone you can't leave, either because you're a minor and dealing with a manipulative parent or the caretaker for someone toying with your mental state, you still have options.

First, find a way to ground yourself. A friend of mine grew up with vicious anxiety attacks and found a way to calm herself down when her emotions skyrocketed.

"I'd look down at my shoes and show myself that I had safe ground to stand on. Then I'd say, 'Today is December 2nd, 30 degrees outside, the current time is 4 p.m....' and so on. It's hard to get emotional about the date and time, so I always started there. Then I'd look at my location. I'd focus on the walls standing straight up, not moving, and think about the firm foundation underneath me. I'd remind myself that my body is strong, I have no debilitating illnesses, and I can walk without help. All of those irrefutable facts came together to help me move out of the attack."

A grounding exercise can be anything. Try holding and looking at a photo of yourself or someone special to you and focus on the details. Or breathe in for a count of four, hold it for four, then exhale for four seconds. You can also try focusing on a plant in your house, a nearby piece of nature, or the sounds of cars driving by.

The objective is to keep yourself present, no matter the situation. Don't let yourself get caught up in a swirl of thoughts and emotions. Remember that that's when you're at your weakest. With the present reality in your hands, you're much stronger and ready to take on whatever situation you have in front of you.

Evidence is another great way to maintain that mindfulness. Keep a diary—a secret one if you like—and write down any odd events that happen with your gaslighter. List the date and time, write out the details, and tell yourself what happened. Don't worry about what your gaslighter might have to say; this is your space, and no one else gets to have an opinion on your notes.

Refer back to this written record whenever your sanity gets called into question. Use this living document as proof that you don't fabricate moments in your relationship. These things happened and there's no denying it.

Another great way to keep a record of what's happening and how is to keep talking to people around you. You might not feel comfortable opening up about your relationship, so find someone you trust and feel confident will listen to you, not judge you. Don't let yourself get cut off socially; every gaslighter depends on you not having a support system. If you push back on that issue and keep in touch with friends and relatives, you'll always have a voice of reason to back you up.

Other pieces of evidence can include photos of anything you might find important. Maybe you're constantly accused of making a mess, yet everything appears clean and organized. Snap a few pictures of the house and keep them for yourself. Show yourself you aren't imagining anything. You cleaned, and you have proof.

Voice memos can also help you keep track of what happened and when. Each voice recording you save to your phone gets an automatic time stamp. You can also record phone calls, though if you hope to use those recordings in a future case, you'll need to check your state's laws. You may have to ask permission to make a recording legal, which defeats the purpose of recording the call.

Any texts, emails, or messages that reinforce a narcissist's negative message can be screenshotted and saved in a file. Make sure you don't put it somewhere where it can be found—label it with a blasé name and tuck it inside a few other files. Again, check your state's laws if you want to use them in any future cases.

FACING YOUR GASLIGHTER

It's time. Time to let the narcissist in your life know that you see them for what they are: an insecure, manipulative person who makes your daily life impossible.

Before you jump into an argument, be ready for any and all reactions. Your narcissist might laugh in your face, deny the evidence, or use it as a chance to play the victim. Your plan of attack is to stay calm, stay honest, and call this behavior out. No more playing along.

Call It Out

To start, you want to let your narcissist know that what they do with you has a name: gaslighting. You see it, and you don't want it anymore.

Many narcissists see a refusal to fight back as a lack of caring. Remember that narcissists will fight tooth and nail for what they want. They will sacrifice friendships, throw colleagues to the wolves, you name it. Your politeness and tendency to look away could signal to a narcissist that you don't see a problem or care enough to deal with the issue.

Let them know you care. Say it out loud.

"Do not gaslight me. It makes me furious when you do that. Admit you did something wrong so we can move forward."

Clear, concise sentences are your friends. Practice and use them whenever you can to shut down any future gaslighting.

When your gaslighter relies on criticism or insults, respond immediately to the technique, not the words.

"It's not productive for us to sit here and criticize each other. I'm ready to talk about this like an adult. When you're ready, you know where to find me." Then get up and walk away. Don't say you're leaving or where you're going; get out the door without apologies.

This is the same technique lots of parents use when kids are out of control. They simply state that the behavior is unacceptable, then turn and leave. Like small children, narcissists crave attention. When your gaslighter sees that their actions only earn them silence and time alone, they'll start to police themselves (at least a little). But this isn't about them—walking away from the vitriol will make you feel better, too. That's what matters.

You can also shut down accusations of fabricated memories. Here's the reality: our brains don't fabricate entire memories. The brain might change the color of a house or swap two people's names, but it won't build the house and create the people for you. Brains don't work that way. Have confidence that what you remember *is* what happened. If your gaslighter throws the "you're insane" argument your way, you can state that.

"I'm not insane. Far from it. I'm a lucid, mentally stable person. And I know for a fact that there's no such thing as a fabricated memory. You can deny the past all you want, but I know what happened."

Hold onto that confidence in your version of events. Tell yourself you have all your marbles whenever you need to hear it. Say kind things to yourself over and over; it helps more than you might believe. It can also reinforce that you won't accept any manipulative behavior. You don't have time for it because you're living your life.

To help you maintain your stand in the argument, here are some phrases that others in similar situations have found helpful:

- "I have heard your point of view many times now, and I still don't agree with it."
- "I'd like to take a break from this conversation."
- "I don't like how much energy I'm putting into proving my perspective, and it would mean a lot to me if you gave me the benefit of the doubt."
- "I get that you're mad. I'm angry, too."
- "I realize you disagree with me, but this is how I see it."
- "I'm not imagining things."
- "Name-calling is hurtful to me. I find it hard to listen to you when you talk like that."
- "My feelings are my feelings; this is how I feel."
- "This is my experience, and these are my emotions."
- "It sounds like you feel strongly about that, but my emotions are valid too."
- "I feel like I'm not being heard, and I need some space."
- "I know what's best for me."
- "This is what I want and what I need right now."
- "I'm making this decision for myself."
- "I'm not responding to that."

- "I want to figure things out for myself."
- "It's hard for me to stay engaged in this conversation; I've already said no several times."
- "I'm finding it difficult to keep discussing this."

Prioritize Self-Care

Remember that all of this is designed to make you—the one on the receiving end of the abuse—feel better. I don't want you to waste time trying to fix your abuser or hanging onto the belief that one day they'll wake up a saint. We can't control others' actions because it's an impossible feat. What we can control is how well we take care of ourselves and how much we value ourselves as people.

Many mistake self-care as self-indulgence, but it doesn't have to be a day at the spa or lounging in the bathtub, (though that might be your idea of Utopia). Rather, take a moment and think about the simple things in life that make you happy.

What is something you could easily do all day without any thought to a reward? For me it's sipping coffee in a cafe and reading a great book while lounging in a soft armchair. For years, I didn't prioritize taking time for myself. It felt selfish and silly. Couldn't I use that time to work or hit the gym?

Yet, when I allow myself a giant cup of coffee, a good book, and a few hours to enjoy them, my whole week gets better. I get more done at work and I feel happier about my accomplishments. My general outlook stays positive and I don't sweat the small stuff. Despite my misgivings about using my free time to be unproductive, it's proven to be the right thing for me.

Remember that taking care of yourself consists of refilling your happiness quota by finding that thing you revel in for hours on end. It doesn't require a salary or an audience; you just love it because you love it.

For example, a good friend of mine makes time to get her skates on and roll around her neighborhood streets like a kid. She knows she's not a graceful skater nor a particularly fast one, but something about the feel of the breeze in her hair and the sun on her shoulders makes all her problems melt away.

Another friend of mine loves walking in the woods. He sometimes has to remind himself to get home, so he doesn't end up in the middle of nowhere when night falls. His wife loves to see him come home—his former stress has vanished, and she swears he has fewer lines in his face.

We need to make space for our partners to find some time for themselves at least once a week, but we also need to do this for ourselves. Remember that no narcissist would hesitate to do what they love for hours on end. Why should you deny yourself?

Good self-care helps improve your mental, emotional, and physical health. If you feel good, you won't stress-eat or worry over small things, and you will have a better handle on emergencies. Self-care does more than help us relax; it gives us the strong foundation we need to build a more resilient and better version of ourselves.

Hobbies can help you begin your self-care routine. If you want your hobby to be something physical, like hiking up a trail or spending time on a yoga mat, make sure you do it with no goals in mind. Do your best to focus on each moment, not how many calories you burned or the number of miles you logged. Instead, pay attention to your internal strength and balance. Notice the quiet around you and try to hold the same calm in your mind.

Other hobbies help the quiet happen as if by accident. Putting together a complex puzzle, sketching something beautiful, or learning a dance quiets our mental noise. You can feel your worries and stress unravel when you put all your attention into these small projects instead of your current romantic or familial drama.

Try to bring other people into your new interest; doing so can keep you motivated and help boost your social life. Whenever your gaslighter tries to discourage you from meeting up with your running friends or your art club, don't respond. Instead, listen to what he's really saying.

"I'm intimidated by the power you're finding in yourself. I've never experienced that, and I'm scared you won't need me anymore."

Chances are, their right. However, you don't have to say that to your narcissist. Rather, keep your interests and self-care to yourself. It's not for anyone else—those things are available to help you and keep you happy.

THINGS TO KEEP IN MIND

First, always remember what drives a narcissist's behavior. Everything behind a narcissist's actions comes from a place of fear. They're afraid they'll be uncovered as a fraud, be alone, don't deserve love, and everyone else is better than them. They've learned to fight that fear by constantly making others feel terrible, but this sham of a life can't last forever, and they can see the end coming.

Eventually, people around the narcissist—even those who love them dearly—start to see through the cracks. The truly adept gaslighters who can toy with emotions better than anyone else might hide longer, but even they get outed as fake and awful.

Remember all of this, because once you start taking care of yourself, standing up to your gaslighter, and putting yourself first, you'll get pushback.

They'll try everything to keep you to themselves and cut you off from your social life or family. They'll try the love bomb again, showering you with the same tenderness you've hoped for all these years. They might threaten you or themselves, say they'll kill themselves or seriously harm themselves if you leave them.

Stay strong. This is the true sign of a gaslighter and narcissist. Someone with a healthy mental state can handle a night alone; they won't be threatened by physical space and quiet. To a narcissist who feeds on the pain of others, this is torture. They see it as a night in which they'll starve while everyone else laughs at their hunger pangs.

Unlike actual starvation, your narcissist won't suffer. Sure, they'll be uncomfortable, but they'll live.

Remember that you won't be happy if you cancel all your plans to sit around and make someone else more secure. You don't get the days you sacrifice to them back; they're gone for good. Don't surrender your time and energy to anyone else. Keep it safe and use it to benefit yourself, even if it means a showdown.

Try stating simply that you have plans you don't want to break. If your narcissist wants to spend time with you, all they have to do is discuss it with you ahead of time, or you can state that it's unfair of them to expect you to give up your night because you wouldn't do that to them. Say it's good to get some oxygen into a relationship because that's what helps keep it fresh. Do anything that will help you feel confident walking out the door.

You might get a sudden submission like, "Fine! Go! I don't care." Take this at face value. Shrug and say, "Great! See you when I get back," then do whatever you want.

Don't focus on whether your actions qualify as right or wrong. Rather, pay attention to how you feel when you're out on your own or with friends. Are you relieved? Breathing deeper? Hang onto those deep breaths and relaxed shoulders. That's how you should feel every day.

To minimize stress and make yourself more independent, separate your money from your gaslighter. This can get messy, but you need financial independence. Remember that many abusers use money—or a lack of money—to keep their victims in a state of dependence. If you make a salary or receive regular payments, keep those funds in an account that only you can access.

Don't loan out your card or make your passwords too obvious. Narcissists don't hesitate to spend a significant other's money. Keep your accounts secure so you can always have a way to fund what you need and pay for what you want.

TIPS FOR DEALING WITH GASLIGHTERS

Having a separate fund to keep yourself financially independent is one of many ways you can help yourself leave a bad situation. Here's a quick list of things to remember to help you manage your emotions and keep yourself safe.

Don't Take Responsibility

Many victims manage to convince themselves that they're the ones causing the problem. Remember—you can only control your own actions; no one else's are your fault. If your gaslighter loses it in public, walks away from yet another job, or hits someone, none of that is on you.

Also, don't make yourself responsible for someone else's anger or outbursts. All adults have access to resources to help them manage their emotions. If someone in your life can't be bothered to grow up, that's not on you.

Don't Sacrifice

Don't sacrifice your free time, personal space, money, and definitely not your happiness. No one ever won an award for suffering. However, plenty of people find their happiness leading them to great friendships, professional success, and enhanced creative expression. Letting someone take that happiness away from you means you'll lose out on all of those opportunities, so don't do it.

Remember—narcissists both want and despise the people who work hard to make them happy. Yours doesn't enjoy your home-cooked food and constant efforts to feed them healthy food, make the home cheerier or make their friends like you. No matter what you do, what they really want is to see you suffer.

That's why a constant state of sacrifice is a death wish. Always settling for less than the best will leave you dried up and lonely with no one on your side.

Put yourself first and watch your life get exponentially better.

Remember Your Truth

Keep that journal of facts and past events and refer to it all you like. Remember that your brain doesn't fabricate entire memories. That means if you remember something, it happened. That's not up for discussion.

Stand on what you know to be true. When your gaslighter sounds confident, that doesn't mean they're automatically right; it means they are certain they can manipulate you and make you feel weak. Hold onto your personal truth and remember that you never have to defend your emotions; your strength will see you through.

Don't Argue on Their Terms

If your gaslighter makes up a few random facts, then tries to belittle you with declarative sentences like, "you never remember anything right," call out what's happening.

"This is gaslighting, and I won't stand for it. If you want to discuss this like adults, I'll listen. Otherwise, we're done here."

Your gaslighter will try to declare some kind of victory or claim that they've won the argument. You never have to accept those statements. When you can see they're based on a faulty premise, you never have to take any of those announcements as true.

Prioritize Your Safety

If, at any moment, you feel you're in danger, get out. Don't pack a bag or announce that you're leaving. Just open the door and go.

Narcissism and constant gaslighting often lead to physical abuse. Don't kid and try to convince yourself that things will change or get better. That's prioritizing someone else over yourself. Like free time and happiness, safety is something you can't get back after you've put it aside. You have to claim and leave with it, no matter what.

Don't Retaliate

In other words, don't play the gaslighter's game. Using their own tactics against them—like throwing confusing word salad in their face or hitting back—won't work in your favor.

A gaslighter loves to fight. They're drawn to it like a beautiful work of art. They want to spend as much time fighting as possible, so don't give in. Your reactions, loss of control, or yelling reinforce all of their statements about your emotional state and lack of mental stability.

Narcissists need friction. Fights turn them on more than anything. They get to play the victim, and can point to past fights years after they happened as proof that you're a disappointment or the aggressor. It lets the worst side of them come to the surface, and they are vindicated in its appearance. After all, you wanted a fight.

Retaliation often leads to violence, which can endanger your life. Prioritize your safety, don't react, and stand on your truth rather than sink to their level.

HOW TO LEAVE

I've thrown around the idea of walking away from a gaslighter, but how can someone really go with their head held high and feel confident they've made the right decision? Remember that our brains can work against us when it comes to toxic relationships. What if this person is our mother or father? What then?

It's hard no matter who it is that deserves to be left behind, but I promise you there's always a way. It's never impossible to walk away from someone, and it doesn't matter how deep a hold they may have on you.

Here's a breakdown of the stages of getting out of this bad relationship and how to start off on your gaslight-free life the right way.

Leave Mentally

Try a quick visualization. Close your eyes and imagine yourself in two years. See what you look like, what you're doing, and who's there with you. What's your home like? How are you physically? Do you have a new look? Have you lost or gained some weight? Are you happy?

Now go back and try to remember—was your narcissist there with you, or were they out of the picture?

If you can't imagine yourself with someone in the next two years, you're not in a good relationship. It's time to start visualizing yourself as a happy single.

I don't want you to replace your gaslighter with someone new. Remember—one bad relationship can inspire us to run into another one. Instead, think of all the great things you could do without a significant other who makes so many demands on you. Think about all the free time and stress-free days you could enjoy and the number of things you could do if you were on your own.

If the gaslighter is a family member, imagine that person miles away. You may not be able to break up with this narcissist, but you can put them at a great distance. See yourself in a new apartment, and maybe even a new state or country. Physical distance makes it much harder to manipulate someone, so find somewhere you can live where you don't see your gaslighter every day. Don't hesitate to get a new phone number or shut down your social media. If you're less available, you're in less of a position to have to deal with insults and painful comments.

Feel Your Feelings

Be aware of how you feel, but don't judge any of your feelings. Allow them to come in and bang around in your heart. Observe how you feel and when. Maybe you wake up feeling hopeful each morning but slowly get beaten down throughout the day. Do you have a long period of your day that's free of gaslighting? How does it feel during those moments?

Don't label any feelings as good, bad, wrong, or right. Feelings exist to give us greater insight into ourselves. However, it doesn't work if we don't listen.

Our emotions also teach us about our triggers. Your triggers are phrases, actions, jokes, or external factors that make you upset, give you knots in your stomach, or make you want to run out of the room. Even things that indirectly remind us of other things that upset us can be triggers. Triggers are essential to learning how to keep ourselves healthy. Everyone deserves a low-stress life, but that means finding a way to live that's as free from our triggers as we can get.

A good friend of mine, Marnie, absolutely detests hearing women described as "crazy" or "insane." I talked to her about this trigger one day and got some insight into how she developed her specific response.

"First," she explained, "it's a catch-all. As soon as any woman does a single thing a man doesn't like, *she's crazy*. And the description normally comes right behind another word—bitch. It's a word I have to hear all the time because I dare to do things like ask for what's mine, have an opinion, or walk onstage to do my standup comedy. You want to hear that you're a crazy bitch non-stop? Become a woman and hit up an open-mic night.

"Second, there's a long history of people labelling women insane or hysterical and treating them terribly. Mental hospitals used to lock up women if they did so much as hesitate to make dinner for a demanding husband or mention they didn't like something. I'm not exaggerating! Society labeled women clinically insane at the first opportunity for decades. 'Hysteria' was considered a physical and mental disorder just a few centuries ago.

"But here's the big one—I had an ex who constantly called my mental health into question. Now, to be fair, he was joking, but the more I told him it wasn't funny, the more he did it! He'd spent his whole life hearing about us *crazy bitches* and how hilarious it was to call them names; he couldn't hear me when I tried to explain it was *not* funny, but hurting my feelings. I had to leave him, which sucked, because it was all fixable."

"And I'm the one who's crazy?"

I hear Marnie, I really do. I also tried to approach past partners and talk out our problems, only to get dismissed by the same person I adored. What's more is that it creates future triggers, making it harder to be around people who upset or tease us, using words that make us emotional.

Remember that those emotions aren't wrong. You're not overreacting or being sensitive; you're listening to yourself and learning what serves you and what you need to leave behind.

Keeping track of your moods can happen in any journal, but journals can be a pain to carry around. If you need some good apps for journaling or tracking changes in your emotions, I have a quick list for you here.

Moodkit—Moodkit asks you how you're feeling, then uses responses based on cognitive behavioral therapy (CBT) to let you know how a therapist might respond to your feelings. It records your changes in a week and month-long chart, so you can assess different periods of your life and figure out when you feel at your best.

Daylio—Similar to Moodkit, Daylio adds a quick diary, easy stats about mental health, responses, and help in changing your lifestyle. Daylio comes in free or paid premium versions.

CBT Thought Diary—This amazing little digital diary can help you track and reduce negative thoughts. If you tend to beat yourself up mentally, you can use this app to build a more positive view of yourself and focus on what makes you grateful and calm.

TherapyBuddy—An awesome app to have when you start or continue therapy sessions. Most of us see a professional once a week or less, so it can be easy to lose track of what we need to discuss. TherapyBuddy gives you a place to track your time out of a session so you can discuss how you felt on a specific day and what happened that could have knocked you out of whack. Not sure what's stressing you out or why exactly you got so upset? TherapyBuddy can help.

RealifeChange—This one goes beyond tracking by coaching you on how to make better choices. If you struggle to take care of yourself, reach for junk food more than you should, or let others treat you badly, this app can turn your weaknesses into strengths. It also comes in free and paid premium versions.

It's Okay to Walk Away

I know many people who, once something goes wrong, dig in their heels and devote themselves to fixing the problem. This can be admirable. We shouldn't give up on kids who struggle in school or refuse to fight for our health. Once in a while, walking away is better than fighting.

How do we know when to walk away, though? It's not always easy. We have to assess the situation. A therapist I saw for years told me the one question to always ask myself is, "Does this disrupt my life?" That's a quick fix to deciding if something is toxic or simply annoying. Remember that an annoying coworker is someone who can't tell a joke, but a toxic one is a person who loves to watch others suffer.

Does your job leave you feeling defeated, micromanaged, or unintelligent? Do you honestly believe no one in their right mind would hire you if you left? Then it's time to go.

When we can't live our lives normally, we have a toxic force biting at our heels. Once you distance yourself, those bites lose their sting. You can recover and move on to something better, but only if you take the first step away.

Keep reminding yourself that staying means disrupting your life. It means committing to a toxic person, not a loving one. It also means you see yourself as someone who does not deserve happiness and love, but you do!

Before you quit and leave your toxic boss behind, talk to friends in your industry. Tell them you're unhappy and want to see if anyone is hiring. Don't gossip about your boss—that puts you in a bad light. Simply mention that you're hoping to go somewhere else.

You can spend your off-hours clicking through job ads anywhere in the world. You don't have to leave the country; rather, use this as a reminder that yours is not the only place to work. There are tons of opportunities out there you might not have even considered.

If you're not dealing with a toxic boss, but more of a narcissist friend or family member, look for opportunities to put distance between that person and yourself. Remember to prioritize your needs over theirs, and you'll start to make better decisions for yourself. It can be hard to call a family member or lifelong friend toxic, but even these relationships can turn on us for the worst. We need to prioritize our own happiness above all. Spend weekends or afternoons away from the person who is emotionally manipulating you and take notes about how you feel when you're far away from them.

Prepare for the Hoover

Whenever a narcissist sees the writing on the wall or gets confronted with their behavior, they may try to bring out the hoover.

If you have a narcissist in your life, you already know this move. Faced with solitude and loneliness, the narcissist suddenly does a 180. All the former insults suddenly turn into lovely praise. Comments like, "you can't do anything right, can you?" become, "I'm so lucky to have you—you're my hero."

It's as if the narcissist suddenly brought out the vacuum and sucked up all that toxicity poisoning you both in an attempt to fix all the problems between you two.

Of course, erasing the problem doesn't fix anything. Exactly the opposite happens, actually; the victim gets a brief respite from the abuse, the narcissist gets to pretend they're truly a good, caring person, and then slowly, both return to their former patterns. After a few days, the narcissist builds up the negative behavior piece by piece, and their victim slowly falls back into depression and a feeling of helplessness. The victim mentions leaving again, and out comes the hoover for another clean up.

The only way to really fix a terribly broken relationship is with intense couple's therapy. I believe that combined with couple's therapy, individual therapy for both parties has to happen too, although that may not be feasible for everyone. And if your partner, family member, or friend isn't open to it, some real, internal work can't happen.

Get Ready for it to Become Worse

After you leave your narcissist, don't expect them to disappear. Exactly the opposite, in fact. Once you've thrown a narcissist's insecurity in their face, you've lit a fire that will quickly burn out of control.

It's often during and immediately after a breakup that abusive behavior becomes more intense. I can see why so many people stay with monstrous partners—if they leave, they take their lives into their hands. Back home where I grew up, one woman went so far as to plan her own funeral after the police wouldn't help her escape her horrifically abusive ex-boyfriend. Unfortunately, those funeral plans came to be—she was murdered in her own home by the man she'd consistently told police officers was dangerous and needed to be in jail.

I don't mean to scare you, but I do want you to be realistic; if your abuse already includes physical attacks, you need to be ready.

Leave when you're alone or can slip out unseen. Don't say anything or make any kind of a scene. Stay away from mutual friends too—gaslighters often use third parties to spy on former partners. You might think you're safe with your ex's casual friend, but they could be the same reason you're in danger.

Block your gaslighter's number or label it "DO NOT ANSWER" or something similar. Remember that even someone who's bad for us can have a pull on us. Seeing that phrase can keep you from having a moment of weakness. Also, ignore any numbers you don't recognize. Your abuser can easily borrow a phone or buy a burner in hopes of tricking you into answering.

If you can, get a new phone and stay with someone your abuser doesn't know. If the gaslighter is familiar with your place of work, alert your colleagues that your situation has changed. You do not want this person approaching you at work or in the parking lot. If you have security guards at work, let them know and give them a picture of the person you want kept away.

Whenever someone asks for details, decline. Discussing it with others can easily open the door to some truly disgusting accusations against you or a disinterest in your situation that could upset you and make it harder to move on. Simply say, "the situation became a threat to my safety." Anything to shut down the conversation and help you feel in control will be good here.

It's a good idea to contact a domestic abuse organization and ask for a safety plan or a safe place to stay. Many will help you find a volunteer with an extra room or offer you housing with the organization. Then, reach out to any support groups or individual counselors who can help you work through the separation, your residual feelings, and resulting fear, exhaustion, or depression. Plan ahead as much as you can, so you can stay three steps ahead of anyone who might come looking for you with the intent of getting you back to your abuser.

ONE MORE THING...

I know it can be incredibly tempting to go back. Many victims eventually return to their abusers despite the dismal state of the relationship. If this happens to you, don't blame yourself. Remember—your mental state is not what it was in the beginning. In fact, you're a different person altogether and will likely never be the idealist partner you were at the start.

Do everything you can to stay away from anyone in your life who actively and intentionally hurts you. Ask friends to encourage you to do things you love. Avoid anyone who slings mud at your old partner or the narcissist—oddly, this can compel you to defend them and even remember the good times.

After you leave, it's essential that you prioritize your self-care. If you can reduce your hours at work or take a sabbatical, do it. You need this time to show yourself what an amazing person you are and that you deserve better. Don't let anyone tell you that it's wrong to be single or away from the person hurting you. That person isn't you. They cannot know what you've been through, nor will they know what's best for you.

Listen to yourself instead. Pay attention to how you feel and why you want to stay away from your gaslighter. I'm guessing you feel better just by imagining it. Now it's time to plan your escape so you can start to heal.

CHAPTER SUMMARY

It's time to take a deep breath. This chapter was intense. Here's what we discussed:

- Distancing yourself from your abuser will happen in stages. Prepare ahead of time.
- Reach out to any local organizations or mental health

professionals for help.
- Prioritize your happiness and make having a stress-free life your goal.

In the next chapter, we will dive deeper into how to recover from the effects of gaslighting.

7

RECOVERING FROM ABUSE

Congratulations. You did it. You got away from the person hurting you and took a stand for yourself. I am so glad you're out and ready to move on.

I should say now, you can't do this alone. More than anything, people recovering from a damaged sense of self, brow-beaten mentality, and sense of hopelessness need people around them who can lift them up. You might want to avoid any intense competitions, anyone who likes to make biting comments, and family members whom you know won't take your side.

Before we get into all of that, let me back up. First thing's first, make sure you're safe.

VICTIM OR VICTORIOUS

Step one is how you view yourself. When you look in the mirror, do you see a victim? Someone stupid enough to fall for psychological tricks? Or do you see someone strong enough to move on from this trying experience?

If you answered yes to the former, it's extremely important that you focus on rejecting that victim mentality. It won't serve you and will open the door to future abuse, which is exactly what you worked so hard to leave behind.

Yes, you should acknowledge what happened and how bad it felt, but you also have to see how much power and strength it took for you to walk away. Think of all the wonderful opportunities you have in front of you, with no negative comments making you second-guess your choices. You know now that you're not just sane; you're great. You can start your new and wonderful life, but only if you put your past in the right context.

Think about how things went with your narcissist. Try to remember a time when you stayed quiet and didn't stand up for yourself. Picture it as clearly as you can, and maybe write about it in your journal.

Go ahead and get mad at yourself. Yell at that memory of yourself for the stupidity or reluctance to say something. Get it all out. Then, do it all again. This time see how your silence kept you safe. Maybe it diffused the situation or allowed you to go on with your day. You weren't hiding in plain sight; you were surviving.

Looking back with this new lens will help you move onto a better, more confident you. Confidence shuts down abuse faster than anything—take it from me. I fought for my self-esteem, and it drove away any potential bad partners. They hated that I didn't need anyone because I had myself.

It's important to celebrate who you are as a person. Find groups, events, literature, or films that celebrate different aspects of you. For example, you come from a Latin background, read some of the amazing books from south of the border or incredible poetry. Listen to some great music and pick up some Spanish if you haven't already.

The same can happen for your gender. If you identify yourself as female, try checking out a women's group, a fun, female-centered hobby, or a club. You can sign up for a women-only retreat if it's in your budget and spend a week with a group of incredible, powerful women and soak in that female energy.

Another option is to find people your age who are working to make society better or more fun. If you're young, look for friends who pursue creative expression like the arts or fun garage band music. Look for people who volunteer, work with the homeless, or help any marginalized group in need of some extra hands.

When you surround yourself with happy, positive people, something magical takes place. Happiness is much more contagious than misery, and once we get a taste of it, we wonder why we didn't seek it out much sooner.

After my graduation, I went a year with no work. I had to move back home and hide my face from anyone who might recognize me because

I was so embarrassed. Not only had I left school emotionally scarred, but I also had no prospects despite my endless hours of research. I needed something positive in my life.

I found a great local group called the Dirt Clods. They met once a week to volunteer for an afternoon and take on big projects that nonprofits, daycares, or other groups couldn't afford to pay for, like cleaning the gutters or disinfecting toys.

The group made me so much more hopeful. So many people came together with the sole purpose of helping. Afterwards, we all headed to the bar for a round of beers and to hang out. I was deeply sorry to leave the group after I got hired at my first job.

The Dirt Clods showed me that I had nothing to be embarrassed about. Sure, I was an unemployed graduate living at home with no job offers, but I was more than that. I was a nice guy, a friend, and someone who saw the value in reaching out and helping. As long as I put my energy into something positive, I could be proud of myself.

Another important thing to do now is learn how to create and maintain boundaries. Your boundaries will keep you safe for a lifetime, so set them carefully.

Think about the people who lift you up, make you feel like a part of the group, and love to include you. Write a list of all their names. It's a good idea to spend more time with this group—even if you only get together once a month, do something to show them they matter to you.

Then, write a second list of the people who make you feel small or unimportant. It's okay to put family members or even close friends on this list. We often build relationships that we don't really need or that outlive their value. Maybe you had a close friend in high school that you don't feel close to anymore—decide to let that friendship go. You don't need it anymore.

For family, think about how you can optimize short visits so you don't have to spend lots of time at someone's home when you could be doing something better for yourself. If you have a sister who demands a ton of your free time, visualize telling her you need time for yourself, your friends, or your work. You love her, but you can't be at her beck and call.

You might have to make some lame excuses like, "I would love to come, but I'm swamped." People will likely see through them, but don't stress; you don't owe anyone your time. That's yours alone.

You also need to set boundaries about activities and behavior. What's unacceptable to you? Do you hate a certain kind of humor, people who make explicit comments, or horror movies? From now on, you don't waste time with any of it. You say no thank you and go look for something you enjoy. This world is too big and interesting for you to hang out with a crowd you'd happily toss out the window or watch a corpse get mutilated while you long for an early bedtime, if neither of those activities are things you enjoy doing.

Now, to maintain your boundaries, you need people who respect how you feel. If anyone dismisses how you feel or doesn't listen to you when you express a clear distaste for what's happening, that is someone undeserving of your time. If you get called names or accused of being "sensitive" when you stand up for what you want, consider that a stamp of approval for you to walk away.

EDUCATE YOURSELF

It's important that you learn about abusive behavior, how it works, and the warning signs before you dive into any new relationships. If you don't, it will be easy for you to fall into another bad situation while convincing yourself that everything is somehow different than before.

If you learn about the habits of an abusive partner ahead of time, you can dismiss them before you get love-bombed or deep into their mental traps. The sooner you can give them the boot, the better. You don't need any more narcissists in your life.

Here's a quick list of titles to get you started:

1. *When Love Goes Wrong: What to do When You Can't Do Anything Right* by Ann Jones and Susan Schecter
2. *The Verbally Abusive Relationship: How to Recognize It and Respond* by Patricia Evans
3. *Scared to Leave, Afraid to Stay: Paths from Family Violence to Safety* by Barry Goldstein
4. *Should I Stay or Should I Go?* by Lundy Bancroft & JAC Patrissi

5. *No Visible Wounds: Identifying Non-Physical Abuse of Women by Their Men* by Mary Susan Miller Ph.D.

I could easily write a whole volume of great books to check out, but I like these in particular. You can also join online support groups, in-person group therapy, or whatever else helps you get a better understanding of what happened and why. Remember—you survived, and that's amazing. The next step is to thrive.

LOVE YOURSELF

I know so many smart, incredible people who see themselves as completely unimpressive. It boggles me! A friend with three jobs will call herself "lazy" because she needs a day to rest. A dad who consistently plays and communicates with his kids will write off his parenting skills as "the fun one," despite the value he brings to their childhood. And whip-smart women will still second-guess themselves at work on a daily basis.

I had a long talk with a therapist about my guilt around my selfishness. I saw any attempt to avoid buying gifts—even if I was dead broke—or a refusal to give up my time as me being selfish. By that standard, I had selfish people all around me, yet I didn't see them in that light. I asked her about how I could reconcile my guilt with my needs, and she gave me an interesting exercise.

"What if," she said, "you just said to yourself, 'I'm selfish.'" She cocked her head to the side and put her hands on her hips, the perfect representation of that me-first attitude. "Just tell yourself that and see what happens. I want you to be selfish."

It took a long time, but I eventually got to a point where I could acknowledge that, yes, my decision to avoid a family function or go on a date instead of seeing a needy friend could qualify me as selfish, but that was okay. Life isn't a test of service—it's whatever we make it.

Practice Radical Forgiveness

It seems bizarre, but the act of forgiveness can help the victim much more than the perpetrator. To radically forgive means to acknowledge that without forgiving the person who wronged you, you'll be the one stuck in negativity and anger, not your abuser.

This can take time, and that's perfectly fine. Try practicing meditation, journaling about the experience, and even writing angry letters to your abuser and ripping them to shreds. Then, look for the sadness your abuser must carry.

People who hurt others harbor their own pain. They likely grew up with horrible abuse, a bad sense of themselves, and constant negative messages or lack of support from those around them. I'm not making excuses for anyone, but it's important that we see the whole picture.

Now try writing about how sad and hurt your abuser must have felt in order to pile all that pain onto you. If you know something about their past, acknowledge the roots of that pain and how it built up over the years. It may be unclear how your abuser's pain came to fruition, but that only shows how hard they worked to hide their pain from you.

Start to see your abuser as someone bumbling around in the darkness—someone deserving of pity. Are you still angry? If so, give it some time, talk it over with a therapist, or discuss it in group therapy. You can't be angry and forgive at the same time.

Once the anger starts to dissipate, find a way to forgive your abuser, but not to their face. Instead, do it for yourself. Write them a letter, declare your forgiveness out loud, create something that represents how you've let go of the past relationship. Don't get your past abuser's friends or family involved in any way or post it on social media; keep it private. Make your experience centered on you and no one else.

Radical forgiveness helps us cut ties with a past that no longer serves us. If you can snip those ties away from yourself, you can heal much more deeply and focus on loving yourself non-stop.

This practice also makes it so we don't live in the past. Do you know someone who lives in their memories? I haven't met many—they tend to spend a lot of time alone, don't do well professionally, and often don't move out of their childhood homes. To live in the past means to refuse to move forward, like insisting on standing in a sinkhole. Don't do it.

LET GO OF CLOSURE

A big part of radical forgiveness is the realization that we may never have the closure we crave. It's too much to ask of a gaslighter. Remember that narcissists thrive on others needing their approval, and once your narcissist sees you begging for a chance to talk and put things behind you, they'll dig in. They'll make you chase them and then refuse to give you what you want. Don't believe me? I tried it.

My ex Kay circled back into my life long after I'd let go of our past issues. Then, she started dating a friend of mine, and we ended up at the same party.

I caught Kay alone in the kitchen and we made polite small talk. Then, I asked her if maybe we could get together and talk sometime so we could go over what happened. I wanted to understand where we went wrong.

I'll never forget the little smile that creeped across her face. She lifted an eyebrow and cocked her head at me.

"What? You want to pick me apart? You think you're a shrink now?"

"No, I just thought—"

"That's your problem, you know. You think all the time. It's very unattractive. But sure. Call me sometime and I'll tell you all the issues we had. Why not?"

She flicked her business card at me and walked away.

The card hit me in the chest, and I caught it, then stared at it for a long time. After a long moment, I laughed. What had I expected? Kay hadn't changed—she still loved to make people feel small. I mean, she thought my ability to think was unattractive? I didn't need to call her.

I knew what the problem was, and it was Kay. She loved twisting emotions and making others bow down to her. And I wasn't going to do it ever again.

Some events in life will never give us closure, and that's okay. It's often beside the point. It's up to us to learn from our pasts and fumbles. If we don't, then we lose out on an opportunity. If our former partner, friend, or family member isn't open to learning with us, then we need to let that person miss out. They're not our responsibility.

FORGET SHAME

I read a great quote from a successful porn star that stuck with me for years: "You can't shame me if I don't feel ashamed."

Bam. That's it right there. Granted, she referred to her profession, but the sentiment is still universal. Shame doesn't live long if you love yourself to let go of any semblance of your own shame. What do you have to be ashamed of? You didn't abuse anyone. You're a beautiful, strong individual. You need to see that every time you look in the mirror.

Shame can also enhance that dangerous anchor to the past. Loving and seeing yourself as a constant work-in-progress, not a failed adult or partner, can keep you moving forward. Yes, you'll make mistakes, but you'll learn from them. That's the most anyone can do.

REBUILD YOURSELF

Maybe you made some mistakes in your past, and perhaps you missed out on some opportunities or shrugged off something important. It's fine. You know why?

Because you get to rip it up and start again.

Gaslighting breaks us because it makes us rely on others to define ourselves. Once we get out of the cycle, we have the opportunity to define ourselves. Try letting go of anything you thought about yourself. Maybe you thought you could never be in a musical production or paint a picture. Perhaps you believed for years that you weren't the academic sort or could never write a book.

Let go of all those former misconceptions and be curious about yourself. What would happen if you auditioned for some community theater? What if that roller derby team could become your new group of friends? Would it be so terrible to buy some paints and try creating?

Go into each of these situations and open up to the idea of failure, not because I want you to fail, but simply because you should. If you fail, it means you tried something outside of your comfort zone, and that's a good thing! We learn a lot about ourselves when we attempt something unusual.

Also, be ready to discover that it's the new you. You could strap on those skates and find you never want to take them off. You might fall madly in love with a streak of red paint on a canvas. However, if you go in with a negative attitude or preemptively decide that you're going to hate it, then that can never happen.

Again, be open to discovering yourself. You've spent so long letting others decide how you should spend your time and who you should see, and this is finally your chance to taste lots of different experiences and see what you like.

Before we move on to the next section, I want to add a quick note—please, whatever you do, don't try to get revenge on your narcissist. Revenge, like a prank or some kind of attack on your abuser, might be fun to think about, but don't go through with it. Going out of your way to make their life difficult, get them fired, or embarrass them publicly can easily backfire. Also, they'll see it as further proof of your mental instability and point to it as a way to absolve themselves of their gaslighting sins.

Trust me—the best revenge is you finding your own happiness. That makes you a clear victor. Don't give your abuser anymore of your energy or time, even if it's meant to hurt them. Focus on building your new, better life.

RECONNECT

I'm guessing your gaslighter expected you to have a minimal social life, if any. If that was the case, reach out to those friends you miss seeing and figure out if there's any chance for you to reconnect. Apologize for your absence and admit you were wrong for not prioritizing a positive relationship. Don't make excuses; focus on how you can bring these people back into your life.

The same can happen with family. If your gaslighter kept you away from your parents, siblings, or extended family, do whatever you need to do to get them back. Having people who love and value you in your life is the best way to rediscover yourself and move forward. Don't use these relationships to commiserate about the narcissist. Instead, talk about how important they are to you and how you want to spend time with them in the near future.

Try planning a monthly get-together, like a family dinner, a trip to the local bowling alley, or a movie night. Keep it easy and casual, no pressure if someone is busy or sick. Focus on making it fun and available to show everyone how much you value their love.

If a friend doesn't want to accept you back or chooses your narcissist over you, respect that person's choice. It may be that seeing you and your past issues is a trigger for this person, they could be working through some personal issues that have nothing to do with you, or the friendship may simply be over. That's fine. Acknowledge the choice and move on with your life.

If a family member does the same, put some physical distance between that person and yourself. There are no laws that say families have to get along all the time. When other family members mention your absence, explain in simple terms what happened.

"Mom decided that the emotionally abusive partner I had was the right man for me, despite how much he hurt me. That's more than I can deal with right now, so I'm just giving myself and her some space."

Focus on how you feel and what you're doing, not other people. Change the subject as soon as you can to talk about something positive and uplifting, even if it's small.

"Guess what? My neighbor got the cutest little dog!"

These comments redirect a conversation that could otherwise hurt for a long time. Keep your sights on making yourself happy and not rolling around in misery. I promise it will work.

THE ART OF VOLUNTEERING

I mentioned my own volunteering opportunities earlier, and I want to suggest that you donate a little bit of your time as well. Reaching out and helping someone in your community is the polar opposite of how any narcissist would spend their time. I once suggested volunteering to a narcissist, and he immediately shot back that he would never "work for free."

A lot of people misunderstand volunteering. It's simply showing up. It's holding a ladle for a couple of hours or raking some leaves. It's sitting next to someone who wants to hear a story.

Volunteering couldn't be further from working. You get to decide when it happens, most opportunities don't require an interview, and people are extremely relieved when you show up. Your presence becomes a gift for everyone.

Serving a homeless person food or repairing a broken hinge on the door of an old building does something to our mental state. It reminds us that one of the best ways to benefit is to reach out to others. Whenever I volunteer my time, I walk away feeling brand new, like I've shed old skin. No, I didn't make any money or network with anyone, but I did something intangible. I used my time and energy to make the world a little bit better. It's got value that we can't underestimate.

Don't shoot for more than once a month's worth when you first volunteer. Many people make the mistake of signing up for a high-commitment situation and then get stressed out by the amount of time required. Keep it simple. Volunteer for a holiday, and then see what other opportunities work for your schedule and energy level.

It's okay if you feel doubtful about giving someone your time. It can seem odd at first, but try it and reflect on how you felt during and after the experience. I already know you'll be shocked at how great your day will go after you put some TLC into your community.

GRIEVE

Whenever something ends—a life, friendship, or period in our lives—we feel the loss. Humans need to acknowledge death in all its forms; it's how we go on living.

You will feel the loss of your narcissist and former connection, and you must acknowledge it. You may find you cry or feel extreme happiness at odd times. You might get melancholic and feel tempted to spend several days alone. Chocolate or fatty foods could begin to call your name non-stop.

You need to feel all of this to the deepest degree possible. Let the tears flow, splurge on some junk food, run whenever you feel up to it, and live in the euphoria for a moment. The loss of your former relationship is important, but so is the person you used to be before you met your narcissist. You'll never be them again—you can't be, you've come too far. The new you is beautiful and powerful, but the old you deserves a memorial.

Find a way to mourn the former you and the life you left behind. Put out some photos of that time and say a prayer of thanks and goodbye to the image in those photos. Feel free to invite someone to join you or do it alone, whatever feels right to you.

You might scoff at the idea of mourning the life you once had, but I stand by this practice. I've seen a huge difference in someone's pre- and post-ritual. I can see a weight lifted in those who've said goodbye to the person they used to be and accepted their new selves. They gained a new light in their eyes.

Light that flame in yourself with a quick ritual. You'll be glad you did.

FORGIVE YOURSELF

After you've said goodbye, forgiven your abuser, and found new connections with the people you love, you need to forgive yourself. I'm shocked at how few people look inward and think, "I forgive you." Yet, they're all so quick to forgive others, even some whom they would be justified in never forgiving!

Why do we struggle to forgive ourselves? I'm not entirely sure, but I have some theories.

We often make the same mistakes we've seen others make. That realization—that we did the same thing as someone who made us frustrated or exasperated, creates resentment. I had the bad example right in front of me. Couldn't I see it?

Of course we saw it, but we don't see ourselves with the same lens as others. Also, when we see others struggle, we don't feel the same emotions as the other person. We forget that mental states, emotional problems, and personal histories play huge roles in bad decisions.

So, what can we do? To start, we can look at those poorly thought out decisions and recognize what outside factors came into play. What were we feeling at that time? What were we carrying?

I'm willing to guess that if you tied yourself to a person who turned out to be bad for you, you needed love. And I bet you can forgive yourself for needing a basic human connection. You wanted to feel cherished and build something with a partner. That's a good thing. Maybe you chose the wrong person. That's also okay. Either way, it's time to forgive yourself.

Self-forgiveness can take time, and you'll have to start by stating it out loud. Say to yourself, "I made a mistake. I forgive myself," when you get dressed in the morning. Write it on the mirror so you can read it over and over as you get ready to step out. Do a forgiveness meditation. Say it as often as you need for it to sink in. Then practice that forgiveness throughout your day when you make tiny mistakes. Did you bump into someone on the street? Say you're sorry, then tell yourself you're forgiven.

If you find pangs of guilt sneaking into your regular emotional rotation, acknowledge the emotion. My old therapist suggests giving it a name and a form. My old guilt is a grimy old man who stands too close to others on the train and tells gross stories. Whenever I feel guilty, he appears in my mind, picking his nose and snarling at me.

To help me manage that old guilt, I sat down with the old man and had a long talk with him. I asked him about his childhood, listened to his gross tales, and empathized with him. Then, I offered to build him a house.

I imagined a beautiful cabin in my old summer camp, then mentally placed my guilt character inside it. I told him I appreciated everything he did for me growing up, but it no longer served me. Now, to thank him, I wanted to give my guilt a place to retire and get some rest.

It worked! I visited the cabin a few times, but my guilt really did stay in that little spot. It made it easier to manage and helped me let go of my old negative feelings of myself. I continue to struggle, but I feel much better now that I know my guilt worked hard to teach me things and can now spend his days in the mountains.

CREATE NEW RELATIONSHIPS

People often complain that it's impossible to make new friends as an adult, but I find it's more than possible if you adjust your expectations.

When we're kids, friends are people who come to our houses at every opportunity, fill up our birthday parties, and call us constantly. Adults don't have to maintain that level of connection. We have families and jobs that require our time.

Think of an adult friend as someone you see whenever you can, not someone you see constantly. Chat with someone in line for coffee or at your new volunteer gig. Reach out to someone in a support group or group therapy and ask if they want to hang out sometime. Keep it low pressure and remember to temper your expectations. That person might say yes and then forget to follow through, but that's okay! Adults are busy people.

Make yourself available and open to new relationships, and they'll come your way. If you're trying new things and being kind to yourself, you'll build lovely, positive energy around yourself that others will want to be around. Let it happen organically, and you'll reap the rewards.

GIVE IT TIME

Remember that it may take years for you to recover from a severe gaslighting experience. It's important that you give yourself the time you need to get back to a good state. Don't rush the process or recovery. Give yourself as much patience as you need.

Most importantly, avoid rebound relationships. I would recommend not dating for a year, but I'm just following the AA rule of no serious romances until you've been sober for a year. I think a year to ourselves is a great opportunity to see what wonderful people we are on our own. Then, when we are ready for a new partner, we'd have learned that our love is a wonderful gift we're giving, not a rote gesture of handing something over.

Your heart is fragile, precious cargo. Handle it with care.

GET YOURSELF SOME THERAPY

I've mentioned therapy a few times in this book, but I haven't gone into any of the nuances involved with finding a therapist or building a relationship with one.

Therapists are a unique bunch of people. They're meant to make us feel completely at ease and yet challenge us to look at ourselves, our habits, and our true desires. I know tons of people who are terrified to walk into a therapist's office, yet it's clear to me that everyone benefits from a therapy session.

Think of therapy like a visit to the mechanic—even if your car is in perfect shape, you still need to change the oil once in a while. If you skip it, all kinds of gross stuff can build up in your engine, and soon your car won't function at all.

Therapists are similar to mechanics. They clean out our emotional gunk, even for those who don't have any mental issues. Our brains, emotions, and internal lives are dark and complicated. Why not let a professional under the hood so they can take a look?

It's important that you find the best therapist for you. Here're a few things to consider before you sign up for any treatments.

Budget—What can you afford? Is once a week feasible, or can you only pay for one session a month? Take a look at your finances and decide if a private session is something you can swing or if you need a cheaper alternative.

Physical distance—Keep in mind that therapy requires an hour. If you're late or have to leave early, you won't get the most out of a session. If you have your eye on a center or private office, make sure you can actually get there.

Groups vs Private—Private sessions will always cost the most. Are you open to a group session? Many community centers, churches, and advocacy groups offer a chance to gather and talk as a group. But, this also means you won't benefit unless you share. If you go the group route, make it your goal to share some deeply personal stories. Check out the group, make sure you feel safe, and introduce yourself. If you feel welcome and secure, go back and start talking.

Alternatives—In this new, digital age, there are some amazing ways you can get therapy beyond the traditional couch or circle of chairs. Now therapy is available in a text message or video chat. These services charge a monthly fee that's not the same as a private session, but not free either. Check out groups like TalkSpace or BetterHelp to see what your options include.

Once you get going with your new therapy, pay attention to how your sessions make you feel. A good therapist will bring up emotions you didn't realize you had simmering just below the surface. You should feel comfortable admitting personal mistakes, openly crying, yelling, and anything else you need. No therapist should ever judge or encourage you to do something you feel is wrong.

I've heard some interesting stories from different people in my life about strange moments in the therapist's office. Some felt judged, whereas others felt pressured to lose weight or change their appearance, which I find appalling.

The majority, however, loved their therapy sessions. Even when I'm low on money, I make sure I pay for my sessions with my therapist. I've seen her for years and have no plans of stopping. I tend to go into sessions feeling certain I'll have nothing too deep to discuss, only to get there and realize I have a million things to talk about!

Therapy helps us learn more about ourselves and pick apart the why behind our actions. A therapist can also help us reflect on our relationships with others and why they serve or hurt. Mine also encourages me to do things like exercise and eat healthy. She's in great shape herself, so I listen to her.

More than that though, she helps me see that I'm an individual worthy of love. She encouraged me to write this book, and I'm so glad she did! This project made me remember why I love studying human behavior and helping others. I need to thank her, but I'll make sure to thank myself as well for all my hard work.

And thank you for reading. I hope this book helped you see the light and love yourself again. You deserve it.

CHAPTER SUMMARY

What a great chapter! I love reflecting on all the ways we can grow, heal, and learn more about ourselves inside and out.

- Practice radical forgiveness as a means of letting go of the

past, then forgive yourself.
- Reconnect with people you love, volunteer your time, and make new friends as you heal.
- Find a great therapist or group therapy that makes you feel welcome and safe.

This chapter marks the end of our book. Please read the following Discussion section for further help on using this book in a club or support group to keep the conversation alive.

FINAL WORDS

I am so flattered you took a chance on this book and gave it your time and attention. I want to help everyone understand gaslighting better and how it works its way into a relationship, turns on the victim, and becomes impossible to escape. If we do get away, we can have amazing lives and loving relationships if we decide to love ourselves like no one else can.

I know that gaslighting can make the recipient believe they're going crazy. I am familiar with that horrible, head-spinning fear that I might be losing my mind and my partner's words may be my last white-knuckle grip on sanity. It's a terrible feeling, and I want to reassure you that anyone who goes through a round of gaslighting feels the same. Gaslighting, more than anything, is designed to make us doubt ourselves.

The other side of that is the never-ending self-doubt. If you can't trust yourself, you start to lean on the narcissist in your life more every day. After all, narcissists are the picture of confidence. Who better to trust?

Sadly, that's exactly what narcissists depend on: that you doubt your own judgment at every turn. It's a horrible way to live and makes us doubt what we like all the way down to the setting on our toaster. Do we really like it lighter? Why not darker? And we continue our day constantly questioning everything.

But what we question the most is the relationship itself. If we've married a narcissist or moved in with one, we start to wonder if this love is truly what love should look and feel like. Should it be this rollercoaster ride of unpredictable emotion, or should it be a calm, canoe ride from one end of a lake to another?

Gaslighting makes us forget the tranquil lake and focus on the screams and laughter of the rollercoaster. We feel silly for looking for an alternative. Surely, this thing that terrifies us deserves our time and attention. It's what we've committed to; we can't possibly throw it away, right?

It gets even more complicated when gaslighters are the parents in a family. Like my own parents, many people grow up with insults, Mom or Dad laughing in their faces and telling them they're not good enough, you name it. Unfortunately, kids experience the damage of gaslighting much deeper than anyone, as it happens when they're much more impressionable. Some parents work their kids so hard that as adults, they believe they have to surrender their freedom and finances by living at home and funding each parent's lifestyle.

Like the gaslit romantic partners, kids whose parents gaslight them regularly no longer trust their own judgment. Statements like, "I want to go to college out of state," or "I'm going to a party," become grounds for endless criticism. The victim walks away thinking, "Are they right? Am I too dumb for college? Did those guys invite me over just to laugh at me?"

Soon, these kids stop making decisions and rely on their parents to decide for them whenever possible.

This leads to extreme isolation for the victim, no matter the relationship. The loss of friends, loved ones, or free time with peers helps the narcissist reinforce their message. That message is that the victim can't manage their own life and needs to give the gaslighter the reins.

Friends or family may help the victim feel empowered or remember that they don't want to hand over control of any kind. So, any positive presence in the victim's life gets the boot.

Ironically, that handover puts the victim's life into a state of chaos. The last thing a narcissist wants is for their victim to feel any semblance of peace. They need their victim constantly questioning their own memories, decisions, and responsibility for any bad moments, mistakes, or accidents. To do that, the gaslighter blames their victim for everything, despite a lack of evidence. Did the electricity go out? Your fault. Did the dogs eat too early, so their food bowls are empty? You must have forgotten to feed them. Are you sad? Don't blame me! You're losing your mind!

You may wonder if the relationship can be saved. I'm sorry to tell you that I have yet to find a couple that worked through narcissism and gaslighting and found their way to a healthy, balanced outcome. It seems the only way to "save" a narcissist is to leave them. Even then, it's unlikely they'll reflect on their actions healthily. Why should they? They're not the crazy one, you are!

In chapter 6, we looked at how to stand up to a gaslighter in a way that doesn't play their game. It requires you to stay calm, state plainly that what they're doing is called gaslighting and you won't stand for it, and to take some physical space whenever you need it. Any attempt to gaslight them back, meet their manipulation in kind, or lash out will only deepen the abuse and could even elevate it to physical attacks.

So no, I'm sorry to say that I'm not here to save your relationship. Rather, I'm here to save you.

I hope this book clarified what gaslighting is and isn't, and why it's important to recognize it when it happens. I want you to be able to call it out right at the beginning and hopefully quickly get away from the person hurting you. I gave you lots of examples so you can walk into a new situation armed with knowledge of what to look out for, like love-bombing.

Other signs include questioning your ability to remember anything, ditching any conversations about the relationship, or quickly changing the subject and refusing to look closer at their actions. A narcissist will ensure you feel confused, lonely, and lost in the relationship. If you struggle to do anything you like, see the people important to you, or eat the foods you like, you're with a narcissist and need to get away.

After you leave, it's essential that you take care of yourself and your mental and emotional health. I covered this more in depth in chapter 7, but the main points are these:

- **Protect yourself**—don't get into any situations where your abuser has access to you, even from a distance. Change your phone number, stay with someone unassociated with them, and alert your coworkers to the situation, so they won't be allowed in your office or place of work. If you have access to security guards where you live or work, give them a picture of your abuser and tell them not to let them in.
- **Focus on healing**—Love and give yourself endless compassion and patience. Keep in mind that it could take a long time for the effects of the abuse to leave your mind and heart.
- **Rebuild yourself**—Reconnect with friends and people you love whom your abuser may have pushed you away from to keep you weak. Explore new hobbies and friendships, volunteer your time, and be curious about who you are as a person. Try new things with an open mind and see what happens.
- **Do the deep work**—Practice some radical forgiveness to let go of the past and see your abuser as pathetic and sad. Grieve and feel the loss of the relationship, then forgive yourself.

- **Find a therapist**—I can't stress enough the importance of finding mental help after a damaging relationship. Find a group, private professional, or online service that can help you rebuild your mental health.

If you can't leave—and I know many of you can't—I encourage you to find a way to put some physical distance between yourself and the narcissist. If you can move in with another family member or good friend, please do. If you can spend less time around this person, maybe by getting involved in after-school programs or tutoring, that's an option, too. Putting space between the two of you will give your mental health a much-needed break. If you're confronted about your avoidance, state simply that it's intentional.

"I don't like the way you gaslight me. I'm spending time away from you to avoid the negative comments."

Don't argue or fight about it. Your narcissist will likely try to start a big argument about your statements. Instead of fighting back, walk out the door. If you're in physical danger, call the police or record the incident with audio or video so you can go get help afterwards.

The moment you can leave, do it. Walk out the door and don't look back. You'll be so glad you put yourself first.

WHAT NOW?

First, I want to say thank you for reading this entire book and ask that you please leave a review on Amazon. Amazon reviews help others find this book and get the advice they need. All you have to do is click the star for a rating, then write a quick sentence about what you thought of the book. It takes less than a minute, but it can make a huge impact on my ability to reach out to others.

Then, take the tools you learned here to move forward and live your amazing new life. Look for the narcissist and gaslighters of the world. Now that you have a clear definition of them, you'll be able to spot them everywhere. Once you see one, you can cross the street and avoid so much as mere eye contact with that person.

You don't have time to waste on toxic people. You need to go and live your beautiful life.

Are you in a therapy group, book club, or crowd that likes to discuss literature? Read on in the Discussion section of this book for more personal testimonies and questions to help spark conversations on the topic of gaslighting, loving a narcissist, and recovery.

DISCUSSION SECTION

The following case studies and questions are designed for use in group therapy, classrooms, or debates. If you use them in your book club or support group, please let me know. I love to hear from my readers.

1. Here's a quote from a victim of a severe gaslighter: "I wished he would hit me." The woman who said it claimed her husband was seen as a pillar of the community, the face of good. She wished for some physical abuse because it would help others see how much he hurt her with his gaslighting. Have you ever felt that way? What signs can we look for in a person to see the damage from gaslighting and emotional abuse?
2. Gaslighting always kicks off with a love bomb. The narcissist showers their future partner with promises of commitment, gifts, and declarations of new, deep emotions. For most of us,

this is too good to resist, and we often don't recognize these situations as dangerous. Imagine you go on a date and get a big, glittery love bomb from the person across the table from you. What signs can you use to confirm that this is an act? What can you say to leave the situation and make it clear that you're not interested?

3. Now imagine a friend of yours just got love-bombed and tells you that they and their date are now an item. You can see in their face that they've been charmed into believing they've met the perfect partner. What can you do to help them see the truth? What can you say if they insist you're wrong?

4. Many narcissists ooze charm. They want everyone to see them as smart, considerate, and beautiful. What famous person can you think of who originally seemed beautiful and ideal to you, only to reveal themselves as ugly and dangerous? How did the revelation happen?

5. Narcissism is most prominent in men, yet plenty of women are narcissists, too. The gaslighting from a woman can hurt a male partner irrevocably, yet men often hesitate to ask for help. What could you say to a male friend in the throes of emotional abuse if one approached you for help? How could you assure him he's not being overly sensitive or overreacting and point out that he's in a dangerous situation? Do you know of any local organizations you could call to get him professional support?

6. Read the following story about my mother, a devoted narcissist, and how she treated me once I became an adult. See if you can find all the stages of gaslighting listed below:

- Love-bombing
- Idealization
- Devaluation
- Lies and exaggeration
- Repetition
- Wearing out the victim
- Escalation
- Discarding Phase
- Attempts to fix the relationship
- Hoovering
- False hope
- Domination and control.

MY STORY

After I graduated from college, I was proud of myself. I felt like I really found myself in school. I solidified my future career—studying human behavior and helping others—and completed a massive research project that my professors adored. Several encouraged me to apply for a graduate degree and become a professor myself, but I wanted to be out in the world and on the front lines of mental health.

To my shock, my mother came to my graduation. She arrived wearing a classy, cream-colored suit and carrying a massive bunch of flowers. When I walked off the stage with my degree, she dramatically handed over the spray of red roses, then planted a big kiss on my cheek. She wiped away a tear and mouthed, "so proud of you," at me, but I'm sure everyone saw it.

I didn't know what to do or say. This was the same woman who originally laughed out loud at the thought of me going to college. She'd insisted I would only drop out, defeated and in debt. Never mind my great grades in high school. Mom felt certain my academic skills had reached their limit. Now? She seemed like a new person. Even the suit looked fresh from the shop.

My friends raised their eyebrows at the flowers. Some were genuinely impressed, but others were confused.

"Is that your mom? I thought you said she was mean and cold."

"No way that's your mom. I can't believe she'd ever be that nice."

Others eyed the flowers with a sad look in their eyes. They could see what a calculated move that presentation really was and wanted me to be careful.

I shook it off. Graduation day wasn't a life sentence. We were all there for a limited amount of time, and then we could go our separate ways. I sat back for the rest of the ceremony and imagined my new life living with my friend Mike in our two-bedroom apartment. We both had high hopes for our futures. I thought about all the books I would write in my new space while Mike walked the nearby trails, protecting wildlife. We'd be unstoppable.

The day I moved into the new place; Mom showed up with a bunch of housewarming gifts.

"Now," she said, "I got you a couch, but before you put it out on the street, you should know that I bought it secondhand. I know how much you hate being spoiled. Oh, and it came with some throw pillows."

Mike's mouth fell open to a perfect little O as he watched several pieces of furniture get carted into the apartment, compliments of my mother. After everything got put in its place, Mom cooked us a big pan of baked macaroni and cheese, (my favorite), and doted on Mike.

"Oh, I love how outdoorsy you are! You must be so strong. Please take my Don out hiking with you. Promise? Oh, you're the best! It will do him so much good." To my horror, she picked up his phone and put in her own number, then made Mike promise to call her if we had any problems. He nodded and seemed happy to pass on his own number.

Had Mom changed? Was she finally the balanced, happy person I'd always prayed she'd become?

Mom started calling me or Mike whenever she got in the mood. The calls went fine at first, and I felt a strange connection to my mother that I'd never felt before. It was nice. I finally felt like I had a mom, not an enemy.

Then, she invited us out to dinner. She knew we were both struggling to find work and surviving on instant soup, so we jumped at the chance to eat dinner.

Mom invited us out to a decent place with appetizers and a dessert cart. We drooled at the rich smells and sank into our soft chairs, a big step up from our secondhand living room. Mom got there early, no surprise, yet she seemed annoyed when we arrived on time.

"I've been here for twenty minutes," she sniffed as we sat down.

"You said 7:30," I held up my phone to show her the text inviting us out. "It's 7:31. We're on time."

She narrowed her eyes at me and signaled to the waiter to bring her another Chablis. Mike and I looked over our menus and I did my best to ignore Mom's fingernails drumming on the table—never a good sign.

"I hope this place is alright. I know it's a bit…"

I waited for her to finish, but my gut knew what was coming. It gave a little twist, warning me.

"It's a bit what, Mom?"

"You know, expensive," she said, whispering the word. "You boys brought your wallets, right?"

Mike and I sank in our chairs. "Mom, you invited us. You said you would treat. What happened?"

Mom gave her rich-lady laugh, a kind of "Haw haw haw," that I hated. "Mike, dear," she went on, leaning across the table to put her hand over his, "it seems my son is back in fantasy land. I never offered to pay." She picked up her menu and chuckled to herself.

Again, I held up my phone. "I've got your text message right here. Let's go to dinner. My treat. What happened?"

Right away Mom shut down. She toyed with her glass as a waiter approached to ask for our order.

"We need a minute," Mike told him. Then he tapped my arm. "You know what, there's a hotdog cart around the corner. Let's go."

I shook my head at my mom. I couldn't believe she'd pull something like that with Mike. Me, sure, she did it all the time growing up, but to my friend? I seethed.

"I know how phone-hacking works," Mom said, not looking at me.

"Oh, so I hacked my phone and faked a message from you? Is that what I did?" I slammed my fist into the table. Mike gave me a kick.

"Seriously. Let's just go."

I sighed. I knew he was right. Mom wanted nothing more than a scene. I wasn't about to give it to her. "Lead the way."

As we left, Mom yelled something after us about her own son, "refusing to spend time with his own mother!" I didn't look back.

Mom called me up a few days later. Against my better judgment, I answered. I tried to talk to her about what happened at the restaurant, but she denied it.

"Your imagination, darling! It's really something."

"You realize I have a witness, don't you?" At that, she clenched her jaw so hard I could hear it over the phone.

"I didn't call to fight. I thought maybe you and I might benefit from some family therapy. What do you say?"

"Family therapy?" I looked at the phone as if some odd filter that made horrible mothers nicer had somehow clicked on. It hadn't. I shook my head in disbelief.

"Mom, I know you don't want to go to counseling. Don't pretend."

"Well," she purred into the phone, in full flirt mode. I shuddered. "It just so happens I've already made the appointment. I know you're into that sort of thing. Do you want the details?"

"Only if you're paying."

"This again? Really, Don. Grab a pen."

I jotted down the details, trying hard not to roll my eyes. She didn't think I'd buy this, did she?

The day of our therapy session came, and I got on the train. I stared at all the mothers on the train holding small children and laughing with their kids. I wondered how many of them were in family counseling.

I arrived at the appointment early, so I pulled out my phone to see how my friends were spending their Saturdays. They all looked relaxed and happy. I put my phone away.

To my shock, my mother walked in.

"Well, what a nice surprise! You're early. I'll let them know we're here." She went up to a receptionist and had an exceptionally quiet conversation with the woman behind the desk. She gestured to me and both turned to give me a glance. Again, I got that twist in my stomach.

"Mom," I started when she sat down next to me. "This is family therapy, right? I only see people here by themselves." I nodded to the waiting room, where a collection of young adults sat far away from one another, legs jostling with nerves.

"Well, I asked for family therapy. I can't be responsible for everyone else." She picked up a magazine and flipped the pages with a firm snap. Fine, I'll shut up.

We heard our names and headed in. The hallway was dark and felt too small for the building. What was this place?

The therapist's office put me at ease. It was a standard setup with a couple of armchairs and a couch. The woman seeing us, I'll call her Dr. X, looked warm and greeted us with a big smile.

Dr. X shook my hand. "So," she said, "you're Don. I'm so glad to meet you."

"Um, yes. I'm sorry, what kind of therapist are you?"

"I'm actually more of a specialist. I help people like you figure out what's real and what's not."

My eyes closed and my shoulders fell. I looked at my mom and saw her as the same woman who consistently trapped me as a kid.

"Really, Mom? You promised me family therapy, and this is what I get?"

"You see!" Mom said, oddly triumphant. "I never said anything like that. I'm certain he lives in some kind of fantasy world, making up all kinds of characters and interactions. I'm terrified of what he might do." She put her head down and managed to conjure up a couple of tears.

"You know what, Mom? Let's do this. Let's talk to the therapist."

I sat down across from Dr. X, who at that point looked completely lost, and told her the truth.

My mother suffered from Narcissistic Personality Disorder. She wanted to hear a professional say that I couldn't function in the world so she could get me back home and rebuild our former codependent relationship. As with the restaurant, she'd gotten me there on false pretenses, and now wanted to get Dr. X on her side. I let the doctor know she was free to agree with my mother. I happened to be an adult who knew his rights—I couldn't be locked up unless the state ordered me into a mental hospital.

Dr. X listened to all of this with a poker face. She gave my mother the occasional glance, but didn't ask her any questions. I kept my tone calm and took long, slow breaths as I spoke.

Mom, on the other hand, paced the room and scoffed at every other comment I made. I walked the doctor through all of Mom's standard tricks. I told her about how she constantly lived in denial and worked hard to make me look bad. She'd done it for as long as I could remember. It was why my father no longer spoke to either of us—he didn't want any connection to his former wife. I didn't blame him.

Finally, Dr. X asked me to pause. She looked at Mom and asked her, "And how do you feel, hearing your son say these things?"

Mom's anger was at an all-time high. She actually looked red. She crossed her arms and looked at me, but spoke to Dr. X.

"Well, I just cannot believe that Don, my own son, could make up such lies about me!"

"Why don't you sit down and give us your side of the story?" the doctor offered. But Mom wasn't about to fall for that.

"Oh, you're not getting a penny out of me," Mom informed her. She headed for the door and looked back at me. "You are such a disappointment!" and out she went.

I looked back at Dr. X who blinked in confusion at the space Mom had just vacated. "She knows we've already charged her for the hour, right?"

I nodded. "Yes. It's all a show. I'm happy to stay and speak with you if you'd like."

Dr. X nodded. "I never get to work with NPD patients. Tell me some more stories about your mom."

I leaned back against the couch and unloaded all my baggage about Mom. By the time I left, I felt amazing. Dr. X gave me some job-hunting advice and contacts, one of which led to my first position as a researcher.

Mom didn't talk to me for a year. When she suddenly called after her long absence, I asked her about the therapy incident.

"I'm sorry, dear," she said, "I don't have the foggiest idea what you're talking about."

Finally, I want to encourage you to share your own story. Looking at the different phases of gaslighting; what steps can you pinpoint in your own history?

Listen to others in your group and repeat the exercise with each of them separately. Is it easier to see the phases now?

SOURCES

A Deeper Look Into Gaslighting. (n.d.). The Hotline. https://www.thehotline.org/resources/a-deeper-look-into-gaslighting/

American Psychological Association. (2018, November 1). Americanpsychologyassociation.org. https://www.apa.org/topics/stress-body

Bain, L. (2019, August 14). *What Is a Narcissist? 8 Key Traits of Narcissism Everyone Should Know.* Good Housekeeping. https://www.goodhousekeeping.com/health/a28690119/what-is-a-narcissist/

Barnes, Z. (2018, April 20). *PTSD After Domestic Violence: Women Share Their Stories.* SELF. https://www.self.com/story/ptsd-domestic-violence

Bennett, T. (2019, November 25). *What's the difference between having narcissistic personality disorder (NPD) and being narcissistic?* Counseling and Life Coaching - Find a Counselor. https://thriveworks.com/blog/difference-between-npd-and-being-narcissistic/

Best books on identifying and escaping domestic violence. (n.d.). DomesticShelters.Org. https://www.domesticshelters.org/resources/books/identifying-and-escaping-abuse

Bridges to Recovery. (2020, October 12). *I Was the Victim of Gaslighting: How Treatment Helped Me Heal After a Nervous Breakdown.* https://www.bridgestorecovery.com/blog/i-was-the-victim-of-gaslighting-how-treatment-helped-me-heal-after-a-nervous-breakdown/

Brockway, L. H. (2020, October 26). *24 phrases 'gaslighters' use against you.* PR Daily. https://www.prdaily.com/24-phrases-gaslighters-use-against-you/

Brooks, H. (2020, January 30). *How I Healed from Gaslighting and Found Self-Love After the Abuse.* Tiny Buddha. https://tinybuddha.com/blog/how-i-healed-from-gaslighting-and-found-self-love-after-the-abuse/

de Canonville, C. L. (n.d.). *What Is Gaslighting? | The Effects of Gaslighting on Victims Of Narcissism.* Narcissistic Behavior. https://narcissisticbehavior.net/the-effects-of-gaslighting-in-narcissistic-victim-syndrome/

Dean, M. E. (2018, January 22). *Gaslighting: A Sneaky Kind Of Emotional Abuse | Betterhelp.* BetterHelp. https://www.betterhelp.com/advice/relations/gaslighting-a-sneaky-kind-of-emotional-abuse/

Drumming, N. (2018, January 17). *635: Chip in My Brain.* This American Life. https://www.thisamericanlife.org/635/transcript

Ellyn, L. (2018, December 17). *This is not what gaslighting is. - Laura Ellyn.* Medium. https://medium.com/@voltairine/this-is-not-what-gaslighting-is-3372e1876791#

Gaslighting. (2018, June 13). GoodTherapy.Org Therapy Blog. https://www.goodtherapy.org/blog/psychpedia/gaslighting

Gordon, S. (n.d.). *Understanding the Manipulative Behaviors Toxic People Use to Control.* Verywell Family. https://www.verywellfamily.com/is-someone-gaslighting-you-4147470

Hartwell-Walker, M. E. (2018, November 6). *7 Ways to Extinguish Gaslighting.* World of Psychology. https://psychcentral.com/blog/7-ways-to-extinguish-gaslighting/

Huizen, J. (2020a, July 14). *What is gaslighting?* Medical News Today. https://www.medicalnewstoday.com/articles/gaslighting

InvajyC. (2019, September 9). *Gaslighting : An emotional abuse to burn your sanity.* ThriveGlobal.Com. https://thriveglobal.com/stories/gaslighting-an-emotional-abuse-to-burn-your-sanity/

Lonczak, H. S. (2020a, November 3). *What Is Gaslighting? 20 Techniques to Stop Emotional Abuse.* PositivePsychology.Com. https://

positivepsychology.com/gaslighting-emotional-abuse/

Mahaffy, K. (2020, August 12). *What Is Gaslighting and How Does It Manifest In Parenting? - Mom's Choice Awards.* Mom's Choice Awards. https://www.momschoiceawards.com/blog/what-gaslighting-how-does-manifest-parenting/

Mays, M. (2020, September 3). *The Impact of Gaslighting.* Partner-Hope. https://partnerhope.com/the-impact-of-gaslighting/

McAuliffe, K. (2020, July 24). *Gaslighting at Work: How to Recognize It—And Stop It.* Career Contessa. https://www.careercontessa.com/advice/gaslighting-in-the-office/

Mindfulness: A Skill You Can Use to Stop Gaslighting. (2020, October 28). One Love Foundation. https://www.joinonelove.org/learn/mindfulness-the-surprising-skill-you-can-use-to-stop-gaslighting/

Narcissistic personality disorder - Symptoms and causes. (2017, November 18). Mayo Clinic. https://www.mayoclinic.org/diseases-conditions/narcissistic-personality-disorder/symptoms-causes/syc-20366662

Peisley, T. (2018, October 10). *Is narcissism common? The answer may surprise you.* SANE Australia. https://www.sane.org/information-stories/the-sane-blog/mental-illness/is-narcissism-common-the-answer-may-surprise-you#:%7E:text=Most%2C%20if%20not%20all%2C%20of,men)%20is%20diagnosed%20with%20NPD.

R., S. (2019, August 29). *5 Things that Motivate Narcissists − Psych2Go.* Psych2Go. https://psych2go.net/5-things-that-motivate-narcissists-2/

Ranya Al Husaini (@AlhusainiRanya). (2019, April 14). *The Seven Stages of Gaslighting*. Sail Magazine. https://sailemagazine.com/2019/04/the-seven-stages-of-gaslighting/

Rethink, C. A. (2020, April 23). *Gaslighting: 22 Examples Of This Brutally Manipulative Mindf*ck*. A Conscious Rethink. https://www.aconsciousrethink.com/6766/gaslighting-examples/

Rodríguez, G. S. (2020, November 20). *Gaslighting: How to Recognize it and What to Say When it Happens*. The Psychology Group Fort Lauderdale. https://thepsychologygroup.com/gaslighting-how-to-recognize-it-and-what-to-say-when-it-happens/

Rundle, E. (2020, October 29). *Manipulation Tactics Narcissists Use To Destabilise You*. She Counselling. https://shecounselling.com.au/manipulation-tactics-narcissists-use-to-destabilise-you/

S. (2020, July 12). *20 Diversion Tactics Highly Manipulative Narcissists, Sociopaths And Psychopaths Use To Silence You*. Thought Catalog. https://thoughtcatalog.com/shahida-arabi/2016/06/20-diversion-tactics-highly-manipulative-narcissists-sociopaths-and-psychopaths-use-to-silence-you/

Stern, R. (2019, January 3). *Gaslighting in relationships: How to spot it and shut it down*. Vox. https://www.vox.com/first-person/2018/12/19/18140830/gaslighting-relationships-politics-explained

stilllearning2b. (2019, April 23). *Five Empowering Ways to Recover From Gaslighting*. Lessons From the End of a Marriage. https://

lessonsfromtheendofamarriage.com/2019/04/five-empowering-ways-to-recover-from-gaslighting/

Streep, P. (2017, August 24). *The Narcissist's Playbook: Ten Tactics to Recognize*. Psych Central.Com. https://blogs.psychcentral.com/knotted/2017/08/the-narcissists-playbook-ten-tactics-to-recognize/

Walker, R. (2018, June 25). *Gaslighting: a subtle, insidious, form of manipulation, hidden in the darkness,*. Medium. https://medium.com/@drwalker/gaslighting-a-subtle-form-of-manipulation-hidden-in-the-darkness-b87dc095553f

Weiss, S. (2017, March 6). *7 Signs Your Parents Are Gaslighting You*. Bustle. https://www.bustle.com/p/7-signs-your-parents-are-gaslighting-you-42457

What is Gaslighting? (2020, September 20). The Hotline. https://www.thehotline.org/resources/what-is-gaslighting/

What Is PTSD? (n.d.). Web Starter Kit. https://www.psychiatry.org/patients-families/ptsd/what-is-ptsd

Winegar, J. (2016, August 18). *Perpetrators of Elder Abuse Are Usually Family Members*. LongTermCareLink. https://www.longtermcarelink.net/article-2016-8-18-Perpetrators-of-Elder-Abuse-Are-Usually-Family-Members.htm

Winters, V. (2020, December 9). *How Growing Up With Gaslighting From My Parents Affected Me as an Adult*. The Mighty. https://themighty.com/2018/12/parents-gaslighting-emotional-abuse/

THE CODEPENDENCY RECOVERY BLUEPRINT

FROM PEOPLE-PLEASING, LOW SELF-ESTEEM & INTIMACY ISSUES OF A CODEPENDENT TO EMOTIONAL INTELLIGENCE, SELF-CONFIDENCE & SELF-CARING OF AN INDEPENDENT

INTRODUCTION

"Daring to set boundaries is about having the courage to love ourselves even when we risk disappointing others."

— BRENE BROWN

Have you lost sight of who you are as an individual? If you find yourself questioning the healthiness of your relationships and struggle to stand up for what you want, you're not alone. Codependent behaviors are some of the most difficult relationship patterns to identify, yet it's rarely discussed and often considered another form of "clinginess". This definition ignores the feelings of guilt and shame that arise from the best of intentions—it does nothing to recognize that even the best intentions can hurt. As you put yourself on the line for the people you love, it can be difficult to tell when the boundaries between you and them have blurred to the point of toxicity. After all, you're motivated by wanting the best for others, even if it means you have to put aside your own values and opinions to do so. However, when you come to rely on outside factors for validation and a sense of identity, these "do good" habits can do more harm than good. You may suddenly feel obligated to stay in a constricting relationship that turns you into a victim and limits your capacity for intimacy. It can feel as though you have no one to turn to because everybody relies on you. That doesn't mean your life has to stay that way. Codependency may be running your life, but you are the one in the driver's seat. In fact, you've already taken the first step by realizing you need to change the path you're on. I know firsthand the transformational effects of recovering from codependency and have compiled the knowledge I've gained over the years so others can experience the same freedom.

Can you imagine basing your day on which side of the bed your spouse, boss, parent, boyfriend or girlfriend gets up on? Codependency is characterized by an individual participating in a relationship that is one-sided; that has a complete lack of mutual respect; and in which one of the individuals nearly relies completely on the other to meet 100 percent of their emotional needs. Codependent individuals live with their confidence and self-esteem depending on another person. Codependency has often been synonymous with the term 'enabler', in which helping through enabling allows another individual to maintain unhealthy behaviors, including not working and other irresponsible actions, drug and alcohol abuse, gambling addiction, shopping addiction, sex addictions (addictions, in general), and abusive tendencies toward the codependent person who is enabling them. Codependency is exhausting because it requires a great deal of energy to meet another person's needs. Here's the good news. Codependency can be treated. It is a behavior that is learned and usually passed down through generations. Sometimes referred to as a "relationship addiction", it affects one's chances of having healthy and happy relationships that are based on mutual respect.

The term codependency has evolved a great deal since its beginning back in 1936. The founders of Alcoholics Anonymous (AA), Bill W. and Dr. Bob started the most successful treatment for alcoholism known today. Shortly afterward, Lois W. (Bill W.'s wife) and Anne B. (Dr. Bob's wife) started another twelve-step group meeting for the family members of alcoholics to attend. Of course, it seems only natural that living with an addict would bring a multitude of problems into any family. By the 1970s, addiction professionals started realizing that treating the addict only was insufficient; the whole family, and possibly close friends needed treatment, as well.

The term codependency has been greatly widened to include many aspects and behavioral traits of individuals living in a dysfunctional family atmosphere. Dysfunctional families often lack boundaries, or the boundaries are so blurred that each member takes on the problems of the others, creating a snowball effect of troubles. Dysfunctional family members suffer from anger issues, shame, fear, and feelings of isolation because their emotions have been ignored and love is often conditional. There are usually underlying issues, such as addiction to food, drugs, alcohol, sex, gambling, or problematic relationships. Other underlying issues include family members suffering from mental or physical illness, various types of abuse, a lack of communication, and repressed fear. They have developed ways of dissociating from difficult emotions and have learned how to not confront any problems. This can lead to serious trust issues and even physical illness. Most dysfunctional families attribute their main focus to the 'identified patient'—the addict or sick one—and then a codependency will develop, and the individual will sacrifice their own needs to devote their time to fixing the sick person. With time, loss of identity sets in and reality becomes distorted.

Codependent individuals seek stimulation from the outside to help them feel better. Some may delve into their jobs and become compulsive workaholics. While they have the best intentions trying to tend to the person having the difficulties, their efforts are often self-defeating. Taking on a martyr's role and becoming the beneficiary of another's needs can become compulsive in nature. We have all heard the phrase 'pulling some strings' to keep someone from having consequences. The issue here is that the problems repeat themselves in a never-ending cycle. The codependent behavior is reinforced by the individual feeling rewarded because they feel needed. As the cycle continues on a destructive course, the codependent increasingly becomes less healthy until they feel no choice but to keep doing it. The codependent person views themselves as a victim; one who is attracted to people in need. It isn't selfish to put yourself first—it's time to prioritize your own life and happiness and stop ignoring your personal needs. Listen to your instincts, and take this first step on your journey to finding independence and fulfilment.

In this book, you will find what you need to learn:

- What codependency is and isn't, as well as its historical background.
- Exercises and practices to help break the pattern of enabling others while learning to assert yourself.
- How childhood experiences contribute to dysfunctional relationships and determine the behaviors that follow you into adulthood.
- The five patterns of codependent behavior, and how identifying them will help you understand the signs and symptoms manifesting in your life.
- Techniques and advice for getting over your need for control and learning to accept people for who they are.
- Identifying the three stages of codependency progression; how to begin the recovery process by reclaiming your sense of identity and self-worth.
- Essential self-care practices that promote self-respect and compassion, even in difficult situations.
- How habits form.
- The Twelve-Step Recovery Program.

1

CODEPENDENCY, NOT CLINGINESS

The healthy characteristics of depending upon one another have been present throughout history; humans have always relied on social support from important relationships. As noted in the introduction to the book, the definition of codependency is a long way from its original meaning in 1936 and 1970s. The significant others of those afflicted revealing dysfunctional behaviors were called *co-chemically dependent*. Shortly afterward, the term was shortened to *codependent*. When the 1980s rolled around, addiction (including alcoholism) was referred to as *chemical dependency*. During this period, the disease model spearheaded the concept of codependency. One reason for labeling codependency a disease is because of its progressive nature. As the individual(s) around the codependent become sicker, the codependent behaviors become intensified. What may have started as overly concerned can snowball into depression, isolation, mental and physical illness in the codependent, and sometimes even suicidal ideations. Another element to the disease model of codependency is that the self-destructive behaviors associated with the condition become habitual, just like the drink or the drug for the addict.

In the 1980s, the codependent personality model was coined and dealt with the condition in terms of diagnosis, treatment, and clinical interventions. This model focused on the predisposed factors in the development of the personality of the codependent. The interactionist model of codependency puts forth a duo of intrapersonal and interpersonal elements necessary in the development and necessary to maintain their dysfunctional lifestyle. During the 1980s codependency, as a condition, was used to delineate people who were in any type of significant relationship with an addict, narcissist, borderline personality and other personality disorders. Codependency definition is aimed toward those whose life seemed unbearable unless focused on their partner; they struggled with individualization. At first, the characteristics seemed to be weak, overly emotional, needed and clingy. In present times, codependency is a common term used by professionals and laypeople, alike. There is some discussion about changing the term to 'self-love deficit disorder', because at the very center of codependency, a lack of self-love is evident. In summation, codependency is a pathological interactional condition developed by the codependent, honing into self-injurious actions that are connected to the psychogenetics of the codependent's dysfunctional family environment whilst growing up.

What determines the severity of codependency in a person?

- Genetics;
- Culture and religious beliefs;
- Family dynamics;
- Dysfunctional families are often predictors of codependent behavior;
- Childhood abuse and chronic physical abuse also promote codependency;
- Past trauma experiences;
- Role models;
- Codependency is a learned behavior, so if you had role models growing up (such as your parents or older siblings) who displayed codependent tendencies, you are more likely to develop them, as well;
- Use of substances, such as drugs and alcohol;
- Many codependent relationships develop when one partner feels they need to step up and support a struggling addict;
- Drugs and alcohol can also make it more difficult for the involved parties to recognize that something is wrong; and
- The relationships a person has had with addicts and other co-dependent people.

Who does codependency affect?

It affects more than just the struggling addict; codependency affects all of the immediate and extended family members, colleagues, friends and anyone else involved in the addict's life. The sad truth of the matter is that one common problem among addicts is the involvement of their loved ones in helping them to protect and conceal their addiction and even accepting it. The members of a dysfunctional family might, without intention, play a part in the addiction of their loved one, therefore, the codependency affects the addict. Often the codependent doesn't reveal that they know there is a problem with their loved one and may ignore or deny the problem even when it is staring them right in the face. The codependent family does not need to take responsibility for the problems their loved one is facing, and they have to keep in mind their own needs. The individual must say out loud that they did not create the problems of the afflicted one and therefore, are not responsible for fixing them. While the codependent has the best intentions in mind when trying to help a loved one, all they really do is perpetuate the afflicted one's illness by trying to protect them. Sometimes refusing to bail them out leads to a much healthier outcome. The longer the codependent rescues the afflicted individual either physically, financially or criminally, the longer the afflicted doesn't learn from their mistakes and continue with the dysfunctional actions. It is sometimes surprising to the codependent that they were enabling their loved one to continue with their addiction or abusive behavior patterns, which was allowing them to continue down the path of destruction. Having a codependent relationship can develop into a dangerous state of being, especially if an addiction is involved. The enabling behaviors cycle and the addiction will continue until a crisis or intervention happens to break the cycle. Unfortunately, and often tragic situations, such as a car crash, loss of employment, divorce, bankruptcy, overdose, and even death of the individual of whom is enabled are the consequences of codependency.

Despite people's best intentions, many often find themselves replicating the same unhealthy patterns in their relationships. If two individuals with maladjusted personality types come together, their dysfunctional traits worsen. *Enmeshment* is a term describing the relationship between family members or couples in which the boundaries are so unclear that the people involved take on the emotions of another to the extent that they experience the anger, sadness, happiness, rage, etc. when the other does. In a dysfunctional family, when codependency is present, the entire group can act as one in ways that are unhealthy for everyone involved. Think about couples you have met (hopefully you are not part of this duo; but if so, there is help.) in which their relationship is so toxic you wonder how on earth they are staying together. Outsiders need to realize that both people in the problematic relationship are there by choice. Some say they are staying together for various important reasons, such as the children, money, fear of divorce shaming, and how much time they have invested. The actual bigger picture is a belief that one or both in the couple think they deserve to be treated poorly.

When born into this world, we are completely dependent on our parents for safety, warmth and food. The bond between an infant and its caregivers is imperative for survival, both emotionally and physically. Hence, dependency on others starts at birth. If, when growing up, the caregiver is inconsistent or unavailable, the child takes on the role of caretaker. This results in the child putting the needs of their parents first. In a dysfunctional family, there is no acknowledgement of feelings or that there even is a problem resulting in the family members holding in their emotions and disregarding their own needs so they can focus on the needs of their parents. When this same child who has been *parentified* becomes an adult, they fall into the same pattern with their relationships.

When an individual doesn't recognize their own wants and needs because they are focused on another person's needs, resentment builds, and the tendency for overreactions or lashing out in anger happens when their partner lets them down in some way. The codependent partner feels a lack of internal control, so they seek validation from the outside by trying to control their significant other's behaviors. When finding out this control cannot be maintained, the codependent becomes disappointed and can slide into depression. While it is completely normal to feel partially responsible for those you love, it is unhealthy when your identity is contingent upon another. Even if you do not feel this way at the start, and even enjoy feeling needed and relied upon, it can be carried to an extremely unhealthy degree as the relationship progresses. Once the relationship has become unhealthy, it can become hard to get out of the dysfunctional relationship, since you feel so relied upon—even when you know leaving is the right thing to do.

It is obvious that relationships can be tricky, and for the codependent, it is difficult to find the right balance between being close to someone and having personal space. If you find yourself leaning toward the clingy direction, here are some helpful suggestions for reeling in your clingy ways and giving your partner some space:

1. Identify the trust issues you need to work on. While it seems that everyone knows how important it is to trust your significant others; if you don't, it becomes impossible to give

them the necessary space for them to live as an individual capable of sharing a healthy relationship with you. A lack of trust usually breeds resentment in your partner. The root of the matter is: "Why is there a lack of trust?" Constantly checking their cell phone messages, Facebook newsfeed, and emails can lead to a horrible existence for both involved.
2. Let your partner have their space. Too much togetherness can put a strain on your relationship and can often lead to feelings of entrapment and suffocation. By giving your partner space, they are less likely to have a negative paired association.
3. Focus on centering yourself. You will be amazed at how much you can learn about yourself when you are alone. Showing your partner that you are not dependent on them for your every thought and need is more attractive.
4. Clinginess happens when the codependent life becomes centered solely around their partner. It is imperative that you have your own interests and goals as a priority. Rather than obsessively focusing on your partner, turn your attention inward toward something constructive.
5. Avoid making your partner responsible for your nervousness or anxiety. Simply employ some healthy stress management techniques to quell your fears and relax your body.
6. Watch your body language, such as an excessive need to communicate affection. Clinginess can be emotional and psychological as much as it is physical. Respect other people's boundaries. Some individuals do not like to be touched too much.

SYMPTOMS OF CODEPENDENCY

Poor boundaries: Boundaries are what divides what is yours and what belongs to someone else. Poor boundary setting is when there is a blurred line between where you begin and someone else ends. Codependent individuals usually struggle with setting clear boundaries. Boundary setting applies to not only your belongings, but your body, needs, money, and your thoughts. Codependent individuals feel responsible for how the people in their lives are feeling and often blame their own feelings or problems on those people. Healthy boundaries indicate what you will and what you won't be responsible for. In the workplace, or in relationships that are very personal, having poor boundaries can lead to feelings of resentment, exhaustion and sometimes anger. In general, having poor boundaries can lead to financial troubles, poor time management, relationship problems, and stress, all of which can cause mental anguish.

Low self-esteem: Self-esteem is a reflection of how you think and feel about yourself. It is essentially a self-appraisal. It is your true opinion of who you are. A low self-esteem is an emotion of feeling that you're not good enough, especially when comparing yourself to others. Sometimes self-esteem is portrayed in a disguise when the person actually feels unlovable. Feelings of shame and guilt and trying to be a perfectionist go hand-in-hand with low self-esteem. Instead of a healthy degree of self-evaluation, the codependent turns to other people for validation and to access their own value. It is other individuals who can make the codependent feel badly or good about themselves; which is why codependent is also described as *other-defined*. Due to feeling disconnected from their inner self, codependents struggle with self-trust and become confused when trying to develop their own opinions. They are unsure of what they really want and have to defer to others to feel liked or loved. Often when they know their own desires and needs, they talk themselves out of them or dismiss them to go along with someone else to avoid any conflict, especially in a tight-knit relationship. The table below compares the signs of high self-esteem and low self-esteem:

High Self-Esteem	Low Self-Esteem
I am fine the way I am.	I am not enough. I have to improve.
I accept praise.	I doubt or deflect praise.
I am efficient.	I lack confidence.
I have self-respect.	I lack compassion and respect for myself.
I am a compassionate person.	I am overly sensitive and judgmental of others.
I trust my decisions.	I am never sure if I am making the right decision.
I am a competent person.	I rely on others to tell me if I am doing OK.
I am honest.	I will say whatever I need to say to gain approval or please someone else.
I know I am of value.	I have low self-worth.
I want to be helpful.	I have to be needed.
I am only responsible for my actions.	I am responsible for the needs and actions of those I care about.

High self-esteem does not change due to external events. People with good self-esteem do not feel badly about themselves when bad things occur because those events are external and, therefore, not a reflection of one's inner being. But, when a person's self-esteem is low and bad things happen, they suffer disappointment or loss and feel defeated. It is important to remember that, when your self-esteem is low, you can become critical of yourself to the extreme, finding fault with all that you do, wear, say or create. Self-loathing can set in, giving rise to feelings of humiliation and embarrassment.

Controlling another person because of insufficient boundary setting and thinking of it as being in a caretaking role is another example of codependency. Feeling the imperative need to tell others what they should or should not do in order to get them to behave the way you want them to. Codependents often need to feel control over others in order to feel OK, themselves. Therefore, they tend to violate other people's boundaries. Codependents have often been through situations in life with individuals who were out of control, leaving the codependent feeling disappointed and sorrowful. They become fearful of allowing other people to let their life events happen naturally and to be who they are. The codependent doesn't acknowledge their loss of control anxiety and thinks they know what is best for someone else. They try their darndest to control other people with manipulations of helplessness, domination, guilt, advice, coercion, etc. and finally end up failing in their efforts to change the person or provoke the desired reaction. The only time a codependent feels safe is when the power is tilted toward them and the significant other has insecurities. When a partner is insecure, the codependent can get to work on "fixing" them. In this instance, the codependent feels they are in control, so they agree and comply with their partner while doing everything possible to give the impression that all is well. They generally do not want a significant other to feel secure so they can keep their fears of rejection and abandonment at bay. They will use non-subtle and very subtle techniques, such as passive-aggression (i.e., the silent treatment) and playing the victim to undermine their partner's feelings of security. Also, they are on high alert for any changes in their partner's behavior or mood that may indicate a turn in the tide in either direction.

Poor communication skills plague the codependent person. When it comes to talking about their own emotions, thoughts, and needs, the codependent individual is afraid to communicate their true feelings in fear of upsetting someone else. It leads the codependent toward manipulation and dishonesty. Codependents struggle with anxiety when it comes to being truthful; they do not want to disappoint anyone. So, rather than saying, "That is not OK," they may pretend that it is OK or give advice on how to be more OK. The communication becomes less than honest and confusing to others. Good communication requires an ability to be assertive and to include the person with whom you are trying to talk to by listening to what they say and showing empathy toward their feelings.

With healthy communication, there is no threatening feelings or the need to agree all of the time. Sometimes compromise is necessary, but there is comfort in expressing your thoughts and opinions, as well as taking the responsibility for what you have said. People's communication styles are developed in childhood. With encouragement, a child learns how to express their feelings, and likes and dislikes in the right manner. This carries on into adulthood. If the child was shamed and came from a dysfunctional family, they develop survival tactics that are unhealthy. Learning to lie and manipulate others to get their needs met becomes a common coping strategy, as well as people pleasing and the inability to handle anger. Relationships become damaged when the patterns of communication are unhealthy. The codependent relationship can become distant, abusive, and controlling without good communication. In turn, this leads to low self-esteem and stops the growth of healthy emotions.

Fear is the underlying force behind the way a codependent communicates. By masquerading as the truth, fear keeps the codependent feeling a false sense of unworthiness and that other people's reactions can destroy their very being. Therefore, fear is often reflected in the communication patterns of the codependent (i.e., walking on eggshells). But, in some instances, when dealing with an angry person, a codependent has made a real habit out of being dishonest and unresponsive, as to avoid any confrontation. If closely examined, the attitudes and feelings behind the way codependents communicate are grounded in shame, lack of commitment, lack of self-worth, anger and fear of abandonment—all based on dishonest communication within themselves. Every time they fail to pay tribute to their own precious feelings and thoughts for the sake of pleasing others, the codependent sells themselves short. Their true self might be periled in agony while the codependent walks around with a smile on their face.

Abandonment: Codependents are dependent on other people's feelings about them. Often, the codependent person has abandonment issues, fear rejection, and obsessively worry about saying or doing the wrong thing (according to someone else's standards). Because of their abandonment fears, they often will stay in an unhealthy relationship, leading them to feel trapped and depressed.

Codependents tend to encounter abandonment in relationships that mirrors the feelings of abandonment they experienced as a child from either one or both of their parents. All children need to feel accepted and loved by both of their parents in order to develop good self-esteem and good self-worth. A parent can't just say "I love you" to their child; they need to do/say more, especially because they are responsible for the healthy development of their child. They need to express their love through actions and words showing they desire a close relationship with their child while respecting the child's individuality. This includes having empathy for the child's needs and feelings. When the parent of a child criticizes, dismisses, or is preoccupied with themselves, they are not capable of empathizing with their child's needs or emotions. In turn, the child is left feeling misunderstood, hurt, emotionally abandoned, ashamed, and alone. Even when giving a child much attention, if the parent is not attuned to their needs, which, therefore, go unmet, it is still *emotional abandonment*. Feelings of abandonment arise when a child experiences feeling unimportant. As the cycle continues, the child, now an adult, fears intimacy. They tend to shy away from partners who want close intimacy because the distance is familiar and makes them feel safe. If the relationship starts moving in the direction of more intimacy, the distance will be recreated through arguments, infidelity, abuse, or addiction, further confirming the codependent's feelings of hopelessness, and self-perceptions of being unlovable. If these components put an end to the relationship, it fuels the fear of abandonment even more, leading to more hopelessness and the codependent's inability to verbalize their feelings.

Caretaking to an unhealthy extreme is a prime example of poor boundaries. Caregiving is not the same as codependent care-taking. It is normal to feel sympathy and empathy for another, but to put their needs ahead of yours is not normal. The codependent is set on fixing someone else, rescuing them, and controlling them even when the person ignores their attempt. Such is the case where addictions are involved. There are critical differences between caregiving and caretaking; the more caregiving and not caretaking the happier and healthier you are. Caretaking is a learned dysfunctional codependent behavior that can absolutely be unlearned. The main goal here is for the codependent to learn to decrease their caretaking while providing caregiving, leading to a more peaceful and more content quality of life. Truthfully, caretaking is the central element of codependency, as it is based on the need for control and is deeply rooted in insecurity. On the other hand, caregiving is based on love and compassion. All relationships involve a degree of give and take. Caregiving doesn't feel like a compulsion or obligation, and instead is the natural flow of support in a dynamic relationship. Codependent caregiving is unbalanced and perpetuates a cycle of imbalance in the relationship. The following are some of the main differences between caregiving and caretaking:

1. Caregiving is inspirational, energizing and feels like love. Caretaking is exhausting, stressful and frustrating.
2. Caregivers honor boundaries, while caretakers blur the boundaries.
3. Caregivers give of themselves freely while caretakers do just that. They take from the person they are helping because there are conditions for the care.
4. Caregivers take care of themselves because they understand that "a happy, healthy me" enables them to be of assistance to others. Caretakers do not take good care of themselves

in fear of being viewed as selfish and having low self-worth.
5. Caregivers actively take measures for solving problems. Caretakers incessantly worry and become preoccupied with thoughts and not actions.
6. Caregivers have a good sense of who they are and know what is best for themselves. Caretakers believe they know what is best for someone else.
7. Caregivers trust other people to help with problem-solving, based on their own capabilities. Caretakers think they are the only ones with the right answers and do not trust others in the care for themselves.
8. The act of giving care lowers anxiety levels and gives the caregiver a rewarding feeling regarding participating in helping another individual. The act of taking care of others creates great angst and/or a depressive state.
9. Caregivers engage more with healthy people either at their own or slightly above their own degree of mental health. Caretakers engage in relationships with needy people.
10. Caregivers are non-judgmental, and caretakers tend to be very judgmental while giving a false appearance of non-judgmentalism.
11. Caregivers show empathy and wait for the one in need to let them know when they need help from them. Caretakers jump into rescue mode as soon as *they* notice a problem in someone else's life.
12. Caregivers are solution driven, while caretakers are attention-seeking in their dramatic actions with the problem.

13. Caregivers refer to "you" a lot. Caretakers refer to "I" much more than "you".

Denial and more denial are prevalent in the codependent personality. Blaming others and never owning the problem allows the codependent to act as if it is all another person's fault, instead of realizing they have the problem themselves. This often happens because they cannot identify the difference between their own issues and the issues of those on which they are dependent upon. Playing the role of a superhero entails looking very good on the outside. All of the giving is bound to start creating resentments within, even though saying yes feels good on the outside. It doesn't take long for other people to expect you to say yes. Part of the codependent feels indispensable, which makes people-pleasing reinforced. What happens is the codependent finds themselves saying, "I'm OK," instead of admitting to feeling overwhelmed. The tendency to ignore their own feelings becomes habit forming (bad habit, at that). It never occurs to the codependent to reach out for help, but the exhaustion starts to reveal itself in outbursts. The remedy for always being "fine" is the admission of feelings, admitting there is a need for change.

Obsessional thinking manufactured from the codependent's anxieties often creates a "fantasy land" within which they live. Incessant thoughts about how different things would be if their significant other(s) did not engage in harmful behaviors is a way for the codependent to escape the pain of the present circumstances. This situation usually leads to painful emotions, low self-worth, shame, and despair. A plethora of negative emotions is attached to rumination about fixing another person. Eventually, when ruminating hasn't fixed the problem, the person ultimately feels numb. Obsessive thinking by the codependent person is a defense mechanism for their painful emotions. Fantasizing and ruminating about how they are going to fix someone keeps them focused on the future and works as an escape from the present. The sad truth about this is, with their attempt to escape any unpleasant feelings, more unpleasant emotions are generated. Worry, in a sense, is a fantasy about what may happen, which in turn heightens the fear factor. The fear becomes distorted, virulent, and ends up as a toxic combination of the false belief that being human is a shameful state of being. This self-defeating and self-perpetuating type of obsessional thinking adds not only to the anxiety, but to further shaming because they believe that being afraid, itself, is shameful and weak.

Intimacy issues surround the codependent. Not referring to sex here; intimacy means feeling open, honest, and close with another. Due to weak boundaries, fear of rejection, and shame, the codependent struggles with the vulnerability necessary to feel intimate. The fear of intimacy goes hand in hand with the fear of abandonment, rejection, and betrayal. This usually stems from early childhood wounds. Sometimes a parent can threaten emotional abandonment if not getting the desired behavior from a child. A child is unable to see themselves as a separate entity from the parents. Hence, the parent's behavior lends itself to the development of self-worth in their children. Sharing who they are is extremely difficult for the codependent because, at their very core, there is a feeling of defectiveness and unworthiness. This is their defense mechanism against rejection and betrayal.

As long as the codependent continues to act subconsciously to their childhood trauma, they will repeat the pattern in their current families, risking a chance of passing the condition down from generation to generation. Since the codependent loses themselves in another due to blurred boundaries, they have a tremendous fear of being judged, which, in turn, closes them off and unable to provide true intimacy. The codependent is confused by the difference between intimacy and sex. They fear that, if they let go of themselves sexually, they might lose their autonomy. They fear being looked down upon by their lover or that they may lose respect. They do not view their sexual partners as being on equal terms. Even though codependents crave close bonds to ease their loneliness and pain, they are too busy caring for others and remain out of touch with what is going on within them, making intimacy nearly impossible.

Shame is also a central feature of codependency. It stems from being in a dysfunctional family since birth. Even though shame is a natural human phenomenon, most people will do anything necessary to avoid it. It is not just an emotion, it is a physiological response implemented by the autonomic nervous system similar to panic, with a rapid pulse, sweating, nausea, poor eye contact, and slumping shoulders all being features of shame. Shame is different from guilt, as shame is a feeling about yourself, whereas guilt is a judgment about whether you have behaved right or wrong. Guilt prompts you to correct an error or fix it. Shame on the other hand is an encapsulating feeling of inferiority, self-loathing, and inadequacy. You feel like hiding, or you feel humiliated, as if other people can outright see your flaws. The strong sense of isolation can be overwhelming.

Toxic shame can ruin a person's life and can cause terrible pain. Shame leaves the codependent with feelings of self-loathing, which is worsened by not being able to verbalize the emotion without further anxiety leading to more shame. Toxic shame is buried deep in the subconscious mind and many may be unaware they are suffering from it. The type of shame experienced by many codependent people has a long duration stemming from childhood. In fact, most codependent individuals have grown up feeling ashamed about their emotions, wants and needs. When grown, they deny their wants and devalue themselves in order to avoid intense feelings of shame. Just memories and thoughts can trigger immense feelings of shame; it does not have to be associated with an external event. Toxic shame spirals out of control, leaving the individual with feelings of despair, depression, and hopelessness. In a normal case scenario, shame leaves us shortly after an embarrassing incident, but the codependent has internalized shame, which is just waiting to be activated by some type of trigger. Internalized shame is often the root cause of low self-worth, leaving the codependent feeling unworthy, unhappy, and unlovable. The lack of ability in allowing oneself to experience positive emotions is caused by a constant repeating message in their mind that they are worthless. It plays like a looped cassette tape pushing the codependent to constantly crave control and tend to others in an effort to reduce those shameful emotions.

Generosity lies at the heart of the codependent—a sincere wish to ease another's suffering. It becomes very uncomfortable for the codependent to witness someone in pain. Helping is rewarding until the help stops working. The codependent thinks of themselves as a superhero because they continuously work to enable another without even breaking a sweat. However, on the inside, they may be getting sick and tired of it. The codependent keeps a smile going until bits of the frustration starts to leak out. All of a sudden, sarcasm without intent happens, and a loss of control over their feelings begins. They get to the point where it is increasingly easier to say yes when meaning no. Anger begins to build up as the superhero feels underappreciated. Craving recognition without asking for it sets up the significant others for confusion and resentment. The codependent "love" is exclusive to other people with little or none left for themselves. The codependent wants their love to be recognized, and so, as such, they may sound off a list of things they have done for someone. It is a conditional love, meaning they want something in return (i.e., what's the payback?). Those loved by the codependent are grateful on the outside, but there is always the underlying feeling of dishonesty or that the giver has some other agenda. This also breeds resentment in the recipients of the codependent. It also leads toward taking advantage of the codependent so as to "teach them a lesson". Often, a recipient of love from a codependent person wants to build up their supply because they do not feel it is genuine to begin with and, therefore, may be cut off at any moment.

People-pleasing is normally a component of low self-esteem in which the individual feels inadequate or unlovable and has to make sure they please people in order to feel validated. For the people-pleaser, saying the word "no" to someone creates severe anxiety. This person will often sacrifice their own needs to oblige other people. Codependent people are strongly motivated in seeking external validation and approval. This insecurity induces conformity to other people's expectations and opinions. They want to please others even when it is uncomfortable for them or it is something they, on the inside, really do not want to do. While people-pleasing, itself, is not a diagnosable mental illness, it is a strong component of the codependent condition. The codependent's people-pleasing can appear much like generosity; however, generosity comes from a genuinely happy feeling of shared enjoyment. For the codependent, people pleasing comes from a low self-worth and from *needing* the approval of others.

The codependent becomes subservient to others, lacking a balance of mutual respect. For many, the wish to please comes from self-worth issues. The codependent hopes that by saying yes to everything asked of them, that will help them feel accepted and liked. Other people-pleasers have a history of being badly treated. Sometime along the way, the pleasers decided that the best way that they can be treated better is to try to please the ones who treated them badly. Over time, people-pleasing became a way of life for them. Take note of the following seven signs of people pleasing:

1. **Pretending to agree with anyone and everyone.** Agreeing with someone just to be liked or out of fear of rejection can cause you to get involved in situations that go against your belief system and values.
2. **Feeling responsible for how others feel.** Thinking that you have the power to make someone else's life happy is a false reality. Everyone is the director of their own happiness. Some people have everything one could want except for happiness.
3. **Constantly apologizing and excessive self-blame** or

thinking you are always to blame is a symptom of a larger issue. You never need to be sorry for being you!

4. **You feel like your activities of daily living are a burden.** Since codependents are people-pleasers, most activities on their schedule are for someone else. It is very difficult for a person with codependency issues to meet their goals as they are busy helping other people meet theirs.
5. **Inability to say "no".** Sometimes the codependent will say yes when they mean no and then have to make up a fake excuse for why they 'can't' follow through with the plans they never wanted to make in the first place.
6. **Fear of another person being upset with you.** Just because someone else is upset doesn't necessarily mean that you did something wrong. Acting some kind of way because you simply can't handle the thought of someone being upset with you is akin to walking on eggshells.
7. **Trying to fit in by behaving the same as the people around you.** It is normal for different environments with different people in them to bring out different parts of your personality. But, the codependent will often get involved with self-destructive behaviors just to fit in, such as eating more than you wish at a friend's house so they are happy that you enjoyed their cooking.

Everyone *overreacts* to small happenings here and there, usually without realizing it. It is fine for a person to feel their emotions and sometimes get angry. However, the codependent expresses themselves in an unhealthy way. With this type of severe codependent style of overreacting, the person tends to lash out at anyone who pushes the right buttons. While this may, to some degree, be effective because you are standing up for yourself, it still comes out as crazy. This means the codependent is still soaking up other people's baggage and letting it affect them. The way anger is unleashed from the codependent is a good indication of being unstable. Serious problems begin to arise when overreacting, such as being at risk for injury from the person you verbally attacked. All the lashing out does is magnify the anxiety and fears of the codependent who is already worried about disapproval. Healthy individuals do their best to avoid overly reactive people because it is demoralizing. They are disinterested in the theatrical drama of the reactive person and will surely label them as unstable and not the type one wants to buddy up with. The more pain the codependent feels, the weaker their boundaries become and that reinforces the lashing out. The lashing out is a sign of external forces permeating the insides of the codependent.

People react to *triggers*, which are unique to each individual's personality and history. Triggers can be imagined as re-experiencing wounds from past traumas, but in the present time. The codependent often feels as if they do not measure up to someone else's standards, triggering shame. Activating the inner critic all of the time can ruin a person's life. A well-documented trigger for the codependent is repeatedly being told they are too sensitive and selfish. Given that they adopted this belief, the codependent will automatically offer assistance, even when it is harmful or counterproductive. When behaviors or feelings are magnified in intensity and duration, people, in general, overreact. If an external trigger brings up a bad experience from the past, overreactions can happen. For example, the war hero who hears fireworks and draws his gun, even though they are safely in their home. *Overreacting* is a symptom of a person lacking the ability to set boundaries. This is noticeable when an individual feels defensive when another disagrees with them or automatically believes to be true what the other thinks about them. The difference between good boundaries and poor boundaries is the realization that people have opinions that are not a reflection of one's self and, therefore, do not feel threatened.

People overreact when they absorb another person's words or feelings because there is no set boundary between the two. When anger cannot be managed, it becomes overwhelming. How individuals react is influenced by their inborn temperament and early childhood environment. Therefore, each individual's reactions are unique to their own personality. Some criticize, explode into rage, blame others, or say things they later regret. The codependent wants to avoid any conflict, so they hold their emotions in where they stockpile into resentments. But, like steam, anger builds up and always finds a way out. Codependents have learned very well how to employ passive-aggressive actions to relieve their anger buildup. For example, a codependent wife may be angry at her husband. Since, she fears verbalizing her feelings, she burns his dinner instead. If the aforementioned denial is in place, and the person doesn't allow themselves to feel or even take a mental note of their anger, and days, weeks, or years go by after the issues, a total meltdown can be in store. Anger can lead to illnesses because the stress related to the emotion wears a person's immune system down and the body's nervous system's ability to repair itself.

CODEPENDENCY AND THE NEED FOR CONTROL

Power plays a part in all relationships. It gives an individual a sense of control in their choices and their ability to influence others and the environment within which they live. It is a healthy and natural survival technique necessary for getting our needs met. Empowerment allows us to feel intrinsically involved in affecting outcomes and managing our emotions in the process. It puts us in a position of efficiency with an internal locus of control instead of overreacting. The codependent, in contrast, feels powerless and thinks they have fallen victim to outside forces. When not lashing out with a false sense of power, the codependent believes their destiny is in someone else's hands. Always acquiescing as to not sound mean, the codependent defers their needs and finds it difficult to make independent decisions. This impaired sense of power can stem from various elements common to codependents, such as low self-worth, shame, dependency, fear (both of rejection and abandonment), approval seeking, denial, and unreasonable expectations of other people coupled with their victim mentality. Most relationships known to the codependent have imbalances of power. With the difficulty they have in expressing their true feelings, it becomes natural for another to fill the void. In these relationships, sometimes a narcissist, alcoholic, addict, or abuser has power over the codependent person leading them to resort to passive-aggressive methods of trying to gain a sense of control. Over a period of time, the lack of power can ultimately cause depression and other physical problems.

In healthier relationships, if there is mutual respect, both individuals engage in ongoing power struggles. This usually revolves around time management, money, household chores, child-rearing techniques, and so on. In avoidance of conflict, some couples agree to separate domains of power. Traditionally, mothers tended to the children and the home, while fathers were the breadwinners. This continues very much today in many cultures, but is changing with the improved earning abilities of women, especially when also caring for young children (social evolution). In present times, men are much more involved in parenting, and women have more power outside of the home, teaching them they can easily function outside of the relationship. Feelings of resentment and imbalance are common issues that coincide with the changing times. This is why effective communication is so important so each partner can feel respected and powerful.

Decisions are made together with both partners assuming responsibility for the relationship and for themselves in a healthy couple scenario. This is where safety, values and needs are developed in a healthy relationship. Here, with shared power, each person wants to express their likes and dislikes, and what each will tolerate from the other. Sometimes, an individual is possibly feeling vulnerable from a lack of respect. The codependent has an impaired relationship with power; possibly coming from their submissive roles growing up where their feelings were criticized, and their needs ignored. Without the encouragement of self-worth and personal power, the codependent is left feeling as if love and power cannot coexist. They have learned the only way to exert power is indirectly. They might have learned that love is acquired only by acquiescing and pleasing others. Historically, this was common in families where girls were encouraged not to be assertive, educated, or self-reliant. The flip side of this is some children learn while growing up that the best way to meet their needs and feel safe is to have power over other people. When becoming an adult, this breeds fear and resentment in their partner, leading the partner into passive-aggressive actions to get their feelings acknowledged.

Many people with codependent personalities have never learned how to assertively solve problems. They very likely had a controlling parent. The codependent may end up rebelling and becoming authoritarian, themselves, which, again, is counterproductive to getting their needs met. They are unable to discern how to get their needs and wants met or how to make decisions for themselves. They give up control of their inner desires and turn to others or freeze (not act at all). Assertiveness requires self-esteem, which makes it difficult for the codependent as the lack of self-worth is one of the key components of the condition. Due to this lack of any sense of power within themselves, control and manipulation become part of the behavioral pattern in the codependent. They focus on external resources for happiness, instead of taking responsibility for their own. The codependent wants to get others to do things or act how they want them to in order to make themselves happy. When these expectations go unmet, the codependent falls into further despair and a further sense of powerlessness. People do not have to give up themselves to have love and power. Actually, love necessitates the exercise of power so we can show that we are responsible for our decisions. It takes power to directly ask for our wants and needs and to honestly express ourselves when setting healthy boundaries.

ROLES PLAYED BY THE CODEPENDENT

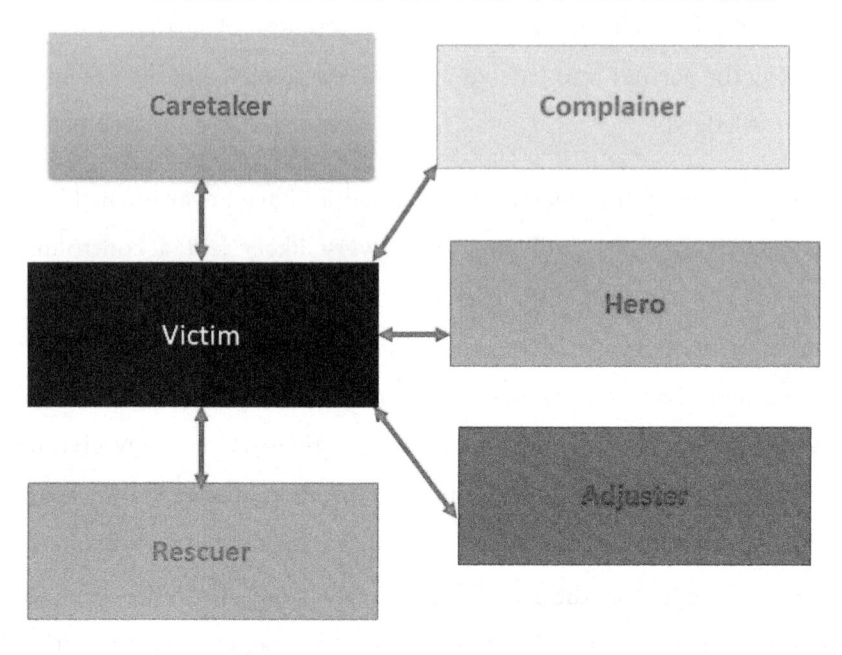

- Caretaker
- Complainer
- Victim
- Hero
- Rescuer
- Adjuster

PREVALENCE OF CODEPENDENCY

It is difficult to establish how prevalent codependency is. Some suggest that, in the U.S., as much as 90% of the population demonstrates characteristics of codependency. The prevalence of codependency is difficult to ascertain partly because of its undetermined definition. Melody Beattie describes a codependent person as someone who allows another individual's behavior to affect them and who obsessively tries to control that person's behavior. Given the prevalence of codependency suggested by experts in the field of behavioral health, it is a condition that needs careful assessment and should not be overlooked when treating an individual, regardless of their presenting problem or any prior diagnosis. It is essential that anyone working in a therapeutic environment understand the characteristics of codependency well enough to have self-awareness of their own potential codependent traits. The severity and development of codependent characteristics overlap and vary. They derive from the codependents' lack of ability to tap into their inner core and primarily include:

- Painful emotions: Anxiety, hopelessness, sorrow, fear and despair;
- Denying that they are codependent and denying their emotions and feelings;
- Blurred or rigid boundaries;
- Poor communication skills; and
- Dependency on others.

When it comes to treating a client or offering expert advice, it is helpful to be able to remember that compulsive behaviors are prevalent in the personality of the codependent. The codependent thinks that they have to be codependent and have no choice in the matter. Even when the behaviors are self-destructive, the codependent will not cease to demonstrate them even when it is destroying their own lives. These individuals are commonly unhappy. They believe they can rescue the dependent person, making them better, when they are only reinforcing the dependency. Making matters even more serious is the belief that they will receive validation in return and when that doesn't happen, resentments start to flourish.

2

WHERE DOES CODEPENDENCY COME FROM?

Codependency most often stems from childhood to the relationships we had with our primary caretakers or parents. It usually occurs when one or both of the parents are under- or overprotective. When parents are overprotective, they restrain their child's autonomy and keep them from building the confidence necessary to go out into the world on their own. Normal anxieties include watching your child try new things, but forbidding them from trying stops them from learning how to complete basic tasks. When a parent or parents are under-protective, they do not provide their children with enough support and, therefore, they structure the basis of codependency. Missing this most important step in child rearing can leave the young one feeling unsafe and alone in the world (a breeding ground for anxiety and depression). Sometimes, a codependent parent will treat their son or daughter more like a friend, over-involving themself in their children's lives, living vicariously through them, and reinforcing dependent characteristics while discouraging them from becoming independent. When this happens, the codependent begins to harbor guilt for not wanting their child to have their own life. If a child grows up with a parent afflicted with alcoholism and/or drug addiction, the child or children stand the chance of being neglected or tending to the dependent parent and thus, the codependent child is launched.

One way codependency is passed down to children could be that it is "inherited" through genetics, which influences personality traits, such as empathy. Another type of inheritance is learning through observation. Children learn how to behave by watching someone model actions rather than learning it directly by experience. While researching the literature associated with codependency, studies noted that a parent's codependent actions, and what they explain to children about helping people, influences those children's behavioral characteristics into adulthood. If, when growing up, a child watches important people in their life over-help, enable and rescue, they become more prone to it themselves, especially when it is one of their parents, who are praised by others for how much they put up with. These behavioral traits are often taken in subconsciously when children are still too young to comprehend their negative consequences. Behaving in a codependent way becomes a habit despite its hazardous results. Professional help is usually necessary for identifying and breaking these patterns.

CODEPENDENT PARENTS

What if you are not in a healthy coupled relationship and are a codependent parent? A codependent parent has an unhealthy attachment to their child or children because they expect a degree of love and devotion to the point that it is destructive to the family as a whole. This usually occurs when the codependent parent is trying to make up for what was lacking in their own upbringing. A vicious cycle is happening, and decision-making processes are likely to become unhealthy because there are blurred boundaries between the parent and child. The message the child receives is one of, "I am not OK unless you are OK, or you tell me I am OK". In turn, the child or children of the codependent learn to pay close attention to the parent and ready themselves to act in a way that will not upset the parent. They don't per se want to 'rock the boat'.

A mother or father who is codependent has a difficult time effecting boundaries or imposing limits when a child misbehaves. So, the codependent parent loosens the rules and limitations so they can revert back to their normal emotional state. Sometimes, the codependent parent will toss their children's actions back at them, making it all about themselves. Due to the fact the parent's sense of who they are is dependent on the relationship they have with their child; they will possibly try to control every aspect of their children's life. If there are happenings in the life of their child that create a sense of anxiety in the codependent parent, the parent will try to gain control so as to provide relief to themselves by getting overly involved. The parent will literally do anything to gain control of their child so they can relieve their anxiety. Sometimes, the codependent parent will try to maintain control by telling their children of the difficult times they had as a child to try and garner sympathy.

Often when one or both of the parents are codependent, their relationship takes a back seat to the children, fearing the marriage or marital relationship will interfere with the parent-child relationship. This can come in the form of a subtle push-away so as to maintain the focus on the child or children. Even when the codependent caretaker is literally wrong, there will be no apology; if there is one it will be insincere, and noticeably so. When a codependent parent has a falling-out with a child, their authority feels threatened, or is viewed as the child acting out of rebellion. A common phrase said during this type of an interaction is, "I feel like I am talking to a brick wall!" A codependent parent will often use guilt as a weapon. Passive-aggression, such as the silent treatment or projecting blame, is often the chosen 'weapon' to use when a child is becoming autonomous. This can happen without the codependent parent even being aware of it. This is all put forth in an effort to control their child or children into doing as the parent forcefully suggests, especially when they are grown. This type of relationship between a parent and a child sets a premise for how a child will relate to life. Each experience a child has provides them with information about future decisions. Therefore, they are at a high risk of using the same dysfunctional behavioral patterns they have learned while growing up with a codependent parent when they become adults.

Family Boundaries

Family boundaries delineate who in the family is responsible for what. They create an emotional and a physical space between each member of the family. Boundaries are a safety net reflecting mutual respect for the feelings and the needs of each family member, while communicating clear roles and expectations. While growing up, a child's boundaries should shift gradually to allow for increased autonomy and privacy, allowing the young person to develop their own set of values and beliefs system. Codependency is a trait that is very helpful to children growing up in dysfunctional homes as they learn to navigate frightening and unpredictable family lives. However, these don't translate positively in adulthood. Enmeshment refers to a family system that has blurred boundaries and the expectations of the leaders of the family are confusing and inappropriate. When a parent relies on a child for support and, at the same time, the child is not allowed to be emotionally separate from their family members, they all become emotionally merged together in an unhealthy manner.

Common characteristics of an enmeshed family system:

- Blurred boundaries;
- Always about pleasing someone else;
- The family members feel responsible for their parents' happiness;
- The child is made to feel guilt and shame if they want a bit less contact with a parent;
- The parents' sense of worth depends on their children's successes;
- The parent **must** know everything about their children's life;
- The parents discourage their children from following their

dreams and goals, and imposing their own wishes on them is a must;
- The family shares private experiences too much with one another, and feelings are expressed in such a way that creates unhealthy dependence, unrealistic expectations and confused roles;
- The children feel that if they don't meet their parents' expectations, they will be emotionally abandoned or shamed; and
- The children begin to avoid discussions where they may have to say "No".

CODEPENDENCY AND SUBSTANCE ABUSE PATTERNS

* * *

LIVING WITH AN ADDICT

Addicts and alcoholics often rely on family members to supply their finances and to support their way of life. This is because their addiction has, in many cases, made them unable to take care of their basic necessities, such as a place to live, food, and money. They depend on the love of their family and want continuous validation of their love and support. Too often, family members feel the need to protect their afflicted so they can be a "good parent, spouse, sibling, friend, etc." The addict is sure of this, and they use it to get what they can and get away with it. Relationships function in give-and-take scenarios; they naturally affect one another. It is important to realize that the addict did not make a moral choice to be one. The addict is not necessarily a bad person, and it doesn't mean they don't love you. You did not cause their addiction, either, and you cannot change it or control it. You can still have compassion for the addict without enabling them in order for you to feel like a good person. Like the addict, the codependent does not have a flawed personality and is not a moral failure. To help you to understand how to start the healing process, you must first know the normal effects of relationships. Relationships connect people in one or more of the following ways:

- An individual will assume some of the qualities of the other.
- An individual will assume a position that complements the qualities of the other.
- An individual will assume a position counteracting the qualities of the other.

The most important thing to understand about these scenarios is that the connection between two people in a relationship changes the people. Everyone is changed as a result of a connection to a person who is addicted to a substance. To help you to understand codependency with an addict, use the same scenarios above, but change a few words.

- An individual will assume some of the *unhealthy* qualities of the addict or alcoholic.
- An individual will assume a position that complements the *unhealthy* qualities of the addict or alcoholic.

- An individual will assume a position counteracting the *unhealthy* qualities of the addict or alcoholic.

To arrive at the next step, replace the word individual with you, and then replace the words addict and alcoholic with the name of your addicted friend or loved one. Addicts often avoid seeking treatment, and so do codependents. It is an uncomfortable process for both. For change to happen, the discomfort must be faced. Thankfully, the discomfort is not permanent as it is just a time of transition. If an alcoholic or addict could stop on their own, they would certainly have done so long before many of the common and serious negative consequences had come along. Actually, when an intervention is accomplished with an addict or alcoholic, it is the first move toward change for the codependent. Difficult at first, the uncomfortable times are well worth the benefits in the long-term and often lifesaving for both. If you are involved with an addict, know it is your partner with the addiction, yet if codependent, you are the one putting a huge amount of pressure on yourself to solve the problem, as if it is your responsibility to restore their sanity. This again stems from abandonment fears and low self-esteem. Unfortunately, the help you are attempting to offer is only hurting the addict in the long run. If the addict does not take the first step by admitting they have a problem with drugs and/or alcohol, their chances of sobriety will be low, to say the least.

When a person with whom you are involved is addicted, they may become hostile and defensive when you attempt to help. Try not to take it personally. It is the codependent's low self-worth that makes it seemingly impossible to understand things from this perspective. Even when you know your partner is sick, you will still feel devastated by their harsh behavior and their rejection of your help. A classic component of codependency is the constant seeking of the partner's affirmation because you depend on that in order for you to feel good about yourself. This is an unhealthy behavior under any circumstance. When your loved one is dealing with addiction, the last thing they need is someone afraid to confront the problem. They do, however, need honesty, which is what you struggle with when letting your codependency stay in control. The love and compassion you feel for someone so close to you are obvious under these brutal circumstances, but your need to keep your abandonment fears at bay can actually lengthen the misery already in place. Commonly, the codependent will become obsessed with trying to fix the addict often to the point of neglecting their own needs.

Addicts can often be extremely verbally abusive and frequently lie to their significant others. The codependent is the one left to clean up their messes. Now is when the one involved with the addict should refuse immediately and let them know this is an unacceptable behavior. But, if codependent, you are probably going to refuse to do what is best, and subject yourself to more abuse while helping them to keep using. Of course, people who abuse alcohol or drugs need help and advice from their loved ones, but in the case of codependency, the efforts made for help are overbearing to the point of acting parental toward the addict as if they are a small child incapable of doing anything on their own. If it gets to this point, you are attempting too hard to control the situation. This is ineffective and may trigger the addict's self-defensive tendencies; a consequence of codependency. Codependents commonly resort to manipulating others to get what they want, using shame, guilt, and embarrassment to play on their emotions. This method ultimately does not get the desired results. Entering treatment just to satisfy the codependent will not be successful. No matter how often you attempt to control the addict's behavior and how your relationship progresses, you are left feeling vulnerable and powerless. Overwhelming fears and feelings of helplessness set in and finally you become convinced that you are trapped. This, in turn, makes for a more unpredictable and uncertain future. As the patterns continue, the codependent may start to lie or blame others for their situations, making it easier for them not to face the consequences of their behavior and remain in a state of denial. Here lies the foremost example of codependency: enabling.

When someone you love is struggling with drug or alcohol addiction, you and other people close to that individual can be of great importance in helping the individual to overcome their addiction and to provide the motivation and emotional support needed to help them with their recovery. This is, of course, provided that the individual is ready to enter treatment necessary for the recovery process. However, codependent relationships have the directly opposite effect, increasing the chances that the person will either never seek treatment or, even after seeking treatment, relapse. It is a lose-lose situation for both the addict and the codependent because it makes it harder for the addict to stop. Enabling makes it challenging for the addict to stick to their treatment goals, unfortunately ending in relapse and a return to self-destructive actions.

For the codependent struggling in a relationship with an addict, both people may go through many negative consequences based on the problem. Some of these potential consequences include:

- Potential for also developing substance, food, sex, shopping or gambling addictions.
- Loss of friends and family relationships with people outside of the codependent relationship.
- Failure to meet responsibilities outside of the codependent relationship.

You have more power than you think you do. Even though you can't cure someone else, or make all their decisions for them, even if you are working with their best interest at heart; what you CAN control are the choices you make and the boundaries that you set in place. In general, codependents work so hard to rescue their addicted counterpart that they end up getting sick themselves. Partners and family members of addicts often struggle with the thought that they cannot help their loved one. A sense of "failing" their loved one can create a vicious cycle of shame, guilt, fear, resentment, and more (see the CoDA five patterns).

EMPATHY

Empathy is the ability to understand, realize and share the feelings and thoughts of another human being, animal, or some fictional character read in a book or viewed in a movie. Some who feel high degrees of empathy may think of themselves as 'highly sensitive', meaning their emotions are affected by the energy of people in their surroundings. It is like walking into an office after the boss 'reamed out' a coworker, and you can feel the tension in the room. It is imperative for people to develop empathy so they can establish relationships and provide compassion. It allows us to help other people by experiencing their point of view, and it comes from within and without being forced. It is important because it enables us to connect to others. It may have originally evolved for survival purposes both when we needed help or detected danger. If you think about a baby, maybe 2 years old, you will notice that they have the sincere ability to try and comfort a parent.

The ability to show support for a friend or loved one is an important part of building positive relationships. It allows us to have rapport with others, making them feel understood. Showing you understand another's perspective further cements the connections we make in life. In present days, external validation is no longer an evolutionary means of surviving, but for many, it still feels like it. The fine line is that, when you put yourself in someone else's shoes, if not careful, it can make you vulnerable and blind to your own needs. Some people will take advantage of your empathy if you are not sensitive to the warning signs. If you put the perspectives and emotions of others above your own, emptiness can set in, and the chance of developing anxiety and depression can arise. The difference between codependency and empathy is that one who feels empathy has a solid sense of who they are without taking other people's emotions personally, or feeling an uncontrollable urge to fix or change them. Each individual is meant to experience their own unique journey in life; even when times of feeling misunderstood occur, we realize it is not evidence of who we are. When others are experiencing emotional circumstances, empathy gives us the ability to give a person our undivided attention by listening and being fully present. If codependency exists, there is an immediate reaction to instantly fix the person with solutions for their problems. The codependent reacts this way because the emotions of the other person at the time are absorbed and are intolerable. The consequences of these self-centered reactions lead the person with the problem to feel unheard (of course, the best intentions were at hand by the codependent). Being truly empathetic means having defined boundaries around what we will accept and what we will not. It gives us an understanding of why a person does a particular thing while also holding *them* responsible for their own actions. Empathy enables us in the understanding that each unique individual has their own version of the truth and that it is out of place for us to enforce our version of the truth on others.

Empathy differs from compassion, but they are closely related. Compassion is how we respond emotionally to sympathy, and it triggers a desire to help. Empathy is an awareness of another individual's emotions while attempting to understand how they feel. There is also a very fine line between being codependent and being a loving/caring person. If you hit the label "codependent" on the human being's empathetic and kind character traits, we might as well label all of the great spiritual icons, such as Mother Theresa and Buddha as codependents beyond repair. Kindness—far from a synonym of codependent—comes from a spiritual or humanitarian place inside each of us (or most of us). It takes perceptiveness to identify codependency from the human characteristics of love and compassion. Nurturing and supporting others provides us with a reward of feeling 'warm and fuzzy'. The world can always use a bit more sensitivity and compassion. A central component of love is noticing other people's needs, and if possible, providing it to them without overextending yourself; keeping a vital balance of caring for yourself while caring for others is key to keeping sane. We have to be careful about casually throwing around the codependent label, as we may miss the fact that we are complex individuals motivated by many incentives. It is a disservice to neglect ourselves in favor of attending to the needs of others. Working diligently to avoid being labeled codependent creates obstacles toward having healthy connections and intimate relations with others.

There is such a thing as *empathy fatigue,* as in having too much empathy. It can be harmful to your health. Leading with the heart and not the head can lead to making poor decisions when in a relationship. You do not want to lose perspective about what is best for you. There are several central elements to finding harmony in your life and reducing any negativity. How about the basics—exercise, hydration, sleep, and nourishment—without which is a state of unhappiness. Here is the key: you have to nurture your mind and spirit, as well. Nourishing your spirit with gratitude creates a barrier against negative emotions that can be destructive to your happiness. It is impossible to feel resentment, envy, anger, and regret while feeling grateful at the same time. They are not compatible with one another. Gratitude is an action word and allows you to actively participate in your life; it tends to magnify the good things.

IS CODEPENDENCY A MENTAL ILLNESS?

The extent to which codependency exists on its own is a subject for debate, with some people feeling it is a disorder severe enough to be categorized in the Diagnostic and Statistical Manual of Mental Disorders, 5th Edition (DSM-5), while others think it is a symptom of other disorders with no scientific research supporting the concept of codependency. The DSM-5 gives a comprehensive foundation for classifications and symptoms of conditions related to behavioral health. As early as 1986, experts in the field of behavioral health contended that codependency should be officially recognized as a mental health condition with diagnostic criteria shared from other disorders, including borderline personality disorder (BPD), histrionic personality disorder, dependent personality disorder (DPD), and even post-traumatic stress disorder (PTSD), qualifying that it has a recognizable personality disorder worthy of placement in the DSM-5.

The DSM-5 does not include codependency; however, it does include DPD. The reasoning behind not including codependency in the DSM-5 is that it has too much in common with other diagnoses causing an overlap to the extent that it does not merit its own place. However, newer studies revealed that, even though codependency overlaps a good deal with BPD and DPD, there are symptoms that are not included in either. This proposes codependency as a unique mental health condition. DPD shares the most in common with Codependency. The main difference is the way they behave in relationships. While DPD refers to individuals who show dependent characteristics toward other people in general, the codependent shows dependent characteristics on a specific individual. Likewise, an individual with BPD has difficulty with maintaining stability in relationships in general and the codependent involves a specified dependence on an individual.

Given the similarities between the condition of codependency and the DSM-5 criterion for DPD, it is noted that the main difference is in the degree of functionality of both the role as a codependent and the enabler role. Once identified, and codependency has been ruled out of the differential criterion, the attributing problems to problematic relationships are considered as relative characteristics of codependency. Currently, codependency is only considered a condition, psychological in nature, where an individual feels a dependence for a certain significant other in an extreme fashion. It is a distorted perspective of one's self that influences every action, behavior, anything said and one's complete path in life, essentially living as only one-half of a person that thinks they are responsible for the feelings and actions of another, eventually leading to low self-worth.

Once more, if the cycle is uninterrupted, the codependent is doomed to passing the condition onto the next generation. The way we interact and relate to people who are significant in our lives determines the degree of enjoyment and pain experienced in life. In the best-case scenario, the people around us are hopefully there to aid us in achieving our full potential. They are there for encouragement, support, and to help us follow our dreams. On the flip side of the best-case scenario coin, we are there to lift them up when they are down and care for them during a crisis. Here lies the dilemma of not getting so caught up in their problems that you are consumed by them.

* * *

QUESTIONNAIRE: ARE YOU A CODEPENDENT?

Answer the following questions and give yourself a score of 1 for each "yes" answer:

1. Do you try to get approval from others by rescuing, tending to their needs and then feeling disappointment when you are not validated?

| YES | NO |

2. Do you spend your spare time feeling anxious about other people or about doing something for someone else because you fear being alone?

| YES | NO |

3. Have you ever been in an abusive relationship and stayed when you knew you shouldn't?

| YES | NO |

4. Was the family you were raised in dysfunctional?

| YES | NO |

5. Have you ever been emotionally, physically or sexually abused?

| YES | NO |

6. Was either one of your parents codependent or narcissistic?

| YES | NO |

7. Is there any type of addiction in your family background?

| YES | NO |

8. Do you tell people too much about yourself before you get to know them very well?

| YES | NO |

9. Do you care more about what other people think about you than you think about your own well-being?

| YES | NO |

10. Does your personal history include many troubled relationships?

| YES | NO |

11. Do you have low self-worth and suffer from shame?

| YES | NO |

12. Have you ever lied to get someone else off the hook?

| YES | NO |

13. Has anyone ever suggested you are overactive?

| YES | NO |

14. Have you ever dated a narcissist?

| YES | NO |

15. Do you say "yes" when you mean "no"?

| YES | NO |

16. Do you believe you did not matter when growing up?

| YES | NO |

17. Do you have problems setting boundaries?

| YES | NO |

18. Have you ever enabled someone to continue drinking or drugging in spite of the consequences?

| YES | NO |

19. Do you try to go above and beyond to make someone else happy before you feel happy yourself?

| YES | NO |

20. Have any of your relationships caused you to lose sleep at night?

| YES | NO |

Now add up your score here _____.

(See Suggested Recommendations in Appendix 1).

3

WHAT DOES CODEPENDENCY LOOK LIKE?

Codependence is a condition that decays the spirit and freedom of those who suffer in dysfunctional relationships and families. It affects the lives of their families, friends, professional careers, their health, and their spirituality. It drains the person of all they have and, if left without seeking help, causes them to become more self-destructive and destructive to others. Some codependents are pushed by friends, therapists, colleagues, or other family members to get help. Codependency occurs when individuals live in the extremes of drama and lack balance in their lives. Often their partners, friends, and families are affected by the dysfunctional control characteristics the codependent portrays, all under the disguise of helping.

There are many roles occupied by the codependent:

1. Victim: Unfortunately, playing the victim role rarely works to the advantage of the codependent. It actually pushes partners, family members, co-workers, and friends away. The following are signs of playing the victim:

- Refusing to take responsibility for their own circumstances; it is always someone else causing the problem, oftentimes pointing the finger in an attempt to make someone feel guilty.
- Often when the codependent is in the victim role, they are paralyzed with fear and believe they are at the mercy of their partner. They feel powerless in this role and, as a result, stop growing.
- When in the victim role, the codependent spurs resentments, holding on to old injustices and manipulating others to feel badly about their behavior. Bringing up past negative memories and excuses as to why they cannot get out of their dysfunctional relationships is the hallmark of the victim role.
- The codependent lacks assertiveness skills when playing the victim and sincerely doubts they have control in their life; therefore, it becomes challenging for them to verbalize their needs, wants, and desires, and they usually remain in a looping pattern of submissiveness. This leads to low self-esteem, anxiety, panic attacks, and depression.

2. Rescuer/Hero: In the case of the codependent and the addict or alcoholic, it is not uncommon for the codependent to literally put the addict in bed after they pass out from over-imbibing.

- "Somebody help me...Everybody help me" is the phrase that ignites the entire realm of stress hormones in the codependent, along with a powerful need to connect to others in the only way they have ever known how. Most are familiar with this role. It is your motherly friend who takes in all of the stray animals and religiously does their partner's dirty laundry. It is the fierce soldier who goes to war every day to save "anything that needs saving". Guilt is not the motivating factor here; rather it is the intense need to be needed. The codependent relies on the rescuer role to give them some sense of self. The codependent needs to rescue more than whomever needs rescuing, in most cases.
- The codependent often feels a drop in self-esteem when there are lags in time between rescues. There is an unsettled feeling that there is something terribly wrong with the situation and the codependent person marches toward finding the next person who needs rescuing.
- The rescuer usually seems to be on a mission to commit to addicts or others whose lives are unmanageable. They always need some form of rescue whether it be in the form of sympathy, money, or an alibi.
- The rescuer role usually develops early in life when feelings of powerlessness were being developed. Imagine a young child who is put in a position of having to rescue their mother or father, siblings, or the entire family. This family is prone to have a big "I can't" as a common phrase in their household. Over time, this rescuer role becomes so embedded in the person that it is the only method they know

when it comes to connecting to other people. Unfortunately, this young person has learned that the only way to meet their own needs is by living vicariously through meeting the needs of others. Therefore, in adult life, the codependent searches for what is familiar.
- The codependent in the rescuer role often views themselves as heroically saving the family image.

3. Caretaker: The codependent caretaker embodies the role of maid, parent, sex slave, chef, accountant, banker, nurse, etc. Everyone feels a certain amount of desire to be needed, but the codependent in this role takes it to the extreme. Caretaking to the extreme can be harmful to your partner and self-destructive to you. In this role, the codependent loses their identity and basically smothers their partner, leaving them no time or room to work on solving their own problems. In the dysfunctional family, as previously mentioned, the codependent learns from an early age that if not needed, they have no value whatsoever. Hence, the caretaker is completely dependent on their partner to be needed.

4. Joiner: The codependent often wants to imagine their partner's dysfunctional characteristics as being normal by simply permitting the unhealthy behaviors and sometimes joining them in their unhealthy actions, such as taking drugs, gambling, or excessive drinking. When in the role of the joiner, the codependent may regularly stop by the store on the way home from work and buy some alcohol, such as a bottle of wine, and have two glasses ready for their addicted partner by the time they come home. Also, they may make sure that the alcohol or drug is in full supply so there is no chance of withdrawals.

WHAT DOES CODEPENDENCY LOOK LIKE? | 259

5. Complainer: In this role, the codependent incessantly blames others for all their problems. It is part of their delusional thinking patterns. After developing resentment, anger, loneliness, and bitterness, they will complain about how underappreciated they are when they have done so much to help. The codependent will constantly complain without ever finding any type of solution. This makes them uncomfortable to be around, but the codependent doesn't care. They are trapped in the loop of thinking if they complain enough, something will change, but it never does.

6. Adjuster: The individual tries to become invisible. The codependent repeatedly adjusts their behavior to avoid abandonment or rejection. They use fantasy to escape reality and tend to deny having any feelings at times.

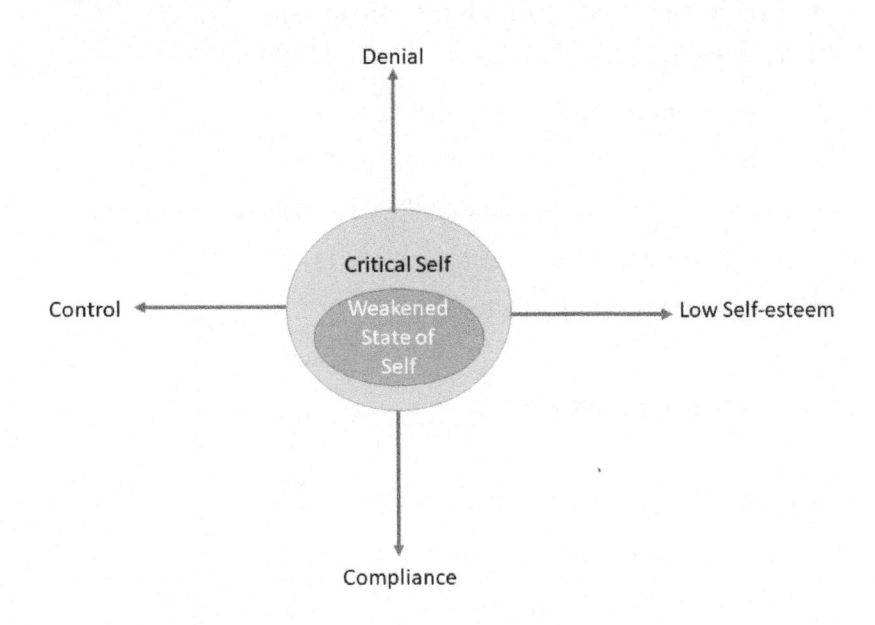

```
                    Denial
                      ↑
                      |
              Critical Self
Control ←———  Weakened  ———→ Low Self-esteem
              State of
                Self
                      |
                      ↓
                  Compliance
```

As previously discussed, a codependent feels responsible for the actions, feelings and behaviors of someone else without practicing self-perseverance. It takes two to take part in a relationship, and the people-pleaser/rescuer personality, unfortunately, is a perfect complement for someone who is completely self-serving. The signs of codependency have been listed in five patterns identified by Co-Dependents Anonymous (CoDA, 2020):

1. Denial Pattern

- Minimize or deny their true feelings.
- See themselves as totally unselfish and committed to the well-being of others.
- Lack of empathy for others' feelings.
- Project their own negative traits onto others.
- They believe they need no help from others.
- Mask their pain with anger, humor, or isolation.
- Verbalize negativity in indirect and passive-aggressive ways.
- Do not recognize how emotionally unavailable the people to whom they are attracted are.
- Struggle with identifying feelings.

2. Low Self-Esteem Pattern

- Indecisiveness.
- Judge themselves harshly, as never being good enough.
- Feel embarrassed when receiving praise or recognition.
- Place extreme value on the approval of others, on the way they think, feel, and behave.

- Think they are not lovable.
- Low self-worth.
- Seek approval to overcome feelings of worthlessness.
- Struggle with admitting a mistake.
- Think of themselves as being superior to others.
- Depend on others for a sense of safety.
- Struggle with procrastination.

3. Compliance Pattern

- Stay in destructive situations too long because of extreme loyalty.
- Compromise their own integrity and values out of fear of rejection or anger.
- Don't do what they want; just do what others want.
- Overly sensitive about the feelings of others and incorporate those feelings into their own psyche.
- Fear of expressing their own opinions, emotions, and beliefs if they are different from those around them.
- Accept sexual relationships when they want love.
- Have little regard for consequences when making decisions.
- In order to gain approval from others or to avoid any type of change, they are willing to give up their own truth.

4. Control Patterns

- Have the belief that individuals are incapable of caring for themselves.

- Manipulate or try to convince others on how to feel, what to think and do.
- Frequently give direction and advice without solicitation.
- When their help is refused, they become resentful.
- Shower gifts and services on people they want to influence.
- Use sex to manipulate or gain acceptance or approval.
- Being needed is a must in order to be involved in a relationship.
- Demand others meet their needs.
- Use their charisma and charm to show others they are compassionate and caring.
- Blame and shame to emotionally exploit others.
- Will not compromise, cooperate, or debate.
- Behave helplessly, indifferently, authoritatively, or angrily to manipulate results.
- Use twelve-step slogans in attempts to exert control over the way others behave.
- Falsely act in agreement with others to achieve what they want.

5. *Avoidance Pattern*

- Elicit shame, anger, and rejection through behaving in such a way.
- Criticize others' thoughts and actions.
- Avoid intimacy in a sexual, emotional, and physical way to maintain distance.

- Permit people, places, and things to become addictions blocking the development of intimacy in relationships.
- Skirt issues when communicating to avoid confrontation or conflict.
- Refuse help of any kind or participation in recovery.
- Repress their thoughts, needs, and feelings to circumvent feeling vulnerable.
- Draw people close only to push them away.
- Have the belief that if you show emotions you are weak.
- Rarely show signs of appreciation.

INTIMACY PROBLEMS

Emotional and physical intimacy with others is often a problem for the codependent. They have a strong tendency to fear judgment and rejection, needing to always appear all-powerful, helpful, and strong. Also referred to as intimacy avoidance, the fear of intimacy by the codependent is characterized as an anxiety around sharing a close physical or emotional relationship with another. It is not that the codependent wants to avoid being intimate, and may even wish for connectedness, but usually pushes their partner away or even sabotages the relationship. Intimacy avoidance can be rooted in several causes, such as a dysfunctional family system of origin, a history of emotional and/or physical abuse, and many other prevalent factors portrayed in the codependent. Conquering intimacy anxiety can take time necessary for exploring and understanding the issues that have contributed to it and for learning how to allow greater vulnerability.

Codependents with fear of loss or abandonment, along with a fear of engulfment are at the center of intimacy avoidance. Rooted in childhood experiences, the codependent is often confused by their reactions to present-day adult relationships. Fear of engulfment is where great anxiety is associated with control, domination, or identity loss in a relationship and can be rooted in enmeshed family dynamics. The fear of engulfment differs from the fear of abandonment in that it is usually rooted in overprotective parenting. Sometimes this may be a parent who seems very generous and loving on the surface but is also overly involved and controlling in their children's lives by not giving them the chance to develop their own unique perspectives in life, which is a vital part of development. There is a severe lack of boundaries in the relationship between child and parent. When a child's individuality is compromised and their identity ignored, narcissism and selfish traits may develop to institute a false sense of self and to assist them in meeting their needs. When fear of engulfment is present, the codependent worries about being smothered and, therefore, becomes very uncomfortable when in intimate situations. The fear of engulfment or of being invaded is characterized by distorted thoughts about losing oneself or being controlled. The codependent has learned to respond to conflict with controlling behaviors that vary from rage and blame, to acquiescence, resistance, and withdrawal. If one of the partners needs some alone time, the codependent feels rejected, abandoned and judged, which triggers other dysfunctional behaviors, including shame, guilt, depression, and panic. When the fear of engulfment and rejection becomes too much, the codependent may decide it is far too painful to have any intimacy at all. It is important to note that the codependent may engage in sexual activity as an obligation or to reinforce their desire to be needed. This leads to a lack of emotional growth, and the cycle is bound to repeat itself.

FEARING REJECTION

There is no doubt that rejection is painful. It is human nature to want to be connected with others and to belong. Feeling rejected by important people in your life and believing you are not wanted is an awful experience. It can seem at times to be physically painful. After experiencing the repeated trauma of rejection as a child, it is no wonder why the codependent wants to avoid ever feeling that way again. The fear of rejection holds many back from achieving success in their lives but can actually overcome it with a bit of work. Most experience rejection over both big and small issues at times in their lives, such as:

- Being ignored when asking a friend to hang out.
- Not receiving an invitation to an event that many people you know are attending.
- Being cheated on in a relationship.

Rejection is painful no matter what the source is. The codependent usually has a higher degree of sensitivity to rejection and feels wounded when others see the incidents in their lives as no big deal. Rejection includes other painful emotions, such as shame, embarrassment, and awkwardness. The first step in allaying your fear of rejection is by acknowledging it. Denying that you're hurt when you really are takes away your chance of productively conquering your fear. While it may not seem so at first, rejection can actually provide you with the opportunity for growth and self-discovery. For instance, you applied for a position in a company that you really want and thought your interview went fantastically, and then you don't get the job. So, you brush over your resume and realize you may need to add to your professional toolkit by learning new types of computer software (the ole 'silver lining in the cloud'). After a couple of months, you now see that many new doors have now opened due to your new learned skills qualifying you for even higher-paying positions. Turning your fear of rejection into an opportunity for growth can boost your ability in trying to get what you want while easing the pain of failure. Try thinking that you will learn a lesson, from the failure, which will benefit you later on.

Codependents heighten their fears of rejection by reading too much into it. Feeling unworthy of love, coupled with a lack of self-confidence creates a sort of paralysis in the individual, leading them to be too fearful of changing themselves for the better. Always imagining the worst-case scenarios or 'waiting for the other shoe to drop' can lead to a very sickly way of living. It has a snowball effect that can make it seem impossible to ever become somehow stable. This cycle of negative thinking spirals into a behavior known as *catastrophizing*. It is usually based on an unrealistic fear.

Catastrophizing is when you always think the worst possible scenarios will happen. It often includes the belief that the situation you are in is worse than it really is and that the challenges you face are more difficult than they really are. For example, you may worry that you are failing in your relationship, and from there you may assume failing in this relationship means failure for any future relationships and that you are a bad person. Many people's relationships fail, but it is not proof that you will not be able to recover. By catastrophizing, you may not have the ability to acknowledge that. The difference between catastrophizing and over-exaggeration is that catastrophizing is usually not intentional or that simple. People usually don't even realize they're doing it because it has become such a habit. It can even affect an individual's health.

CYCLE OF CODEPENDENCY

Codependents often have good intentions while perpetuating this cycle. They want to take care of a loved one who is experiencing difficulties (substance abuse, mental illness) and do this by 'covering' for them, making excuses, working to reduce consequences from action or inaction, etc. However, these attempts to help their loved one actually have the opposite effect in the long run. The needy individual continues on their destructive path with no incentive to change, as they rely on the codependent to take care of everything. The more needy the individual becomes, the more the codependent feels they are getting a reward and validation from being needed (often subconsciously). After some time, the caretaking reaches a point where it is compulsive, and the codependent feels trapped and helpless while simultaneously feeding into the cycle of behavior. Codependency is a symptom of the S.A.D. (Seduce-Abuse-Discard) cycle functioning in the background.

Seduction phase

During the seduction phase of the S.A.D. cycle, the narcissist or taker (similar to a parasite) targets a codependent to add to their supply of ego inflators. The supply will include anything the codependent has that the taker desires, such as money, status, good looks, culinary skills, attention, and sex. One of the key components to this part of the cycle is the amount of attention the codependent receives while being lavished, praised, and having time spent on them. This provides a sense of euphoria within the codependent because it mirrors their internal fantasy of being loved. In their grandiosity, the taker may say the codependent completes them, and that they are exactly what the taker has been looking for (i.e., "You are my soulmate!"). (Notice the term *what* they have been looking for, not *who*). The taker wants what they want, and they want it NOW! Early marriage proposals, wanting to move in with each other, wanting to spend every minute of the day together; before long... "Darn, I had a really tight month financially, do you think you can help me out, and could I maybe stay at your place?" This is a prime example of enmeshment with goal being entrapment. Here is where the codependent begins to lose their identity.

Abuse Phase

The abuse phase of the S.A.D. cycle is where the taker's use of the codependent starts to become abuse. They no longer feel such ego inflation from conquering their prey; the rush is over, and now they start becoming easily annoyed. The codependent is now committed and has become increasingly emotionally dependent and obsessed with fixing any problems. The taker becomes secure enough to reveal who and what they really are. This is awfully confusing to the codependent, who turns to their inner belief that they were not good enough. The codependent starts to try and change themselves to fit the taker's wants, hoping to resume the seduction phase. This phase of the cycle triggers the codependent's abandonment fears and validates their feelings of unworthiness. Here, the fixer or rescuer begins to take charge. One goal the taker has during the abuser phase is to increase their control over the codependent; the more worn down they are, the easier they will be to control. The more abuse, the more shame the codependent feels, deepening their feelings of inadequacy. The codependent simply tries even harder to fix the taker, fix themselves, and delve deeper into their fantasy that the taker truly loves them, but is just having difficulty showing it. The taker uses their narcissistic skill set and plays into the situation by:

- Blaming the codependent;
- Attempting to make the codependent question their reality;
- Verbally abusing, e.g., "You are a wussy!";
- Attacking the codependent's character;
- Making the codependent the villain;
- Denying accountability;
- Making false promises;
- ...and the list goes on.

The Discard Phase

The biggest fear a codependent has is to be discarded. It causes a feeling of paralysis, turning into submissiveness. Abandonment threats trigger a deeper feeling of shame and powerlessness. This is in line with the same element that gives the codependent that feeling of euphoria during the seduction phase, as well as the stress and sorrow during the abuse phase. Codependents feel as if they will not survive abandonment by their significant other. This comes from the trauma of childhood emotional and/or physical abandonment. This awful feeling of incompleteness and isolation looks to the taker for wholeness and completion. The natural process of individuation when a child learns they are separate and unique to their parents was impaired. Now that the codependent thinks they have met a person who 'really' cares and gave them all of that praise in the seduction phase, their dysfunctional childhood is reactivated. During the discard phase, all of the love and care is taken back, often quickly, and the codependent is sent spiraling into despair and emotional isolation. However, the act of discarding the codependent is not always permanent. Sadly, the codependent can be wooed back within minutes to the seduction phase.

In the discard phase, the untreated codependent can fall into self-pity. Most individuals have at least one person they know whose main topic of conversation is themselves. Hearing someone say, "Woe is me" all the time can drain everyone they are around of their energy and happiness. Attention-seeking and condolence-craving are the primary symptoms of the codependent in the discard phase. For some reason, the codependent feels some sense of relief from their sense of victimhood. It is associated indistinguishably with their patterns of behavior linked to their growing-up years. When focusing on what you think to be fair in life and feeling confident that your situation is worse than anyone else's, you are drowning in self-pity. This can be a complete 'turnoff' to those around you. The sense that you are always being slighted shows in your body posture and facial expressions without even having to verbalize your feelings. If somewhere in your mind you believe that your self-pity will keep you from being discarded, you can't be any further from reality. No one wants to be around a frowning person. Low self-worth and depression are quick to follow. Isolation will become prominent as you will slowly have to come to terms with the fact that a change is necessary.

Always venting how pitiful your life seems to your partner or other significant people in your life, rather than taking action to improve your situation, will put you in a state of mental weakness, and it is also unattractive. There is a saying in the Twelve-Step philosophy: "Accept the things you cannot change (Bill W., 1939)". Not every problem in life has a solution; hurricanes still come, loved ones still pass away, but the key to keeping a healthy mental state is acceptance, not self-pity. At some point in each individual's life, tragedy happens. Knowing you will survive and grow under any conditions is what getting better is all about. Mental toughness requires keeping self-pity at a minimum. No one ever said life is easy, everyone is taking the mental, physical, and spiritual journey together. There is a myriad of good examples out there of ways to triumph during tough times, so how long you suffer depends on you, even though it may not seem like it at the time. There are those who stay comfortable in their grief and never seem to be able to rebuild, and unfortunately after being discarded, find themselves in another abusive codependent relationship. Self-pity gives you a reason to not even attempt to conquer your goals. The difference between a healthy mind and one dwelling in misery is that the mentally fit person sees others and their accomplishments as an inspiration rather than those minds dwelling in the misery of envy.

THE DYSFUNCTION DANCE: CODEPENDENT VS. NARCISSIST

The dysfunctional-codependent-versus-narcissist dance requires two opposing personality types but an inherently balanced duo: the codependent rescuer/fixer and the narcissist/taker. It is tough to say, but the truth is that those suffering from codependency often find themselves wrapped up in a torrid relationship with a narcissist. Narcissists are comforted by the term codependence by feeling admirable for not being one. A narcissist is a person who is so excessively self-involved that their desires trump anyone else's with whom they are involved. Some of the characteristics of a narcissist include: entitlement, a lack of empathy, and compassion. Ironically, while codependency and narcissism are often thought of as opposite, there are similar behavioral traits in both. Some of these include blurred boundaries, the need to control or depend on others for validation, and denial. Really the only difference between narcissism and codependency is the narcissist's lack of empathy and sense of entitlement.

Codependents and narcissists both can be seemingly charming, warm, and caring at the beginning of a relationship. The narcissist appears this way in order to be in good favor and gain appreciation. The codependent does this in efforts of lavishing attention on the other to start the dependency ball rolling. Whereas the codependent easily becomes prey to the charm of the narcissist, the narcissist quickly falls for the codependent's offers of complete control. The codependent will voluntarily sacrifice boundaries, personal goals and desires, even their own needs, in order to please the narcissist, who in turn, loves the role of the 'be-all' to the codependent. Sadly, this 'honeymoon' phase is really a trap, which is bound to end in misery. Once the codependent has conquered winning over the relationship status with the narcissist and vice versa, the codependent is now in the role of self-sacrifice, and the narcissist no longer needs their charm so overtly stated as in the beginning; the narcissist now believes they are entitled to the codependent. Regrettably, the craving for admiration, attention, and love craved by the codependent will most likely never appear again. The more the codependent desperately tries to revive those sentiments, the more attention is given to the narcissist and less is received by the codependent.

Narcissists are harmful to the codependent, as well as self-centered and controlling. The codependent who is self-sacrificing, giving and enveloped with the needs and wants of others, have blurred boundaries (a recurring theme in this book); the codependent does not know how to disconnect emotionally with the narcissist. Like a bad habit, codependents repeatedly show up on the dysfunctional dance floor attracted to partners who counter-match perfectly to their submissive, acquiescent style of dance. The codependent finds this particular type of partner, to dysfunctionally dance with, very appealing. They are continuously attracted to the dominance, confidence, and charm so easily displayed by the narcissist. When the two pair up, the dance experience can boom with excitement...at least at the start. After many go-'rounds, the 'thrill of the dance', as expected, transforms into major conflict, drama, and entrapment. Even so, neither dare to put an end to it.

With the two paired up, the codependent/narcissist dance plays out flawlessly with the narcissist always maintaining the lead with the codependent following (always being careful not to step on the narcissist's toes). Their parts in the dance seem all too natural to the pair because they both have been practicing for it their whole lives. Seemingly instinctual, the codependent voluntarily gives up their power leaving the narcissist to thrive upon it. As usual, the narcissist receives much more than they give. The codependent is seemingly stuck dancing for song after song naïvely hoping for their partner to finally understand they have needs, too. With the heartbreak of unfulfilled hopes, the codependent quietly and bitterly swallows their misery. They are basically cemented in a pattern of sacrificing and giving with no chance of ever receiving the same from the other. While pretending to enjoy the dance, they are really harboring feelings of bitterness and sorrow for not ever leading the dance. They feel as if they know for a fact that they will never find another caring dance partner. They have developed a form of learned helplessness due to their low self-worth and pessimism, which ends up keeping them in the dysfunctional dance with the narcissist. Although the codependent wishes for balance and harmony, they sabotage themselves consistently by choosing relationships with individuals to whom they are attracted initially, but in the end will resent. Without self-worth or feelings of independence, the codependent is not able to choose a partner capable of mutual respect. The fear of abandonment and feelings of powerlessness is an extension of their youth where they yearned to be respected, cared for and loved.

As for the codependent, there is no end in sight to this relationship due to the fact that they will deem it as a personal failure. Remember it is the "job" of the codependent to rescue the relationship. The narcissist will 'stick around' as long as they keep being the center of attention and getting their needs met...but, just providing slight encouragement enough to keep the spark of hope alive in the codependent. The narcissist doesn't feel responsible for any wrongdoings due to their lack of empathy, so there is no reason for them to change. This leaves the couple's relationship ending in the hands of the codependent. However, due to fear of being alone and a lack of self-worth, the codependent feels they are better off trapped in a loveless and one-sided relationship. Usually, the relationship does not come to an end until the codependent has reached a breaking point, and even then, are highly unlikely to seek professional help or join a support group.

4

THE STAGES OF CODEPENDENCY

For romantic relationships and friendships, these stages are more easily observed and identified than in family relationships, as later discussed. In the early stage, the codependent starts to become increasingly involved in an unhealthy obsession with someone. Dysfunctional behavior is rationalized or denied. They start to give up their own hobbies, friends and interests. In the middle stage, self-blame, guilt, and anxiety play a bigger role in the relationship and when receiving nothing in return, disappointment and resentment start to grow. The codependent may start being dishonest, manipulative, blaming and nagging in attempts to change the other person with whom they are involved. A strong potential arises for harmful eating, dieting, compulsive gambling, or shopping, and excessive use of drugs and alcohol. The codependent may try changing their loved one by nagging or manipulating them. They may be dishonest about their partner's behavior to family and friends. The late stage of codependency begins to affect the individual physically and mentally. Often, disorders related to stress, such as headaches, stomach problems, insomnia, sciatica, muscle fatigue, and heart disease, can arise. If addiction is happening, it will worsen. The codependent's self-worth hits rock bottom, hopelessness sets in, and the individual stops caring for themselves. At this point, the codependent urgently needs help.

The following describes the stages of codependency:

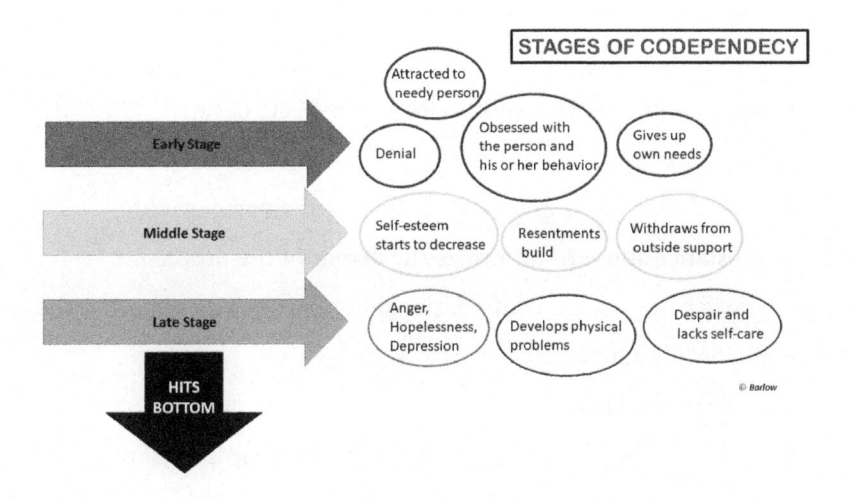

STAGES OF CODEPENDECY

- **Early Stage**: Attracted to needy person; Denial; Obsessed with the person and his or her behavior; Gives up own needs
- **Middle Stage**: Self-esteem starts to decrease; Resentments build; Withdraws from outside support
- **Late Stage**: Anger, Hopelessness, Depression; Develops physical problems; Despair and lacks self-care
- **HITS BOTTOM**

© Barlow

Early Stage

- Looks like a normal relationship, with increased attention and dependency on a partner and a strong need to please.
- Codependents may find themselves attracted to needy people, or be overly involved in a friend's life and wanting to help them, offering help, gifts and meals.
- Over time, the codependent becomes increasingly dependent on them for emotional validation and begins to give up

independent hobbies and activities in order to focus more on the other person and with them.
- Attempts to please the person.
- Obsessed with other's behaviors.
- Rationalizes and doubts own perceptions.
- Denial about codependency, but concern grows.
- Family and social life are affected.

Middle Stage

- Increased effort to minimize painful aspects of the relationship.
- The codependent may start covering for a partner with substance abuse to minimize the extent of the problem.
- Hides painful aspects of relationships from others.
- Anxiety, guilt, and self-blame increase.
- Self-esteem lessens.
- Tries to control by nagging, blaming, and manipulation.
- Feels resentment at inability to control the person.
- Enables and manages the person's responsibilities.
- Withdraws from outside family and friends.

Late Stage

- Develops physical symptoms.
- Digestive and sleep problems.
- Headaches, muscle tension, or pain.
- Eating disorders and Temporomandibular Joint Disorders

(TMJ).
- Obsessive-compulsive behavior or other addictions increase.
- Feels angry, hopeless, and depressed.
- Despair and lack of self-care.
- Increased conflicts.
- Further decline in self-esteem.

CODEPENDENCY, CHILDHOOD TRAUMA AND POST-TRAUMATIC STRESS DISORDER

In the context of family members, the development of codependency often happens so early that they aren't easily broken down into stages. Trauma is injurious in many ways, from psychological, to emotional, to physical and relational. Any kind of trauma can lead to codependent relationships. These relationships can develop in a family system or an intimate relationship. Unfortunately, too many individuals suffer from childhood trauma, and not enough of them were provided with the resources to cope with it. Experiencing trauma as a child is one of the main causes behind codependency. A strong reason is that childhood trauma is usually family-centered neglect, abuse, substance abuse, verbal and emotional abuse or constant arguing. This often results in an adult who is very helpless or an adult who needs to be needed. A review of the literature revealed that traumatic childhood experiences, have a long-lasting impact on individuals, including:

- Chronic physical illness;
- Bipolar Disorder;
- Borderline Personality Disorder;

- Depression;
- Chemical Dependency;
- Suicidal ideations and/or attempts; and
- Post-Traumatic Stress Disorder (PTSD).

Sometimes something can be noticed that has only a vague reminder of a past situation that was traumatic and can trigger the mind's readiness for a freeze, fight-or-flight response. Examples include: a triggered flight response to perceiving a threat, causing an intense need to flee; a freeze response takes over in the form of dissociation, numbing-out, or oversleeping; a fight response happens when the response is one of aggression fueled with adrenaline. Many individuals suffering from trauma develop an ability over time to use a combination of these responses based on the nature of the circumstances.

Another triggered reaction seen in the codependent, that stems from childhood trauma, is learning how to relinquish the fight response. This means no backtalk, due to a lack of the development of assertive language skills. The child has also learned from an early age that they cannot outrun a parent and hopelessly must stay in the harmful atmosphere. Therefore, the child must bypass the defense mechanism of the fight response, causing them to slip further into the freeze response, slowly drifting into a dissociative state, which can later develop into an addiction to numbing substances, such as marijuana, alcohol, and opiate, or other sedative-type drugs. Finally, the child learns, after realizing they cannot run, hide, or fight their way out of the trauma, that they may be safer if they are helpful, useful or needed, leading them into a life-long struggle of servitude. All boundaries are surrendered, and the child has become a parentified housekeeper, friend, parent to other siblings, and sounding board and landing in adult life as a codependent destined to repeat the cycle if they do not seek help. This all starts before the child has any insight and develops into immediately becoming servile when there is any hint of danger.

It is awful to think of a human being behaving like an animal that remains loyal to an abusive master out of fear of being harmed. Clarification of this concept is necessary but not enough for recovery. Some codependents understand their habit of giving up on themselves, but seem to, without consideration, forget everything they have learned about appropriate differentiation in their relationships. To break free from subservience, the codependent has to have the cognitive insight to identify the fear that triggers the aforementioned responses to trauma and practice increasing their skills of responses, which are more functional.

One possible result of experiencing trauma is dysfunctional relationships. Even when only one individual in the pair has experienced trauma, it has a ripple effect for all of the people close to that person. Significant others can experience secondary effects from the trauma, or feel traumatized by witnessing their loved one's reaction to trauma. Forming healthy relationships and bonding with others is one of the most challenging parts of life. When traumatized, a person can form loyalty to others in an unhealthy way, which is called 'trauma-bonding'. This means that the traumatized individual has a tendency of having abnormal attachments to another when in the presence of exploitation, danger, or shame. There is a tendency for more abuse, dishonesty, obsession, and self-sabotage when entering into this type of relationship. Another unfortunate aspect of codependency is resulting from another's addiction. In this relationship, the codependent offers a type of dysfunctional helping where they enable or support another person's abuse of substances, irresponsibility, defective mental health or under-achievement. Healthy relationships, which are supportive in nature, are essential for a person recovering from trauma. However, too frequently codependency is the result of complex trauma and childhood trauma.

5

LOOKING FOR A LIFELINE

The importance of getting help cannot be underestimated when it comes to codependents. Each treatment protocol is unique to each client. These symptoms are completely reversible with help from a professional and the assistance of support groups. A specialist in the field of codependency can help you recognize and verbalize your concerned feelings, thoughts and actions. If there are secondary psychological issues, such as depression, anxiety, and/or PTSD, medication may be considered alongside therapy. It is possible to regain your own identity, improve your self-esteem and gain ownership over your needs, thoughts, feelings and desires. By working with a therapist and attending support meetings, you will learn how to stop enabling behaviors, set appropriate boundaries, and reform healthy relationships with those you love. Eventually, your happiness will depend on you. Your life will include things that interest you, attainable goals, and the innovative energy with which to pursue them.

Codependents do not usually get help for themselves until they 'hit bottom' or there is a big enough crisis, or they are suffering to the breaking point. Sometimes, they are not even aware, or they are in denial about the abuse or their significant other's addiction. Recovery starts with breaking through that denial and becoming educated about the reasons behind the condition. Learning through reading the literature is a good start, but the real change happens when you seek therapy and attend Twelve-Step programs (later explained in this chapter), such as Al-Anon and CoDA. Codependency doesn't just stop automatically when an individual leaves a dysfunctional relationship. Recovery requires ongoing support and maintenance. After years of recovery, the codependent's thinking and actions start to internalize, and the skills learned lead to new and healthy habits. Even so, codependency can return quite easily if you enter into another dysfunctional relationship; relapse happens without due diligence. There is no such thing as a perfect recovery. Slipping back into old behaviors simply offers a new learning experience! With recovery, hope is renewed, and focus is shifted back onto yourself. There are three stages of recovery:

THE EARLY STAGE OF RECOVERY: PRECONTEMPLATION

In the early stage of recovery from codependency, the denial starts to break down. You are ready to face reality and confront the issue that is necessary in order to change it. This early stage may be encouraged by another person in recovery or a close friend that knows of your suffering. This is a real wake-up call, also known as hitting bottom. Change becomes of the utmost importance and instead of minimizing the issues, you decide to face them, even with them being as difficult and painful as they are. Starting recovery begins by obtaining information and asking for help.

As the codependency gets worse in severity, as do the consequences. During the early stages of recovery, the codependent has had to come to terms with their reality that life has become unmanageable, that they have been in denial and minimizing the dysfunction in the relationship. The person may even know at this point that they are codependent. However, a person in the early stage of recovery still wants to remain in the chaos rather than try and change their circumstances. Briefly, the perceived comfort of continuing to remain in the relationship is thought to be better than the consequences.

* * *

See the following table for the comparison of the stages of codependency versus the stages of recovery.

Progression of Codependency	Recovery from Codependency
Finds themselves attracted to a dysfunctional relationship.	Hits bottom and asks for help.
People-pleasing.	Educates themselves about codependency.
Obsessions about the significant other.	Starts therapy and/or Twelve-Step Meetings.
Doubts and rationalizes their own perceptions.	Begins to feel hope.
Denial about the other's addiction, abuse, and other dysfunctional characteristics.	Breaks through denial.
Gives up their own friends and activities and becomes engulfed by the other's needs, wants, and desires.	Learns that recovery is a selfish program.
Family life is negatively affected.	Starts to focus on themselves.
Falls deeper into dysfunction and codependency.	Begins to build their own identity.

THE MIDDLE STAGE OF RECOVERY: CONTEMPLATION

Transitioning from the early stage to the middle stage is one of contemplation. This stage is considered when the consequences of the relationship are much worse than they had thought. In fact, the codependent is starting to be very aware of the bad effects that the relationship is doing to them, however, they are not quite positive that the bad effects outweigh the codependent's habitual comfort of staying in the abuse. It is during this stage that the codependent starts to open up to the idea of recovery; while they have not actually thoroughly decided to get help, the person has started to feel that recovery has to be inevitable at some time in the future.

They may even openly start to verbalize they have a problem. However, if any attempts are made to push the codependent into getting help, they will usually have some type of excuse as to why they have to put it off until sometime in the future. Sometimes, it may even seem like a valid excuse.

During the middle stage, the codependent also begins to learn about building their self-esteem, own boundaries, identity, and how to express their feelings with a healthy assertiveness.

At this point, the codependent starts to move in the direction of preparation; they realize that the consequences of staying in the dysfunctional relationship are far worse than any benefits they can think of. With addiction, they come to the conclusion that changes in behavior are necessary for their health.

Now, there is an acknowledgement that help is needed. Hence, thus beginning the preparation stage. Once here, the codependent realizes that getting help will be life changing. It is also at this time that the codependent begins to become proactive by educating themselves and starts to search for different available resources.

The Middle Stage of Recovery: Action

During the action stage, the codependent dives into recovery by seeing a professional, joining a Twelve-Step group, and using various other tools available, such as codependency workbooks and life coaching. But the action stage is more than just getting help, rather the codependent makes a commitment to change their lifestyle, one which will provide a healthier, happier and more productive future. During the action stage, the codependent is also looking for other ways to enhance their new lifestyle, such as exercise, nutritional plans, and career goals, along with re-establishing relationships on a healthier foundation.

Independence, mental hygiene, spiritual fitness, and self-dialog are all important aspects of recovery from codependency and are also heavily influenced by physical condition. Most people realize that exercise is good for their body, however, it is the relationship to their mental state that is underestimated. Our ancestors instinctually hunted and gathered, continually expending energy to meet their needs. The human body is clearly designed for that type of energy expenditure. Plus, exercise releases the brain's natural endorphins, such as adrenaline, serotonin, and other inherent antidepressants. Rather than taking a pill to feel better (unless prescribed by your doctor), take a nature walk if you are feeling down. The best way to keep exercising is to make it a habit or part of your daily routine. Keep it up, along with positive affirmations and soon you will notice a big difference in how you feel. Showing up is what counts, worry about how long and how much later. Most of all try and make it an enjoyable event so that you will look forward to it as rewarding.

THE LATE STAGE OF RECOVERY: MAINTENANCE

Now that the codependent has passed the early and middle stages, which included precontemplation, contemplation and action, they must now take on the responsibility of maintaining their newly acquired independence. This stage is of great importance, because if not taken to heart, it can lead to relapse. Fortunately, there are many resources available for this stage of recovery: CoDA, Al-Anon,

Alumni groups, therapy, aftercare, religious affiliations, and other support groups. Much like needing to practice a new skill, the codependent in this stage must practice maintenance. In the late stage, self-worth and happiness no longer depend on someone else. What is gained is the capacity for both independence and intimacy. The codependent will experience their own sense of power and self-love. They will experience an expansive, uninhibited innovativeness, with the ability to produce and pursue their own goals.

What is a Twelve-Step Recovery Program and Does It Work?

Codependents Anonymous (CA), Narcotics Anonymous (NA), and Alcoholics Anonymous (AA) are among mutual self-help groups, which operate under the guidelines of twelve steps and twelve traditions. The twelve steps encourage honesty, faith, and self-probing humility. These groups are led by peers, are free of charge, and meet on a regular basis. These twelve faith-based steps were to be followed by recovering alcoholics. The basic premise is a step-by-step guideline that introduces practices meant to create more self-awareness and a willingness to accept help. These practices also focus on consciously changing thought and behavior patterns, and maintaining recovery once achieved.

Most interestingly, when AA was founded in 1936, many were unsure and cynical that those addicts could find recovery based on a set of spiritually based principles. Doctor prescriptions? Sure. Behavioral therapy? Of course. But relying on a higher power for recovery? At the time, many psychology experts believed that alcoholics could in no way be helped by a support group that was as 'touchy-feely' as AA. However, to the surprise of all, AA and other twelve-step groups soared with ever-increasing popularity. As of today, there are in excess of 2 million AA members with 115,000 AA groups, and that is not counting NA, CA, Coda, Gamblers Anonymous (GA), and many others. There are literally thousands of meetings for every morning, day and evening in every location. Often, the group halls are open 24 hours during holidays. They produce social events, such as Christmas parties, Valentine's dances, barbecues, and other chemical or misbehaved free get-togethers. AA believes that there is no cure for alcoholism, and remaining sober requires perpetual self-awareness and effort. These programs are based on community, bringing together people from all walks of life who share a common struggle. Listening to success stories from others makes recovery feel achievable. Sharing setbacks and failures reduces the feeling that you are 'unfixable'.

A review of research indicated the main factor of change is the primary aspect of mutual-help groups. The studies reviewed concluded that by even adding one friend in recovery to your social circle increases your chances of staying clean by 25%. In addition to meeting other people who are struggling with the same issues as they are, codependents can contact other members and get a sponsor whenever they need inspirational support, which is much like group therapy on an informal level. This is one of the many reasons CoDA and Al-Anon are so effective. After reviewing the literature, it is quite obvious that dismissing Twelve-Step programs as unscientific because they are faith-based is inconsistent with the large body of in-depth research acquired throughout the past 25 years.

WHAT ARE THE TWELVE STEPS?

Through meetings in a group with others who are in the program, an individual who joins a Twelve-step group usually gets a sponsor who works together with the codependent and guides them through the **Twelve Steps**. These include:

1. We admitted we were powerless over others, that our lives had become unmanageable.
2. Came to believe that a power greater than ourselves could restore us to sanity.
3. Made a decision to turn our will and lives over to the care of God, as we understood God.
4. Made a searching and fearless moral inventory of ourselves.
5. Admitted to God, to ourselves, and to another human being, the exact nature of our wrongs.
6. Were entirely ready to have God remove all these defects of character.
7. Humbly asked God to remove our shortcomings.
8. Made a list of all persons we had harmed and became willing to make amends to them all.
9. Made direct amends to such people wherever possible, except when to do so would injure them or others.
10. Continued to take personal inventory and, when we were wrong, promptly admitted it.
11. Sought through prayer and meditation to improve our conscious contact with God as we understood God, praying

only for knowledge of God's will for us and the power to carry that out (CoDa.org).
12. Having had a spiritual awakening as the result of these steps, we tried to carry this message to other codependents and to practice these principles in all our affairs.

The Twelve CoDA Traditions:

1. Our common welfare should come first; personal recovery depends upon CoDA unity.
2. For our group purpose, there is but one ultimate authority, a loving higher power as expressed to our group conscience. Our leaders are but trusted servants; they do not govern.
3. The only requirement for membership in CoDA is a desire for healthy and loving relationships.
4. Each group should remain autonomous except in matters affecting other groups or CoDA as a whole.
5. Each group has but one primary purpose: to carry its message to other codependents who still suffer.
6. A CoDA group ought never endorse, finance, or lend the CoDA name to any related facility or outside enterprise, lest problems of money, property and prestige divert us from our primary spiritual aim.
7. A CoDA group ought to be fully self-supporting, declining outside contributions.
8. CoDependents Anonymous should remain forever nonprofessional, but our service centers may employ special workers.

9. CoDA, as such, ought never be organized, but we may create service boards or committees directly responsible to those they serve.
10. CoDA has no opinion on outside issues; hence, the CoDA name ought never be drawn into public controversy.
11. Our public relations policy is based on attraction rather than promotion; we need to always maintain personal anonymity at the level of press, radio, and films.
12. Anonymity is the spiritual foundation of all our traditions; ever reminding us to place principles before personalities.

Twelve Promises for a fulfilled life: People pledge to engage in the following twelve promises while recovering:

1. I have a new sense of belonging, and any feelings of emptiness or loneliness will eventually fade away.
2. I am no longer controlled by my fears, and instead I overcome them to "act with courage, integrity and dignity".
3. I know a freedom from codependency and unhealthy dynamics.
4. I release feelings of shame and guilt, as well as regrets about the past. I cannot change what has happened, but I can act so it doesn't happen again.
5. I feel genuinely lovable, loving and loved. I accept myself and others as we are.
6. I see myself as an equal in current and future relationships.
7. I maintain healthy and loving relationships, without needing

to control what those people do. I learn to trust those around me.
8. I recognize it is possible to heal and change while maintaining healthy boundaries with my family.
9. I recognize I am "a unique and precious creation". No one in the world can be me, besides me.
10. I know my own worth without needing the validation of others.
11. I trust myself innately and believe that I am able to guide myself.
12. I experience more serenity, strength, and spiritual growth each day.

Exercise

1. Write down a list of the things your loved one does that trigger these feelings of failure so that you can reflect upon them during your recovery journey.
2. Sort these things into 3 categories
3. Things I can control;
4. Things they can control; and
5. Things neither of us can control.

Possible actions for Change

- Limiting contact: removes opportunities for you to ask questions or offer unsolicited advice.
- Set physical boundaries. Decide how much energy and time

you want to give to each individual in your life. If someone is toxic, set firm boundaries about the length of time you will spend together.

- Establish emotional boundaries. If you cannot limit your time spent with a toxic individual, set limits on how much emotional energy you are willing to spend on them. In your spare time, do not spend it complaining about them. Remember, you can regulate how *you* feel. Your day does not depend on what side of the bed a toxic person gets up on!
- At first, you may feel as if you are abandoning that person, but in order for them to live a fulfilled life they have to be able to make decisions for themselves.
- Reduce friction between you and your loved one.
- Work on self-control not on controlling others. Set your focus on how you react to others—assert yourself or walk away—it is *your* choice.
- Follow through with what you say or plan. Repeated warnings or threats to stop lending money—just to do it again—makes matters worse. Be a person of your word, or you will be adding to the relationship's dysfunction.
- Regulate your thinking. If you catch yourself having destructive thoughts, create a healthy self-dialog, reminding you of your decisions and telling yourself you are no longer a victim.
- Practice healthy coping skills. People can and will still be draining on your emotions, even when you have set good boundaries. It is imperative that you practice strategies that will help you cope and stay strong.

- Use various coping skills, such as mediation and writing a gratitude list.
- Tend to your health.
- Stay true to your set of values by prioritizing them.
- Build your mental muscles. If you do not exercise your mental muscles, they will atrophy just like physical muscles. Give up negative habits that are draining your mental strength. The stronger you become, the less draining are toxic people, giving them less power over you; they are then less likely to take a toll on your health.
- Use your support system. Rally your support network. It will feel so much better to vent to someone who values you.
- Let yourself be strengthened by your motives. Control your decision-making power, rather than letting it be controlled by someone else. Personal power has nothing to do with what someone else thinks, it has everything to do with your beliefs, that you will not be a victim.
- It is important to understand that takers usually see in other people what they do not want to see in themselves (projection). You can be the most generous, kind, and nicest person in the world and the taker will nearly 'kill' themselves trying to turn you into a monster. Understand why they're seeing what they see in you.

Have you ever noticed that, when something isn't working for us, we have a tendency to do the same thing more before we try another way? The same goes for the codependent; things may get worse before the taker stops the abuse. They will try every manipulation known to mankind to try and control you. Take their increase in tyranny as a sign that their old ways will no longer work, and they will move onto the next victim. Keep up the good work so they know you are sticking to your guns. Teach those with an unhealthy dependency on you that you are not responsible for their habitual crises and that you will not partake in their pity party anymore. Do offer to help or ask a lot of questions; you are not dealing with a normal individual. Toxic individuals will tear down your boundaries before you even realize you have them built. Know just what you will take and what you won't, and how far you are willing to let someone intrude on your boundaries; listen to that practiced self-dialog, "It just isn't worth it anymore".

You are still a compassionate, understanding, respectful and kind human being, but be all of that to yourself first. Compassion exists wonderfully with strength. You can dismiss certain behaviors, people and their requests, without becoming someone you don't like. It will be empowering to feel OK about your boundaries as long as you haven't hurt another in the process. Remember, sometimes helping is hurting. Own your weaknesses as well as your strengths; everyone is a work in progress. Know that your weaknesses cannot be used against you; that is how the taker tries to gain power. They will work tirelessly to play down your strengths while amping up your weaknesses. Once you are aware of your flaws, nobody can use them against you. There is no reasoning with a toxic person. Make your stance and stand strong. You are handling a person whose motivation is controlling and taking advantage of what is not good for either of you. Try not to focus on anger and resentment; focus on the solution. If you know or think you are about to make a poor decision, focus on the consequences, not on the person who is trying to ruin your life.

Surround yourself with like people; those who give the way you do. You may not be able to actually decide on how much freedom you have in specific parts of your life, but you can choose who is in it and who is not. Then you can choose, from those who are in, to which ones you want to open up your heart. You know you have no control over the past, but you can control how much you let it affect the present and to what extent it will impact your future. Forgiveness is about letting go of thinking things will be different. Self-love is necessary for forgiveness, because it is accomplished with strength. However, don't forget the way you have been treated and use those memories to add clarity to your life. Remember the codependency patterns of fear and the patterns of the taker. At first, they charm, then provide attention, love, and affection. Next, they gain your trust, and then they drain you of all that you are. Be aware of the cycle, so it doesn't repeat itself.

MAKING AMENDS

An important part of recovery is taking action toward making amends. It is essential to your mental health. Think of it as something you are doing for yourself, not just the person to whom you are making amends. Each time you conquer uncomfortable circumstances, you grow spiritually. Taking that step of owning your mistakes, makes it much easier to progress forward. Everyone involved in a previous mistake benefits when amends are made. Thinking that you are that one person in the whole world who doesn't owe anyone an apology has you standing a good chance there are some resentments looming around in your life. Own your mistakes, make amends, and then put it behind you; it's cleansing. This is an action-based step in your recovery process. The circumstance was difficult enough and now it has had time to brew into potential resentment. Ignoring it does not make it go away. The person who feels upset or injured will harbor those feelings as they grow stronger with each day that passes without resolution.

It can be terribly uncomfortable, and if you have been going back and forth in your mind as to whether or not to make amends, chances are it is time to do so. Fearing anger in the other and allowing procrastination to take over associates with negativity in your mind. Facing the fear builds your character in a strong and healthy direction. Just know that you have probably associated mistakes with being a bad person, or that saying you're sorry is a sign of weakness. This is part of the shame-based developmental aspects of being codependent. In actuality, it is just the opposite; making amends is a sign of great strength and fearlessness and that you are moving in a positive direction.

SELF-DOUBT

Self-doubt is connected to self-dialog in a negative manner. It also becomes like a bad habit. Individuals who can become comfortable with self-doubt can become, in essence, lazy. Why bother trying something if you are already convinced it can't be accomplished. To remedy the problem of self-doubt, it first has to be acknowledged. It takes perseverance and inner-strength. You have to hold yourself accountable for not putting a stronger effort into your endeavors. Some individuals believe only in dreams of new jobs or moving across the sea, but, then there are those who realize their dreams without doubting their abilities to make them come true. Participate fully in your life, and do your best to not be on the sidelines of envy wishing you never doubted yourself.

Trying your best means not trying to be perfect; that only increases self-doubt because perfection is rarely attainable. Do you know many happy perfectionists? Also, if you are regularly comparing yourself to someone else, it will be nearly impossible to cure self-doubt. Why tell yourself you are unsuccessful in life because you do not have that big pool that your neighbor has? But still, try to strive for the pool that you want in your backyard and make it a reality. Having compassion for yourself will be rewarded with positivity and will interrupt self-criticism. If you bump into a case of self-doubt, examine the truth behind it, and ask yourself, "What is the worst that can happen?" Self-doubt is grounded in unfounded predictions of fear and failure. Before you hit the road, take a look at a map. Then, you will not doubt your path.

FEELING OVERWHELMED

These days, most people are very busy and, therefore, it is easy to feel overwhelmed, making it difficult to keep things in the right perspective. The key to coping during these stressful times is to take 'baby steps' and to take your time. Feeling overwhelmed can be all-consuming, draining you of your energy and distorting your reality. Left unattended to, it will also lead you to burning out or 'freaking out'. It can also be a bit tricky to identify because the way it looks and the way it feels come in various forms. At times, feeling overwhelmed may seem like it is 'all too much', and you do not know what to do next. It can come in the form of fatigue, impatience, irritability, and lack of focus. This often happens when the codependent is trying to meet everyone else's expectations, and there is not enough time spent on themselves. When it happens, life seems like one big struggle and feels like you are barely treading water with 1,000 pounds strapped to your back. Thinking can come negatively in black and white when feeling this way: "I am the worst partner, mother, employee, friend, etc.!" Every person is going to be overwhelmed at some point in time, and yet when in the midst of it, you can feel like you are completely alone. The codependent will keep telling themselves, "I should be able to handle this." This only adds fuel to the fire and makes them feel even worse.

Codependents have come to believe that they must be helpful and selfless and that other people's needs are much more important than their own, thinking they have to be amenable, obliging, 'good' people. This conditioning from early childhood has taught the codependent the false belief that they should be able to do everything known to man, to please everyone at all times, and to do it with a smile on their face. And so, if they cannot, because, of course, it is not possible, they become overwhelmed and feel like a failure. Reliable and responsible are 'must-dos' for people who are codependent, thinking if they disappoint anyone, they are a bad person. If you are in a relationship as a partner or parent or family member, and you're trying to be perfect—handling other people's stress—all the while comparing yourself to them, and then beating yourself up because you don't think you're good enough, your identity and happiness will surely fade.

The question is what do you do? The first thing to do when trying to reduce your feelings of being overwhelmed is to question yourself about what is important right this second. Not what you or someone else should or wants you to do, but what are *your* needs in this moment. Maybe it is time to take a few deep breaths in your nose and out of your mouth or have a cool glass of water; try going for a walk, meditating, or any of the stress-reducing techniques mentioned in this book. Next, question yourself about the basics, such as sleep/rest, food, and water, or have you been gassing up with sugar and caffeine? Then, decide on one baby step you can take to rebalance yourself, even if it is in just one aspect, and 'just do it'. If you do not meet your basic needs, coping can be a real problem. When feeling overwhelmed, your mind cannot cope with the demands of your emotions and body, so commit yourself to taking a baby step to move you out of being overwhelmed.

By taking action and actually participating in a stress-management plan, you are taking back control of your life so that the problem of feeling chronically overwhelmed no longer rules your life. Then you will be able to figure out specifically what is making you feel overwhelmed and institute the steps necessary for reducing it. By acknowledging that you have too much on your shoulders, because you believe you have to say "yes" to every request, you can start the process of sticking to your boundaries by firmly and politely, saying "no". You do not need to give a long-winded explanation to anyone as to why something is too much; it doesn't make you a weak, selfish, or bad person. It simply means that you have a finite amount of energy and time. As discussed later in the book, asking for help is an indication of inner-strength, not a weakness. Trying to conquer feeling overwhelmed on your own is, itself, overwhelming! So, start by recognizing when the feeling starts, asking for help, and naming the baby steps that you will take to guide you gently back into a state of peace and calmness.

SELF-IMPROVEMENT

Everyone talks about improving themselves in one way or another. Rather than setting unrealistic goals, try a few of these simple steps; all you need is willingness, consistency, and determination, and the quality of your life can change for the better.

1. Have the willingness to work hard, and this means for you not for others. Like everything else in life, if you want success in anything, you have to put the work in to get it. This doesn't mean to exhaust yourself leaving you feeling down in the dumps.

2. Make sure you have a healthy support system. Sharing the load by communicating and taking feedback on how you are doing helps and is important for self-improvement. We can all use encouragement to keep us going during tough times. It is important to have people around us whom we respect enough that we would listen when they tell us how it is even when you don't want to hear it.

3. Do not overthink your situation, adapt to it. People hit difficult periods in life, such as the loss of a job or divorce. Rather than overanalyzing the problem, accept and adapt to your circumstances. Briefly

ask yourself if spending a vast amount of time analyzing a situation in any way can change it; if the answer is no, do not waste anymore of your emotions trying to change something with an outcome that you are powerless to attain.

4. Effective time management is very important. We have only a short time on this planet, so use it wisely. Take a look at your day; is it a daily grind? It is most likely time to try something new and to make it something you enjoy. Evaluate how much time you waste on worrying, obsessional thinking about another person's behavior, ruminating about rescuing, etc.

5. Stay consistent with your improvements. If you have decided to take a 15-minute walk each day, don't quit after three walks. Stick to your commitment. Can you imagine how many people pay good money to join a gym and only go to it for the first few weeks after having paid for a year's membership?

6. Locate your happy place where you find serenity and contentment, as long as it is a healthy place. Try meditation and, with your eyes closed, develop a beautiful happy place to go to in your mind that you can go back and visit regularly.

7. Embrace each emotion, even the difficult ones. Sometimes your emotions can bring out your joy and sometimes your fears. Embrace each one, as they come up in your life, wholeheartedly so you can understand them and then let them go. Do your best not to resist them because 'what you resist, persists'.

8. Always be ready to step outside of your comfort zone. The concept of stepping outside of your comfort zone can be a paralyzing fear for

some, however, it is necessary for any major change. You don't have to go skydiving. However, it is not a bad idea to try something you once feared, like doing something alone just for you. It doesn't have to be way out of your comfort zone, but it does need to be a challenge for you.

9. Stay present and live in the here and now. It is within this moment that gratitude can be felt for all that you appreciate and in the beauty of the simple things in life. Being mindful of what is happening in your life right now and taking yourself to where you belong will bring about a better quality of life instead of the incessant worry and stress about your past or your future (both do not exist right now).

10. Try learning something new. Learning new things makes your world much bigger and can build your self-confidence and self-esteem. Going to a Twelve-Step group and meeting new people will have you feeling on top of your game and wanting to share your experience, strength, and hope with others that they may find peace and happiness, too.

The following are helpful exercises for identifying and working through potential codependency traits:

11. Write down the symptoms you have learned, and you relate to. Not all will be relevant. Identifying the symptoms most apparent in your life makes it easier to look for solutions tailored to your experiences.

- Optional follow-up: Family history exercise.
- Look at the list of symptoms and identify any that you

remember observing in family members, especially when you were younger. Understanding why your family/parents acted in a certain way makes it easier to unlearn that inherited behavior.

12. Practice self-care.

- An important component to breaking the cycle of codependency is realizing you are complete on your own. By practicing nourishing and caring for yourself, you will gain a sense of empowerment.
- Techniques for self-care can include: meditation, breathing exercises, taking a class, going to the gym, nature walks, and other solo exercises will improve your self-worth, along with your mental and physical health.

13. Develop decision-making skills.

- Take note of instances when you are depending on another person when trying to make a decision.
- Try going with your gut and inner self when determining your best choices.

14. Cultivate independence.

- Do things by yourself that you usually want to do with someone else in order to feel comfortable. Try hiking, going out to eat or going to the movies alone. When you learn you can enjoy things on your own, you will discover a new relationship with yourself.

15. Consider therapy for past trauma.

- People do not need some drastic reason for seeing a counselor. There comes a time when every codependent notices the relationship they're in is not meeting their needs.
- A therapist can assist you in working through traumas from your relationships and childhood that are possibly causing you to act in codependent ways, as well as helping you define relationship patterns and establishing boundaries moving forward.

16. Exercise for resolving obsessional behaviors. (Note: If you've been sexually abused, this exercise should be conducted under the guidance of a professional.)

- Find a quiet and safe place where you can sit uninterrupted.
- Meditate on your true inner feelings, including fear, anger and sorrow.
- Think of a time when you were growing up that you felt the same way.
- What age were you?
- Who was the person or people responsible for these feelings? Were you told to stop crying or acting like a baby, or were you told you are overly sensitive?

- Were you made to feel shame, thereby making you repress your feelings?
- Next, tap into the emotions instead of repressing them and allow yourself to honestly really feel them. Anger may surface and tears may fall, but it is imperative that you move through the feelings until they are spent.

17. Relationship inventory.

- Make a list of people in your life who are important (spouse, lover, colleagues, family members and friends).
- Think about each relationship for a couple of minutes.
- Note the individuals on your list whom you believe to be dysfunctional.
- How many suffer from addiction or any form of mental illness?
- Note unbalanced relationships where you do all of the giving.
- Put away your list for 48 hours, then;
- Pick the most stressful relationship.
- Write down a boundary to set.
- Practice how to tell that significant person about the boundary with someone in your support system whom you trust (knowing they may not like it). I suggest that you put your list away for at least 24 hours. (This is a significant first step in your recovery from codependency.).

18. Stress-reducing relaxation.

- The path to conquering codependency lies in being able to relax and start a loving relationship with yourself.
- Be seated in a relaxed position and shut your eyes.
- Relax each muscle in your body starting with your toes and moving toward your face.
- Breathe through your nose and silently count 1 and then breathe out of your mouth slowly and count 1 and repeat. Do not try to control your breathing.
- Do this exercise every day for 10 minutes.

19. How to start focusing on yourself.

- When with someone else, remind yourself not to keep watch on the other person.
- Imagine putting that person's wants and needs in the hands of a higher power.
- Mindfully practice being non-judgmental.
- Write down your feelings in a journal.
- Take time-outs when starting to react to another's emotions and journal.
- Journal affirmations.

6

REWRITING YOUR LIFE STORY

"Whether we realize it or not, we all impose a narrative on our lives."

— JOAN DIDION

As you have come to understand from previous chapters, codependency is rooted in the belief that you are not good enough on your own. You feel unworthy when not serving others, and this lack of self-love allows you to give up healthy self-care routines in order to focus on other people. The extreme codependent feels empty inside, void of healthy feelings, and existing only for others. They do not exist as an individual and use other people like a drug or alcohol. The codependent feels that other people make them feel good and assist them in covering up their own feelings. The more they do for other people, the more highly they think of themselves. What story do you tell about yourself?

The beliefs most ingrained in our subconscious often form by the time we are 7 years old based on the behaviors we have observed around us. Attachment and bonding to caregivers are critical for survival, and we adapt our behaviors to work around the needs and actions of that caregiver. In unhealthy families, children receive acceptance and rewards from those around them, and they learn they have no power over how they feel. Since feelings and emotions are ignored in dysfunctional families, it is an unsafe environment in which to be vulnerable.

The conversations we have within ourselves mirror our experiences in life. Almost every step taken in life is simultaneously based on a memory. Our first experiences come from touching, smelling, tasting, and seeing, each of which triggers an emotion. The emotion then sparks a feeling that it labels as right, wrong, happy, or sad. Then, you apply a meaning to each of those experiences. Next, a meaning is registered to accompany each of those experiences. "I was adopted so my parents must have wanted to get rid of me." Or, "My parents adopted me because I am very special." Think of a time when you heard that voice inside of you saying, "be afraid". That voice has stopped you from many wonderful life experiences. This triggered anxiety is your mind's way of protecting you from repeating a mistake or a negative action. But it also reinforces that 'be afraid' story that you shouldn't do something. The good news is you get to choose your journey because you are the author. Your story doesn't only tell you why or how events happened in your life, it tells you which experiences were important. Either from a self-taught lesson or a spiritual awakening, the way you describe something to yourself is what makes it a memory.

You can begin the process of rewriting your life story by examining your interpretations of past experiences. Traumatic experiences can be repressed but still seriously influence your behaviors. One bad memory can have a snowball effect and create an anxiety disorder, triggering emotional terror. Everyone has bad memories, such as your first traffic ticket, first hangover, first trip to the dentist, etc. Once you learn how to rewrite your tale with an outcome that is full of resilience and heroic, you can achieve true peace. How you interpret events is up to you. It is possible to train your thought patterns to change the feelings associated with a memory to one with effective coping. If you have recalled a traumatic memory, start an inner dialog that tells you the lesson learned and how much stronger of a person it made you. Look back and revise your story to include how awesome, beautiful and intelligent you are. However, a traumatic memory is very different from a 'bad' memory and often needs an intervention on a professional level. Acceptance is the central component for coping with a traumatic memory. Your life story is a combination of your past reconstructed—how you perceive your present and how your future is imagined. All three exist together at the same time; they are linear and co-occurring, not separate. When you change the meaning and story of your past, your present and future are changed simultaneously and vice versa. Changing the meaning of your present and future story alters the meaning of your past at the same time.

Your story is constantly changing based on life experiences. No, you cannot change the facts of your past, but you can change the story you tell yourself. Your entire view of the world and your identity is a story with a meaning. Ask yourself: Is this story benefiting you? Is this the way you want to tell your story? Most likely, most of what you believe is based on the narrative you tell yourself; all of which are based on your past experiences. If you had trauma without any empathetic support to help your frame of mind can lead to dysfunction, fear, shame, guilt, and a whole gambit of unhealthy manifestations. You don't always have to have a plan for your day. Sometimes, it's best to let the day come to you...to let go of any obsessive thinking about how things should play out. When you are at peace with yourself, you can create what is around the next corner for yourself. You can pre-think your story and look for opportunities that are positive and healthy. There are those who seek comfortable atmospheres, and there are those who create comfortable atmospheres. You have to make the decision about which one you will seek.

Recovery means doing a 180-degree reversal of your dysfunctional patterns so that you can reconnect with your inner being, honor and self-care, and begin to behave from your core self. Healing from codependency redevelops your autonomy, authenticity, ability to be intimate, and integrated and harmonious thoughts, feelings, values, and behaviors. When it is time to edit your story, try not to distort reality, otherwise you may find it difficult accepting the best parts of you and accepting who you are. If you lie to yourself about yourself, you can have a rude awakening. Personal characteristics develop over the years into habits. Anything done repeatedly shapes into a habit, so mind your actions that had negative consequences. Poisonous narratives turn into low self-worth, self-doubt and self-pity. Spend time training yourself to notice distorted thinking. Some individuals believe they are the main topic of conversation and thought in everyone's lives. You have to address that distorted reality if it applies to you. Learning how to conquer irrational fears can be challenging. Anxiety and fear have much in common, however, they are not the same. Fear derives from perceived threats, while anxiety is a result of a fear that is anticipated.

Exercise: Challenging Limiting Beliefs

- **Step 1:** List beliefs you have about the world that inform how you act. Write this down in a journal or on a piece of paper (writing by hand makes more of a psychological impact).
- Ex: I am worth something when I am helping others.
- Ex: No family is truly happy.
- Ex: I can't be alone.
- **Step 2:** Recognize that these are things that FEEL true but are NOT. They are just beliefs. Write down where these beliefs may have come from (parents, siblings, home environment, teachers, etc.)
- **Step 3:** Come up with a belief that is aligned with what you want, rather than what you're working with right now. On that piece of paper, write a belief that challenges the ones you currently believe.
- Ex: I am worthy of space regardless of my actions.
- Ex: I can thrive independently of others.

You want to acknowledge this new belief and feel it. This won't be a process you do once and are finished with forever.

- **Step 4:** Take different actions.
- Act as if your new belief is true.
- Ex: How would you act if you truly felt you were worthy of space no matter what?
- You would most likely stand up for yourself, set boundaries, and be OK saying "No".
- Even small steps will help to undo the old belief and solidify this new, empowering thought.

Your old ways of dysfunctional coping, those entrenched in you, will keep tugging away, trying to send you into a panic. Once identified, you can calm the storm. Next are some breathing exercises that are proven to work by triggering the parasympathetic nervous system, which influences your body's ability to calm down and relax. The anxiety associated with our flight-or-fight response is ruled by the sympathetic nervous system. It is in the exhaling that works on anxiety.

Breathing Exercise 1: Lengthen your Exhale

If you take deep breaths too fast or too many of them, it can cause you to hyperventilate. When feeling anxiety and attempting to quell it by taking deep breaths too fast, we can increase the anxiety when we are actually trying to calm it.

1. This process can be done in any comfortable position.
2. Before taking a deep breath, fully exhale instead. Exhale all of the air out of your lungs, and then naturally inhale.
3. Inhale for 5 seconds
4. Exhale for 7 seconds
5. Do this for 3 minutes.

Breathing Exercise 2: Belly Breathing, Using your Diaphragm

1. Put one hand just above your belly button and the other hand in the middle of your chest.
2. While slowly breathing in with your nose, pay attention to your stomach rising.
3. Exhale through your mouth with pursed lips pushing all of the air out.
4. To make this breathing start to happen automatically, it takes daily practice for up to five minutes.

Breathing Exercise 3: Calming

1. Starting at your feet and moving up to your shoulders and face relax every muscle.
2. Take a slow deep breath while imagining the air coming in through the soles of your feet, traveling up your legs, through your stomach, and into your lungs, relaxing every muscle as the air passes through.
3. Slowly exhale, imagining the air leaving your lungs back into your belly, then your legs, and out of your feet.

4. Repeat until you are noticeably calm.

Breathing Exercise 4: Mindful Breathing

1. Put yourself in a comfortable position either sitting or laying down.
2. Slowly inhale through your nose, noticing your stomach expanding.
3. Slowly exhale through your mouth.
4. Repeat the pattern.
5. As your thoughts move into your head, notice there is no judgment, then release those thoughts and focus on your breathing.

WHAT IS SELF-CARE?

Did you know that 44% of people think self-care is possible only during leisure time? Many people associate self-care with 'treating yourself'—for example: getting a manicure, taking a bubble bath, or indulging in chocolate. These can be good practices to unwind after a long day, but don't actually target your mental or emotional health. People often just think about what will feel better in the moment and want to numb themselves instead of being proactive. True self-care is about taking actions that create a nurturing experience in the moment but also set you up for continued success. Many people believe it is selfish to make time for self-care. One coach proposes, "It's actually a selfish action not to engage in self-care because in order to care about the people in your lives, you have to care for yourself." With stillness comes a clearer picture and insight, and being active in your own care helps you to learn how to communicate, interact, and reach out. Mindfulness is by being emotionally present.

Self-care is deliberate actions needed to tend to our physical, mental and emotional health. Implementing self-care is essential to reducing anxiety and enhancing your mood. It is also important to the relationship you have with yourself and other people. It is not just knowing what self-care means; it is also what it doesn't mean. Self-care fuels you rather than drains you of your positive energy and well-being. It also is *not* selfish. It is knowing what needs to be done in order to take care of yourself and therefore to take care of others, too. By practicing self-care, you will learn how to cope better with everyday stressors. Some think self-care is about how you can feel better only immediately. Some think numbing the pain in the short-term works. However, self-care is proactive and requires you to examine the cause of your pain. It is an action that makes you feel better the next day, not wishing maybe you shouldn't have imbibed so much the night before. Self-care should not be an activity that is separate from your daily routine; it should be part of it. It means knowing what your limitations are and recognizing when you are doing more than you can handle and then trying to find out how to slow yourself down. This means getting the right amount of sleep and rest not only for your body, but also for your mind. Proper nutrition cannot be underestimated. Food is the factor on which all human life depends. Overindulging once in a while is natural, but on a regular basis can cause emotional, social, and physical consequences. By practicing your new self-dialog techniques, you will not be relying on cues from the outside, making food no longer a psychological band aid. It is about making decisions that show you that you value yourself.

Self-care includes finding ways to decompress yourself throughout the day, not just after a long day at work. How do you decompress, rest your mind during a stressful day? Even when time is limited, you can stop what you are doing and stretch for a minute or two to refresh your mind and body. Do this throughout the day. Think of an exercise you can do to tune out the noise, like stopping what you are doing and getting a cool drink of water. Your brain needs to pause. Give some thought about stress-reducing techniques you can utilize when and where you sit or stand to do your work. Is there something you can change in the environment, maybe a flower or two? It is so important that you take the time necessary to know yourself better. Learning about yourself prepares you to know your personal limits and how to recognize your own level of sensitivity. Make a list of things you think are fun, and make a serious effort to include them in your daily grind or at least once a week. Make this plan routine, something you can look forward to each day and that does not have to be complicated. Feeding your spirit is one of the most important aspects of self-care. This may be in the form of taking a nature walk, praying, watching the sunrise or sunset, writing your gratitude list, meditating, listening to inspirational music, or audio tapes, and/or going to a twelve-step meeting. Self-care is taking the time to appreciate you.

Three major areas of self-care:

1. Care for your body.
2. Healthy diet, exercise and sleep habits.

3. Codependents will often give up sleep and other healthy physical activities in order to devote more time to the other person in a relationship.
4. These three basic routines can transform how you feel mentally and physically, but are also usually the first to be given up.
5. Care for your inner self.
6. The process of recovering from codependency.
7. Care for your community.
8. Engage in NURTURING, HEALTHY friendships and connections with your family and community.
9. The key is to be aware of codependent behaviors and stop them before they happen.

ASKING FOR HELP

A major hurdle most codependents face is acknowledging that they cannot do this alone. Because we are highly social beings, we rely on each other for learning and growth. Helping someone else does feel good and is very likely a key aspect in the evolution of our species, as hunting and gathering together was necessary for our survival. If we are hardwired to ask for help, why then is it so hard to do? First of all, we live in a world that praises self-reliance, and self-preservation. The smallest thought of asking for help can chip away at our ego and make us question our strengths and coping mechanisms. Yet, in modern times, where we are seemingly all digitally connected, the truth is that no one person can go it alone. Learning how to ask and accept help will be one of the most important skills you can use in recovery. Mind the reality distortions when it comes to asking for help. It is much easier than you may think.

Fear is the main reason so many are reluctant to ask for help. Fear of being turned down and rejected, which is personified as weak, vulnerable or a fraud leads to self-loathing. Here, fear trumps reason, and the mere risk of emotional pain activates our fight-or-flight response. Also, people can find it very difficult to articulate their needs in a way so that another can offer constructive assistance. This again is tied to your false belief system that your feelings, needs, and thoughts are outright obvious to others. No one can telepathically receive your plea for help, and therefore, you should not feel disappointed when others are not sensing your issues. Distorted thinking is usually based on irrational fears, and they cause painful and unnecessary emotional confusion. Putting unrealistic expectations on others or yourself causes undo emotional havoc. Individuals who believe that society as a whole needs to conform to their beliefs or their set of values are thinking narcissistically and being impractical. Discussing what you believe and standing up for yourself is a healthy characteristic, but, pushing your values and beliefs onto others can lead to chronic arguments and make people feel uncomfortable being around you; again, it is important to manage your expectations. Spend time journaling about your distorted thinking patterns, and you will realize you are far from the topic of everyone's lives. Anxiety is often based on an irrational fear and learning how to conquer anxiety is a challenge. Be prepared for your old thinking habits to keep tugging at you. This is dysfunctional and has probably become entrenched in you like a bad habit.

TIPS ON HOW TO ASK FOR HELP

- Be specific and concise. Clearly communicate your request in a concise manner. You need not overly explain so the party whom you are asking knows exactly what you mean and can accurately prepare for the amount of time and energy the task may take. Let them choose how much support they can lend, and, if there is something mutually beneficial; be willing to negotiate.
- You need not apologize when asking for help. As soon as you apologize, the excitement for the helping person diminishes. Needing help is nothing to be ashamed of, but apologizing casts a negative light on the action and makes it seem like you think you have done something wrong.
- Similarly, do your best not to minimize your request with phrases such as "I hate to ask…" or "Can you do me a favor". This implies that their help is menial and takes a sense of joy away from the act of helping someone or makes them feel obligated to say yes.
- Don't make it a transaction, make it personal. Emailing or texting for help is not a good idea unless you are filing a written request. Explain why the person with whom you are asking for help is uniquely skilled for the task. This tells the person they are special not just some way of achieving means.
- Don't emphasize reciprocity. While we tend to think that making the deal sweeter, by returning the favor, is a good strategy, this kind of communication makes your request

seem transactional. People don't like to feel indebted to others, and a show of genuine appreciation for their aid rather than assign their efforts a monetary value is better received.
- Follow up with the person's past just expressing your thanks. People do long to feel validated and effective when they help another. Take the time to let them know what impact they have had upon your life or community.
- Practice getting ahead of the problem. If you have a situation or task that you know will be difficult for you, reach out before it becomes a full-blown challenge. This can be as easy as telling a friend that you have an upcoming family event, and asking if they can text you to check in. This approach avoids feelings of failure by having support on stand-by when the situation arises.

Exercise

Think of a problem or situation you need help with, but are struggling to ask for support for it. How would you respond to a friend who asked you for that same help? It's easy for us to be kind to others and hard on ourselves. Remind yourself that, at the end of the day, we're all just doing our best, and that can make it easier to show yourself this compassion.

WHAT IS HEALTHY GIVING?

Discussing healthy giving is very important for any codependent in recovery, especially since it is in their nature to give. The reason for giving is usually when contributing to another's well-being or personal growth. This is sometimes the trap for the codependent. Whether giving money, affection, or time...giving can be very dangerous for you, if you're a codependent. Wanting to be recognized for giving and feeling disappointed when not is the catch, as well as expecting something in return. In recovery, you will recognize that healthy giving is a choice. Give gifts of money, time, and affection because you want to from the heart, and based on a thought-out conscious decision. Secondly, healthy giving is for your own benefit and not just the recipient's. Actually, it is not even necessary for the person you are giving something to even be aware of it. There should be joy in your ability to give freely. Thirdly, you can only give what you have at the moment. That can come in the form of a prayer or good thoughts for an addicted loved one or in a smile to a grouch. Maybe it is in the form of forgiving someone for something incidentally done without any harmful meaning. There are many ways to give without giving up yourself, your power or your sense of calm. Lastly, healthy giving is done without expectation, unconditionally. There lies the blessing in giving. The motivation behind it is kindness, love and compassion, and treating those as you wish to be treated. The following are some healthy gifts for giving:

- Hugs;
- Acceptance;
- Encouragement;
- Affirmations;
- Listening;
- Compliments;

- Prayers;
- Forgiveness;
- Hospitality;
- Letters or cards;
- Time; and
- Volunteer services.

CODEPENDENCY SELF-ASSESSMENT QUESTIONNAIRE

Answer the following questions and give yourself a score of 1 for each "False" answer to odd-numbered question and each "True" answer to even-numbered questions:

1. I care more about my feelings than I do other people's feelings. **True / False**
2. I am not positive about my feelings sometimes. **True / False**
3. I am happy with my intimate relationships **True / False**
4. I look OK on the outside when I am miserable on the inside. **True / False**
5. I am OK with the type of relationships I have. **True / False**
6. I would never go on a trip/vacation alone. **True / False**
7. I am able to handle challenges directly and in a calm manner. **True / False**
8. I am not where I want to be in life. **True / False**
9. I have no problem ending an overwhelming relationship. **True / False**

10. I often say "yes" even when I mean "no". **True / False**
11. I usually feel pretty healthy. **True / False**
12. I am unsatisfied with my current relationship. **True / False**
13. I have no problem expressing my anger. **True / False**
14. I hate being alone. **True / False**
15. It is not at all difficult for me to not intervene; 'not my problem'. **True / False**
16. I wish I could change the past. **True / False**
17. My family communicated openly and effectively. **True / False**
18. I question my reasons for doing so much for other people. **True / False**
19. I take time to enjoy myself at least once a week. **True / False**
20. I find critical decision-making hard. **True / False**

Tally

Now add up your score here_____

A combined score of 20 and up indicates strong codependent characteristics as revealed in a review of the literature (Johnson, 2014; Lancer 2019; Livingston, Hall, & Ross, 2020).

7

THE ROAD TO RECOVERY

Recovery is a lifelong journey that involves the restoration of relationships with yourself, your higher power, and others. The three restorations are a part of your journey; they are interdependent. In order to grow in one type of relationship, you must also be growing in the other two. Recovery is about finding a healthy balance in all three relationships and finding productive and innovative ways to keep the balance. Some examples include finding a healthy balance between tending to others and tending to yourself, what you can and cannot change, and work-life balance. Every being is on a journey; the thing about recovery is being aware of it. Life is full of peaks and valleys. Those in recovery are OK with knowing it is dangerous but today choose to stop and smell the roses.

At the end of each day, doing 'good', and living 'good' comes down to a balancing act between emotion and reason, between your needs and the needs of others, and between problems and solutions. With recovery, there is a good chance of achieving this balance if you stay on course and do whatever is necessary to protect your recovery and stay consistent with your values. It is about being resilient, having the ability to bounce back in the face of adversity. Simply put, resiliency is the capability of coping with and rising to life's challenges you encounter during the course of your life, and coming back from them even stronger. It depends on various skills and draws from different sources of help, including meetings, counselors, sponsors, physicians, and the relationships you have with people around you.

There are four fundamental concepts to resilience:

1. ***Awareness:*** Acknowledging your surroundings and what is inside of your own head.
2. ***Thinking:*** Having the ability to rationally interpret the events going on in your life.
3. ***Reaching out:*** How you communicate to others to help you meet the challenges that you face, because being resilient is also about knowing when to ask for help.
4. ***Fitness:*** Your physical, mental, and spiritual ability to face life's challenges without becoming ill.

RECOVERY FROM CODEPENDENCY INVOLVES FOUR MAJOR STEPS:

Abstinence

The goal of recovery is to establish an internal point of control and bring your attention and priorities back to you. Having an internal locus of control means that your actions and behaviors are primarily motivated by your needs, values and feelings. This is the goal codependents are working toward in recovery. It is important for the codependent to learn how to meet their needs in a healthy way. There is no such thing as perfect abstinence because it involves people's dependency and not just putting down the drink or the drug. People need to be able to depend on one another in a reasonable manner and therefore, learn how to compromise in their relationships. In this case, recovery is about learning how to detach and not obsess about your relationship. Recovery is also about independence and self-direction rather than people-pleasing and manipulation.

Detachment

Many codependents associate detaching from another person as leaving them or no longer caring for them. True detachment isn't about cutting the other person off—it's about protecting yourself and your mental and emotional health. When you practice detachment, you stop projecting the feelings of others onto yourself and your worth. This is the process of learning to respond to people, not react to them. The difference is that reactions are instant, driven by the beliefs and biases of our unconscious minds. They are based in the moment and don't involve thinking about the repercussions of a behavior. They are survival-oriented. People in codependent relationships often respond in reactionary ways because they are so caught up in wanting to please/appease the other person. Responses are slower and more deliberate, involving the conscious mind in the decision-making process. They consider your own well-being as well as the effect on those around you. Externally, these responses may look the same, but they feel entirely different. Responses allow you to maintain control and stop yourself before continuing the subconscious behaviors you are trying to fix.

Exercise: Evaluate Your Responses

This exercise focuses on analyzing your reactions and requires you to take an honest, non-judgmental view of yourself. It is best done in writing, in a journal dedicated to recovery. The more you practice, the easier this process will become:

1. Reconsider the last situation in which you reacted negatively. For example, if someone chose not to do what you thought they should, and you got angry and felt defensive.
2. Write down the situation, how you reacted, and how you felt afterward. Then write down how you wish you had responded in the moment.
3. Take some time to think about why you reacted the way you did. What thoughts caused you to say or do that? What emotions were you experiencing?
4. Having identified the thoughts/feelings behind your reaction, look at possible beliefs that created those thoughts and feelings. Even just being aware of this makes it easier to be prepared in the future.

Awareness

Denial is one of the major patterns of codependency, as discussed in Chapter One. Codependents deny their own addiction to taking care of others and deny their own feelings and needs to stay in the cycle.

The simple fact that you're reading this book means you've already accomplished part of this step! Being able to identify that you want to change is a huge achievement. To reverse destructive habits, you need to be able to recognize what those habits are. The most damaging obstacle to self-esteem is negative self-talk and self-criticism. Starting to recognize the good things in life facilitates a big role in your happiness. Showing that you appreciate what you have will add to your overall life satisfaction. However, make sure not to confuse appreciation with gratitude. Appreciation is noting the good characteristics something, or someone has. Gratitude is a feeling of gratefulness for a person or a thing. While appreciation is a behavior and gratitude is a feeling, you can feel gratitude without showing appreciation. Gratitude becomes appreciation when you act upon it by bringing forth feelings of appreciation. For example, you may be grateful for your home, and, by taking care of it, you are showing appreciation. Appreciation is about acknowledging the value, significance and quality of things and people.

Exercise: Thought Awareness/Mindfulness

Meditation practices and guided journaling are the most effective ways to become aware of your thought patterns.

1. Find a comfortable seated position on the floor or in a chair where your spine is straight, and your shoulders and jaw are relaxed. Set a timer for five to 15 minutes (five for beginners is best).
2. Take five deep breaths to ground yourself. Try to focus on the sensations of the entire breath—the air coming in

through your nose or mouth, your chest rising and then falling as you exhale. This will help you practice awareness of the present moment (which makes it easier to respond, rather than react, to things).
3. Continue breathing naturally, focusing on the rhythm of your breath. See what thoughts come into your mind.
4. As thoughts come up, notice and acknowledge them without engaging. If you think of an upsetting situation, acknowledge the thought but don't go down the rabbit hole of negative emotions.
5. Observe your thoughts compassionately, and try to be aware of your inner dialog. What are you telling yourself in the moment? What emotions are present, and where in the body do you feel them? Approach your thoughts with curiosity. Where are they coming from? Are these thoughts really 'you', or are they part of the story you've been telling yourself?
6. If you notice you've gotten caught up following a specific thought, return your focus to your breath without shame or judgment.

Acceptance

The healing process is rooted in self-acceptance, and showing yourself compassion and understanding even in difficult times. This step is a journey all on its own, and one that can be made easier through therapy and group practices. Codependents must come to terms with the fact that they cannot solve everybody's problems. Acceptance is not the same thing as approval; you can't please everyone out of the fear they will not like you. To be real, you cannot control how other people feel about you no matter how hard you try. Acceptance doesn't happen overnight, or in a week, or sometimes even a month, it is a work in progress, and it takes effort, missteps, and baby steps. The acceptance of 'what is' defines the concept of acceptance. It doesn't mean resigning yourself to what is because that means you are taking a passive stance toward your circumstances, which is derived from hopelessness. Acceptance is a positive technique necessary to move toward taking charge of your life again. It doesn't mean your approval of the facts, just the knowledge that they exist whether you like them or not. It doesn't mean acceptance of abusive or inappropriate behavior. While this misconception is common, some are not always conscious of their abuse and do not recognize it as such. Therefore, they do not face it. With acceptance, you can make behavior changes, seeking support and safety, and begin to set boundaries.

Action

In order to grow and recover, you must combine insight with action in your day-to-day life. In some ways, this step is the most difficult, because it requires us to engage in the present moment. This means setting internal boundaries and keeping commitments to yourself. When you have no respect for yourself, it is easy to let other people create an identity for you. You have to consciously say "no" to your inner critic and the negative habits in your life. Get to know yourself. As you continue on this journey, create opportunities to reconnect with your inner self that you have repressed for so long. Intentionally explore what you like, what you value, what you want from life and relationships, etc. Practice: Set aside time each week for an activity that's just for you. In the beginning, you may try a new activity each week as you relearn what resonates with you. Recovery isn't all or nothing. Even small changes can create lasting effects in your life. Practice consistency over achievement. There is no finish line you need to rush to, just a steady pace to follow.

Exercise: Say "No" To One Request

When you state "no", you are saying it to only one option. By verbalizing "yes", you are saying no to every other choice. Codependents often find themselves committing to too many things and making time for too many people. This exercise is meant to help break the gut reaction of saying "yes" to any request.

- **First approach.** Choose a period of time that you will set aside for yourself each week. Regardless of what situations may arise, say no to anything that would eat up that time. This will not only help you practice healthy boundaries, but also create an opportunity to do some self-care.
- **Second approach.** Set a goal each week to say no to one request, and increase that number as you feel more confident in asserting yourself. When you say no, reflect on how it feels in your journal. Do you feel guilty? Think about why that might be.

Labeling

If you label your negative thinking, you can tame it. When you have an unhealthy thought that goes along with the negative emotion, mentally "label" it as a story. Then, create a self-dialog to let it go. If you repeat this process, you will be able to diffuse the story and eventually overcome the negativity. Labeling a painful process/cycle makes it easier to find solutions and steps to break those patterns. The life you live today is basically the sum of your habits. How successful, healthy, and happy you are is directly related to your habits, what you do repeatedly every day, whether it is a thought or an action, and the characteristics you portray. If you want to improve and form healthier habits, there is a helpful foundation that can make sticking to new habits easier.

Self-Forgiveness

The definition of forgiveness is usually defined as a deliberate action to let go of feelings of resentment and anger toward a person who you believed did you wrong. However, while many codependents are very good at forgiving their partners or other significant people in their lives, it is commonly much harder when it comes to forgiving themselves. It is very important to learn from your mistakes and errors, and how to let go, forgive yourself and move on. Self-forgiveness is not a sign of weakness nor is it letting yourself off the hook. It doesn't mean you condone the wrongdoing. Self-forgiveness is about acceptance of what happened and your part in what happened, and now you are ready to let it go and proceed with your life without ruminating in guilt over the past (which cannot be changed). Forgiving yourself and letting go of your acknowledged mistakes can lift you up and improve the way in which you think about yourself. One strategy for self-forgiveness implies four essential actions (the 4 Rs) that will assist you:

1. **Responsibility**: This is facing the reality of what you have done, which is the hardest part of self-forgiveness. The time for rationalizing, justifying, and making excuses for your behavior to try and make them somehow acceptable is over. It is time to 'face the music'. Acceptance and taking responsibility helps avoid excessive shame, guilt, and regret.
2. **Remorse**: You may feel guilt, shame, and other negative feelings as the result of taking responsibility. Remorse can act as an avenue to positive actions and an overall behavior change. Feeling guilty essentially means that you are a good individual who made a mistake, it is the shame that has you feeling like a 'bad' person. This gives rise to feelings of unworthiness, depression, aggression, and addiction. It is important to remind yourself that mistakes don't make a person bad nor should they undermine your personal sense of value.
3. **Restoration**: An important aspect of self-forgiveness is making amends to the person you feel you have wronged even if that person is you. Just like forgiving someone else for doing you wrong, forgiving yourself is equally important. It is likely to stay with you too, as you may feel as if you earned it. Rectifying your mistakes is one way to help you in moving past your guilt. This way, you will not have to think back and wonder if there was more you could have done.
4. **Renewal**: All people have things that they regret, but falling into self-loathing and self-pity can damage your self-worth and motivation. It is necessary to find a learning experience out of each negative situation by first

understanding why you did what you did so you can prevent the behaviors moving forward.

Recovery from codependency is not as clear as it is for the addict. The addict has a clear-cut picture of what they need to do and is not confused about whether or not they are using drugs and/or alcohol, partaking in gambling or other addictions with measurable consequences. Relapse in the form of obsessive worrying, self-pity, resentments, as well as other negative emotions can creep back into the life of the codependent before they realize it even happened, if they do not consciously work with a program of recovery on a daily basis. There may be other gray areas for the individual with codependency, such as, "Where does appropriate concern end and obsessive caretaking begin?" The challenges are considerable and cannot be handled alone. Fortunately, there is an abundance of helpful resources on the subject available to facilitate the recovery process for the codependent.

Respect and Codependency

In recovery, you will learn how to live respectfully and mindful of others. Being respectful of another person does not entail becoming a doormat. People in recovery learn to never demean themselves. Recovery is about redeeming your self-worth enough to have self-respect and respect for others. Recovery gives you the freedom to stand up for your convictions when other people treat you with disrespect. What can be more demeaning than codependency? It will drain you of your self-respect, especially if you allow someone else to treat you as less than. Through the twelve steps, you will gain the power back and learn to respect yourself. You will gain a choice in whether or not to esteem other people not just so they will approve of you or love you back, but, because respect is essential to all human interactions. There is not much mystery in recovery because it seeks only to accomplish. All beings are worthy of respect. The relationships you seek should be with others who offer mutual respect, not ones doing you a favor or wanting something in return. Everyone has to carry their own load. But, you can still and always be mindful enough to support and encourage others on your journey through recovery.

Letting go of Perfectionism

Being a perfectionist is no healthy way to live. Eventually, you will have to give the imperfect world an imperfect you. The difficulties in life are what make us grow. So, one of the best things you can do for yourself is to give up any false expectations and learn how to forgive and accept yourself as a compassionate person capable of seeing other's perspectives beyond your own. Waving a white flag to an imperfect universe will free you up to enjoy life as it simply unfolds. When you learn how to accept your own limitations, you will be free to be comfortable with yourself and give the freedom of comfortability to those around you. Leave your judgmental attitudes and idealism to the birds, and accept imperfections as a part of the beauty in life. Acceptance goes a long way toward healing any unhealthy desires you may feel compelling you to change, manipulate, fix, rescue, control, or alter another person's behavior or events in your life of which you cannot change. Clinging to past events is far too much pain for anyone. Yesterday's answers and solutions have landed you only looking for more. Practicing honesty and hard work in your life leads to better self-esteem, self-respect, and inner peace. The good news is that new answers and new solutions await you. Try to patiently encounter your future, rather than trying to control it obsessionally. To have serenity, you must fill your feelings with complete awareness while realizing you do not have to act upon them, act them out or judge them. You simply recognize your feelings and quietly accept them. Notice the circumstances producing them, and make a conscious decision on whether or not to respond.

Your personal perception of right and wrong is referred to as your moral compass. This includes your values, beliefs, traditions, and behaviors that, after much inner thinking, point the compass in either the right direction or the wrong direction. The question you need to ask yourself before you take action is, "What information do I need to make the best decision on what to do?" The answer to your question is communicated to you from your past, both good and bad memories that were similar in nature. Your understanding of how to act "healthy" and how you use the information to improve upon yourself in some way guides your behavior. These information sources together help you to decide how you can apply what you already know to any given circumstance. It is imperative that you practice self-honesty here about what you are capable of doing and what you are not, and the consequences of your behaviors in the past, so as to not repeat any previous mistakes.

Exercises: Feeling better:

- Making your bed helps you to feel accomplished and organized.

- Reading for 15 minutes during lunch is the break your brain needs from worrying.
- Daily exercise keeps you ahead of the problems life has to offer.
- Handwrite your daily goals. Follow a regular sleeping pattern even on the weekends. Re-evaluate the impossible.
- Practicing positive thinking is key to stress management. Take a block of time and use it each day to practice positive thinking. It is one of the most important aspects of recovery, happiness, and peace.

REBALANCING YOUR LIFE AND YOUR PERSPECTIVE

The focus in your life must be removed from the other person in your codependent relationship. Codependents have to make a decision wholeheartedly to switch the focus back onto themselves. The more self-educated you are, the more you will become aware of your self-defeating propensities. Giving up your codependency may at first make you feel like a monster, but as we noted before, you cannot take care of someone else while neglecting you. It can be challenging to pull back from someone you care about and to stop blaming them for your problems. People bring their family skeletons and ghosts from the past into their current relationships, and all of those traumatic and disappointing experiences affect how you interact with someone else. It is not until you can untangle the emotions connected to bad life experiences, that you can grow out of the codependent cycle. Ask yourself what role you were expected to play in your family of origin.

Examine unhealthy patterns reflected from your past into your current relationship.

Therapy and sharing at meetings are also good ways to dedicate your time to recognizing these patterns. Unloading expectations from your childhood will help you put your own needs ahead of others. Some people resist this idea because it feels like they are being selfish. Prioritizing yourself doesn't mean you have to ignore or be hurtful to others. When you are your most authentic self, the people who care about you will be even happier. Consistently denying your own needs takes you out of touch with what *you* want, and eventually leads to exhaustion and resentment. Give yourself permission to enjoy the journey. Make time for some irresponsible fun, something that will enhance your happiness, something you enjoy. Personal growth is always a process, and you may not be exactly where you want to be. Give yourself credit for how far you have come in life and appreciate the small victories.

Work toward having balanced expectations of others. Strive for healthy tolerations. You may have tolerated too much or not enough in your past or expected too much or not enough. Did you swing back and forth from taking mistreatment to refusing to even tolerate normal imperfections humans have? Even if you feel better in either extreme, it's not healthy. If you open your mind to the process of recovery, you will, at some point in time, start to transition from extremes toward balance; it is an 'aha moment'. Learning how to not confuse contentment with boredom is one of the best gifts of recovery. Breaking the chaos addiction, not having to be the VIP at your own pity party, is another gift of recovery. You are able to find your own unique journey to balance as you start and continue your recovery. Say to yourself, first thing in the morning, "Today, I will work on patience and working toward my goal of balance in my life."

People commonly sacrifice their authenticity to fit in, almost without thinking, and have been programmed in life to do so. Self-awareness sounds like a self-defining term. But it requires becoming educated to learn how to practice it. The essential aspect of being authentic is when you find what you love in life and stop basing your emotions on the expectations of others. Working too hard to try and be what others define as authentic is not how it works. Staying true to yourself or emotional self-transparency is not only about being honest to yourself, it is about the ability to receive and accept feedback, having empathy, and being humble. A chameleon protects itself by changing colors, not to protect another. Don't change yourself for another person, change for yourself. The reward is a more authentic and happier state of being, as well as improved coping skills. Make emotional self-transparency be your mission in life for staying authentic. This means having to identify all your character defects, influences, and then examining them. It is important to be able to adapt, but staying true to yourself in the process is the key to being authentic.

Balance in a Relationship

The way you know a relationship is healthy is that, when things are good, you should feel balanced and grounded. There are always going to be changes along life's journey, and sometimes they are big changes. In a relationship that is balanced, both partners give and take and change in the process together. Love does have a transforming power, so choosing a partner you can grow with is of the utmost importance. Remember, your friends and family become their friends and family and vice versa. Your partner's ability to listen, support and honor you will be the lift you need when times get tough, but if they tend to invalidate, criticize, ignore and/or abuse you, it will take you to a place that no one wants to go. This is why it is critical that you both pitch in, giving and taking the same amount of energy and support. One-sided codependent relationships, as we have fully discussed in this book, are far from healthy. A balanced relationship takes brutal honesty.

Codependents often realize but fail to mention that the power in their relationship has shifted since the seduction phase. It is not far-fetched for the codependent to adjust their schedule according to their partner's, canceling important events just to do something trivial with them. This spells bad news for the relationship. The taker in this relationship feels a need to maintain control and will eventually lose all respect for the giver, and the giver will begin to seed resentment. At that point, there is already serious trouble brewing. It isn't easy to regain equal footing just through arguing or acquiescing when you mean "no". The following are some warning signs:

1. Not visiting or accepting invitations by friends to go out, because you don't know if it is OK with your partner or you don't know their schedule yet. This also tells your partner that they do not even need to check with you prior to making any plans.
2. Do you find yourself always answering with an "I don't know" when asked to make simple choices such as what to

order on a menu in a restaurant? You might just be trying to be easy to get along with, but easygoing can sometimes mean putting someone else in control over your needs, wants, and desires.

3. Are you a person that literally follows the lead of others? Do you wait for your partner to always cross the street first or for them to turn a certain direction in the mall? Who picks the table when dining out? If you said yes to any of these, it is time to take your life back. Try taking the lead next time.

4. If your partner is only calling you when it is most convenient for them, there is a problem. Do you answer the phone or panic to answer the phone in fear you will miss a call from your partner? If you answered yes to either of these questions, your relationship is unbalanced.

5. Does your partner think it is their right to take their temper out on you? It certainly isn't anyone's right to take their frustrations out on another person. If you are uncomfortable with your partner's tone, guess what, it is a BIG deal. Tell them to stop and if they choose not to, leave the room.

The first step in creating a balanced relationship involves both people in verbalizing and listening. If the communication is not balanced, the relationship cannot be balanced. The main reason for a relationship is to create an atmosphere where both partners complement each other. It is all too common that individuals are preparing a rebuttal while their partner is talking and therefore cannot really hear a word the other is saying. People who do not know or practice skilled listening miss out on great and interesting things in life. If you genuinely listen, you will be better at problem-solving and conflict resolution. To help you to develop your listening skills, make sure to pay attention to non-verbal cues, as well as focusing on the person's words. This will aid in understanding better. Various meanings are portrayed at any given time in a discussion (were they kidding or being sarcastic?). Rephrasing a question when answering it, tells the person who asked the question that you fully understood its meaning. Take a look at your strengths and weaknesses and how they influence your decisions. To listen genuinely takes remembering what was verbalized in the conversation. Rephrasing assists your memory recall about the context of the conversation. Jumpstart your skilled listening with a bit of information gathering from various places, such as your partner's eye contact, hand gestures, facial expressions, and tone. Your partner will feel better understood if you are looking into their eyes when they speak. Take into account your partner's culture as it plays a big part in how they communicate.

Consider non-verbal gestures:

- Your hands say more than your face. Placing your hands behind your head may indicate boredom. Clasping your hands together signals dominance.
- Watch out for a blank stare and pursed lips as it may indicate anger.
- Tilting your head back when listening signals condescension (looking down your nose at someone).
- Poor eye contact and looking around when someone is talking portrays disinterest and a lack of respect (except, in

some cultures, such as the Native American Culture, where eye contact is considered a lack of respect).
- Don't think by interrupting you are showing an interest because it makes others feel misunderstood.
- Listen without judgment. Mentally criticizing impairs effective listening. It directly interferes with understanding your partner, and it takes a conscious effort and practice to get good at it.

The feeling you get when someone is giving you their undivided attention is one of ultimate respect. Poor listening skills will kill your relationship. It is the main strategy for showing you care about the person talking. Feedback validates your understanding of the conversation. The best way to show that you have listened to someone is to ask pertinent questions when they are finished talking. This tells the person they were understood. Being balanced in a relationship does not mean you always agree. In fact, you often have to come to terms with disagreeing. Balanced relationships are not conflict-free; conflict precedes all change and sometimes it is the main factor in balance restoration. The key to effective disagreeing is to mind any aggression and always maintain mutual respect. Make space for disagreeing and try to understand the other's point of view. If you are going to debate —debate with respect.

Your partner may not always, if hardly ever, do what you want. You also may not always do what they want you to do. However, having a balanced relationship requires you to consider your own wants and needs as well as your partner's. If your significant other makes decisions regularly without conferring with you, they obviously care more about having it their way than having harmony in your relationship. Unfortunately, this is all too common in codependent relationships where there is a lack of balance. Also, having balance in your life is not just about your relationship, it is about having a balance between your relationship and the other parts of your life. It is critically important to your emotional health for both people in a relationship to have independence from each other outside the relationship. If you both have a life outside of the relationship, you are able to maintain your authentic self and bring various learning experiences to your relationship. It is not always going to be perfect. There should be plenty of occasions where you need 'some space' or when you are not feeling 100% 'warm and fuzzy' about each other. That is OK. Remember, life is peaks and valleys, as are relationships.

Positivity Exercise

Sit comfortably with an aroma diffuser and list five positive thoughts to carry with you throughout your day. Share in a group meeting and with your friends that you practice every day on improving your positivity. The list of stress-related ailments is lengthy. There are thousands of books on stress management. But, the importance of self-dialog in recovery and stress management needs to be emphasized.

The Four Stages of Habit

Cue	Craving	Response	Reward
1	2	3	4

Timeframe ———————————————————→

These stages are the foundation of every habit and your brain walks through them in the same pattern each time. Firstly, the cue is what triggers your brain to begin a specific action. This small amount of information predicts a certain reward. During times of primitive man, this pattern was necessary for survival as the brain paid attention to signals that cued the places of rewards such as water, sex, and food. Today the reward cues are more in line with money, status, approval, love, praise, and power. These rewards in a way also lend themselves to survival or at least improving the quality of our lives. Your brain is constantly taking note of your internal and external atmosphere for clues as to where rewards may be. Because this clue lets us know a reward is around the corner, it naturally triggers a craving.

Cravings are the next stage in the loop of habit-forming, and they are the inspirational force backing up every habit. Without motivation (craving), we are not prompted to act. The craving is not the habit but the change in you that it creates is. It is not an alcoholic drink the addict craves; it is the feeling the drink provides. The motivation behind turning on the TV is the entertainment provided. Each craving is connected to some desire in changing your internal feelings. Cravings are unique to each individual, but the cues are pretty much the same. For the coffee drinker, the sound of the coffee maker can be a strong trigger to spark an intense craving for the beverage. They mean nothing without your interpretation. The feelings connected to the cue are responsible for the craving.

The third stage is your response. This is the specific habit you act out, which can be in thought or action. How much difficulty is associated, and your level of motivation are the defining aspects of whether or not and how you respond. If a specific behavior requires more effort either physically or mentally, then you might not respond. Habits only happen when we are able to perform them. If you want to run a mile but you have a broken leg, then, you are just out of luck. Bad habits get in the way of accomplishing your goals. They also jeopardize your mental and physical health. All of your habits—both good and bad— have a reason in your life. There is some secondary reward. Sometimes it is physical, such as the 'ahh' feeling some get from an alcoholic beverage, and some are emotional, such as the adrenaline one gets regularly when in an abusive relationship. Some habits elicit both types of response, for instance, checking your email every hour may make you feel more connected and stops you from feeling like you may miss out on something, and so you repeat the cycle. However, think of how much productivity is lost due to this habit.

Lastly, a reward is delivered to the response. Rewards are the main purpose of each and every habit. You notice the reward with a cue; then you crave the reward, then you obtain the reward. The reason for the reward is to satisfy a craving. Energy is provided by water and food; a raise produces more respect and money and working out improves your fitness and dating prospects. But the more immediate service is the satisfaction of the craving. Also, being rewarded stimulates a memory telling us how to achieve the reward again in the future. As you go about your daily routines, your brain is constantly monitoring and reminding you which behaviors deliver pleasure and satisfy cravings. Disappointing and pleasurable feelings are part of the feedback that helps you decide useful behaviors from useless behaviors. The reward completes the habit-cycle feedback loop. If the behavior lacks in any of the aforementioned four stages, a habit will not be formed. If you remove the cue, you will never start a habit. If you make an action very hard, you won't be able to do it, such as not buying ice cream to begin with. If the reward doesn't satisfy your craving, you will not have any purpose for doing it again.

How to Unlearn a Bad Habit

Unlearning a bad habit is just as important as learning a productive one. As mentioned above, a repetitive action creates a routine, which manifests as a habit over time. Getting rid of a bad habit is a learning process, and most often it is never comfortable. But that distasteful quirk can be exterminated with a bit of patience and perseverance. The codependent has bad habits, the same as the addict does. The first step in countering a bad habit is to own up to it. Taking responsibility to acknowledge that it is, in fact, a *bad* habit allows you to notice who you were before the bad habit became one, and that will give you the strength to label the toxic tendency. Coming to terms with your reality gives you a clear understanding of why change is necessary. Like with addiction, identifying your triggers is a step toward unlearning a bad habit. Take a good look at your negative tendencies, and you will come to see them as the source of your problems. If you know your triggers you will be able to act upon them when they arise. Similar to smoking, going cold turkey is challenging, but, if you substitute a positive trait for your toxic traits, you can get a hold of your undesirable ways. For the smoker wanting to quit, they will need to find other anxiety-reducing positive characteristics to replace the toxic one of smoking, such as taking a walk and taking advantage of the enormous amount of smoking cessation resources. Seeking the help of a professional isn't a bad idea if your bad habits are self-destructive.

In order to overcome a toxic habit, planning is a must. Be prepared for failure, and do not let that stifle your motivation. People often fail the first, second, and even third time they try to quit a bad habit, especially if that habit is in the form of toxic relationship addiction. Shake it off and start again. Being creative and diligent with your planning can save you from having to go back to the drawing board. Being innovative and meticulous with your planning can save you from starting all over. Learn from a failure or a stumble, it is not the end of the world (even if it feels like it) ...you're only human. Step back from your bad habit slowly and keep stepping back until it is gone. Self-dialog will take you a long way in calming the triggers. The more you tell yourself you are committed to change, the more likely your attempt to curb your toxic quirks. Again, be fearless about asking for help. Tell your support group about your goals to end a bad habit because they will undoubtedly be in your cheering section. Keeping positive people in the loop about your challenges allows them to motivate you to keep pushing.

Another way to kick your bad habit to the curb is to employ a healthy substitute. You need to plan ahead of your response stage, such as instituting a breathing exercise rather than lighting up a cigarette. Also, blot out as many triggers as you can. If you are trying to shed some pounds, don't buy ANY ice cream for example. If you are spending too much time in front of the TV, put the remote away. Simply put, make it easier on yourself to break your bad habit(s) by avoiding the triggers that ignite them. The comfortable couch in front of the TV is a perfect example of how your environment supports some bad habits and makes good ones more difficult. Change your environment, and you can change your habit. Sit at a desk when you read instead of in your bed.

Keeping track of your journey will help you to succeed in extinguishing the bad habit and replacing it with one beneficial to your happiness and serenity. Simply take to journaling your process and progress. Overcoming an unhealthy habit should be your main priority, but don't focus on the toxic behavior alone; put your energy and time into your efforts, not on targets or deadlines. Just take it a step at a time without overthinking. Stick with the winners. The codependent must work on limiting their interactions with toxic people because they serve to only amp up your toxic habit. Find creative ways to stay upbeat even in the face of adversity. You need to note your process when defeating the demons in your life, while honoring your achievements along the journey.

A good way to defeat bad habits is by surrounding yourself with people who have what you want, the way you want to live your life. See yourself as a success by visualizing yourself on top of your game, smiling in face of your success, building your new identity. Know that you do not need to be someone else's doormat, you need only become your authentic self. It is often thought that a person has to become a completely new individual in order to change their ways. But the truth is that you already have it in you to be that person without those bad habits. It is so important to monitor your self-dialog so that you do not judge yourself for not being better; remember it's baby steps. If you do employ negative self-judgment, finish the thought with the word 'but'; for instance, "I am foolish, and no one likes me, but I am working on stopping my negativity". Plan for falling off the horse every once in a while; what separates successful people from those who are not, is getting right back on the horse. Simply tracking your bad habit will help you to be more aware of the behavior and will give you many ideas for how to stop them.

Activity: Write down and answer the following:

1. When do you act out your bad habit?
2. Here's a simple way to begin: Put a piece of paper and a

pencil in your pocket and write down how many times per day/week your bad habit appears. At the end of each day/week, add them up to see your total.
3. The goal for this part of the activity is not to make you feel badly about yourself or to feel guilty for your actions. The goal here is to become more aware of the circumstances surrounding your bad-habit actions.
4. How many times per day/week do you act out your bad habit?
5. Where are you when you act out your bad habit?
6. Who are you with when you are acting out your bad habit?
7. What triggers you to act out your bad habit?

Social Support

The term "social support" often is discussed in terms of relationships. Social support means having people or a group of people to turn to when you are struggling and to help give you a wider focus and positive self-worth. Social support betters the quality of life and provides a safety net against adverse life events. For the codependent, a strong support network can be of critical importance to helping you through the difficult obstacles that arise in your recovery journey. Lacking a support network can lead to isolation, relapse, and loneliness. Social support differs from your support group, as it is with the people you turn to outside of the Twelve-Step environment. It is made up of peers, friends, colleagues, and neighbors. It needs to be cultivated, whether you are under stress or not. It will provide you with a better foundation when struggling because you know that you have a network of people there for you. A social support network does not need to be formalized. Having coffee with a neighbor, a phone call with a friend, and volunteering at a local charity are all ways to foster and develop lasting relationships with others.

The benefits of a social-support network include the following:

- Improving stress and coping mechanisms;
- Alleviating the effects of relationship distress;
- Promotes optimal mental health;
- Increases self-esteem; and
- Promotes healthy behaviors.

Having a strong social network will help to improve the quality of your life by assisting you in combating stress. Here are some helpful suggestions for creating your social-support network:

- Get involved by volunteering for a cause that is important to you. It will connect you to people who share common values and interests.
- Join the gym. Adding exercise to your daily routine will bring you a healthier lifestyle and be a great place to meet new friends who also have good health on their mind.
- Enroll in an educational activity. This will open up opportunities to meet and engage with others who share similar interests.
- Search the Internet for sites to help you stay connected with community resources and allow you to be privy to codependency literature.

All too important to note is that a social network is about the 'give' and the 'take'. Successful and meaningful relationships are a two-way street. The following are the foundation for social networks.

- Call people back who reach out to you. Return emails and stay connected.
- Identify with others, don't compete. Be happy for others' successes, not envious.
- Practice your listening skills, noting what is important to the person who is sharing their experiences or thoughts.
- Keep in mind your ability to overdo it. Do your best to keep your codependency at bay and not overwhelm your friends with controlling phone calls and/or emails.
- Take time to appreciate your social network by saying thank you and letting them know they are important to you.

The goal of establishing your social-support network is to decrease your stress level, not to add to it. Keep an eye on your energy meter so that you do not end up in a draining scenario. This means to avoid those relationships within which people are negative, critical, and needy. Steer clear of gatherings focused on drinking alcohol or doing recreational drugs. Taking the opportunity to create a social-support network is a smart investment not just for your emotional well-being but also for your physical health and longevity. When you are the one provided support or receiving support, you will reap the benefits.

Twelve-Step Support Groups

We have already touched on the background of the twelve-step support groups and how they have been proven to be effective in helping codependents. There are different types of groups; each type being designed to help a different type of unhealthy relationships. Al-Anon is a support group for those whose lives have been damaged by an alcoholic. They share experiences common amongst them and work together on creating a positive change. Alateen is for teenagers whose lives have been damaged by an alcoholic. Teenagers meet other teens with situations in common with them. Nar-Anon is a twelve-step support group for friends and families of addicts and has the same programming as Al-Anon and Alateen. All three of the abovementioned groups are essentially for those who are feeling desperately concerned about the addiction problem of someone very near to them. When entering the group, you are no longer alone but amongst real friends who understand your problem as few others could. Confidence and anonymity are always respected. Assurance is provided that there is no situation too challenging and no degree of unhappiness that is too great to overcome.

Codependents Anonymous is a twelve-step program of recovery from codependency. It is where those with codependency issues can share their experience, strength, and hope in efforts to find freedom where there has been servitude and serenity where there has been mayhem in their relationships with themselves and/or others. Many codependents have been looking endlessly for ways to solve the conflicts stemming from their childhoods, and in their relationships. Commonly, they were reared in dysfunctional families, often where there was substance abuse, some were not. In either case, individuals who seek out such support groups as CoDA have realized in their lives that they have compulsive behaviors deeply connected to their dysfunctional family systems. People who commit themselves to this simple program have usually tried to use their partners, friends, and sometimes even their children as their primary source of well-being, value, and identity to restore the emotional losses suffered in childhood. CoDA provides a method for learning how to live life rather than just survive it. CoDA members are encouraged to grow at their own pace and recover from their self-destructive lifestyles. The twelve-Step sharing technique is a way to identify compulsive control issues and find freedom from the painful aspects of their past.

Online Support Groups

There are various online locator tools to find meetings in your area or anywhere on the globe. These tools include links for AA, NA, Al-Anon, CoDA, Naranon, and many more. (See link below)

https://recovertogether.withgoogle.com/?utm_source=houseads&utm_medium=ads&utm_campaign=onlineresources&gclid=Cj0KCQiAifz-BRDjARIsAEElyGKr0VGMLxR6xM_yp2m1wIePhwrO3xbFyr8qp63PMJggIB3DbGRS81EaAt1cEALw_wcB#online-meetings

CoDA is available online at https://coda.org/find-a-meeting/online-meetings — CoDA.org.

Meetings are available in many different languages and many different topics. When you sign into your first group meeting, you will be welcomed to a safe place. Some meetings are completely virtual, while some are in person or even both.

At that first meeting is where you will learn about The Twelve Steps, The Twelve Traditions, The Promises and more. These steps, traditions, promises, and principles are the foundation of the program, in which great comfort can be found, one day at a time, as you start your journey on the path to codependency recovery. There are structure and ground rules in the meetings. There should not be any cross-talk (talking to others while someone is sharing). When you're new, you may feel the urge to question or identify with someone when they are talking. The goal is to identify and not compare, speaking only about your own experience, strength and hope. The value in these rules helps the codependent to be honest in their sharing. Some meeting formats go around the room allowing each person a chance to share. Sharing is optional. If you wonder about your personal situation, share about it first. Someone may offer something amazing to you about it.

The meetings start with introductions and readings from The Twelve Step literature resources. You may be asked to introduce yourself, and you may want to let the group know this is your first meeting. Other readings are The Twelve Steps and the Twelve Traditions. Twelve-Step programs are spiritually based, so you will commonly hear statements about a 'higher power' or God. If you are uncomfortable with this you can apply your own concept of God, such as Creator, Spiritual advisor, and the list is endless. There is no right or wrong way to work the steps, and you do them at your own pace. Spirituality allows you to strive far beyond material things. Becoming spiritually fit will help you to figure out your meaning in life, and with it, the satisfaction and happiness that come with fulfilling your purpose. Your unique spiritual guidance, from within, will help you to choose how to best act toward yourself and others. Just like a muscle in the body, spirituality can be strengthened and developed. But instead of lifting weights, you are participating in willpower, and it's better than running to the finish line; you are pursuing your purpose in life.

Meeting Makers Make It

For many codependents, recovery starts with your first attendance at a meeting. It really doesn't matter how you came to the twelve-step group; meetings will become the anchor of your recovery work. It is suggested in the beginning that you attend a meeting every day for 90 days. After which, many codependents start to ease up on their attendance and show up only during a crisis. However, staying spiritually fit is much better attained through attending meetings on a regular basis. If you only drop in during a life-or-death situation, it is very likely you will not have the same support and understanding from the group as you would if they have gotten to know you. Make a mental note that it is only one hour a day in exchange for 23 hours of happiness, joyousness, and freedom. Hope is found in meetings, and there is where you have the opportunity to spread the recovery message. At meetings is where you will likely find your sponsor.

Often the first time you hear someone at a meeting share about a topic, it is something you may have already been thinking about. You may feel amazed that another person actually does know how you feel. This is the identification component of recovery. Make sure to take names and numbers. You never know when you might urgently need someone to talk to, so you are not facing a potential relapse alone.

Aside from keeping you sane, most people feel better after attending a meeting, even when they did not consider it to be a great meeting. Investing in the meetings of the group you joined, also called your homegroup, and the fellowship is like putting yourself in the middle of the solution. Showing up regularly allows people to know you well enough to tell when you are struggling or suffering. Plus, it makes it easier to reach out for help when you are there. Your homegroup is a special place where you make a commitment to attend meetings regularly. Many people in recovery want to give back "what was so freely given to them" and stay after the meetings to clean up, such as putting away the chairs, wiping down the tables, and making coffee for the next meeting. This is referred to as service. This way, you are still making a difference in your life and the life of another codependent, no strings attached. Also, in your homegroup, you can learn how to share and get along with other codependents (i.e., learning how to agree to disagree). Members in a homegroup often feel a healthy sense of family and enjoy getting together for risk-free social events where they love and support one another.

Importance of Sponsorship

No one likes to be controlled. But you can seek guidance in the rooms of one of the twelve-step groups or with a sponsor. Sponsors are there to guide you through the steps and teach you how to live a fulfilling and happy life and can be a great inspiration for spiritual fitness. It is your choice who you pick to be your sponsor. It is smart to ensure they are aligned with your own values and goals, and that they will build you up and not bring you down in any way. Getting a sponsor is one of the most important aspects of recovery. It is how you learn to work the steps. When members of a twelve-step support group use a sponsor, the meetings tend to be very healthy as beginners already feel a sense of fellowship.

Sponsors are there for you when you need help in understanding the process or when you have a weak moment. They have the ability to be objective and dissociated from any feelings of responsibility for another's happiness and recovery. They also do not act in any abusive, controlling or critical ways that can end up with them acting like a therapist or rescuer. They are excellent examples of recovery, sources of caring support, and respectful of the member's anonymity and unique pace in recovery. The best place to start your search for a sponsor is in your homegroup. Many clubs or meeting places have lists of potential sponsors and when online you can ask the person chairing the meeting. Over a period of time, you may hear someone share something that you feel in common with and may want to check them out as a potential sponsor. Just like there is no perfect person, there is no perfect sponsor.

What to look for in a sponsor:

- They are sponsored themselves.
- Ideally, they have already worked through the twelve steps.
- Have more than a year of recovery.
- Recovery is their #1 priority.
- Have what you want in your recovery.

- Are the same gender, or otherwise not attracted to you sexually.
- Respect your right to confidentiality.
- Have the ability to listen and understand with compassion without giving advice or any rescue attempts.
- Help you to recognize codependent behaviors without shaming or blaming.
- Do not judge if you are also a member of another twelve-step program.
- Accept your individual pace.
- Communicate specifically and clearly.
- Ask questions only for a better understanding, not to manipulate or control.
- They know how to have fun in recovery.
- They have a power greater than themselves.
- Have a program in recovery that you admire.

TWELVE-STEP (FIRST STEP) EXERCISES:

Step One: "We admitted we were powerless over others, that our lives had become unmanageable" (Bill W., 1976, p. 21).

Step one is the only step you can take on your own before joining a group; which is recognizing the problem. The twelve Steps start with admitting you are powerless over others. Therefore, the end is really your beginning. Most often, codependents start the first step when they hit bottom; just like the addict. Insanity defined is doing the same cajoling over and over and expecting a different result. Accepting the truth that you are powerless over others is the end of your misery and the start of your freedom. You can dwell in self-pity until the cows come home and basically just look at the other person just standing there and watching. The only person who you can really control is the one who looks back at you in the mirror. Becoming truly emotionally independent has to come from within and from letting go of your expectations in relationships. Of course, everyone can have expectations of others that are reasonable. But, if others do not keep to their commitments or they are addicted, you are the only one who can manage the unmanageable. You can work step one and realize your life became unmanageable because you gave control over who you are to another person and now it is time to take it back.

Step One Exercises:

1. Recently, have you been attempting to influence someone or something, and even repeatedly tried with less than your desired results? Write an answer to each of the following:

- What have you been trying to influence?
- Who have you been trying to influence?
- What have been the results?

2. Who in your life or what in your life has been causing you barely tolerable stress? Who do you believe is victimizing you? Whom do you feel under the control of? Write an answer to each of the following:

- Who and what is/are causing you to feel crazy?
- Who is controlling your emotional well-being?

- What are you running from?

3. What would happen to you if you stopped trying to influence or control someone or some event? Write an answer to each of the following:

- What would you have to go through if you stopped trying to fix someone?
- What would happen to you if you stopped letting someone else control you?
- Which areas in your life reflect unmanageability?
- *Emotional health;*
- *Spiritual health;*
- *Financial well-being;*
- *Physical well-being; and*
- *Professional growth.*

CODEPENDENCY AND TREATMENT

Treatment involves individual and group therapy, education, and support where the person suffering from codependency can learn to identify behavioral patterns that are self-defeating. Sometimes, codependent individuals also suffer from drug and/or alcohol addiction, or their loved one is an addict who encourages them to use substances, too. Codependents may fall into the addiction trap due to their state of depression and stress encountered in their dysfunctional relationship. Just like getting treatment when hitting bottom with codependency, likewise the codependent should seek treatment for substance abuse.

Recovery is the joyous experience of finding unexpected meaning and value in the worrisome times and in the pain. It is about discovering what you thought to be unfathomable and sharing it with other people with whom you choose to have interactions. Recovery is about your decision to live your life to the fullest, one moment at a time. Living abundantly is what recovery is all about, but not in the pursuit of wealth; it is about the pursuit of happiness in being who you are right now and letting tomorrow come as it may. Some codependents are able to recover by joining a twelve-step program. Some codependents recognize their ailment through reading books, articles, blogs, and watching videos on the subject. Others begin recovery when their dependent partner becomes clean and sober. However, many times, codependency requires treatment on a professional level.

Psychotherapy, or talk therapy, can help individuals understand why they feel the excessive urge to fulfill everyone's needs while putting their own aside. A therapist can assist the individual in identifying codependent characteristics, and in understanding where in the first place these behaviors were adopted. Learning self-compassion is essential in healing and in changing dysfunctional patterns of behavior. In psychotherapy, an individual can learn how to acknowledge and accept repressed emotions. The therapist helps them to understand why and where codependent patterns developed in childhood and have now transferred into adulthood. Since codependents often suffer from low self-worth and tendencies toward perfectionism, learning self-care is essential to recovery. Individuals can role-play with their therapist and practice kindness in their self-dialog and forgiveness for their own mistakes. Over time, talk therapy can help lessen the codependent's urge to overcompensate. A therapist can also facilitate individuals in improving their relationships with their partners and family members. They may educate the individual on how to support others without enabling them. The therapist in psychotherapy may also help the person to improve their ability to be assertive.

Group therapy is one treatment protocol shown to be an effective treatment technique for codependency. The dynamic of the group gives the codependent a chance to form healthier bonds with others in a safe and appropriate environment. Improved communication is often a key goal of family therapy. Issues that have never before been talked about in the family may be discussed in therapy. Sometimes, one person changes (such as getting sober or encouraging someone to be more independent), and it has a ripple effect on the entire family dynamic. Group therapy allows the special opportunity to provide an individual with validation from other members who have similar treatment goals and who are experiencing similar difficulties. These sessions are led by one or more facilitators who are specially trained for implementing proven techniques for managing challenges specific to codependency. In the beginning, the thought of participating in group therapy can seem daunting. After all, who wants to 'air their secrets' with strangers or people they hardly know.

Group therapy allows the members to provide support to one another. Listening to others with common issues can help you realize that you're not alone in having struggles, whether you're grappling with an addict, an abusive partner, low self-esteem, or another codependency issue. Many people who have participated in a group-therapy setting experience a sense of relief. When discussing problems with others, the group functions as a sounding board and can help you view things currently happening in your life that you don't see. You get a broader range of perspectives on your circumstances that can help you cope better with your problems. A group approach to therapy can propel the member forward through encouragement. Listening to others discuss how they overcame their dysfunctional helping can be an inspiration for others to push themselves harder toward recovery. Group therapy not only eases feelings of isolation, but also facilitates the member to practice healthy communication with people, so that the member can see that it is possible to get along with others. It is also less expensive than one-on-one therapy sessions. Groups provide a metaphorical mirror, and the member gets to see themselves through the eyes of another.

Some group therapy approaches utilize *cognitive behavioral therapy* (CBT), which facilitates the new learning of specific skill-building strategies. Other group therapy approaches institute the twelve-step model, previously discussed, with the goal of acceptance, increasing self-esteem and the verbalization of feelings. CBT helps the codependent change negative and dysfunctional patterns in their thought processes and belief system necessary for changing their behavior. The CBT treatment approach aims to educate the codependent individual on how to acknowledge their own problems as separate from other people's problems. CBT is a type of talk therapy that is used to treat individuals who need help with their thinking patterns, emotions and behaviors. While many think of individual therapy as exploring repressed memories from childhood, CBT focuses on exploring solutions for today instead of continuous processing of the root cause of where the codependent traits are coming from. The CBT approach is designed in a structured manner with a limited number of sessions. Identifying negative or distorted thinking patterns, so the person can see difficult situations more clearly and learn how to effectively respond to them, is one of the essential components of CBT. It aids the codependent in recognizing how their thinking patterns are affecting their actions. While the way you're thinking and responding may be based on past experiences, CBT doesn't focus on your past, it focuses on finding a solution now.

In a CBT setting when first meeting with a therapist, the codependent person will likely spend time filling out assessments so the therapist can get to know their circumstances. The therapist may also inquire about their physical, mental and spiritual health, and if they have any coexisting mental health issues, such as depression, anxiety, addiction, PTSD, bipolar disorder, borderline personality disorder (BPD) or any other conditions that may affect their feelings and behaviors. The reason for these assessments is to aid the therapist in formulating a specific treatment plan tailored to the person's specific needs. It may take more than one session. The more honest and open codependent is from the beginning, the less difficult it will be for the therapist to gather enough information to start moving them forward in their treatment goals.

Like most therapeutic processes, CBT can be challenging and emotional to go through. Learning how to change your thinking patterns about circumstances in life that have been very painful can be difficult. But, if you stay the course with your treatment plan, you can find the relief you never thought possible and experience life-changing and long-lasting changes. Here are some important things to bear in mind with CBT:

- **Honesty is a must.** If you are unable to be honest with your counselor, CBT will not work for you. It is not the type of therapy where the facilitator has to explore your thinking patterns over the course of many weeks or months trying to get an accurate picture of your life. This can prove to be very challenging for a person who is used to guarding their thoughts due to fear of rejection or a loss of control. But, the therapist is highly trained for assisting you with processing negative thinking and replacing it with beneficial and appropriate thoughts.
- **Follow through with the work provided.** If journaling is suggested by your therapist, then by all means, journal. It is in your best interest to complete your assignments so that you can enjoy the fruits of your labor.
- **Ask questions.** If you are involved in the participation of CBT the entire time, you will reap the most benefits. It is OK to question the process because your therapist is not going to shame, intimate, blame, or ignore you. Also, by asking questions, your treatment plan can be continuously revised to meet your needs.

Family therapy examines the dynamics of the dysfunctional family. Each member of the family learns how to acknowledge their patterns of dysfunction and works on improving their relationships. The goal of family therapy is to improve communication between members and to bring up difficult issues that have never been appropriately addressed. When and if one member of the family changes their behavior, it affects the whole system. Family therapy's goal is to lower the stress and provide conflict resolution by improving the interactions between members of the family. Family therapy doesn't necessarily mean only blood relatives, it can mean any system within which family-type dynamics occur. Rather than primarily focusing on the individual's role in the problem, family therapy identifies systems and patterns in the problems that need adjusting. Family therapy can be helpful for all involved on many different levels. Family therapy sessions facilitate the following:

- The development and skills to maintain healthy boundaries.
- Communication and family cohesion.
- Improve problem-solving skills by having a better understanding of the dynamics in the family.
- The ability to understand and build empathy.
- Conflict resolution with the family.

Some techniques use a *multi-family* therapeutic approach where an intensive focus is on the specific dynamics at work within a family. This strategy widens the perspectives of the family members and aids in the understanding of the treatment process. It also creates an empathetic and understanding community environment in which the family members can interact, provide constructive feedback, and process their experiences in a safe place with families who share similar concerns. The families essentially learn from each other. Being involved with a family member's treatment can very often feel like an isolative experience. It is common for the codependent's family members to feel overwhelmed, angry and scared. Though every individual's and their family's journey through treatment is unique, many of the experiences can overlap. This is why multi-family therapy sessions can help members know they are not alone. At first, the members of the family may feel uncomfortable and anxious sharing their difficulties, the codependent in treatment has already become family with group processing and may often take the lead in sharing first in the multi-family group setting. There is something very powerful in family members hearing similar experiences of other families struggling through the codependent-treatment process. Listening to one another in this type of group setting helps families learn about particular challenges other families are suffering, and can therefore, better accept the process. Multi-family sessions can assist in the development of understanding and compassion, by listening to other individuals who are struggling with codependency. When families have a chance to be a part of a greater group of individuals facing similar circumstances, challenges, and making similar efforts to change and grow, there is a propensity to leave feeling inspired and encouraged to continue.

SELF-EVALUATION

It is up to you to identify your needs, and then figure out a healthy way to have them met. It is far from reasonable to think that any single person is capable or wants to meet your every request. You are responsible for asking for what you need, as well as whether or not to respond to other people's requests. If you try to manipulate another person to be there for you, that is codependency rearing its ugly head. There is a big difference between asking and demanding something from a person. If someone is unwilling to be there, you need to change your expectations; do it for yourself. It is important to begin to let go of feeling that you have to rush through life, letting go of the constant urgency to win the rat race. A major problem about being part of the rat race is that you lose yourself because you're trying to become like everyone else. If you have to get up each morning and act out someone else's life, you are no longer in touch with yourself, and it feels awful. Living in 'your own skin', the way you choose to live, you will understand the meaning of self-pride. Getting out of the rat race means being unapologetically yourself and sharing your story, both the good and the bad. This way, you can connect to people on a different level by being yourself and not anxious about sharing your wrongdoings as well as the things you have done well. Only talking about your success stories is on the surface level. Going deeper and talking about the mistakes you have made, the tough times, and misjudgments is a cleansing process.

'Attitude' is a frequently overlooked secret of serenity. By choosing to maintain a healthy and positive attitude about everything in life, in the past, and in relationships, you can essentially control the quality of your recovery on a moment-by-moment basis. Of course, you cannot always control the situations life throws at you, but you can control your attitude about them. If you don't, life can become invariably out of control and messy. It is merely a matter of making a choice on how you will react to situations presented in life. Sometimes, a particular circumstance will come your way that is so toxic or painful that you will have to permanently leave the situation just to stay sane. If the source of the problem is too much to bear, you can leave, guilt-free, so you are practicing self-preservation. If you think you can realistically improve your situation to be healthier, that's fine, but if you keep trying to fix something that cannot or will not be fixed, in spite of your best attempt, that is when it becomes insanity. If you spend your time in negativity, thinking only about the future and the past, there is no room for the present. Think about what exists right now because it is the only reality. The past is gone, and no one knows what lies ahead. Your brain is so powerful that it has you sensing physical pain from a memory of your past. It is completely understandable for individuals to spend some amount of time thinking about the past and projecting about the future. Past experiences, whether good or bad, are a necessary survival tool. Without them, we cannot learn from our mistakes.

In order to soften your attitude toward yourself, it is important to go after the things you enjoy. By doing things you genuinely enjoy, you allow yourself the chance to experience your own pleasures and other people in an unconditional way. Create a baseline for your self-worth that you consciously cannot descend below. Feeling a sense of worth does not mean you are ego-centric or full of yourself. An ego-centric believes they are the best at everything whether it is true or not. Valuing yourself means you are going to try and do your best, but a single action does not define you. Try and be a role model to yourself with a new way of behaving. This will ease feelings of not being good enough for yourself and for those around you. We are a success-oriented society, but we are not a commodity, and we need a society that can tell the difference between the two and assists us in seeing that one person does not define another. By appreciating yourself and practicing self-care, you can create a positive change that has an outward ripple effect.

Everyone compares themselves to other people, and you can be sure that those who you think have everything surely do not. If you look at other people through the eyes of understanding and compassion rather than judgment and jealousy, you are better equipped to see them for who and what they are—humans, just like you. Always know there is more right with you than can ever be wrong with you. Many codependents zero in on their perceived flaws. It is helpful to note the positives about yourself and love the fact you are alive and able to take whichever paths you choose in life. Before you can achieve anything in the present, you must first rid yourself of the shame and guilt you feel about your past. Even if it is small, have something to look forward to. Similar to caring for yourself, having something to look forward to can be very rewarding. There is a ridiculous amount of pressure in this world to perform, which is very difficult in challenging times. But the mind and the body do find enjoyment in small things, such as your morning cup of coffee, taking the scenic route, and sleeping in. Tell yourself it's OK to enjoy the moment. The meaning you assign to events in your life impacts you more than you know. When it seems like all is doomed, your outlook decides your response. Make room for your new behaviors, if your old ones are no longer serving you. Try your best not to hold on to bad habits. When it seems like your life is falling apart, it is actually laying the groundwork for its reconstruction.

Take a page from Al-Anon's Twelve Steps and practice progress and not perfection. Striving for perfection leads only to feelings of worthlessness and self-pity. Realize that just by putting yourself on the right path is an accomplishment in itself. Instead of putting yourself down and falling down, pat yourself on the back for coming as far as you have and continuing to make progress. Telling yourself that you will only fail will not make you more successful. If you say to yourself that you are not living up to your full potential, it will not help you climb the ladder. Telling yourself you are not enough will not make you enough. It may sound almost easy, but the only road to achieving love for yourself is to love yourself, regardless of where you have been, where you stand, and even when you know you want to change. You are enough, and every time you tell that to yourself, loving yourself will become easier.

FINAL THOUGHTS

Codependency, if left untreated, gets worse. It can lead to severe depression, anxiety and potentially even suicidal tendencies. However, codependency is a condition that can be successfully treated with individual, group, and family therapy and by participation in twelve-step meetings. Usually, treatment protocols rely on a variety of therapy techniques. Client-centered therapy, as well as CBT, can be effective in treating codependency. Twelve-Step programs, such as Al-Anon Nar-Anon, and Codependents Anonymous, are beneficial to the successful treatment of codependency. Trauma therapy may also be advised for individuals who have experienced abandonment or abuse. If you have lost sight of your authentic self and question whether or not your relationships are healthy, remember there is help out there for you. If you are suffering from your own form of clinginess and feel trapped in a one-sided relationship, chances are you are codependent. Even though you're motivated by wishing the best for your loved ones, your do-good habits have become toxic to all involved. After reading this book, it is sincerely hoped that you know you have people and places to turn to in your darkest hours. When you learn to deeply value yourself and become less reactive to other people's opinions and do not take rejection personally, you become willing to lose another rather than lose yourself. The tools supplied in this reading will help you to turn self-loathing into self-love and to begin to take back control over your life and your decisions, to return to your authentic self. In fact, you've already taken the first step in gathering the information provided here to start your recovery journey.

When an individual is caught in the trap of codependency, they believe their own needs are not important. Even though the codependent often looks like the 'healthier' of the two partners, they struggle with their issues that cause them to believe they are less important than the other. Their insatiable need for approval trumps all other needs. By continuously diminishing their own wants, needs, and feelings, and looking to someone else for validation, the result is an unhealthy relationship for both. All in all, being codependent is not good for anyone involved, despite the false acts of gratitude they may receive for being so skilled in giving. Recovery from codependency takes deep self-examination and thinking things through, rather than simply acting upon an impulse to rescue. Recovery is about no longer taking everything in life so seriously; it is about learning how to love, live, laugh, and about having fun on your journey. You can find something that you enjoy doing, that is healthy, and do it for the sheer pleasure you receive.

There will always be times when giving feels like the right thing to do, and yet, there are times when that very same action is codependent. In order to distinguish between the two, an individual must be able to delve into their inner wisdom. If unable to reach inside for solutions, asking for help is imperative. Twelve-step meetings, therapy, sponsorship and researching the Internet are all excellent ways to approach the matter. Taking the time to think about your feelings and needs, and how to best address them each day, is a helpful tip for the codependent. Always remind yourself that you have a choice and the power to say "No", even when it is very hard to do so. Practice pausing before answering "yes" to anything asked of you. There is nothing wrong with saying, "I have to think it over and get back to you". Then, examine the action you may take in the situation if you were not afraid or felt obligated. Use spiritual exercises, such as journaling, nature walks, meditation and quiet contemplation to tap into your inner wisdom. Do your best to tolerate another person having a bad day or unhappy feelings without you being there to fix them.

Those who suffer from codependency can receive the help they need from many of the aforementioned resources. Twelve-step programs, such as Al-Anon, CoDA, Nar-Anon, and other non-professional fellowships, offer no precise diagnostic criteria or definition for codependency. They do freely share from their own experiences the characteristic traits and behaviors that describe their own histories of the struggles they face and have faced with codependency. Twelve-step recovery begins with self-honesty about their inability to maintain healthy relationships with themselves and with others. Finding the cause for much of their grief lies in longstanding destructive behavior patterns.

Being codependent is an emotional and a mental problem that affects the interactions and connections made with others in an interpersonal relationship. It creates major difficulties and creates great discomfort with themselves, resulting in unfulfilling and often abusive circumstances. Hopefully, by reading this book, you will be more likely to verbalize your true feelings and not be afraid that it will upset someone or hurt them in any way. Otherwise, you end up bottling up your feelings, and then they come out in the form of an illness or rage. By reading this book, you have learned:

- What codependency is and isn't.
- The history of codependency and how it has evolved over time.
- What a healthy, balanced relationship looks like compared to a toxic, codependent one.
- To understand why you act the way you do, and the possible causes of codependent tendencies.
- How to recover from being codependent and focus on your own life again.
- Different options for recovery and how to use counseling, treatment and group settings most effectively in your life.
- How to self-assess your behavior in relationships and reflect on what caused you to become this way.
- The steps to recovering from being codependent.
- How to say "No" and set boundaries with the people in your life without feeling guilty.
- The importance of getting a sponsor or professional therapist.

SOURCES

American Psychiatric Association. Diagnostic and Statistical Manual of Mental Health Disorders. American Psychiatric Association. 2013.

Bacon, I., McKay, E., Reynolds, F. et al. The Lived Experience of Codependency: An Interpretative Phenomenological Analysis. Int J Ment Health Addiction 18, 754–771 (2020). https://doi.org/10.1007/s11469-018-9983-8

Bandura, A. "Social Learning Theory". Englewood Cliffs, NJ: Prentice Hall. 1977

Barnett, J.E., Baker, E.K., Elman, N.S., & Schoener, G.R. "In pursuit of wellness: The self-care imperative". Professional Psychology-Research and Practice, 38(6), 603-612, 2007.

Beattie, Melody. "Codependent No More: How to Stop Controlling Others and Start Caring for Yourself". (Center City, MN): Hazelden, 1992.

Belyea, D. "The Effect Of An Educational Intervention on the Level Of Codependency Among Graduate Counseling Students". Wayne State University Dissertations. 2011. https://digitalcommons.wayne.edu/cgi/viewcontent.cgi?article=1208&context=oa_dissertations

Cherry, K. "Taking the Steps to Forgive Yourself". Very well mind, 2020. https://www.verywellmind.com/how-to-forgive-yourself-4583819

Codependents Anonymous Inc. "Recovery from Codependence". Codependents Anonymous Inc. 2013. www.coda.org

Cleveland Clinic. "Dependent Personality Disorder". Cleveland Clinic. 2014. http://my.clevelandclinic.org/neurological_institute/center-for-behavorial-health/diseaseconditions/hic-dependent-personality-disorder.aspx

Field, M. "My Day Depends on Me: How to rewrite your life narrative". Balboa Press, 2019.

Friel, J.C. "Codependency assessment inventory: A preliminary research tool". Focus on the Family and Chemical Dependency, 8(1), 20-21. 1985. https://doi.org/10.1016/S0899-3289(10)80005-7

Johnson, R.S. "Codependency and Codependent Relationships". BPDFamily.com. (2014).

Hinkin, C. & Kahn, M. "Psychological Symptomatology in Spouses and Adult Children of Alcoholics: an examination of the hypothesized personality characteristics of codependency". Int J Addict. 1995 May; 30(7):843-61. doi: 10.3109/10826089509067010. PMID: 7558473.

Lancer, D. "Shame: The Core of Addiction and Codependency" Psychology Today, 2019. https://psychcentral.com/lib/shame-the-core-of-addiction-and-codependency/

LePera, N. "How to Tell the Difference Between Empathy & Codependency" mbgMindfullness (2019). https://www.mindbodygreen.com/articles/difference-between-empathy-and-codependent-behavior-for-hsps

Lindley, N. R., Giordano, P.J., Hammer, E. D. Codependency: Predictors and psychometric issues. Journal of Clinical Psychology, 55, 59-64. 1999. https://doi.org/10.1002/(SICI)1097-4679(199901)55:1<59::AID-JCLP5>3.0.CO;2-M

Livingston, A., Hall, C. & Ross, G. "An Exploratory Assessment of Codependency in Student-Athletes". Athens Journal of Sports - Volume 3, Issue 3– Pages. 2020 207-224https://doi.org/10.30958/ajspo.3-3-4.

Loverde, M. "What Is Codependent Personality Disorder?" Family Intervention (2019). https://family-intervention.com/blog/what-is-codependent-personality-disorder/

Prest, L.A., Benson, M.J., Protinsky, H.O. "Family of Origin and Current Relationship Influences on Codependency". Family process. (1998) [Pubmed]DOI: 10.1111/j.1545-5300.1998.00513.x

Jenner, N. " Controlling Codependency: Keeping Others In Line". Dr. Nicholas Jenner (2019). https://theonlinetherapist.blog/controlling-codependency-keeping-others-in-line/

Rosenberg, R. "The Human Magnet Syndrome: Why we love people who hurt us." Morgan James Publishing (2013).

Staff, H. (2008, December 7). Letting Go of Perfectionism, HealthyPlace. Retrieved on 2020, December 19 from https://www.healthyplace.com/relationships/serendipity/letting-go-of-perfectionism

Sarkar, S., Mattoo, S. K., Basu, D., & Gupta, J. "Codependence in spouses of alcohol and opioid dependent men". International Journal of Culture and Mental Health, 8(1), 13–21, 2015. https://www.tandfonline.com/doi/abs/10.1080/17542863.2013.868502

W., Bill. Alcoholics Anonymous: The Story of How Many Thousands of Men and Women Have Recovered from Alcoholism. New York: Alcoholics Anonymous World Services, 1976.

SUGGESTED RECOMMENDATIONS

Please note: Your tallied results from this questionnaire cannot be considered as any type of diagnosis and, therefore, should not be understood as such. They merely indicate the potential need to investigate codependency further. The tallying system was based on a review of the literature, and points were assigned to symptomology most often reported as problematic signs of codependency.

Score: Below 6

If your score was below 6, you most likely know how to set your boundaries and may just be very sensitive and empathetic of others.

Score: Between 6 and 11

You may be ruminating about other peoples' opinions of you. Boundaries are sometimes difficult to establish. Your self-worth is not where it should be. You see yourself as a rescuer as a positive characteristic, even when it is not.

Score: Between 11 and 20

Your self-esteem is low. Codependency is flaunting itself in many areas of your life. You most likely are struggling with anxiety and approval seeking. With this score, it is recommended that you gather more information regarding codependency, including attending an Al-Anon or CoDA meeting and/or talking to a professional.

Score: Between 11 and 18

If you scored between 11 and 18, you definitely face challenges with feeling invisible, low self-esteem, and are with codependency issues most likely in many areas of your life. You may suffer from anxiety, rumination, and an ongoing need to gain approval from outside of yourself. In spite of being overly empathetic to the needs of other people, there is a good possibility you feel continually let down by others in your life. You may be someone who absolutely believes is doing everything right, but yet, no matter how hard you try, you never feel good enough for yourself or for others. Shame, guilt and self-doubt may be a constant in your life. You are someone who will benefit greatly from learning about how to heal from the patterns that were created when you were a young, powerless child.

RECOVERY FROM COMPLEX PTSD

FROM TRAUMA TO REGAINING SELF THROUGH MINDFULNESS & EMOTIONAL REGULATION EXERCISES

INTRODUCTION

Is your daily life impacted by previous traumatic experiences? Post-Traumatic Stress Disorder (PTSD) is more common than many people believe, with an estimated 3.5% of the population, or approximately eight million Americans, suffering from it (Hull, 2020).[1] Researchers discovered a particularly severe form, known as Complex PTSD, with even more serious consequences.

Do you have difficulty developing and maintaining solid relationships with other people? You may find it very hard to trust anyone other than yourself and to be intimate with them. These interpersonal problems have also very likely affected your sense of self-esteem, which makes you feel worthless or "less-than" the people around you. You're experiencing flashbacks to your painful past and getting trapped in negative thought loops.

Struggling to function in daily life can be incredibly frustrating, especially when others around you seem to be handling the ups and downs just fine. It's not because you are unworthy, or not as smart as other people, or because you lack some kind of ability that everyone else seems to have. Your troubles are due to the traumatic events in your past and the way that the human mind evolved to cope with issues like these.

You may already have begun to learn about PTSD if you're aware of the trauma that's impacted your ability to function. Complex PTSD is less known to most people, so you might or might not have run across it in your reading. It's usually the result of traumatic events such as sexual or physical abuse in childhood, domestic abuse, or living in chaotic environments or as a refugee. You're probably not sure where to start healing, or even if it's possible.

Although you might not have anyone close to you who is suffering due to a similar situation, there are others who are. You're not alone in your pain. Fortunately, researchers now know a lot about PTSD and Complex PTSD, and better yet, how to treat them. In this book you'll learn about your condition and what you can do to unwind these pathways in your brain.

You'll understand why you have the physical, emotional, and mental symptoms that have been plaguing you. There are exercises and suggestions to help you regain control over your life, so that you can start moving forward instead of being held back by frightening memories.

The first chapter is dedicated to what PTSD really is, and the difference between it and Complex PTSD. You'll learn a little about the history of the term and how the medical field treats these diseases. They lead to a number of other conditions if left untreated, and you'll learn what those are as well. As you discover more about the typical ways in which Complex PTSD manifests in your body and mind, you'll realize how much earlier events have affected your development.

Then you'll learn about how people get Complex PTSD and how it develops. It's true that two people can experience the same traumatic event and one may end up with a disorder and the other won't. It's not because the one who is ill is weak or mentally disturbed, but rather some brain wiring that isn't working properly.

Those who develop a traumatic disorder experience what's known as the "trauma loop" which begins with the experience and activates the "fight-or-flight" reactions in the brain. But with the disorder, the brain doesn't come out of the defensive reaction and continues to loop through the memories and defenses.

Next, you'll learn about the symptoms of PTSD. Though trauma disorders are primarily located in the brain, many if not most people also suffer physically. You may find that some of your illnesses or bodily aches are actually manifestations of your trauma, and not due to some other cause.

The difference between PTSD and Complex PTSD is mainly the inability to regulate or control your emotions. This is known as *affect dysregulation*, and you'll understand how it impacts your life. Typically, it appears in one of two forms. Either you're under-regulated, which often shows up as a lack of impulse control, or you're over-regulated and shut down feelings or reject them outright. If you don't clearly remember the trauma that happened when you were young, dysregulation is probably a factor.

In addition to emotional difficulties, you likely have a negative concept of yourself as a person as a result of your experiences. You have self-destructive thoughts that up until now you haven't been able to reframe, which leaves you with low self-esteem and feelings of guilt and shame. You'll find out where these concepts come from, and more importantly, how to deal with them in a constructive way so that you can begin thinking more positively.

You'll further discover why you've had so much difficulty in relationships. It's very common for those with Complex PTSD to lack fulfilling and intimate bonds with other people, whether romantic or platonic. Since most people need these connections for happiness and even survival, it's vital that you learn how to establish trust with others so that you can eventually develop these bonds. In chapter six you'll find some methods for opening up and moving forward.

Finally, you'll discover what recovery means and looks like for trauma survivors. There are more suggestions for tactics you can use to heal and avoid the trauma loop. You'll be able to improve your ability to assess the situation objectively and find the facts, which will help you take your anxiety out of the equation and let your logical brain take over. This allows your brain to exit its fight-or-flight mode.

At this point, you might be wondering if I'm an expert on the subject of healing from trauma, and why you should trust what I have to say. I am the survivor of a traumatic upbringing, with an abusive and manipulative parent. I spent years suffering from anxiety, mood swings, panic attacks, and all the other issues you've probably experienced as well.

Fortunately for me, I was able to recognize that my symptoms were the result of PTSD and I began to research the subject. Through my study, I was able to develop healing and coping strategies that helped me leave the trauma loop behind. What I learned made such a huge difference in my life that I wanted to share it with others who are going through their own traumatic journey.

I love helping others identify and recover from relationship and behavior patterns that are toxic and unbalanced, just as I have. In fact, everything you're about to discover about achieving a sense of freedom and self-worth is based on my own journey of overcoming PTSD and finding peace.

Because I'm so excited to be able to help you move forward, I want to encourage you to get started right away. The longer you put off reading the rest of the book, the longer you'll feel frustrated by daily occurrences that other people seem to be automatically able to deal with. You'll delay your understanding of how you got here and how you can escape your painful present. By starting right away instead, you'll overcome your difficulties that much sooner. You'll be able to form strong bonds and a support system that's there for you when you need it. So, let's get to it!

"You can't patch a wounded soul with a Band-Aid."

— MICHAEL CONNELLY

1

WHAT IS COMPLEX TRAUMA?

The word "trauma" is used a lot in popular culture. It sometimes refers to a type of hospital care, and sometimes it's used to describe an ordeal. However, Post-Traumatic Stress Disorder is a specific diagnosis with a specific meaning of the word "trauma." Complex PTSD is a very particular type of condition and comes with its own symptoms and results. Understanding what trauma really is and how Complex PTSD is separate from PTSD will help you view your condition from the proper perspective.

WHAT IS TRAUMA?

The standard dictionary definition is "an experience that produces psychological injury or pain."[1] However, by this benchmark, even relatively small incidents such as being ignored by someone you thought was your friend, or having a romantic partner decide to walk away, could be considered trauma!

For the purposes of this book and the diagnosis of PTSD, instead I'll use the more specific claim of a semi-permanent change in the person's nervous system due to a psychological or physical injury or event. In other words, the effect of the trauma incident is strong enough to actually alter the person's body, not just cause a brief pang of sadness or despair.

Many trauma events occur once and their duration is a short period of time, such as having a car accident, being mugged, or the death of a loved one. Other traumatic events that many people go through include:

- Divorce
- Losing a job
- Family/parental abandonment
- Abuse
- Assault
- Childbirth/surgery complications
- Incarceration
- Witnessing a crime, death, or other accident
- Other violence.

Almost everyone will experience one of these at least once in their lives, but not all who have suffered such an event will go on to develop any form of PTSD. Later in the book you'll learn more about the factors that may increase your likelihood of developing PTSD or

Complex PTSD. They include repeated or ongoing trauma, such as domestic abuse.

The human body and mind go through a certain natural process after a traumatic ordeal, and some of these reactions are similar to PTSD. In fact, the disorder has to be diagnosed after a period of thirty days following the event because the symptoms are so similar. For people who don't go on to develop PTSD, these natural reactions decrease over time until they're back to baseline as they were before the event.

Always on guard (hypervigilance)

Your mind is trying to protect you from experiencing another trauma, so it's especially aware of potential dangers and threats in your environment. This feels very strange for many people who have never been particularly concerned or aware of the perils around them, but it doesn't mean you're going crazy. It's just a natural consequence of going through an ordeal.

The hypervigilance doesn't have to be related to the actual event. For example, suppose you've recently gone through a divorce. You might be walking down a sidewalk at dusk, as you've done many times before, but you hear footsteps behind you and start to panic that someone's after you. Your brain is more sensitive to any kind of threat after a traumatic event, even things that never previously bothered you.

Unwanted thoughts or memories of the event

Typically, these are triggered by something that reminds you of the event. It can be anything: a person, a smell, a noise, a place, etc. These can occur as flashbacks or any other kind of memory. Again, this isn't a sign that you're going crazy or that anything is wrong with you. It's a response that happens because of the way our brains are wired (more about that in the next chapter!)

If you were in a car accident where you were hit by a white SUV, for example, you might have flashbacks every time you see a white SUV on the road. Or if you had a pine air freshener in your car, that scent could trigger a memory, whether you're in someone else's car or in a store that has pine-scented candles. If you had a passenger in your car, the subsequent sight of that person might trigger an intrusive memory.

It's not possible to know ahead of time what the trigger will be, but when the memories come up, recognize that they're related to the trauma itself.

Being on edge (hyperarousal)

You'll feel keyed up after an ordeal because your brain is preparing you to take action. Threats seem like they're everywhere, because when you're in this state of hyperarousal you're better able to react to danger. The hormones and physical reactions that accompany this state are perfectly fine when they occur from time to time or dissipate after a period of time. It's only when they're chronic that they can do long-lasting damage to your system.

Just as with hypervigilance, you're on edge about things that may or may not relate directly to the event that you endured. After a divorce, for example, you might be on edge every time you walk down the sidewalk that you previously never thought about. Or if you're in a grocery store and someone gets too close to you, your body might start the fight-or-flight reaction process.

Feeling endangered

Traumatic events leave you feeling unsafe. It may have been a physical event such as an assault or a car accident. Or it could be something like a death or divorce that leaves you feeling unsafe emotionally, because a part of your identity has just been taken away. Before the event, the world probably seemed like a reasonably safe and secure place, but now that illusion has been destroyed.

Many people feel that no place is safe after such an event, and so almost any location or situation seems dangerous. Even if you previously felt fine there, it now may fill you with anxiety or appear threatening to you. It's particularly common in places that remind you of the ordeal you went through.

For example, if you were assaulted in a park behind some trees, you may no longer feel safe in a forest or park where you don't have a clear view of your surroundings. Or you might not feel safe in a small grocery store where the space is tight, and you can't see over the shelves to scan for threats.

POST-TRAUMATIC STRESS DISORDER (PTSD)

While the symptoms in the last section are typical for anyone who's experienced trauma, there are additional factors that lead to a diagnosis of PTSD. These reactions are typically more extreme for those with PTSD, compared to the people who will find their symptoms decreasing over time and eventually returning to their "normal" state of being.

People who are likely to develop PTSD may find themselves with three additional behaviors on top of the reactions noted above.[2] Anyone who's experienced a trauma should be on the lookout for overdoing them to ensure that they reach out for help.

Avoidance

While it's pretty natural to avoid anything that reminds you of your ordeal, you can cross the line into avoiding anything and everything. That's what is likely to result in the disorder.

For example, someone who's experienced a mugging in a dark alley will avoid dark alleys for some time after the event. This is a normal reaction. Avoidance becomes a problem when the person starts avoiding any places where dark alleys exist, such as an entire town or city. Or won't go anywhere in the dark.

Once you get started on avoidance, you may find that you start avoiding more and more until you end up isolating yourself. It's one thing when a specific part of the world is dangerous and you avoid it, and something else when the entire world is dangerous, and you must avoid it.

Loss of interest

It's normal to feel a little reluctant to try new things in the aftermath of a traumatic event. The unknown is a little scary anyway, even before you've endured an ordeal. It's a problem when you don't want to do the things that you previously enjoyed.

If you're a dog owner who enjoys taking your dog on walks or to the dog park, no longer wanting to do that is a sign of depression. Or you might no longer want to hang out with your friends at a favorite cafe. Being detached from your interests in activities and people can also cause you to isolate. Then you'll lose the social support that you need after a trying time, which can lead to an eventual PTSD diagnosis.

Unhealthy coping strategies

These typically go along with avoidance. You don't want to have those intrusive memories anymore, or feel like you're in danger all the time. You may end up trying to numb yourself with substances, or other unhealthy behavior like shopping too much or gambling.

These behaviors might make you feel okay or numb for a short period of time, but of course after a while the effects wear off and you need to numb again. That's how these types of things can easily spiral into addiction.

They also don't help you solve your problem or heal yourself, so it's very easy to end up with PTSD when you can't curb your habits. Instead of diminishing over time, the reactions and thoughts that you're trying to avoid using substances or shopping actually grow stronger over time, not weaker.

Those who are diagnosed with PTSD may end up with some additional conditions as well. One study found that those with PTSD were eight times more likely to have three or more other diagnosed disorders during their lifetime, such as substance abuse, mood disorders like major depression or anxiety, and personality conditions like borderline personality disorder.[3] These are known as comorbid conditions.

There are specific criteria for diagnosing the existence of PTSD. The World Health Organization (WHO)/International Classification of Diseases (ICD) states that the disorder has developed when the person is having difficulties with functioning in daily life in terms of school, work, in the social sphere, or at home and has at least one of the following three responses.[4] Note that if the person is still able to function, or experiences only one or two of the following symptoms, the diagnosis of PTSD is not warranted.

1. Re-experiencing

Memories or thoughts of the trauma continue to occur. This can be through repeated nightmares related to the event, flashbacks, or unwanted memories in conjunction with feelings of severe fear or horror. While the occasional flashback or nightmare is common, those with PTSD can't seem to get rid of them.

2. Avoidance

Deliberately avoiding any kind of thought, memory, feeling, situation, or activity related to the event is also a symptom of PTSD. While common in the month following an ordeal for anyone, someone with the disorder does their best to pretend that nothing happened and to avoid anything that might remind them of the event for a longer period of time.

Keeping yourself too busy or preoccupied to think about what happened is another way of avoiding the trauma. It also can lead to blocking out parts of the event, or even the entire thing.

3. Hyperarousal

Being jumpy, easily startled, or excessively vigilant when it comes to threats for longer than a month after the event is also a part of the PTSD diagnosis.

This can interfere with sleep and concentration because any little thing can wake a PTSD sufferer up or distract them from their task. They may also be more irritable than usual as a consequence of constantly being jittery or on edge.

In the United States, the fundamental handbook for psychiatric disorders is the Diagnostic and Statistical Manual of Mental Disorders, known as the DSM. It's periodically updated and currently we're on version V, so you might have seen the DSM-V referenced in your research. The DSM-V largely agrees with WHO/ICD on the symptoms that lead to a diagnosis of PTSD, but they do differ slightly when it comes to Complex PTSD.

COMPLEX PTSD AND DIAGNOSIS

The idea of Complex PTSD, or C-PTSD, is more recent than PTSD itself. In 1988 Dr. Judith Herman of Harvard University suggested that a different diagnosis was necessary for repeated or ongoing trauma, which can cause more severe psychological harm than the single occurrence types of events that typically lead to PTSD. Trauma that occurs over a longer period of time or repeats itself is known as *complex*, and experiencing complex trauma is more likely to result in C-PTSD.

You'll learn more about these situations and their harm in a later chapter. However, the following are some examples of ordeals that may cause even more psychological damage.

- Domestic violence or abuse
- Human trafficking
- Neglect during childhood
- Extremely chaotic and/or violent environments, such as a living in a nation at war
- Being a refugee.

Originally, the exploration of C-PTSD was mainly on childhood trauma, particularly sexual abuse. Yet as research continued, it became clear that the duration of the ordeal, or how long it was endured, is a better predictor of C-PTSD compared to the nature of the trauma (e.g., childhood abuse.) When the trauma continues for a longer period of time, the survivor is under chronically high levels of stress and remains anxious and captive, either emotionally or physically. This set of factors results in the more severe harm experienced by those with complex trauma.

In the DSM-V, C-PTSD is not considered its own separate diagnosis, but is grouped under Disorders of Extreme Stress, Not Otherwise Specified (DESNOS). There are a variety of symptoms that fall under the DESNOS criteria after a traumatic event.

Difficulty regulating emotions or impulses

Being able to adapt emotions to the situation you're in is key for emotional regulation and an important factor in being emotionally intelligent. People who are traumatized are often unable to adjust to their current circumstances and express their emotions in a positive way.

Having issues with impulse control can show up in a number of ways. You might find yourself having unusual amounts of angry outbursts, taking too many risks, or being sexually promiscuous. Or you might end up directing these impulses inward and engaging in self-destructive behavior or becoming preoccupied with suicidal thoughts.

Before the event, you may have had a high EQ (emotional intelligence) and been able to regulate your emotions appropriately. The aftermath of your experience has badly affected your EQ. Or you may have had difficulties prior to your trauma as well, which have become worse as a consequence.

Changes in consciousness and focus

The typical response here is amnesia or having entire blocks of time wiped from your memory (even if only temporarily). It tends to come on suddenly, and it can last a few brief minutes or for months.

Or you may feel disconnected from your own body, your emotions, or the world around you. This symptom is also associated with feeling like you've lost your identity or sense of self, or you're confused about who you are. It's known as transient dissociative episodes or depersonalization.

In order to be diagnosed with DESNOS you'll experience at least one of these alterations.

Self-perception issues

Most people have some issues with how they perceive themselves from time to time, and this is not a disorder but a feature of life. For example, someone who's just been broken up with might feel unworthy or ineffective. For someone without a disorder, these feelings go away in a relatively short period of time.

In contrast, those with a DESNOS diagnosis have poor perceptions of themselves most of the time, which prevents them from living a so-called "normal" life. They feel ineffective or that they're permanently psychologically damaged. There is usually guilt and shame, especially around the traumatic event.

They don't think anyone else is going through what they've gone through and won't understand. This type of thinking, while common in C-PTSD, makes them more isolated and less likely to reach out for the help that they need. At least two of these issues with self-perception, as described above, must be present for the diagnosis.

Difficulty relating to other people

There are a variety of ways in which this difficulty manifests in C-PTSD sufferers, and at least one must be active to be diagnosed. One of the symptoms is the inability to trust other people.

Human beings are naturally social animals, even the introverts. You'll learn a bit more about that later in the book. Since we are social animals, we depend on the bonds we have with other humans to be healthy. Those connections can only be established with mutual trust and respect. Therefore, someone who has lost the ability to trust as a result of their disorder is cut adrift from what can help keep them healthy.

Another response is known as *re-victimization*. This is what happens when the C-PTSD sufferer continues to be a victim, or repeatedly endures victimization after the first trauma. Although popular culture often places the blame squarely on the victim, the extreme distress caused by the original trauma results in defense mechanisms that don't work as intended and leave them open to further harm.

Research shows that the best predictor of future trauma is a history of previous trauma. Children who are abused often grow up to be revictimized as a teen and/or later in adulthood (Fadelici, 2020.)[5]

Guilt over the ordeal often makes people pay attention only to their own thoughts and feelings, which causes them to ignore red flags or threats from others in their environment. Shame often results in isolation, which increases the likelihood of being vulnerable in a way that ends in re-victimization.

The other side of the coin is that the sufferer victimizes others, instead of being re-victimized. This helps them retain a sense of control over their own lives.

Physical symptoms

Although many people often think of mind and body as being two separate entities, in reality these two are very tightly connected. The brain sends signals to the body, but the body also provides feedback to the brain. Those who have C-PTSD often experience *somatization*, or the appearance of physical reactions to their trauma.

Did you know that you have neurons (nerve cells) in your gut? That's part of the reason the disorder may show up in the digestive system with pain or another condition. Additional reactions include chronic pain, cardiovascular symptoms like high blood pressure and inflammation, and sexual ones such as loss of sex drive.

The diagnosis of DESNOS requires the patient to have at least two of the physical symptoms, or somatization.

Changes in understanding the meaning of life

At least one of these reactions is necessary as DESNOS criteria. Some people have an overwhelming feeling of despair or hopelessness. They cannot even imagine a world in which hope exists, or that they themselves are able to heal. It seems like all their symptoms whether physical, mental, or emotional will never go away or dissipate in intensity and there's nothing to live for.

Another way that this reaction shows up is in a complete loss of faith or other sustaining beliefs. After a difficult event, many people may undergo a temporary loss of faith or anger towards a deity or spiritual ideal. But those with C-PTSD have a chronic loss of belief and can't see how they would ever make it back to their previous spiritual or foundational practice.

Unlike in the DSM-V, C-PTSD is recognized as its own disorder by the WHO/ICD. In addition to the three criteria for PTSD of re-experience, avoidance, and heightened threat awareness, C-PTSD sufferers also experience all three of the following:

1. Inability to manage or control the duration or intensity of "negative" emotions such as anger, fear, and sadness (known as affect dysregulation)
2. Negative concept of themselves
3. Inability to trust others.

You can see that these overlap with the DESNOS diagnosis. Ultimately, identifying many psychological or mental conditions is not an exact science, whether you're using WHO/ICD or DSM-V criteria. However, it's clear what kinds of issues accompany the aftermath of trauma and result in PTSD or C-PTSD. If these symptoms and reactions are preventing you from functioning in your daily life, you'll need to learn to heal from and cope with your ordeal. Fortunately, research has shown us the way to recovery.

CHAPTER SUMMARY

The human body and brain produce certain reactions to traumatic events that are common for everyone who experiences a car crash, death of a loved one, etc. Those with trauma who are unable to return to baseline may be diagnosed with PTSD, and those whose ordeals last for a long time or repeat are at risk for C-PTSD.

- Trauma causes changes to a person's nervous system, and

may be the result of a divorce, abuse, and other events including witnessing a crime or accident.
- Common symptoms of trauma include being very aware of threats, hypersensitivity to the environment, intrusive memories and thoughts of the event, and feeling unsafe.
- The common symptoms may dissipate over a month or so, as they do for many survivors, or they may intensify and interfere with daily life, in which case a Post-Traumatic Stress Disorder diagnosis is often warranted.
- PTSD is accompanied by other symptoms as well, and generally is a consequence of a trauma that occurs once and for a finite period of time, such as a car accident or assault.
- Longer-term or repeated traumas may develop instead into C-PTSD, which can be more severe and has additional symptoms.

In the next chapter you will learn how and where C-PTSD comes from.

2

WHERE DOES C-PTSD COME FROM?

It's important for anyone experiencing C-PTSD to understand what's going on in their brain and body, which is helpful in the process of healing from the trauma. These symptoms are a consequence of how the human brain evolved and how it works in some people. Even up until the last century, scientists believed that the brain couldn't generate new nerve cells (neurons). Fortunately, we've since discovered that's not true. Which is great news because it means that you can potentially make changes to your brain to make recovery possible!

If you think of yourself as a car—especially a newer model that has an electric or partially electric engine and technologies such as parallel parking assist or drift warnings—your brain is the engine, and the rest of the car is your body. Let's pop open the hood and take a good look at the engine and how it works.

HOW THE HUMAN BRAIN EVOLVED

You might remember (or not) from your school science class that humans, Homo Sapiens, evolved on the African savannah. At the time, humans had to defend against predators that might kill us, and also had to find ways to feed ourselves. Those who did so the best were the ones that survived to pass their genes onto the next generation, so those of us here now are the descendants of the humans that best adapted to their environment.

Due to the way that we evolved and survived as a species, our minds and bodies were shaped by the environment. Just a reminder, again from science class, that evolution happens over many generations, not just one or two. A generation for Homo Sapiens is about twenty years. Therefore, a century is only about five generations. The surroundings in which most people now live began with the Industrial Revolution, which was in the 1700s. So, we've really only lived this way for three hundred years, roughly fifteen generations, and the recent technology explosion is only a generation or two ago.

The consequence of this is that the human brain evolved to fight off predators on the African savannah, and we're using them in an environment where we have no predators (except maybe each other!) and we have a very different life from our ancestors. We're constantly on the go, checking our technology, working long hours because we're not tethered to daylight anymore, and consuming whatever we want. We don't have to hunt down our food, and calories are plentiful.

But that's not what the human brain adapted for. We survived in small groups of about 150 people or so, because bringing down large predators is a pack activity. Not something one person can do on their own. Back then we didn't have supermarkets and didn't know where the next meal would come from. The human brain thus evolved to finding sweet, fatty, and salty tastes very pleasing, because that meant we'd be able to get enough calories.

Also, as a result of not knowing where the next meal is coming from, the human brain likes to conserve energy as much as possible. That way you're not out there burning too many calories and starving to death when you might not eat again for many days. Obviously, this has led to some physical health issues for modern people, particularly in the developed world where calories are plentiful, but there are also repercussions for the modern brain as well.

Because the human brain is basically still back in the savannah, it treats all threats as the same. It can't tell the difference between a life-threatening situation and one that is scary but probably won't kill you. If you are afraid that you're going to be fired, for example, your brain thinks you're about to get eaten by a tiger and makes adjustments accordingly. Unfortunately, the survival instincts that worked very well on the savannah don't work so well in the modern world.

There are a number of ways that the brain can get things wrong, including systematic errors in thinking known as *cognitive bias*. These errors are baked into the brain as a result of how we evolved. In other words, it doesn't matter how intelligent you are, your brain automatically makes these mistakes.

For example, one bias is known as recency bias, where you weigh what happened recently more heavily than something that occurred further back in time. Suppose you've had depression before and were able to function with it through medication, or therapy, or both. Once it was successful, you might have dropped the therapy and been fine for a while. But recently you became depressed again, as commonly happens. But you'll think about your current depression more and not the previous time when you recovered from it, because the depression is what happened lately.

Another bias is to remember the negative more than the positive. You can see how that would have benefited ancient people, so they remembered what happened after they ate the wrong berry and wouldn't eat it again. Or avoid the place with all the hissing snakes in it. You can also see how that would make life more difficult for people who have a tendency toward depression or anxiety in the first place.

HOW THE BRAIN WORKS

All animal brains in the most basic sense work in the same way, through sending electrical or chemical signals that "tell" various organs or systems what to do. There are a lot of different sections in the brain responsible for a variety of things, most of which you're not aware of because they happen at the unconscious or subconscious level. (I'll be using these terms pretty much interchangeably.)

When it comes to survival, one of the key structures is the *amygdala*. It's a little almond-shaped part of the brain responsible for motivation and emotions, specifically fear. The amygdala is a part of the *limbic system* in your brain that deals with emotions and memories. (Some people refer to the limbic system as part of the "mammalian brain" which is more advanced than the lizard but not a thinking organ.)

If you're scared or feel threatened, the amygdala is on it. Sensory data can bypass your thinking structures and arrive directly at the amygdala for a faster response. This little area of the brain is responsible for the fight-or-flight reflex (sometimes also known as the fight-freeze-flight reflex.) When you're threatened and fearful, the amygdala helps prepare your body to escape (or kill) a predator. Remember, the brain is still back in the savannah and thinks fear means death is imminent.

There are a number of things that the brain does to get the body ready. The *sympathetic nervous system* in your brain and body is activated, causing hormones like cortisol and adrenaline to be released. This results in a faster heart rate, blood pressure, and breathing rate. Because you might have to sprint away from the predator that's threatening you. Blood is sent to your muscles, legs, and arms. Your focus tightens so you're paying more attention to the threat than to other things that may be going on around you.

Once this stress response has been activated, it normally takes 20 minutes to an hour to return to baseline, if it's functioning normally (Cherry, 2019).[1] Note that none of this is consciously controlled by you as it all happens automatically. Researchers now know that while the occasional stress response is perfectly fine for you (and can even help you do well in high-stress situations like a presentation or a race), chronically elevated stress hormones are dangerous to your health.

We share this structure with animal ancestors, as well as other parts of the brain that operate unconsciously, such as the regulation of body temperature, breathing rate, repair of cells while you sleep, and so forth. You might have heard of the "reptilian" or "lizard" brain, which is what all of these things are contained in. In his book *Thinking Fast and Slow*, the psychologist and economist Daniel Kahneman refers to the lizard brain as System 1.

Most of System 1 occurs subconsciously. Tasks are carried out without your conscious knowledge, including the generation of emotions, formation of memories, and reflex reactions. System 1 is fast. It works on rules of thumb (heuristics) so the brain can make quick decisions.

Very important when you're on the savannah and you see some grass waving. Your brain will guess that it's a tiger ready to eat you and prepare you accordingly. If it turns out that it was just the wind, that's fine. You survived either way, and in ancient times the stress response didn't have much of a downside. After you escaped, everything would settle down.

What your brain doesn't want is for you to stand around trying to figure out what you should do. The likelihood is that you'd die (when faced with a hungry predator) and your brain would really prefer you to survive, thank you very much. It doesn't want you to try to make long lists of pros and cons of what would happen if the grass is or is not hiding a tiger, or consider the advantages and disadvantages of fleeing.

Those kinds of reasoning decisions are made with System 2, which includes the human part of the brain that people use for logic, thinking, and reasoning. It is much slower than System 1—agonizingly slow when you're faced with a tiger about to eat you—and it is an energy hog in comparison.

Much of our logical thought processes are contained in the prefrontal cortex, which is connected to the limbic system and is integral to higher-level, *Homo Sapiens* thinking. It's where self-awareness is located, the regulation of emotion occurs, and where conscious beliefs sit, among other things. The prefrontal cortex doesn't mature until age 25, unlike other human organs and systems which reach maturity significantly earlier. This is the part of the brain that typical modern humans need the most in order to function in the 21st century.

It was long thought that people arrived at logical, "modern" decisions through careful analysis, rational thinking, and so forth. Hence lists of pros and cons when trying to decide whether to take a new job in a different location, the comparison of advantages and disadvantages of new vs. old, and other reasoning tools that people use. In this model, the prefrontal cortex and higher-level thinking of the conscious mind were the drivers on decisions like these.

However, we recently discovered that this is mostly not true. It turns out that decisions are mostly made at the subconscious level, based on emotions (Camp, 2012).[2] A neuroscientist discovered that people with damage to their emotional centers could not make decisions, even after considering pros and cons of one option versus another. Conscious decision-making is basically after-the-fact justification for whichever choice the subconscious made. (Advertisers know this and try to hook you with emotion, before providing the facts and features that will satisfy the logical part of the brain.) The fact that emotions come first is key to understanding why C-PTSD can develop in some people.

As you might imagine, all that logical thinking, which is a fairly recent evolutionary project, takes up a lot of resources in terms of energy (calories). Recall that earlier you learned that the human brain evolved to conserve energy. Therefore, it tends to default to System 1, which is faster and uses up fewer resources. In other words, your brain prefers to use heuristics for rapid decisions rather than logical thinking. Most importantly in any discussion about anxiety or emotional regulation, when you're under threat, whether physical or psychological, the brain tends to shut System 2 off. Rational thinking is unnecessary for survival on the savannah when faced with a hungry tiger. Energy is shifted to the stress response so you can get away from the predator quickly.

Most of us in the developed world face more psychological threats than physical ones, yet our brain still treats threats as though they're physical. When System 2 is offline, you can't really think through the consequences of your actions. You can't regulate your emotions or control their expression very well. Even though the modern world requires more use of the human brain and logical reasoning, when you feel under threat, you're at the mercy of emotions and autonomic reflexes.

In addition to emotions, the amygdala plays a part in processing memories. Another part of the brain's limbic system which is also involved in memories is the hippocampus, which is mainly responsible for short-term or episodic memories. Though they both can act independently, these two brain areas can also team up. Memories are better recalled when they're stored along with an emotion (either good or bad), so the amygdala and hippocampus help form long-term memories.

THE BRAIN AND TRAUMA

After a traumatic experience, the sympathetic nervous system (SNS), including the amygdala, remains on high alert. This is why everyone experiences things like hypervigilance and hyperarousal after an ordeal. With normal functioning, the SNS will gradually return to baseline and stress levels dissipate. If they don't, and the SNS remains stuck in the trauma response, the entire brain is in stress mode, which affects the physical body as well.

Being constantly in a high state of arousal from trauma response, the amygdala is constantly reacting to potential threats and danger that it continues to search out. When your body is constantly at a high threat level, it has a hard time regulating itself. Your body gets tired, because producing all the stress response takes a lot of energy. Stress hormones make the brain's hippocampus less effective at consolidating memories, which means the brain has difficulty receiving the signal that the danger is over. In addition, these effects on the hippocampus may cause the brain to suppress the memory of the ordeal in order to cope with it. All of these issues occur at the subconscious level, so they're not anything that you have control over.

There are a variety of unconscious operations that happen during sleep, from encoding learning from the day to making repairs on the cellular level. They're all necessary for mental and physical health. Although many people in the 21st century may brag about how little sleep they get, they're doing themselves quite a disservice. Often those with PTSD and C-PTSD have difficulty sleeping as a result of the disorder.

One of the things that happens in the brain during sleep is the maintenance of neural pathways in the brain. This is a part of habit formation as well. Pathways that go unused will be pruned back (so they don't waste unnecessary energy) and pathways that are used are strengthened and may eventually become habits. Because clearly something that's being often used must be important!

Unfortunately, of course, for those suffering from all forms of PTSD, the pathways that are being strengthened during the sleep you do get are the negative ones that result in poor self-perception, increased startle response, and so forth. The brain responds to the trauma that has occurred in ways that will protect it (and you), but when it can't return to a normal state the protection won't work the way it's designed to.

Another consequence of complex trauma is that it can alter people all the way down to the genetic level. We all have genetic inheritances from our parents through DNA, which sometimes includes genes that have been implicated in diseases like Alzheimer's and dementia, certain cancers, and others.

However, not everyone who has a copy of these genes will actually contract the disease. In the last century you might have heard of the debate between nature vs. nurture, or whether DNA (nature) has more influence on a person's life than their upbringing (nurture). It's a bit more complicated than that, as it turns out. The environment that a person lives in and other outside influences can turn some genes on or off. Some people with a DNA inheritance of dementia don't get the disease because those genes aren't turned on.

One of the factors that can alter gene expression is complex trauma. Those with C-PTSD, as you learned in the last chapter, are more likely to be diagnosed with additional illnesses. This might be a potential result of trauma switching genes on or off. Fortunately, the gene expression of on or off is based on chemical signaling. While you can't change your DNA, you may be able to change the signaling that was affected by trauma.

Complex trauma is not just the ordeal that someone has gone through. It's also their fixation on it, and the compulsive return to the terror and drama over and over again. When you have C-PTSD, the brain can't let go of stress responses or return to normal, so instead the emotions repeat and become reinforced.

WHEN THE BRAIN CAN'T LET GO

At the end of a life-threatening situation, a healthy nervous system will "finish" the fight-or-flight response by literally shaking off the additional energy generated. The limbic system sends a signal that causes shaking or trembling (which is where "shaking like a leaf" after a fright comes from). This tells the body that the threat is gone and that the stress response is no longer necessary. Then the nervous system returns to normal.

You can see this in animals—after they're triggered by a threat, they will shake themselves to rid their bodies of the excess energy. If animals are unable to shake off their ordeal and return their nervous systems back to normal, they might actually die (Shaw, 2019).[3] By contrast, humans tend to become ill.

In people with C-PTSD, their brains form what's known as a trauma loop. You've already learned that after a trauma, the brain fires up its defenses, especially the fight-or-flight reflex. It's the resulting patterns afterward that determine whether the trauma leads to C-PTSD. In short, the loop looks like this:

- Stress response activated
- If situation dealt with, return to normal (no PTSD)
- If not, stress response still active and emotions build
- If emotions build long enough, sense of helplessness/being overwhelmed triggers inertia defenses: submit or become hopeless
- If the brain submits, defenses deactivated, and brain returns to normal (no PTSD)
- If it becomes hopeless, defenses remain activated
- If defenses remain activated and brain cannot find a way to be safe, they are permanently activated and continue to loop, leading to C-PTSD.

You can see, going step by step, how the brain's survival mechanisms can turn against us in certain situations. After the trauma occurs and the fight-or-flight reflex is activated, you can become more afraid, rather than shaking off the danger after it's gone. This often occurs for trauma that goes on for a long time or repeatedly, since the brain must stay in stress response for longer periods of time. It can also happen when the person feels that they can't escape or fight the situation. There's no way to "finish" the SNS arousal because neither fight nor flight is possible.

Consider someone who is the victim of domestic abuse. Most abusers can be charming, which is how they are able to attract their victims, and they don't abuse their partners all the time. The victim's stress response is nearly always present, because they tend to walk on eggshells around the violent partner in the hopes of avoiding being a target. Even when the partner isn't currently lashing out.

Or someone who's living in a war-torn country. There's no safety available anywhere within the borders, and so staying alive means that the person must constantly be on high alert for threats. The brain isn't able to dismiss the stress response, because the danger simply does not go away unless the person is able to find refuge somewhere else. Though being a refugee is also a factor for developing PTSD, because they're traveling to places they're unfamiliar with, and the brain can't relax its vigilance when constantly dealing with the unknown.

These are just a few examples of how people can be in situations where their brains are on high alert for danger over long periods of time. It's not something that our early ancestors really had to deal with, because they'd run away from or fight the predator and deal with the situation. Afterwards their nervous systems, no longer faced with imminent threat, could signal that the episode was over, and they were safe.

For our ancestors, feeling the fear and responding appropriately took care of the matter. But for modern humans, it doesn't always work that way. C-PTSD develops over time, because it takes time for a stressed brain to believe that there is no way out and no hope of escape. That's why the duration of the ordeal is more important than how it occurred.

Feeling like you're under constant threat and having your body constantly pumping out stress hormones to prepare for fight or flight doesn't just cause physical harm, but emotional harm as well. With your body's lizard brain activated, it's harder to think rationally about anything, including the specific situation in which you find yourself. Recall that emotions come first, and so in these circumstances, fear can lead to anger, frustration, discontent, and sometimes more fear.

As these emotions wash over you frequently, you may feel overwhelmed and overcome by a sense of helplessness. These feelings trigger more intense emotional defenses. Your brain wants you to survive so it can survive, and it will try to find solutions to avoid being in danger. But at this point, escaping the situation isn't possible and you're no longer capable of initiating action. Instead, the brain ends up thinking that submitting to what's going on is best, or maybe becoming immobilized will save you.

Now your brain has left behind the defenses of arousal (fighting or fleeing) and is activating defenses designed for inertia, like collapsing or fainting. You've still got plenty of emotions roiling around, like anger, disdain, and hatred yet still need safety, which means sadness, pain, and defeat. Typically, at this inflection point there are two options: one is to submit, and the other is to become hopeless.

1. Submit

If you accept the situation as it is and are able to control the fear and sense of hopelessness, the brain recognizes this as a threat reduction and will stop raising its defenses. In time, your system will return to baseline. Similarly, if you see a way out through the submission, your brain will deactivate the defenses.

For example, someone who is being abused will stop resisting and attempt to do everything they're told. They may make plans to leave or even take revenge against their abuser, which also deactivates the inertia defenses. Over time their stress response will return to normal, though this may take months to years.

2. Become hopeless

When the terror and exhaustion are too overwhelming, a person can lose all hope instead. Unfortunately, this sense of hopelessness instructs the brain to continue to keep the stress response going. So, you'll keep those defenses activated and lose sight of everything except survival, no matter the cost.

When someone can't find a way to stay or feel safe, when they can't think of a way out of their circumstances, the defenses will stay permanently activated. They're in self-defeating survival mode, rather than able to find a way out. This is what causes the typical symptoms of the disorder of numbing, disassociating, depersonalization, memory loss, and others. The brain is doing what it takes to keep going, and these symptoms are all methods of survival for someone who's lost all hope with eternally raised mental defenses.

You may have heard of the saying, "neurons that fire together wire together." The more often the trauma loop is repeated, the stronger the neural pathways of the loop become. The brain strengthens the pathways because they're being used more often, which embeds the loop even more deeply into the mind.

The brain learns to function under these conditions and the repetition of this loop between emotions and defenses is what creates complex trauma. The constant release of stress hormones destabilizes other bodily functions such as digestion, sweating, heart rate, and others.

With complex trauma, you're eternally on high alert with no one to trust and no hope for your future. This loop of traumatization affects not just your physical health, but your perception of yourself and the world around you, your emotions and your ability to reflect on your own thoughts and actions and other behaviors.

EFFECTS OF CONSTANT STRESS RESPONSE

As you read earlier, there are a number of things that occur in your mind and body when you experience hyperarousal for long periods of time. It strains your ability to adapt to your environment, which leads to a variety of health conditions. PTSD particularly affects the system that is known to lead to irritable bowel syndrome, fibromyalgia, and chronic fatigue when not functioning properly. It may be the cause of otherwise unexplained pain, especially in muscles and bones.

People with PTSD have higher rates of cardiovascular disease, especially with high blood pressure (McFarlane, 2010).[4] They also tend to have high cholesterol and triglycerides, which often develops into cardiovascular and other diseases. PTSD is a risk factor in obesity, which is another precursor for illness. Individuals with high stress levels have an increased mortality rate compared to those who don't experience chronic stress response.

In addition to heart disease, PTSD sufferers also experience higher rates of other conditions, as the elevated stress response increases the risk for a number of other ailments. The hormone cortisol in particular has some well-known negative effects if the body continues to pump it out on a regular basis. Too much stress also contributes to additional inflammation throughout the body, which is a known factor for a number of unhealthy conditions (Hannibal, et al, 2014).[5]

Inflammation widens gaps in the barriers between blood and the brain, as well as those in the intestinal walls. These allow larger bodies and toxins to cross these barriers, causing further inflammation and damage. The dysfunctional cortisol responses are also linked to acquired immunodeficiency syndrome or AIDS (Ibid).[6]

Inflammation releases "free radicals," which are molecules containing oxygen and an odd number of electrons. The free radicals can then attach to and interfere with other molecules. Moderate amounts of free radicals actually help the body take care of itself, for example by allowing attaching to and destroying an invasive microbe (Pham-Huy et al, 2008).[7]

However, too many free radicals cause *oxidative stress*, which damages cell membranes and other structures within the cell. This leads to certain degenerative illnesses. Oxidative stress has been linked to certain kinds of cancers because it can alter the DNA of a cell and disrupt its behavior. In addition to smoking tobacco, the oxidative stress from inflammation caused by asbestos is known to contribute to lung cancer (Ibid).[8]

Too many free radicals and the resulting inflammation is also known to be a factor in lung (*pulmonary*) diseases such as asthma and chronic obstructive pulmonary disease (COPD). They are also known to affect the brain in a number of ways in addition to depression that lead to illness. Alzheimer's disease (and other forms of dementia), Parkinson's disease, multiple sclerosis and ALS or Lou Gehrig's disease.

Free radicals may also induce your cells to essentially turn on each other, which is what happens with auto-immune disorders. Your body no longer recognizes its own cells and believes them to be invaders, which it then tries to fight off as it would an actual invader. Rheumatoid arthritis is an autoimmune disease where joints and their tissues are continually inflamed, as an example.

Oxidative stress run rampant is also known to contribute to a variety of kidney (*renal*) diseases, such as chronic kidney failure. It can even damage your eyesight by inducing the formation of cataracts. It's a factor in additional systems throughout your body, including other cancers, diabetes, and premature cell aging. Your immune system also gets stressed out, which means you might be at higher risk for infections because your body can't fight off bacterial or viral invaders.

All the oxidative stress that your body endures with too many free radicals doesn't necessarily mean that you'll end up with any of these specific ailments. However, it makes you more likely to develop them over time compared to someone whose cortisol levels are functioning properly. Any and all of the conditions that are generated from an elevated stress response may also lead to bodily pain. It's important to understand that physical effects are a very real manifestation of the changes that occur when the brain is under constant stress and awash in hormones that are intended for short periods of time.

In addition to all the physical effects of PTSD, there are a number of mental ones as well. In a later chapter you'll learn more about the symptoms of PTSD and C-PTSD. The symptoms can also be effects that come on after a period of time in which the disorder hasn't been addressed or treated.

As with the physical effects, suffering from any form of PTSD doesn't mean that you will go through all of these situations. You're more likely to develop them if you have PTSD than not. Also, you may only have one of the following effects, or you may have more than one. There are a variety of factors that contribute to the disorder, and your particular combination isn't necessarily the same as anyone else's. How PTSD manifests and its results are different for each person.

Depression

Everyone feels "down" or "blue" some of the time, even if they're otherwise mentally healthy. Major or clinical depression is different from the garden-variety blues. Those with major depression can't function normally as a result of a continuous feeling of sadness and a loss of interest in activities or people that formerly brought happiness and pleasure.

Other symptoms of depression include weight changes that you didn't intend, because you may have a total loss of appetite or you might be hungry all the time. Your sleep is disturbed, meaning you might not be able to sleep well or in contrast that you sleep too much. It's sometimes accompanied by feelings of guilt and shame, and difficulty concentrating or thinking.

The occasional sleepless night or binge on ice cream when your date didn't go well is normal. It's when your symptoms continue for at least a couple of weeks that you could be diagnosed with depression.

Anxiety

Just as everyone gets the blues from time to time, everyone experiences anxiety at least sometimes. People who are otherwise mentally healthy get anxious before public speaking or before a date, or for some other event.

Anxiety disorders occur when the worry is persistent, especially about daily issues, and excessive or intense. The anxiety interferes with normal everyday functioning and are out of proportion to the actual (potential) danger of the situation.

Substance addiction

As noted earlier, substance problems and addictions are common coping mechanisms for many people, even those without PTSD. The preferred substance might produce euphoria or just a numbness, but either way it's a temporary fix.

The more you use and abuse the substance, the more those neural pathways get strengthened. That's why it's often easier for people who have been using it for a short time to quit the substance, because they haven't strengthened the pathway as much.

In addition, these substances alert the brain to pleasure, which means it releases happy neurochemicals like dopamine. The reward system of the brain, of which dopamine is a part, is a way to encourage pleasurable habits. When dopamine is released, the brain is essentially saying, Yes, we like this. Please do more of this!

You can see how that can lead to addiction, because your brain is telling you that it wants more of the substance. With many of them, you need more and more to get that dopamine release, so you need more and more substance to feel better.

Eating disorders

As with anxiety and depression, nearly everyone has "fat days" and feels like skipping food to get back on track. Or they overeat due to emotions, which may be pleasurable or not. It's the extreme behavior of attaining a specific body shape or weight control that marks eating disorders.

It sometimes represents a feeling of control for someone who otherwise feels that they don't have much control over their lives. But they can control how much they eat, or how much food is absorbed. Eating disorders develop over time and can start off as simply wanting to be a bit thinner (Jade, 2019).[9]

You might have heard of some of the disorders, such as anorexia nervosa, where the person severely controls their food intake. The guidelines for adult women are to consume 2,000 calories per day, more or less, depending on factors like height and how sedentary they are. Someone with anorexia usually tries to take in less than half that amount. You may also have heard of orthorexia, where someone begins eating healthy but then develops an obsession with healthy eating that interferes with their daily life.

On the other end of the spectrum are disorders such as binge eating disorder and bulimia. You may binge or overeat excessively and feel like you can't stop even when you've had enough. Bulimics tend to binge and purge, so that they can eat what they want but don't absorb the calories.

Self-harming

This can take a variety of expressions, but it too is a coping method for emotional pain, if not a healthy one. It's hurting yourself on purpose, which can (like some eating disorders) give you a sense of control in an otherwise chaotic life.

Those who self-harm may cut themselves with sharp objects, burn themselves, pick at hair or skin, and pick at wounds to prevent them from healing. It's not so much a mental illness as it is an unhealthy coping strategy. For some people, self-harm can stimulate their endorphins, so they (temporarily) feel better as a result.

Suicidal tendencies

Although most people don't talk about it, apparently plenty of human beings have fleeting thoughts of ending their lives sometimes. For those who are emotionally healthy, it doesn't leave a lasting impact and the person can easily move on.

But for others, especially those with PTSD, these tendencies can recur or be present for longer periods of time. This is obviously dangerous, because the combination of the tendency plus a means of ending life can have disastrous consequences.

People who do end up committing suicide usually can't think through the consequences of the action to consider how friends and family would be deeply upset. Or they may believe that they're all alone in the world and no one would miss them if they went, which is usually not the case.

Lack of social interaction

A support system is key for optimum health for human beings. Even introverts need a few people that they can count on, and extroverts tend to have more people in their social circles. Going it alone is mentally and emotionally difficult, and even people without PTSD have cognitive distortions that make them unable to see reality when they're alone for too long.

Because PTSD sufferers tend to feel guilt and shame (among other emotions), they also tend to withdraw from their friends and family.

Many also have depression, which means that the things they used to enjoy are no longer pleasurable. So, they stop going out and visiting friends or reaching out by telephone to their connections.

As with many other factors in PTSD, the longer you go without social support, the more difficult it is to restart it or get back in the swing of things.

For example, you might think of someone that you know casually. You might feel a little awkward about picking up the phone to call them. If you haven't called in a few weeks, picking up the phone is even harder than if you'd called them a few days ago. And if it's been months since you connected, you might feel so awkward that the phone is impossible to pick up.

With PTSD, this happens even with people you know well, or even love. You don't call them or pick up when they call. Maybe one day you're feeling like you might want to talk to them, but now it's been weeks or months. You're wondering how you're going to explain this gap in connection, and it seems so difficult that you decide to do it another day. Which never comes, because the distance grows the longer you wait.

Separation or divorce

Unfortunately, many people who don't have PTSD don't understand it or how it shows up in different people. If you have a partner who knows nothing about it except for what they see on TV, they might have a skewed perception.

Other partners might understand the disorder to a point, but not be able to cope with the symptoms that show up. Or think that what's going on is "all in your head," not recognizing that there are physical effects from PTSD as well.

Sometimes, people with PTSD act out in a way that their partners think is dangerous to them or their children, and they want to leave the marriage to ensure their family's safety.

Although separation and divorce don't typically help the PTSD sufferer heal, they are fairly common in these situations.

Lack of relationships

The inability to trust people that's associated with the disorder often results in having fewer connections with others, whether platonic as just friends or romantic. As noted earlier, social interaction is important, and having strong bonds with at least a couple of people is key for mental and emotional health.

PTSD interferes with these bonds when it's not treated. You feel like you can't trust others, and you withdraw from them. Close friends may continue to try for a while, but if you don't respond they may eventually give up, leaving you without a support system.

Without friends and partners, it's easier to isolate even more and get stuck in your own head. Which isn't a great place for PTSD sufferers to be.

In addition to these effects, PTSD often shows up in conjunction with other mood or mental disorders, known as *comorbidity*. These include eating disorders, other depression or anxiety illnesses, and

Obsessive-Compulsive Disorder (OCD). It's not always possible to tease out which one came first, but some of them are known to make a diagnosis of C-PTSD more likely in someone who has them compared to someone who doesn't, as you'll find out in the next section.

CONTRIBUTING FACTORS TO COMPLEX PTSD

Earlier we discussed the nature vs. nurture debate, and that C-PTSD can alter genes to the point of turning some off or on. Similarly, there are factors that can lead someone to be more susceptible to the disorder compared to others. Some are genetic in nature, but others are environmental. Not everyone who may be more genetically susceptible will end up with it, because they've received nurturing that essentially keeps those genes "off". Conversely, people are diagnosed with it without any genetic factors contributing.

History of anxiety or depression

Both having a family history and having a record of these conditions yourself is often found in people with C-PTSD. Being anxious or depressed and adding complex trauma is not a recipe for solid mental health!

Regulation of chemicals and hormones

Depending on how your brain releases chemicals and hormones, especially when under stress, you may have a higher likelihood of the disorder.

Tendency toward neuroticism

People who are "neurotic" tend to be moodier than average. They often feel anxious, worried, jealous, angry, frustrated, and/or lonely. Though every living person sometimes has these feelings, they're usually short in duration and easily dismissed for people who aren't very neurotic.

By contrast, neurotic people worry a lot. The emotions may be intense or last for a longer time period, or both. It's much harder for someone who is high in neuroticism to shake off these feelings or let the anxiety go. It's often an inherited trait, though it doesn't have to result in C-PTSD.

Repeated trauma in childhood

You learned that trauma over a long period of time, or repeated traumatic events, are more likely to lead to C-PTSD. Children can end up with the disorder as well as adults, especially since they're still learning coping skills.

Complex trauma interferes with learning how to deal with life too. It's unlikely that a child whose brain has been disrupted in this way is capable of processing later traumas in any kind of healthy way.

Lack of support system

After someone has experienced a traumatic event, it's important for them to process what happened in a way that's healthy. Being connected to other people also gives them a sense of hope, and a safe environment to process in.

Those who tend to cope with their lives by themselves, or without seeking out support, are more likely to develop the disorder (Tull, 2019).[10]

Dysfunctional family

When the family isn't a safe place to be, it's much more difficult for someone who's experienced trauma to work through it in a healthy way. This can be the family of origin, or current family.

Either way, the inability to heal the trauma is more likely to result in C-PTSD. You're with your family every day (for the most part) and living in a toxic or dysfunctional environment can be re-victimizing.

Dangerous job

Most of the original PTSD studies were done on military veterans. You may have heard of "shell shock," which many World War veterans came home with. Today we call that PTSD instead, but either way it can be understood as a response to the trauma of combat. My own grandfather (who was in combat in WWII) was known to have suffered shell shock. Similarly, combat seems to increase the likelihood of C-PTSD.

Other occupations that are more likely to lead to the disorder are law enforcement and firefighting.

CHAPTER SUMMARY

C-PTSD is actually a result of the way the human brain is wired to survive. When the stress response system is activated after a trauma

WHERE DOES C-PTSD COME FROM? | 441

and not able to shut itself off, the chronic load has a variety of mental, emotional, and physical effects.

- Though we live in the age of computer technology, our brains were designed to keep us alive on the savannah and to flee or fight when the fear circuit is activated.
- The human brain reacts to trauma with a stress response, which is supposed to deactivate when the danger is past.
- The stress response doesn't deactivate for a variety of reasons, and if the brain starts cycling through the trauma loop, the person is likely to develop PTSD or C-PTSD after a long period of time.
- Being on high alert causes a constant wash of stress hormones like cortisol, which can lead to diseases like diabetes, Alzheimer's, cardiovascular disease, cancer, and others.
- There are both genetic and environmental risk factors for C-PTSD which lead to a higher likelihood of having the disorder after trauma.

In the next chapter you will learn about the symptoms for PTSD, and later in the book you'll discover the additional C-PTSD symptoms in greater detail.

3

SYMPTOMS OF PTSD

Before we get into the specifics of Complex Post-Traumatic Stress Disorder, you need to be familiar with the symptoms of PTSD. You learned in an earlier chapter that to be diagnosed with C-PTSD, the symptoms of PTSD also must be present. In other words, everyone with the complex form of PTSD has PTSD, though not everyone with PTSD has C-PTSD. In this chapter you'll better understand what the signs of PTSD are and what they mean in real life.

As a reminder, the three markers of PTSD are continuously reliving the event, trying to avoid all reminders of it, and being hyper aroused or on high alert most of the time. In order to be diagnosed with PTSD, you must exhibit all three of these symptoms in one form or another.

EXPERIENCING THE TRAUMATIC EVENT REPEATEDLY

For people with PTSD, the trauma doesn't just fade into the background after a month or so, the way it does for those without the disorder. There are numerous ways in which the event keeps coming back for the traumatized person. It can be incredibly frightening as well as energy-draining to be continually reminded of what happened. This is also known as *re-experiencing*.

Though people without PTSD may re-experience the trauma, it's usually brief and occurs soon after the event. It doesn't happen to them over and over again, or months down the line, and it may not be as intense.

Flashbacks

Unlike a memory, flashbacks seem like they're happening in the current moment. It replaces the current situation that you're in. Many people can't tell that they're having a flashback while it's occurring, because it appears so real.

The emotions are the same as in the original event, and usually the sensations are as well: sounds, scents, tastes, images, and physical reactions. That's why it's so hard to tell when you're having one, because it plays out in your mind just as it did in real life.

Researchers have discovered that flashbacks tend to center on the moment when the person first realized in the initial event that they were in danger. Due to this phenomenon, someone who's currently in the middle of a flashback may suddenly start taking action, which injures them or others. They're trying to avoid a danger that's occurring to them *right now.*

Of course, the person suffering from PTSD doesn't mean to lash out or harm anyone else. They're reliving an event that happened in the past as if it's in the present and trying to avoid whatever the results were. Unfortunately, someone without the disorder and who's never experienced a flashback often doesn't understand what's occurring. They might believe that the one with PTSD is trying to hurt them or the people around them.

Why does this potentially harmful phenomenon occur? Your amygdala and hippocampus are the main sources for these repeated, intense re-experiences. The amygdala is activated in the fight-or-flight reflex, but your hippocampus is repressed by the lizard brain that wants you to survive first.

Since the amygdala is also involved with emotions, what you end up with is a strong, emotionally negative memory without a clear sequence of events because your hippocampus was offline. You've got the memories of sights, sounds, smells, etc. that are associated with the event, but no timeline or context that you'd normally get from your hippocampus.

Therefore, when you're triggered by an image, sound, or scent that's reminiscent of the event, your amygdala fires up the negative memory, senses that you're in danger, and activates the stress response.

So you're sweating, your heart speeds up, and you're breathing heavily so you can escape the hungry predator that your amygdala thinks

SYMPTOMS OF PTSD | 445

you're facing. In fact, depending on the original trauma, you might actively try to defend yourself against it, not recognizing that you're not currently in that previous situation.

It's because your hippocampus was shut down by the stress response. If it had been functioning normally during the original event, it would provide context to the amygdala's memory. It would recognize that you're no longer in the same danger and signal your body to deactivate the stress response. But because it was offline originally, it can't provide the context that you're in a different place and time.

The amygdala doesn't receive the message that you're not in danger now, and so you're stuck with the strong negative emotion that your brain's generating (Chi, 2019).[1]

Combat veterans are known to experience flashbacks once they're in civilian life. The sound of a gunshot, or 4th of July fireworks, or even a car backfiring reminds them of the shots they heard during the war and those memories often come rushing back. The smell of fireworks can also trigger these memories.

Of course, you don't need to be a combat veteran to suffer from repeated flashbacks. I used the example of being in a car accident with a white SUV in an earlier chapter. If you witnessed an event such as a wildfire that ravaged your town, you might have flashbacks if you smell wood smoke in the air or sit close to a fireplace. Leaves crackling could bring back the crackling of flames and result in a flashback as well.

Someone who was assaulted by a person wearing a specific cologne may experience flashbacks whenever they're in a crowd and somebody else is wearing the same scent. Or by going to a store where the cologne is sprayed in the air.

You may not even be aware of what the trigger is. Maybe you were in a car accident in the middle of Gilroy, California (known for its garlic) or there was an air freshener in the car that you didn't pay any attention to.

Smelling a scent later, even if you don't remember it having a connection to your traumatic event, can trigger a flashback because your subconscious remembers it. This goes for all other memories as well: images, sounds, etc., not just smells.

Recurrent nightmares

These types of dreams are threatening and/or scary. People often have very physical reactions to their nightmares. For example, you might shout out in your sleep, or thrash around, or wake up soaked in sweat.

It's estimated that only about 5% of the population have nightmares. As you might imagine, the numbers are much higher for those with Post Traumatic Stress Disorder, as roughly 71-96% of sufferers experience nightmares (Veterans Administration, n.d.)[2] In addition, people who have experienced trauma are more likely to have more than one nightmare a week.

If you have PTSD and a co-occurring condition such as panic or anxiety disorder, you're more likely to have nightmares compared to those with a single PTSD diagnosis.

Having threatening dreams after a drama is somewhat different than a "regular" nightmare, because they seem to occur earlier in the night in different stages of sleep. If you have PTSD-related nightmares, your sleep is also affected.

You don't get as much sleep as you need, and you tend to wake up more during the night and stay awake longer when you do. You have a lot of restless leg activity as well. Not only are you not getting the amount of total sleep that's best for your health, but you're also missing out on deep sleep, also known as *slow-wave* sleep (Jain, 2014).[3]

Humans cycle through different stages every time they sleep. The first stage is really just dozing off, and it's easy to be woken up. As the night (or time asleep) goes on, future cycles may not include the first stage.

The second one is non-REM, where the body relaxes more. Deep or slow-wave, also known as delta sleep for the waves that the brain produces, is the third stage and is necessary for restorative sleep.

The final stage is REM (rapid eye movement), where brain activity picks up and vivid dreams may occur. This stage is crucial for cognitive functions like memory and learning. Getting enough deep and REM sleep is important for good health mentally and physically.

Deep or slow-wave sleep is when the body repairs muscles and helps them grow. Almost all of your growth hormone, or 95%, is released during this period of the sleep cycle (WHOOP, 2019).[4] In addition to muscle repair, this stage is thought to bolster immunity as well as creative thinking and memory.

Without enough deep sleep, it's harder for your mind and body to make necessary repairs and give yourself the rest you need.

For all trauma survivors, the dreams contain elements of the trauma itself. People diagnosed with PTSD are more likely to experience their nightmares as a replay of the event compared to trauma survivors without the diagnosis.

As an example, someone who survived an assault might dream about being powerless, being held at gunpoint, being beaten, or some other scenario that involves the frightening aspects of the ordeal. Someone with PTSD is more likely to dream of the actual event itself.

Unwanted thoughts and memories

These occur when you're not really trying to recall the event. They can occur at any time and be triggered by a variety of stimuli. Or they may have no apparent trigger at all. The thoughts may force you to revisit the event, and you could end up ruminating on the ordeal, which increases the feelings of being overwhelmed and helpless.

You might recall from earlier that the prefrontal cortex helps regulate actions, which it can do by stopping an activity that might be regretted later. In addition to stopping actions, it plays a role in stopping unwanted thoughts via the hippocampus.

This process relies on the neurochemical Gamma-aminobutyric acid (GABA), which acts to inhibit nerve cells. When the brain doesn't have enough of this neurotransmitter, its ability to stop the unwanted thoughts is much lower (University of Cambridge, 2017).[5]

One thought that often comes up for those with PTSD is "Why did it happen to me?" or "What could I have done to prevent this from happening?" In many if not most cases, there's nothing you could have done to change the outcome.

For example, someone who is being abused, sexually or otherwise, might think that it's their fault for dressing, speaking, or acting a certain way. However, the abuse is always due to the abuser themselves, not the victim. The person being abused could have been acting, dressing, and speaking normally and the abuser would have found something to critique.

In other traumas due to accident, natural disaster, etc., there's still usually nothing that you could have done differently to prevent it from happening. Unfortunately, you cannot go back in time and change it even if you could identify something that would have altered the situation.

Some people with PTSD have unwanted or intrusive thoughts more frequently than flashbacks or recurrent nightmares. They can come up differently for everyone, and many with PTSD find that this symptom is aggravated when they're under more stress than usual.

For example, an adult survivor of childhood sexual abuse may experience these thoughts and memories whenever they're being physically intimate with their spouse. But another adult survivor might experience the memories and thoughts randomly throughout the day.

Unforeseen triggers

This is troubling for many people with PTSD, because it's not always possible to prepare for triggers ahead of time or to know what they are. What is a trigger? Anything that cues up your symptoms, like the intrusive thoughts described above.

There are two types of triggers. One is internal, or things that you experience within your body. Memories, thoughts, and emotions can trigger symptoms, as can physical sensations. For example, feeling angry or abandoned, out of control or vulnerable can lead to re-experiencing the trauma. So can tense muscles, body pains, or a pounding or racing heart.

The second type is external, or things that happen outside your body. Earlier you learned that almost any feature of the ordeal can bring it back to you in terrifying detail: a scent, a sound, a taste, or an image. In addition to those, things like holidays, anniversaries, and arguments.

Something others who don't have the disorder often don't understand is that the trigger doesn't have to be related to the same trauma that the survivor experienced.

News and nowadays social media often run stories that cause re-experiencing for anyone with PTSD. A story or image about any kind of trauma can trigger someone with the disorder. For example, someone who survived an assault can be triggered by a story about someone being abused or living in a war-torn country.

The news, whether you get it online, streaming, or via social media, is tuned to emphasize the negative. Earlier we talked about the negative being part of human survival strategy on the savannah, so that we'd stay away from things that would kill us.

We still have that negative bias, and in fact studies show that when given the option, we will choose negative stories over positive ones (Stafford, 2014).[6] Even people who insist that they prefer to hear good news!

Advertisers and the media know this, of course. They know that people pay more attention to negative stories, so if they want to make money (and they do) they need to run more negative stories because that's what people want. If you have PTSD, it's probably a good idea to limit your news intake from whatever sources, which will help you avoid triggers you didn't see coming.

AVOIDING REMINDERS OF THE TRAUMATIC EVENT (AVOIDANCE)

The second group of markers for a diagnosis of Post-Traumatic Stress Disorder is the active avoidance of anything that might remind a survivor of their ordeal. Avoidance is a method for isolating from any situation or feeling that might otherwise give you a reminder. There are several ways in which someone engaging in avoidance might try to evade their memories in an attempt to cope with their distress.

Why is this a problem? Avoidance often leads to more avoidance. It tells the brain that something isn't safe. The more messages that the brain receives that the world is unsafe, the more dangerous everything feels. It can lead to a downward spiral until the survivor isn't leaving their house or talking to anyone or enjoying the things that they used to love to do.

Emotional avoidance

PTSD sufferers often try to push down or ignore all emotions, whether they're related to the trauma or not. However, "feeling the feelings" is actually a very important part of the process of recovery. Trying to avoid the feelings can make PTSD symptoms worse, or last longer, than if they're dealt with.

Ignoring emotions, whether from trauma or not, doesn't actually get rid of them. Instead, they continue to build up. And at some point, they can no longer hold it all in and the emotions explode out of them.

Sometimes people seem very calm or serene, but they'll suddenly blow up for no apparent reason. (Anyone can try to ignore their emotions, not just someone with PTSD.) That's a case study in trying to push away emotions until they can no longer be hidden away.

Emotions are like a big pot of water on the stove, boiling away. You can try to put a lid on the pot, but if there's no ability for the steam to escape, the pot will eventually just blow the lid off due to the pressure from the steam. But if you leave the lid open a bit, or there's a vent in the lid, you don't have the same problem. Feeling emotions is a way to vent all that steam and prevent it from building up.

Just as it's very hard to keep the lid on a pot that's boiling hard and producing lots of steam, it takes a lot of energy to push away feelings.

Sometimes people end up abusing substances to help them avoid feelings, or they have no time left over for family or friends or work.

When your energy is all tied up in keeping emotions at bay, you can't really handle other emotions in your daily life like frustration, and so you feel like you're constantly on edge. It's similar when you're trying to avoid thoughts or memories as well, because actively trying to push them away requires a lot of energy as well.

Intimacy avoidance

Having PTSD often makes its sufferers afraid of being enmeshed with another person. While it may seem in some ways natural to avoid intimacy after sexual assault or abuse, other kinds of trauma can also result in avoiding close connections with others. It can be made worse by attempts to self-medicate through substance abuse or being sexually promiscuous.

Sometimes those with PTSD feel that they're being engulfed in a relationship, or they develop a fear of abandonment. Either of these can result in avoiding intimacy by leaving the relationship or preferring to be isolated from others and celibate.

Another way someone with PTSD might deal with intimacy is to leave a relationship as soon as it starts to get serious or they feel engulfed in it, then immediately find another partner to avoid being abandoned.

There are some common ways that intimacy avoidance gets played out. For example, the spouse who spends all day at work and barely interacts with their partner at home. The mother who ignores her husband and concentrates on their children. Abusers can be intimacy avoidant, as can their victims or the ones who chase after them.

In addition, there are signals in behavior changes that can tell the partner of someone with PTSD that the symptoms are being aggravated. They might stop holding hands, kissing, or making other kinds of physical contact, and no longer want to do things together or talk the way they used to.

They may get overly anxious if the non-PTSD partner is late or can't be contacted, or become dependent on the partner to take care of everything for them. They could start criticizing and finding fault with their partner, or become either overly protective or afraid of their partner.

Though some of these signs may appear to be the complete opposite of another, all of these are ways that PTSD can show up differently in different people. Though not all of those with PTSD will become intimacy avoidant, it's definitely not uncommon.

This can be very difficult for the intimate partner as well, unless they learn more about the disorder and why its sufferers react in certain ways. Couples who are able to work through the distress together can even find that their bond becomes stronger than ever.

Staying away from people, places, and things

This symptom of PTSD is known as *behavioral avoidance*, in contrast to emotional avoidance which is the attempt to ignore or evade thoughts, feelings and memories of the event.

SYMPTOMS OF PTSD | 455

As you might guess, there's overlap between these types of avoidance. Someone who is trying not to trigger any thoughts of the event will probably try to avoid situations where they believe they're likely to re-experience the trauma.

In the previous section you learned about the various triggers that can bring back the traumatic memories, from thoughts to feelings to smells and sounds. Trying to avoid setting off these triggers often results in staying away from any type of situation where you think there's likely to be a trigger.

The 9-11 terror attacks generated PTSD for many Americans, even those who weren't geographically near the sites involved. Someone previously living in New York City might have moved away to prevent reminders of the tragedy. Or to simply avoid that area of the city.

Someone who was assaulted in a specific environment will likely try to stay out of that place and anything similar to it. For example, anyone who was assaulted in a big warehouse at work will probably try to stay away from the warehouse. They might ask for a job in the office. Or they might quit that job entirely and go work somewhere else where there's no warehouse. They might avoid big box stores which are very like warehouses.

Suppose that the warehouse involved lumber, so that the smell of cut wood was associated with the assault. That person would probably also stay away from any place with the smell of fresh-cut wood, such as a lumber yard or home store. If the warehouse played a certain kind of music, they might want to avoid any place with that music, whether it be a store, a restaurant, or anything else.

They may also want to ignore anyone that was associated with the assault, even if the other person wasn't actually involved. For example, if the survivor was speaking with a co-worker prior to the assault, in their minds the colleague is associated with the event and they'll try to stay out of the way.

As noted earlier, it's not always possible to know when the cue will happen. And since there are such a variety of ways that those with PTSD can be triggered, something that might have been OK shortly after the assault can end up being a trigger itself.

For example, suppose that pop music was playing in the background during a traumatic event. At first, the survivor simply avoids the places that remind them of the ordeal. But later they're in, say, a grocery store and they hear the pop music which triggers them. Now the grocery store may be off limits to them as well.

Remember that PTSD forms after a period of time; it doesn't happen overnight. Likewise, the cues that might set a survivor off can change over time as well.

Changing routines

In an attempt to avoid the persons, places and things as discussed above, people with PTSD may change their daily habits in order to try to prevent themselves from being triggered.

A classic example of this is someone who's been in a car accident and no longer feels safe in a car, either as a driver or as a passenger. They will now need to get around by foot, bike, scooter, or public transportation. None of these methods are faster than a car, so taking alternate forms of transportation can be very time-consuming.

Which usually means that they'll need to rearrange their day to make sure they get to work or their appointments on time. They may need to get up earlier in the morning and change the time of day they exercise and do all the other things they normally take care of in a day.

At first, changing routines may not seem like it makes that much of a difference. But depending on what you're changing, it can completely change the way you live on a day-to-day basis. You might have to drive an hour out of your way every day to avoid a specific building or area that triggers you. Some people end up changing shifts at work, which can wreak havoc on their normal routines.

Restricted range of emotions (affect)

There are a couple of different ways to talk about emotions. One is *affect*, which is "An immediately expressed and observed emotion." (Washington University, n.d.)[7] The other is mood, which is more of a sustained emotion and not necessarily expressed.

The way people show a normal or broad range of affect is to use gestures, body movements, changes in tone and facial expression. Those with restricted affect show less variability in their expressions and less intensity as well.

Imagine someone with a normal affect receiving an award. You can picture them smiling, beaming, maybe even crying tears of joy. They may stand taller once they have the award in their hands, signifying the pride they feel in themselves. In their speech, thanking others for the award, their voice changes tone, rises if they're asking a question and falls afterward. They might show their award to the audience, make big gestures as they talk, etc.

Someone with restricted affect won't display their thanks or pride in such a way. For one thing, they may not be feeling much gratitude or happiness, if any at all. They might not smile, nor speak in a way that sounds like normal conversation with changes in tone and so forth. They're unlikely to make big gestures or change posture.

This is often frustrating for a PTSD survivor's loved ones. They might plan special treats or outings and be disappointed when the survivor doesn't seem to be grateful or excited about it. It's difficult for someone who has normal affect to understand why someone would be restricted. Especially if the one with PTSD enjoyed these types of treats before the event.

Not seeing a future for themselves (foreshortened future)

How can a trauma survivor get back to a quote-unquote normal life? While their loved ones often have very specific ideas of what they should do, someone with PTSD can't necessarily see a way back. Unfortunately, their loved ones are often wrong about what will help them to heal because they don't have expertise in the disorder.

Many people with PTSD feel that no one understands them and that in a way they're cut off from society. Therefore, the usual goals such as having a house, a spouse, kids, a college or graduate degree are pretty much off the table as far as they're concerned.

They feel that their life will be cut short. The severity of this symptom can vary. Some survivors may have a milder version, where they believe that something will happen to them but they're not sure when or how.

Others may experience a more severe belief of a foreshortened future, where they are convinced they'll suffer a premature death and have a specific time frame for it.

Either way, this feeling leads to depression and isolation.

HYPERAROUSAL

This is the state of heightened anxiety that your mind and body replay when thinking about or being reminded of the trauma. Although it's no longer happening, your body responds as if it were. You learned earlier about cortisol, and another chemical that the body releases is adrenaline, or epinephrine. Adrenaline affects the immediate response to danger: your pupils dilate, blood pressure is increased, etc.

In PTSD sufferers, cortisol is low. It's meant to help regulate stress over the long term, so the lack of it can make symptoms worse. The lower level of cortisol and higher levels of epinephrine lead to a system that doesn't function properly. Those with the disorder are very sensitive to certain stimuli, so their brains overreact and continue to pump out adrenaline. Which, in turn, continues to activate the fear responses.

Those who are hyper aroused can't control their responses to certain stimuli because their baseline state of arousal has changed.

For example, suppose someone without PTSD is attending a seminar and they hear a noise at the back. They'll turn to look at the source of the noise. If the noise was caused by someone entering the room late, their arousal returns to normal as they know they have nothing to fear. They'll turn back to the presenter without thinking more about it.

If on the other hand they see someone with a gun, they'll stay aroused, because they are in the presence of danger. Their fight-or-flight reflex kicks in and they'll react appropriately. For someone with PTSD, confirming that the noise is innocuous, by seeing the latecomer, doesn't actually reduce the arousal. They can stay aroused, as if danger is present, even though the stimulus is benign.

Hyperarousal shows up in a number of different ways. These effects can feed into and off each other as well. For example, being easily startled is a sign of being hyper aroused, and it's also a signal that you're hypervigilant.

Irritability

Sometimes people refer to this as agitation. It can be intense frustration and annoyance, and even anger, maybe over the smallest things. When taken to the extreme, irritability results in violence and aggression. It's the symptom that military spouses report is the most damaging to the relationship they have with their veteran (Moore, 2015).[8]

Many people, not just those with PTSD, are irritable at times. Chronic irritability is often related to health issues, from stress and low blood sugar to diabetes and depression. You might experience physical signals along with your irritability such as an increased heart rate, breathing fast, an inability to concentrate, or sweating.

Chronic anxiety

As with many other symptoms of PTSD, everyone occasionally gets anxious. Doing something new, or preparing to speak in public, or interviewing for a job are common generators of short-term anxiety. Breathing gets faster, your heart rate speeds up, and your body prepares for the situation. Those without anxiety disorders such as PTSD return to baseline after the situation is over.

Long-term anxiety, which is common for PTSD, can be dangerous to your health because of all the stress chemicals that your brain releases on a regular basis. People who already have heart disease are at higher risk for an event such as a heart attack.

Your digestive system is also affected, which leads to stomach pain, diarrhea, nausea, and loss of appetite. As you learned earlier, a constant wash of stress chemicals such as adrenaline weakens your immune system over time, so it's easier for you to get sick. In addition, vaccines might not work as well when your immune system isn't working properly.

Anxiety often causes insomnia, depression, and headaches too. In addition, people with chronic anxiety may lose their sex drive and become fatigued during the day. Sometimes anxiety results in a panic attack, which is a feeling of extreme terror accompanied by physical symptoms.

Difficulty with falling or staying asleep

There are a variety of ways in which someone with PTSD might have issues sleeping. It might be harder to fall asleep in the first place, or they could wake up earlier than they wanted to. The disorder causes some sufferers to wake up a lot during the night and not be able to fall back asleep or take a long time to do so. As a consequence, the sleep they're able to get isn't restorative or restful.

People who aren't able to sleep at night often try to sleep during the daytime instead. Which makes it harder for them to fall asleep at night, and so on in a vicious circle. Worrying about sleep or being afraid to sleep due to potential nightmares about the trauma, make the issues worse but are very common for people with PTSD.

The edginess that comes along with hyperarousal interferes with the ability to get to or stay asleep. In addition, being so reactive to stimuli often means that the trauma survivor wakes up easily to noises or other stimuli.

Research shows that those with PTSD are more likely to have *sleep apnea* (Tull, 2020).[9] This condition results in breathing repeatedly stopping and restarting during sleep. People who snore, are overweight, smoke, drink too much or have diabetes are also at higher risk.

In the obstructive type, the muscles of the throat relax and block the airways. Central sleep apnea happens when the brain doesn't send the correct signals to the muscles, and the complex type has both these symptoms.

Doctors can test you to see if you have sleep apnea. Some of the symptoms include snoring, interrupted breathing during sleep, waking with a dry mouth, morning headaches, insomnia, and irritability.

Sleep apnea leads to a higher risk for many illnesses such as cardiovascular disease and high blood pressure. It can complicate surgery when you need an anesthetic.

Angry outbursts

Anger is a very common reaction for anyone who's been through trauma. For some survivors, the high levels of arousal that you experience may actually lead you to try to find situations that you need to be alert for to ward off danger. Others may prefer to numb the sensation with substances or other addictive behaviors.

When a person is under threat, the best response can often be an aggressive reaction. Those who experienced trauma as a child may never have learned any other way of responding, and they often act impulsively, without thinking. Other aggressive reactions include backstabbing, doing a bad job on purpose, self-blaming, and harming yourself.

One of the mental issues for trauma survivors is that they can't tell when their thoughts have been affected by the experience. They believe that they're responding to the situation in front of them, but they're still reacting to what happened.

For example, in combat it's important to follow the rules and obey the leader in order to survive. A veteran at home may lash out angrily at their spouse and family when they disobey or question the rules.

Because trauma so often involves a loss of control, many PTSD sufferers end up trying to enforce control rigidly after the situation. Because you're being inflexible, you'll likely get hostile responses from those around you. Which feeds back into your inability to trust others.

It's another vicious cycle, especially when you are horrified by your outburst and determined to keep an even tighter lid over your emotions, including your anger. Unfortunately, this will make future outbursts both inevitable and excessive.

Being able to work on your anger (which you'll discover more about later in this book) will help you avoid responding to triggers with intense or explosive anger. In turn, you'll be able to build better relationships.

Easily startled

Everyone gets startled sometimes. Horror movies activate the startle response with a "jump scare," where the monster suddenly appears, or the hero suddenly disappears (often accompanied by ominous music on the soundtrack.) For most people, the event has to be higher stress in order for the startle reflex to kick in.

Someone with PTSD has an extreme or excessive startle response, where they overreact to something that happens suddenly. The strong response to a mild stressor (that doesn't affect people without the disorder) can happen at any time to a sufferer, whether the environment is like the traumatic one or not.

The exaggerated startle response, as you might imagine, is linked to the stress and fear responses. A stress hormone known as CRF[10] makes your amygdala more sensitive to the neurochemical norepinephrine, which triggers the stress response. This link between CRF and norepinephrine is also involved in areas of the brain that get involved with drug abuse, which may be why people with PTSD are also at higher risk for alcoholism.

You might refer to yourself as "jumpy" when you have the excessive startle response. A slight noise behind you could cause you to whirl around and be ready to fight or flee, whereas the same noise for someone else doesn't register as a threat.

Involuntarily trying to cover the back of your neck or your throat, parts of your body that are vulnerable, is a reflexive way to react to being startled. In addition to experiencing this more often, you might also feel more distress after a startling experience.

For example, most people watching a horror movie will settle back down after a jump scare, or even laugh at themselves for having the reaction. But someone with PTSD might be genuinely upset and unable to go back to watching the movie for some period of time.

Constantly on the lookout for threats (hypervigilant)

This isn't just being extra vigilant. It's more extreme than that. People who are hypervigilant are often exhausted because they are constantly scanning for threats. Hypervigilance interferes with their ability to function in daily life.

You know you're suffering from hypervigilance if you're experiencing one or more of the following signs:

1. Overestimating potential threats

You're on the lookout for things that are either unlikely to happen or exaggerated. For example, you might find yourself insisting on a seat in the restaurant with your back to the wall so that you can see everything happening around you and no one can sneak behind you. Is it likely that you're in danger in the restaurant? Unless you're a Mob boss, not really. Similarly, you may insist on remaining near the exits in a store, restaurant, movie theatre, etc. Although it's highly unlikely that anything will happen to you, your state of hyper-arousal prevents you from assessing risk in a logical way.

2. Avoiding perceived threats

You may also find yourself trying to avoid any place that might be perilous, even if there's no current threat. For example, you might skip any kind of public gathering, even if it's for something as innocent as watching the lighting of the town's Christmas tree. Or for something that you previously enjoyed, such as an outdoor concert.

In the extreme, this manifests as agoraphobia, where you don't want to be anywhere you perceive as being difficult to escape. People in this condition rarely leave their homes because calculating escape routes from new or unfamiliar places can be too taxing.

3. Increased startle reflex as discussed above

4. Sustained adrenaline response

> When there's no threat to be seen, you're still experiencing the symptoms associated with adrenaline release: dilated pupils, fast heartbeat, and so on. This was explained in the example under Hyperarousal when someone with PTSD in a seminar can turn to see that a noise was due to a latecomer, but several minutes later their heart is still racing and they're breathing fast.

When people are hypervigilant, they can enter into a state of paranoia where they feel that they need to arm themselves, whether the weapons are legal or not. Or they may decide extra locks for doors and windows are needed, or that a sophisticated (and expensive) alarm system is necessary, or even install a panic room to escape to when something goes wrong.

PTSD DIAGNOSIS

In order for a person to be officially diagnosed with Post-Traumatic Stress Disorder, they must have at least one reaction or symptom from each of the three categories. In other words, you need to experience hyperarousal, avoidance, and re-experiencing the trauma. You may have one symptom in one area and multiples in the other two areas, but you must have at least one in each category to be diagnosed.

As a reminder, re-experiencing may occur through recurrent nightmares, flashbacks, intrusive or unwanted thoughts and memories, and unforeseen triggers. Avoidance can be emotional, intimacy, and behavioral. Symptoms can include not touching or interacting with a partner, shutting down emotions, changing routines, exhibiting a restricted range of emotions, and seeing only a foreshortened future.

Hyperarousal can manifest in a variety of ways. You may feel irritable, have chronic anxiety and sleep issues, have episodes of explosive anger, be easily startled and hypervigilant.

While some of these symptoms at the mild or moderate end are common for humanity in general, experiencing them intensely or for a prolonged period of time may indicate the presence of PTSD.

CHAPTER SUMMARY

There are three categories of symptoms that comprise a diagnosis of PTSD, and they're also a part of the C-PTSD diagnosis. The trauma survivor needs to present at least one behavior or symptom in each category to be classified under Post-Traumatic Stress Disorder. These symptoms also must last longer than a month for the diagnosis because those without the disorder often undergo the same symptoms, but theirs resolves in about a month.

- People with PTSD continue to re-experience their trauma as if it were currently happening, which often results in excessive reactions to the existing situation which can be violent.

- Those with the disorder try to stay away from anything associated with the trauma, which is known as avoidance and includes the pushing away of emotions.
- Someone with Post-Traumatic Stress Disorder experiences hyperarousal, where their brains are very reactive to even mild stimuli and continuously releasing stress and fear chemicals.
- While mild or short-duration episodes of many of these signs are experienced by a lot of people, not all of whom have an anxiety disorder, the intense and long-lasting characteristics of the symptoms are key for PTSD sufferers.

In the next chapter you will learn about affect dysregulation, which is one of the key markers for C-PTSD.

4

AFFECT DYSREGULATION

Now that you understand the various symptoms that manifest for trauma survivors who have PTSD, you'll learn about the additional symptoms that mark sufferers of C-PTSD. "Affect dysregulation" may sound like a very complex term, but recall that *affect* just refers to the expression of emotion. *Dysregulation* is similar to dysfunction, meaning that something isn't being regulated properly. More simply, we'll be discussing emotions that aren't properly regulated. People with C-PTSD are incapable or impaired when it comes to controlling emotions, or the expression of them.

WHY EMOTIONAL CONTROL AND REGULATION IS SO IMPORTANT

You might be wondering why not having control over your emotions is so crucial to your functioning that the inability to do so is a symptom of C-PTSD. You might be asking yourself, "What's the big deal if I lose control once in a while and explode or yell at my family?"

In fact, there's not really much anyone can do to control their emotions. You might recall from earlier chapters that emotions are automatically generated, so it's not possible to simply stop anger from appearing, or frustration or sadness. However, you can control your actions. If you can regulate your emotions, you control how and when you express them. People with good emotional control rarely lash out at others, even when they're feeling angry or disappointed. They also don't lash out at themselves, or turn the anger inward, which can result in depression and self-harm.

You've probably heard of IQ or intelligence quotient, which basically measures how well people can perform logic and reasoning tasks. It's considered to be pretty much fixed at birth. But you may not have heard of EQ, which stands for emotional intelligence, and can be developed and improved over time. It refers to how well a person can manage their own emotions and help others with theirs.

Having a high EQ is necessary for strong relationships, because those who have a lot of emotional intelligence understand what's going on with others as well as themselves in a nonjudgmental way. They're able to communicate well with others and build the bonds that we humans need to feel good and be happy with our lives.

It's also a growing need in the business and leadership world, because the old command-and-control style of leadership, at least for civilians, has largely been discarded in favor of a style where leaders inspire their followers instead of ordering them around.

There are four or five requirements for EQ, depending on who you ask, and emotional regulation is one of them. Without being in control of your emotions, your emotional intelligence will be poor. That affects your home life, your work life, and everything in between.

1. Self-awareness

This trait means that you are aware of your emotions, and also how they are affecting you and those around you. You're aware of how your actions affect you and others too. you're not trying to push away your feelings, or pretend that they don't exist, because they do.

Self-aware people understand when their feelings are affecting them. For example, they know when they're sad or angry, and ask for a time-out or a delay if someone wants them to make a decision. They're able to recognize when a strong emotion might prevent them from taking the right action, and give themselves some time to sort it out first.

They're also knowledgeable about their own strengths and weaknesses. Sometimes it's hard for trauma survivors to remember that they have strengths, especially when they're feeling overwhelmed and out of control. Yet everyone has something that they're good at or a good quality to them, like kindness or compassion. Or being physically strong in some areas, or intelligent, or having a creative mind or an artist's eye.

Self-aware people also understand where they're weak. They may choose to try to improve in these areas, or they might ask for help from someone they know is strong in that area.

For example, people who aren't good at numbers or money can ask their friends and family who are strong in these areas to help them make sure they're on a good financial footing. They know that they can help others who are struggling in areas where they're strong, and that everyone has some of both.

You also know what your own values are. What's most important to you? Supporting your family? Being honest? Caring for those less fortunate? Staying humble and right-sized, where you neither puff yourself up nor put yourself down?

2. Self-regulation

This is all about staying in control of your actions. Feelings and thoughts come up in the human brain all the time, but that doesn't mean they must be acted upon. They're not always true or based in reality, so reacting to them without pausing or thinking can often lead to the wrong decisions.

Interestingly, being in control means that you're more aware of your emotions, not less. That way you can evaluate the likelihood that the feeling you're experiencing is likely to help you or harm you. When you're so numb to what's going on within you and don't understand the emotions that are occurring, whether you acknowledge them or not, you have no way of knowing how they're impacting your actions.

By contrast, when you know that you're angry, you also know that you're more likely to lash out at your family members even over small stresses that really don't matter in the grand scheme of things. So, before you open your mouth, you can consider whether what's about to come out is going to be beneficial or not. And if not, implement some strategies to help you cool down instead. (You'll learn about these strategies later in this book.)

By being in control, you can act according to your values. If one of your values is prioritizing your family and you're able to self-regulate, you stop lashing out at them over small details.

You also give yourself time to make good decisions based on the actual facts of the situation at hand, and not look at the circumstances through the lens of your emotions. And you'll be able to hold yourself accountable and stop blaming others when things go wrong.

This is invaluable at work. No manager wants to put up with a worker who's constantly blaming others for their errors. They prefer employees who can own up to their mistakes, which means they can learn from them and prevent similar errors in the future.

3. Motivation

Being able to pursue your goals is also critical for the emotionally intelligent. You don't need someone standing over you telling you what to do all day, which most of us find annoying anyway!

Motivated people also want to do good work and get the job done right. It's actually easier to get it right the first time, because having to correct mistakes results in more work.

4. Empathy

Building those important bonds with other people requires you to be able to step into their shoes and see things from their perspective. When you're busy trying to ignore or push away inconvenient emotions, you really have no emotional space to spare to think about other people.

Just like you, people want to be seen and heard. Listening to them and understanding their feelings is key to this. But how can you understand someone else's feelings when you can't understand your own?

5. Social skills

Being able to communicate well with others is important in all aspects of life: family, romance, work, even going to the grocery store. People who have good social skills are able to manage conflicts in their own relationships.

They know how to praise others, and they can accept negative feedback and use it as an opportunity to learn, rather than feeling attacked.

Plus, when you're able to be vulnerable, others can be vulnerable too. That helps you connect with others. No one can really build a bond with someone whose surface appears to be perfect and shiny. When you let others in, they feel they can bond with you and relate to you.

Earlier we talked about emotions as being like a pot of boiling water, and trying to cover it with a lid simply means all the pressure builds and the lid eventually blows off. When you're in control, your emotions may be boiling, but you're actually not trying to fit a tight lid on the pot.

When you can regulate properly, you're able to tweak the flame underneath the pot so that the water doesn't boil over. You're controlling the source, so you affect how much power the boiling water has.

You can turn down the flame so there's not as much steam coming out, instead of trying to suppress it by covering it up.

The ability to regulate how you express yourself is key. When you avoid feeling your emotions, there's no way that you can control them or understand how they affect you and the others around you. Only someone who acknowledges their emotions will be able to regulate them. Affect dysregulation prevents you from understanding, acknowledging, and regulating how you behave.

Bear in mind that regulation does not mean ignoring your feelings. When you can regulate them appropriately, you are aware when they come up for you, but you don't necessarily act on them. You have the emotional ability to adjust the flame or soothe yourself, instead of allowing the water to boil out of control.

HOW DO YOU LEARN SELF-REGULATION?

The ability to control how you express your emotions is not an innate ability of humankind. Typically, those who are strong in this skill learn it from their parents or caregivers.

If you've ever been in close contact with a baby, you know that they are incapable of soothing themselves. They cry when they're wet, when they're in pain, when they're hungry, or when they want something. They can't stop themselves crying, so the parent has to change them, feed them, rock them, give them a pacifier, or whatever the baby needs at that moment.

As babies grow into infants and then children, they learn more skills to help them cope. You might see a young child sucking their thumb, which is a method of self-soothing. Their parents, teachers, and others around them can help them continue to grow and mature.

Having a nurturing environment is key for learning how to cope with emotions. A child who grows up in a healthy way learns that they can ask for help and get it. They discover that they can be comforted by others when they face challenges, and also how they can comfort themselves. A nurturing caregiver teaches them how to think about puzzles and problems to solve them rather than being overwhelmed.

A child who doesn't grow up with nurturing parents or caregivers don't learn these skills. Instead, they may learn that there is no help available when they ask, and they'll stop asking. They are not able to find comfort in others or in themselves, which teaches them that the world is not a safe place and other people can't be trusted.

Due to these issues, childhood abuse, maltreatment, or neglect is a common factor in those who have been diagnosed with C-PTSD and is known to cause affect dysregulation (Franco, 2018).[1] It's also possible for trauma to be transmitted from the parent to the child, because trauma survivors who struggle with their own coping skills cannot help their children develop in a healthy way.

WHAT IS AFFECT DYSREGULATION?

Also known as emotion dysregulation, it's the inability to deal with emotions such as sadness, anger, or fear. You can't always control either the intensity of the feelings, or how long they stay with you.

Rationally, you might be aware that you need to shake it off in order to move on, or to have a healthier relationship, but the emotion stays with you instead. The effects of having the feelings remain for a long period of time can be very intense.

The inability to deal with emotions is another aspect of your brain trying to protect you. In order to prevent the uncomfortable feelings from appearing, all emotion gets shut down. It affects memory as well, which is the reason many sufferers don't remember the event(s) later.

For example, suppose that you end up having an argument with your brother about something, large or small. When you think about where the fight fits into your life, it's nothing that can't be solved or maybe even brushed off. But you're unable to let it go.

Thinking about the argument might prevent you from sleeping at night. Or you can't stop thinking about it while you're at work, which causes you to make silly mistakes that you'd normally avoid. You might even be telling yourself to stop thinking about it, or shake it off, or move on. But you can't.

This seeps into your interactions with him when you have a family picnic or outing. You might get to the point where you keep escalating until the two of you end up shouting unforgivable things to each other, and end up damaging the relationship badly, possibly beyond repair.

Or you're desperate not to let that happen, so instead you choose to numb yourself. Maybe you start drinking too much. Or you decide to numb out by hitting the casino or heading to the mall to shop 'til you drop. You might be thinking that you cause less harm this way.

Unfortunately, even if you believe you're only hurting yourself, usually you're still affecting the whole family. When you're drunk or high most of the time, you're unable to truly participate in family life because you're not really there even if you're physically present.

Or you're physically absent, plus you're spending so much money that eventually you're drowning in debt. You could easily end up at the point where you can't pay for your basic necessities, such as heat or electricity or a roof over your head.

There are a number of symptoms that point to someone who is suffering from affect dysregulation. Some of these are also involved in the categories of PTSD (avoidance and hyperarousal) and they can also feed off each other. You've already learned about a few of these symptoms in earlier chapters, so the details are not repeated here.

- Depression
- Anxiety
- Excessive shame and anger

Shame is the sense of being worthless, small, or powerless in a situation. It's usually a reflection of feeling that other people are looking at you negatively, with disgust or disdain. That doesn't necessarily mean that the person who feels shame is actually worthless or a subject of disdain, but they believe they are.

Shame produces physical changes in the body as well. It's often accompanied by a sense of time having slowed down, so that the feeling of shame is actually magnified. People feeling shame also experience an increased heart rate, and sometimes sweating and/or blushing as well.

The brain sees shame as a threat, probably an interpersonal danger, and activates the fight-or-flight reflex as a response (Traumatic Stress Institute, 2007).[2] Because feelings of shame are disorganized and often intense, the shame isn't precisely encoded in the memory. It can spread and be connected to other memories that didn't originally have shame attached to them.

It shows up in speech typically as a barely audible voice that speaks with a lot of pauses and repetition, and the listener often can't make out the words.

Traumatic events often lead to shame for their survivors. The trauma makes them feel helpless or powerless, which in turn they feel makes them weak or ineffective. These feelings are associated with a sense of shame.

- Self-harm
- Sexual promiscuity or other excessive sexual behavior

These behaviors are another way to avoid uncomfortable feelings or push the trauma away. It's common, especially for those who developed C-PTSD as a result of sexual violence or abuse. However, even those with a different trauma use sex as a way to numb out or try to ignore their emotions.

Eating disorders

Like many of the other symptoms of affect dysregulation, eating disorders are a way to respond to the powerlessness and helplessness induced by a traumatic event. Starving yourself or making sure that you eliminate calories in some way (such as purging) are ways to assert control over yourself.

Another reason eating disorders are often an issue for C-PTSD sufferers is that they're a common reaction to rape and other sexual abuse. Although the exact mechanism isn't yet known, the association of eating disorders and sexual trauma is well-documented (Hower, 2018).[3]

Substance abuse

Whether the drug of choice is legal (alcohol, prescription medication, and marijuana in some locations) or illegal, overusing drugs to numb the uncomfortable feelings is a well-known, if unhealthy, coping mechanism.

It provides temporary relief, but once the effect wears away, the user is no better off. This often leads to escalating use in an attempt to stay self-medicated at all times. With some substances, the reward system of the brain is altered, and you need higher and higher amounts of the drug to be able to stop feeling your feelings.

Excessive perfectionism

Like eating disorders, an unhealthy level of perfectionism is a way for survivors of traumatic events to take back control of their lives. There are people who are naturally disposed towards perfectionism. Trying to do your best at all times is not necessarily a bad thing.

Everyone makes mistakes, so the healthy response is to learn from it and move on. But for C-PTSD sufferers, the need to achieve the goals is intense and failure to meet them is grounds for self-loathing and criticism. They see errors or less than 100% as a character flaw, not as a steppingstone for improvement.

When you spend a long time in a situation where every mistake can lead to severe consequences and everything you do is criticized, the natural result is a fear of failure. Excessive perfectionism is a way to try to evade conflict and punishment.

Some signs that you're experiencing perfectionism to an extreme level include:

- Expecting more from yourself than you would from someone else in the same situation
- Expecting others to give you negative feedback even when you've exceeded
- Taking so much time over your work that you put off fun and interesting hobbies or activities
- Rechecking your work over and over
- Stressing out about whether a routine task is done to perfection
- Over-performing to the extent that you realize later you didn't need to do so much work.
- High levels of interpersonal conflict

Complex trauma often results in a survivor who is both afraid to trust others and have relationships, as well as fear of being rejected or criticized. It's very hard to build or maintain bonds with other people when you have these fears, which leads to a lot of conflict.

You might be arguing with parents, siblings, your own children, your spouse, friends, colleagues, or anyone who crosses your path. An overstimulated fear response prevents you from giving other people the benefit of the doubt and to hear criticism and/or rejection when none is intended.

Suicidal thoughts and attempts

Suicide may be another way of exerting control for someone who previously felt powerless. Suicidal ideation happens when you often think about committing suicide, how you would do it, possibly role-play various scenarios and test them out.

There are a variety of ways that emotional dysregulation shows up in ordinary life. They're often characterized by outbursts that are out of proportion to the circumstances. Suppose that your partner cancels a date because they're not feeling well. Someone with good self-regulation would be disappointed, but then move on to call a friend to hang out or watch a movie. They'd shake off the feeling of being disappointed or rejected because it's just one date.

However, someone with C-PTSD is more likely to assume that means the partner doesn't love them anymore and start crying and eating ice cream. Or cut or burn themselves, consider suicide, or retreat to the bottle. Because they're constantly in a state of high arousal, these types of events seem much more momentous and threatening than they do for someone who doesn't have that elevated response.

Or consider a scenario where you're at the post office and they don't have the package for you to pick up as they should and ask you to come back the next day. A regulated response would be to feel the disappointment but recognize that this kind of thing happens and go on about their day. But someone with affect dysregulation is more likely to start shouting at the clerk and throw a pen at them.

The signs can be more subtle than that. Survivors of complex trauma often believe that they don't belong in a given situation. Everyone else seems to be having a great time and you might be feeling alone and unwanted. Maybe you're at the company holiday party and everyone else seems to know everybody there and having a lot of fun. Meanwhile, you feel like you don't belong there and when you go home, you binge on food or drugs.

UNDER-REGULATION OF AFFECT

There are two ways in which affect dysregulation can present: in over-regulation and under-regulation. A DESNOS diagnosis (per the DSM-V) refers to under-regulation as an alteration in regulation of affect and impulse.

When affect is under-regulated, the C-PTSD sufferer loses control over their emotions and expresses them in an intense manner, overwhelming their ability to reason through the situation. There are two ways in which trauma survivors demonstrate their under-regulation. One is through extreme emotional distress such as fear and rage. The other is behavioral, resulting in impulsive and aggressive actions.

This is a well-known consequence of childhood trauma especially. If the infant's caregiver isn't available to help soothe high arousal states, the intense negative experience requires all the child's mental and emotional resources to withstand the dysregulation. The combination of the trauma and the lack of caregiver response prevent the child from learning how to manage the various levels of arousal.

When your emotions are under-regulated, you don't have good coping skills to deal with uncomfortable feelings and you're not able to self-soothe. The above example of losing control in the post office is an under-regulation experience. You can't manage the feeling of disappointment or control your actions over it, and you fly into a rage even though the situation doesn't call for it.

It's not just anger that people with under-regulation struggle with. Fear or anxiety can bloom into full-fledged terror out of proportion to the trigger. Consider going to a "haunted house" around Halloween that's been designed to induce a few scares. They normally have spooky music, some monsters that suddenly pop up in front of you, and other jump scares like you might see in a horror movie.

Someone without the disorder might experience fear when a scaly hand suddenly reaches out for them from behind a curtain, but once they realize it's just a part of the attraction, they can relax, and the fear dissipates. But if you have C-PTSD, something like that could very well trigger a panic attack or other manifestation of extreme terror that leaves you unable to function normally.

For those with C-PTSD, impulsive behaviors like bulimia and binge-shopping are often an attempt to distract themselves from the negative emotions. They're more likely than other people to act impulsively when they're experiencing feelings like sadness or anger, whereas people without the disorder who simply have a tendency to act without thinking do so no matter what they're feeling.

The short-term reward of the impulse also counters or distracts from the feelings that the survivor doesn't want to accept or think about. For example, when you cut yourself deliberately the physical pain can make you feel better, at least briefly, and prevent you from experiencing the negative emotion or thinking about the trauma.

When it comes to aggression, there are two types of aggression that people can have, whether or not they've survived a trauma. One is *impulse aggression,* which is pretty much what it sounds like - emotional and reactive. This type is uncontrolled or spontaneous. The second is *premeditated aggression,* in which the reaction is planned and controlled. People can be both.

Combat veterans with PTSD show signs of impulse aggression, but not usually the premeditated type. Which makes sense, since in this kind of affect dysregulation emotions are uncontrollable. However, women with trauma backgrounds demonstrate both kinds of aggression (Miles, et al, 2017).[4]

What does aggression look like? It's an act of hostility that can do damage to another person (though you can also be aggressive toward yourself.) It's behind a range of behaviors from verbal abuse all the way to violence. However, aggression is often a defense reaction and isn't always meant to hurt someone else, especially when it's impulsive. If in the post office example, you attacked the clerk verbally, that's an aggressive act too.

There are four types of aggression, and women and men are equally aggressive. However, women are more likely to use indirect or verbal forms (Good Therapy, 2019).[5]

1. Accidental

This kind of aggression is not meant to cause anyone harm, and it's often just the consequence of being careless. For example, if you're running for the bus, you might accidentally bump into someone else who's standing on the sidewalk.

2. Expressive

This type is intentional, but it's still not meant to hurt anyone. In the post office example, throwing a pen across the table is intentional but there's no real intent to injure the clerk.

3. Hostile

Someone in the throes of hostile aggression means to inflict pain, whether it's emotional or physical. Malicious gossip is hostile, as is bullying. Also, reacting aggressively when provoked is also hostile. Verbally abusing the post office clerk is clearly hostile.

4. Instrumental

This type comes from a conflict over things or what someone perceives as their right. Suppose that you have a parking space at work that you think of as yours, because you always park there, even though it's not specifically assigned to you. If one day a coworker parks in "your" space, you might respond by starting a nasty rumor about them or "accidentally" bumping into them in the hallway.

OVER-REGULATION OF AFFECT

In contrast with under-regulation, those who over-regulate try to ignore and shut down their emotions. They don't want to acknowledge when the feelings occur or deal with them in any way. Over time, they're often less able to determine when they're experiencing emotions and what the emotions actually are. They shut down so they don't have to re-experience the feelings and the trauma that occurred.

DESNOS also includes alterations in attention or consciousness in the list of symptoms, which is known as over-regulation. These changes can include both amnesia and dissociative episodes. There's a variety of ways in which C-PTSD sufferers might experience dissociation, which is when you feel detached from things.

It's not something that you transition to automatically after your fight-or-flight reflex is activated, but rather it's something that happens over time. It's another way in which your brain is trying to protect you from the trauma. The more you feel disconnected, the more you dissociate.

On the mild side, the interruptions in consciousness which is the foundation of dissociation result in daydreaming or briefly "spacing out." More severe reactions include feeling disconnected from your body or the processes of your body.

One type of dissociation is known as *depersonalization*, which is a detachment from your identity or yourself. For example, you might have an "out of body" sensation where you feel like you're floating away from your body, or watching it do things as if you're watching a movie.

Or your body may seem like it's no longer yours, and you're wondering why you're attached to it. Maybe you no longer recognize yourself in the mirror, or you have to keep checking the mirror to make sure there's a reflection so you can satisfy yourself that you are real.

You might have the sense when you talk that it's not really "you," but a robot or something that's not you is in control. Other symptoms include feeling like parts of your body are much larger or much smaller than they actually are.

You might not feel "real," which is an aspect of dissociation known as *derealization*. Sometimes people experience this when they feel that real life is actually a dream, because everything around them (and possibly themselves) doesn't appear to be real. Or you might feel disconnected from loved ones, like there's a glass wall between you. You can see them, but you can't reach them, and they can't reach you.

Your surroundings might seem blurry or colorless or fake, like it's a stage or movie set. Conversely, some people have a very sharp awareness of what's around them and everything seems very clear and high-definition.

Derealization is often accompanied by distortions in space and time. Something that happened relatively recently seems like it was years ago. Or objects in your surroundings seem either much farther away or much closer than they actually are.

With dissociation you can lose time as well. The missing time can be a few minutes, to a few days, to large chunks of your childhood.

In the most severe cases, you might switch between different states of self, also known as "alters." This is usually diagnosed as Dissociative Identity Disorder, which you may have heard referred to as Multiple Personality Disorder.

When you continue to dissociate over a longer period of time, you may develop amnesia as well. This might show up as an inability to feel certain emotions, because you've left behind the ability to feel. Or you may experience it as not remembering what happened to you, or both. The memory of what happened is not gone completely, but your brain is shifting focus to things that you can better handle.

But just as you need to feel your emotions in order to recover, at some point you need to remember what happened to you so that you can deal with it. The amnesia is both a method of coping as well as an obstacle on the way to recovery.

To someone who's never experienced dissociative amnesia, the idea that you could actually forget a serious trauma may seem ludicrous. Yet it happened to a childhood friend of mine, whom I'll call Rhonda. I didn't know when we were growing up, as most outside a family don't know, that she was being sex trafficked by her mother and stepfather. For all outward appearances, she belonged to a normal suburban family and led a normal suburban life.

Her family moved overseas in high school and for a while we lost touch. The trafficking continued until she was in college, and in adulthood she didn't remember any of this had happened. Then she married and had children, and with the children came the flashbacks and other symptoms. Fortunately, she was able to find a therapist who could help her work through the trauma and help her protect her own children.

As with many of the other symptoms of C-PTSD, dissociation doesn't just happen to those with a type of anxiety disorder. Everyone daydreams sometimes, which is actually positive for the brain and helps you be more creative. Similarly, "spacing out" briefly is a pretty common occurrence.

Many people experience a fleeting feeling of being outside their bodies, or that their surroundings are dreamlike instead of real. However, for someone without the disorder, these episodes are typically fleeting and rare.

For sufferers of C-PTSD, however, these sensations interfere with their ability to live their life normally. They may keep coming back; they're often very distressing; and they can't be shaken off.

CHAPTER SUMMARY

Affect dysregulation is a part of Complex Post-Traumatic Stress Disorder, because sufferers for a variety of reasons are not able to regulate themselves emotionally.

- Emotional regulation is a key factor in emotional

intelligence, which is an important component of life and work in the 21st century.
- Humans are not born with the ability to regulate their emotions but learn it from healthy parents and other authority figures.
- Those whose parents don't self-regulate typically don't learn these skills either, and instead they're subject to affect dysregulation or the inability to manage emotions appropriately.
- There are a number of signs that someone is dealing with affect dysregulation, which can range from depression and self-harm to excessive perfectionism and a lot of interpersonal conflict.
- One type of dysregulation is known as under-regulation, which is demonstrated by aggression or lack of impulse control.
- The other type is over-regulation, where the survivor tries to shut off the feelings, and may end up dissociating from themselves or their surroundings or experiencing amnesia.

In the next chapter you will learn about another symptom of C-PTSD, which is negative self-concept.

5

NEGATIVE SELF-CONCEPT

It's true that nearly everyone on the planet feels badly about themselves from time to time. Not getting the date, or the job promotion, or muffing a presentation in front of the boss: all of these happen and cause some negative thoughts and self-talk. But for trauma survivors, the negative self-concept runs much deeper than the occasional sense of disappointment or that you should have tried harder.

It's the lens through which you view everything that happens in the world, as a reflection of your own bad, weak, powerless, ineffective, shameful, self. What recovery includes is the realization that these things you've been telling yourself, or that you believe about yourself, are not true. It's the trauma speaking, and your brain's attempt to make sense of it.

WHAT IS SELF-CONCEPT?

It's the way that any one person evaluates, perceives, or thinks about themselves. It begins taking shape in infancy, with the realization that you're separate from other people and you're yourself all the time. This *existential self* is the most basic aspect of selfhood, and recognition starts as soon as you're two or three months old (Mcleod, 2008).[1]

You smile, and your caregiver smiles back. You touch the mobile in your crib, and it moves. Babies begin this fundamental aspect of self in relation to their surroundings, both people and things.

Next comes the awareness of the *categorical self*, where you see that you're also an object in the world, just as your crib mobile is, and you become aware of yourself and the properties that you have, or how you can be categorized.

Age and gender are usually the first two categories to be applied, as you discover that you're two years old and you're a girl. In young childhood, the categories are concrete instead of abstract: age, gender, height, hair color, favorite toys. As people grow older, they start adding the more abstract characterizations to their sense of self: introversion, animal-lover, enjoys working with their hands, etc.

There are three components to the self-concept of humans (Ibid).[2]

1. Self-image

This is how you view yourself. And it may not reflect reality, especially for trauma survivors. It's influenced by a variety of factors, such as parents, friends, colleagues, media, social media, teachers, supervisors, etc.

All these factors have a varying degree of impact. Parents, especially in early childhood, have a great deal to do with your self-image. Caregivers who treat their children well and support them are more likely to raise kids who have more of a positive self-image, compared to parents who neglect or abuse their children.

"Who am I?" is a basic question of self-image, and the responses tend to come back in one of two ways. One is social roles, or a response of "I'm a teacher," "I'm a son," and so forth. The other group is personality traits, such as "I love animals" or "I have a sense of humor" or "I'm impatient."

People also describe themselves in terms of physical characteristics like height, hair and eye color and also in the abstract, such as "I'm a child of the universe." When they're younger, the descriptions are more likely to be personality-related, whereas the older folks usually respond in terms of social role.

2. Your value

This is also known as self-esteem or self-worth. It's your measure of how valuable you are in the world.

Those with positive self-esteem tend to be more confident, optimistic, self-accepting, and less concerned with what others think about them. Telling people that they're good enough actually isn't much of an esteem-builder, whereas mastering things and becoming more competent in some areas does help increase a person's sense of self-worth.

You can probably guess how people with low self-esteem feel about themselves. They're more likely to lack self-confidence, be pessimistic, want to be someone (or anyone) else, and worry about what others think of them.

In addition to the influence of parents and caregivers, there are four factors that affect self-esteem.

3. How others react to us

When people seem to want to be around us, or are asking for our opinions, listen and agree with us, that usually makes us feel worthy. By contrast, if they avoid, ignore, or talk over us, that leads to lower self-esteem.

There can be something of a vicious circle here for someone who's feeling alienated or alone. They're less likely to approach others or to seem approachable, so other people tend to leave them alone. Which in turn makes them feel even more isolated.

4. How we compare ourselves to others

If our "target group" for comparison is richer, better-looking, more confident, etc., then we're more likely to have lower self-esteem. In contrast, when the reference group is doing worse than we are, that's positive for self-worth.

Social media has exacerbated this issue. What most people post on their feeds are carefully curated images of themselves at their best. In the holiday photo, all the kids are smiling, and the dog is lying down quietly. The vacation spot is gorgeous and dreamy. Or the businesswoman carries a "statement" handbag and is wearing a gorgeous designer outfit.

Of course, people sitting in front of the computer (or phone) in their pajamas with unwashed hair will feel bad by comparison. It's important to realize that those snapshots are just those: snapshots. They're not indicative of real life either.

That holiday photo is the one out of 100 shots taken, because in all the others the youngest kid is trying to run away and the older two are hitting each other while the dog is trying to eat candy out of someone's pocket.

The lush vacation spot is packed with mosquitos and the travelers came back coated in calamine lotion. They just decided not to capture that bit on camera. The businesswoman is carrying a fake designer purse that she picked up from a street vendor and rented the designer outfit for the photo shoot. Don't get too carried away by the perfection on social media because it's artificial anyway.

5. Social roles

Let's face it, some roles carry more social sparkle than others. People look up to airline pilots, medical doctors, senators, TV anchors and the like. By contrast, no one wants to admit they're unemployed, work at a low paying job, or were in prison or a mental hospital.

When you inhabit a role that people look up to, you probably have higher self-esteem compared to someone in one of the roles that isn't seen as desirable.

6. Identification

We tend to identify with the careers that we have and our titles, as well as our roles in life and our groups. That's why many successful people have a hard time transitioning into retirement, because they no longer perceive themselves as having the "successful businessperson" identity.

Sometimes people have C-PTSD and aren't diagnosed right away. They may go years thinking that they're "crazy" because of all the symptoms discussed so far in this book. They may believe that their role is the one of "crazy aunt" or "alcoholic sister" or "black sheep of the family." They see their very identity as a person as a negative.

7. Ideal self

This is the person you want to be. For most people, whether or not they've experienced trauma or been diagnosed with a disorder, there's a gap between their self-image, or how they view themselves, and who they really want to be. (Unless you're Dolly Parton, in which case you are your ideal self.)

In many cases, the greater the gap or *incongruence* between the self-image and ideal self, the less worthy they feel. The closer a person can approach their ideal, or even if they feel like they're working to get closer, the more self-esteem they'll have.

Everyone experiences some incongruence because no one ever really lives up to their ideal selves. In order for there to be *congruence*, or significant overlap, between the actual self and the ideal self, the person must have a high positive regard for themselves.

But for those with C-PTSD, there's often not much overlap at all because their self-concept is very negative.

NEGATIVE SELF-CONCEPT

This is very common for anyone with C-PTSD, because they often feel helpless, guilty or ashamed. They may believe that they're at least partly, if not wholly, to blame for their trauma. And it follows logically that if something so bad happened to them and it was at least partially their fault, then they must be a bad person.

It's not true that a trauma survivor is a bad person, but you can see how these kinds of negative beliefs can lead to that conclusion. Many survivors feel that they're isolated and alien from other people. Especially since everyone else seems like they're functioning OK in daily life and survivors aren't.

In social interactions, people express how they feel or think about you, even in childhood. When you're picked last for the baseball team, your peers are telling you that they think you're a bad athlete. If your parents are always criticizing your grades, they may be telling you that you're dumb, or they might see you as lazy since you could have got a better grade if you tried. If your teacher praises the stories you write in English class, he's telling you that you're a good writer.

Not all of these expressions are necessarily true. You might be a great swimmer or track runner, but your hand-eye coordination is too poor for you to be good at baseball. Your parents may have received bad grades themselves and want you to do better than they did.

Comparing yourself to others and allowing them to influence how you think about yourself is natural, but it can make you think more negatively about yourself than you really should. But when you buy into these negative thoughts that others have about you, and develop a further sense of negative self-concept, you may end up feeling a lot of shame.

You learned a lot about shame in the last chapter and how severely it can affect people. Even in someone without a history of trauma, it can lead to behaviors like self-harm, including eating and substance abuse disorders, and suicidal ideation. The effect is even stronger when trauma is added into the mix.

Once the lens that you have to view yourself is tainted by negative self-concept, it's hard to see things clearly. Because you feel badly about yourself, all your interactions with other people seem negative, or that other people don't care about you. The smallest sign of neglect or omission helps support the bad image of yourself that you carry around.

Even if someone is genuinely trying to help you, when you believe that you're not worth much, you'll be suspicious. You'll want to know what they have to gain by doing so, since you don't believe that anyone could want to help someone like you out of the goodness of their hearts. Your past and your trauma taught you that other people simply can't be trusted, and you've learned that lesson very well.

You'll find some techniques at the end of this chapter to help you stop the shame spiral and develop a more positive image of yourself. Remember that the negative image is the one that's false, because it's the one that developed from the trauma you survived. It's the better self-concept that is the true one.

CONSEQUENCES OF NEGATIVE SELF-CONCEPT

We all know what confident people look like. They don't mind (or at least appear not to mind) entering a room full of strangers and introducing themselves. They're the ones volunteering for new projects at work and walking around with their spines straight and their shoulders back. Confidence brings optimism and trust with it, and these types of people have a positive self-concept of themselves.

On the flip side, there are a variety of ways in which someone with a negative view of themselves acts and thinks. They also hold true for people who don't see themselves accurately (which is true for most people with a negative self-concept) and for those who don't really understand who they are.

Fear of rejection/abandonment

All human beings have the fear of rejection or abandonment to some degree. Recall that our *Homo sapiens* ancestors survived by joining together in small groups. Being shunned by the others in the village or being abandoned by the tribe might very well have meant certain death in those days. One person doesn't have much of a chance against a hungry predator.

For trauma survivors, rejection confirms the belief that they already have of themselves as being unworthy and/or unlovable, or that they're really all alone on the planet. It's associated with psychological pain and suffering, of which most C-PTSD sufferers already experience enough of without adding on rejection.

There are plenty of ways that someone with this fear can try to avoid it, whether knowingly or not. They can abandon other people first, before the other has a chance to hurt them. Or they can draw back and create distance from others. Or hold back their true thoughts and feelings.

For example, a trauma survivor might pick a fight with their best friend which leads to a rift in the relationship. That avoids the risk that they'll be abandoned. Or they never talk about their pain with friends, who then wonder why someone who's so "together" is so distant and cold.

Reluctance to take risks

When it comes to uncertain outcomes (which is really what risk is about), the untraumatized human brain has two contradictory systems that sometimes conflict. On the one hand, the brain is wired for preferring novelty. New things are exciting, and you get a reward of pleasure neurochemicals when you experience them. It helped motivate humans as a species to explore their world and learn.

On the other hand, your brain wants to keep you alive. Going into the underbrush where you can't see what's happening could result in being eaten by a tiger, so there is a part of the brain that's risk-averse too.

Consider the people you know or have heard about who enjoy doing things like bungee-jumping, free climbing mountains (without safety ropes), or surfing huge waves. Or who don't mind getting in (and then out of) steamy love affairs, or who always want to take on the latest difficult project at work.

You can probably guess that their novelty system is much more active. They're happy to take on these risks that might seem way too big for other people, so clearly the risk aversion centers aren't taking over.

What else might you think about them? Do they seem timid or shy? What kind of self-concept do you think they operate under? Even if you don't know them personally, you can probably spot their confidence in themselves. They're willing to take on these risks because they're sure they can pull it off. They have a very positive self-concept.

On the other side of the coin are all the people whose risk adversity is much stronger than the pleasure they receive from trying new things. Some of this might be due to the fact that they don't realize it doesn't actually take that much novelty. You don't have to go bungee jumping in the Grand Canyon but can take a new route to work or to the store.

Those with C-PTSD aren't convinced they can take risks and come out unscathed. They've been scarred by the trauma, and having a negative self-concept prevents people from being able to get past that fear of risk. They don't think of themselves as being successful or having the capacity to conquer challenges. It's much safer to avoid as much risk as they can.

Extreme self-protection

When it comes to interpersonal relationships, there's a spectrum of the ways that people can act. At one end of the spectrum is self-exposure, where the person allows themselves to be fully vulnerable to the other. They let down their guard and permit the other person to get to know who they truly are.

The other end is self-protection, where the person doesn't trust the other one fully enough to let them in or expose weakness. For many trauma survivors, exposing weaknesses leads to more trauma, so they usually come down much closer to this end of the range.

Someone who's trying to protect themselves, in addition to not trusting other people, is always looking for potential threats coming from others. It's similar to hypervigilance but takes place in the relationship arena.

If your fear is that your romantic partner will leave you, you're constantly looking for signs that you're right. Are they wearing a different perfume or cologne than they were yesterday? Why did it take them an extra fifteen minutes to get home at rush hour? Why did they suddenly decide to wear a tie or scarf they haven't worn for months—are they meeting someone?

Or you may try to distance yourself from another person, even a friend. You're concerned that they're going to hurt you, and so you back away. You might believe on some level that creating some distance between you will lessen the inevitable pain when they leave or abandon you.

Once you're convinced that the person is ready to bail on you, you might start treating them rudely or knock them down a peg. You're thinking that it'll hurt much less when they eventually do take off, because they weren't that great to begin with and really, they've done you a favor by removing themselves from your life.

There are times when people do need to protect themselves in a relationship. The other person might be an energy vampire, taking up too much time and thought. Or they might be abusive, or they may be trying to work a scam. It's wise not to get close to these types of people once their true nature is revealed.

However, for many C-PTSD sufferers, they protect themselves against every single person they know and meet. There's no chance for them to find the kind of intimacy that will help them recover, because they can't allow themselves to be even a little bit vulnerable.

Difficulty with relationships whether romantic or platonic

Extreme self-protection is one obstacle that gets in the way of nurturing relationships. And when you're convinced that you're worthless or weak, you don't understand why anyone would want to be your friend or partner. Your lack of trust gets in the way.

Another issue is that you may (again, unintentionally) seek out relationships that will be destructive or harmful. People without a disorder who tend to be positive in their outlook find it very hard to spend time with someone who's constantly down on themselves. The positive types want to "fix" their friends, and then get frustrated when nothing changes.

Traumas are difficult for people who haven't gone through them to wrap their heads around. Because your positive friends have probably always been that way, they really don't understand how someone could genuinely feel that badly about themselves.

They often give advice, such as to get more exercise or more sunshine or think about the things you're grateful for. These tips often do work for someone without a disorder who's temporarily feeling blue or sad. But they're ineffective for someone who's experienced complex trauma.

After trying and failing to get you to think better about yourself, the way that they feel about you, they might give up or at least spend less time with you. You've probably heard it said that misery loves company, so another person who thinks badly about themselves is more likely to hang out with you. Or someone who is attracted to people with negative self-concept because they're bullies or otherwise have their own issues about healthy relationships.

Either way, negative self-concept is a recipe for unhealthy relationships.

Unconstructive thinking patterns that reinforce the negative self-image

You've already learned about the way that neural pathways that get used become stronger, while those that aren't are weakened and pruned back. This happens whether the pathway leads to constructive or unconstructive results.

The more you think negative thoughts, the stronger they become and the harder it is to think positively. It's a vicious cycle.

For example, you feel like you're alone and isolated because of the trauma that you've been through. You meet someone for a date at a local restaurant, and you're nervous about what they might think of you. They turn their head to catch the waitress's eye while you're talking, which you see as a sign of rejection.

Now, everything they do is under scrutiny. Did they look at the cute person at the next table for just a little too long? Did they drop their spoon on the floor because they were careless, or didn't want to look at you anymore?

You might start drinking to take the edge off, but in any case, it's clear to you that they don't like you and there's no chance of a second date. So, you pick a fight or start arguing with them over nothing to cut them down to size, and that's the end of the date.

You can't sleep that night thinking about how they didn't like you or think you were worthy. What you saw on the date only reinforced your view that you're unlovable. And so, the cycle continues, as you continue to search for clues that you're right about yourself and wind up confirming your beliefs.

Less able to solve problems

Thinking is hard for the human brain. It requires the use of a resource that we haven't really had for all that long, compared to how long the lizard brain structures have been on the planet. It's slow work. The brain would really rather conserve energy and go back to using the lizard brain and rules of thumb instead of all this tiring reasoning and problem solving.

If there's no way that the brain can solve a problem using this slow, inefficient system, then why should it waste its time with that resource? If you look at the problem and can't even see how you could start to solve it, what's the point? You give up before you start. There's no point in doing all that work when you're not going to resolve anything.

This is especially true for trauma survivors who don't think very much of themselves. They don't think they're smart enough to solve puzzles that seem a little more complex, so they won't try to in the first place.

The other factor is that with all the hyperarousal and activity that's going on in the brain, there's less capacity for the brain to switch over to logical thinking and problem solving. It's already using up a lot of fuel keeping you alert to danger.

When you're under threat, the brain doesn't think you have time for all the slow processing of facts that problem solving requires. It wants you to survive, and logic can come later after the tiger's gone. Of course, for C-PTSD sufferers, the tiger is never gone so there's never a good opportunity for using reasoning skills.

Can't address their own wants and needs

Have you ever thought about what an earthworm wants when you see it on the sidewalk? Whether it likes the sun, or wants some food, or maybe the company of another earthworm? You've probably never given much thought to what an earthworm needs, because it's not really worthy of your consideration. It's too low down on the food chain for you to think about.

Unfortunately, many complex trauma survivors feel they're roughly on the same level when it comes to value or worth as an earthworm. Why should they think about their own wants and needs, much less express them to someone else? Who cares about worms?

They may not even be able to admit to themselves what their wants and needs are. For example, someone who's feeling alone and alienated doesn't want to think about their desire for intimacy with another person. That will probably make them sadder and more depressed, and even more isolated than they already are.

They're certainly not going to express these needs to another person, because they've learned that other humans are not trustworthy. Talking about what they want might just be an open invitation to be rejected or abandoned by others, so it's much safer to ignore them.

Did any of these effects resonate with you? Do you feel like you're in a downward spiral and that everything you do and everyone you talk to is just reinforcing the negative image you have of yourself? Remember that a wholly negative image is a false one. You may feel like you're a worm, but you're not. Maybe you'll never actually be your ideal self, but you can get much closer to it and feel that you're much closer to it than you do right now.

COGNITIVE DISTORTIONS

It's very common for survivors of complex trauma to think in ways that don't always line up with reality. Thinking that someone doesn't like you because they turned their head away briefly while you were speaking is a cognitive distortion. What you're thinking is inconsistent with what's actually happening in reality.

You might think to yourself that as a result of your trauma that you'll always be afraid. Whenever that thought appears, you'll likely experience a mix of uncomfortable emotions, such as shame, helplessness, frustration, and sadness. The more this thought reoccurs (and as you know that neural pathway gets stronger and stronger the more it's used), the more you will be afraid.

Similarly, once you start thinking that you'll never be able to get over your depression, you'll start thinking more about feeling depressed and your inability to change it. You'll feel sad, hopeless, and down. The more you feel this way, the more likely you are to begin (or continue) isolating yourself from others. You'll start finding excuses to avoid the activities that previously brought you joy. Which, in turn, will make you feel more depressed.

But when you step back from these thoughts, you can see that they're cognitive distortions, or maladaptive thoughts. Because you probably haven't always been depressed in the past, and experienced times when the depression lifted, even if you're prone to it.

Likewise, it's not realistic to think that you will always be depressed for the rest of your life. Even if it's not treated, depression has a tendency to come and go. You learned earlier in the book about recency bias, which is a systemic thinking error where what's happened most recently seems the most important. That can affect your thoughts as well.

There are a number of these distortions that are common to humanity, whether or not someone is suffering from C-PTSD. As with many of the symptoms and effects you've already learned about, most people without the disorder will occasionally have these thoughts themselves. But for them it's usually fleeting, or something they can shake off relatively easily. But if you have C-PTSD, these thoughts can greatly affect your actions, and you can't let go of them quickly or easily.

Catastrophizing

When you immediately assume the worst outcome for yourself, particularly if something goes wrong, you're catastrophizing. Even if it's not the most likely outcome, it's the one that you're drawn to, ignoring others that are more realistic.

For example, suppose someone you know without an anxiety disorder lost their job. If you're friends with them, you would probably assure them that they would soon get another job. They might simply need to rework their resume, start networking, or take some other actions now that they're unemployed.

After the shock of losing their job is over—and I've certainly lost jobs before myself, so I know how much of a shock it can be! —the friend will get into action to find another position. It might take some time, but they'll work on it. This is commonly what happens when people lose their jobs; eventually they'll find work.

For someone who catastrophizes, though, the mind automatically goes to the worst-case scenario of never finding another position again, for the rest of their lives. They might go even further and decide that the job loss means that they'll lose their home and family and eventually end up in a homeless encampment.

These terrible outcomes are certainly possible, but they're not likely. The problem with dwelling on them is two-fold. One, all the rumination continues to make the neural pathways stronger, so traveling down the road to catastrophe in your mind becomes easier and easier.

The second is that if you believe this is your likely destination, then you won't take the actions that lead to better results. You don't ask someone to help you improve your resume. You don't search job boards on the Internet to find who's hiring people like you. And you ignore the networking opportunities in your area. Avoiding all these things makes the adverse events more likely, which is the exact opposite of what you want.

All or none (black or white)

In reality, life is made of nuances and shades of gray. Though taking too many drugs is considered bad, not everyone who does so is a bad person. Getting top grades is common for smart people, but occasionally doing badly doesn't make you dumb. In many situations, there are more than two possible results.

However, those with C-PTSD often take an all-or-nothing approach when it comes to life, especially for themselves. Either you're bad, or you're good. Either you're smart, or you're dumb. Either you're weak, or you're strong. If you get a raise or get promoted at your job, you're successful, if you don't, you're a failure.

Another aspect of life on this planet is that humans make mistakes. All of us get things wrong, say the wrong thing, don't understand the context of the situation which leads to an error, and so on. No matter whether you're good or bad, smart or dumb, weak or strong, no one gets it right all the time.

Therefore, in reality no one is all good or all bad, totally smart or completely dumb, utterly weak or strong. There are times when good people do bad things or make bad decisions. This holds true for everyone, whether they have a disorder or not.

When you start thinking that any bad move (like taking drugs) turns you into a bad person, or that weakness on your part when it comes to something like intimacy makes you a weak person, you're strengthening the deconstructive pathways. And just like with catastrophizing, you begin acting in a way that runs counter to what you really want.

Once you perceive that you've become a bad person, you might feel guilty and ashamed and prevent yourself from doing things you like because you don't think you deserve them. Or you might increase the "bad" behavior, because in for a penny, in for a pound.

Minimizing the positive, or "filtering"

When you feel badly about yourself it's hard to see anything in a positive light. Whatever's happened to you previously that was good you decide was due to luck or chance, being in the right place at the right time or knowing the right people.

You might believe that you got the job you love because you knew someone at the company, not because you have a degree or solid experience in the subject and did your best to wow them at the interview.

Or you went out to lunch with a friend of yours and they mentioned that they don't like your new hairstyle. You found the rest of the discussion pleasant and fun and enjoyed yourself, but once you get home all you can think about is that comment about your hair. You fixate on the one unpleasant detail until it's almost all you remember of your lunch. Now you're angry or upset at your friend and thinking about what a horrible meal you had with them.

Which isn't what really happened that day. But as happens with this type of cognitive distortion, you magnified the small, negative detail until it cast a shadow over the entire experience.

Labeling

Everyone labels themselves and other people. It's a shortcut for our minds that helps conserve energy, and we rely on rules of thumb to get us through the day. Everyone who drives a certain type of car is a jerk. People who go to Ivy League schools are smart. People who go to Ivy League schools are rich. Anyone who wears unusual jewelry is interesting.

The issue is that people with C-PTSD are overly rigid in their labels and don't allow for the kind of nuance that exists in reality. You're probably particularly rigid when it comes to labeling yourself, thinking things like "I'm a loser" or "I'm weak". As you can probably see, this goes hand-in-hand with all-or-nothing thinking.

Taking things personally

Of course, from time to time most people take a comment that wasn't aimed at them as a personal attack or statement about them. Yet for many with C-PTSD, nearly everything that goes wrong or is a negative issue is directly related to something they've done, or because there is something wrong with them.

For example, you may text a friend of yours and not hear back immediately, which is unusual for them. If you take this personally, you might rack your brains to figure out what you said to anger or upset them. You'll reread your message several times to see what you said that was offensive. If you try hard enough, you can probably come up with something.

After you've worked yourself up into believing that you did something wrong, and potentially catastrophizing it into feeling that this friend has dumped you and will never talk to you again, you get a text from them saying that they were in a meeting where phones had to be silenced. Or they were driving somewhere and couldn't respond.

The reality is that other people's behavior is usually more about them than about you. Just as you're mostly concerned with yourself and you're the most important person in your life, other people are mostly thinking about themselves, not you or anyone else. Believing that you're the reason other people do what they do is not a true reflection of what's going on.

Misunderstanding control

Just as you don't have control over anyone else's actions, they don't have control over yours. But a common cognitive distortion is believing that control is located anywhere else besides the person themselves. There are two related fallacies when it comes to control.

One is the fallacy of external control, where everything that happens to you is the result of someone or something else and there's nothing you can do to change it. You didn't get promoted because your boss, or others in the organization, don't like you or preferred the other guy who did get the promotion. Whatever occurs in your life is fate and you're completely helpless to make any changes.

When you don't take responsibility for your own actions, you can't grow as a person and you can't get what you want. It may be true that your boss likes your colleague more than you, but that could also be due to the fact that you often show up late to work and you take more time to get everything done.

While there certainly are things that happen in life that are beyond anyone's control, like accidents or natural disasters, the fact is that the only one who has control over your actions is you. Whether or not your boss likes you doesn't affect whether you get up in time to make it to work (at least not directly), and it doesn't affect whether you get your work done in a timely fashion or if you take too long playing around on social media.

The internal control fallacy is where you believe that your actions directly affect other people's emotions, thoughts, and actions. Because you said something negative, you made the other unhappy. Or you did something that caused another person to feel badly about themselves.

Believing that you affect other people's lives to such an extent is the flip side to taking everything personally. Your friend may be unhappy because their spouse lost a job, or their grandfather died, or they read an article that made them feel sad. None of these things has to do with anything that you said or did.

Reading others' minds

Similarly, it's not realistic to believe that you know what's going on in anyone else's head. Even if you believe that their actions or words are a clue, you still might be getting it wrong.

For example, you might conclude that your counselor thinks you're a waste of time. This might be based on nothing more than your own distorted view of yourself. Or maybe during a session the counselor fidgeted in their chair or looked out the window as you were talking.

But you have no way of knowing that the reason they fidgeted or glanced away is because they think you're a waste of time. They might be fidgeting because they've been sitting in the desk chair for too long.

Maybe their leg started itching and fidgeting was a good way to scratch it. They looked out the window because seeing the landscape helps them think about what you were saying. In other words, there are a lot of reasons why people do things, and many of them are not related to you.

Or it is related to you, but they haven't reached the conclusion that you believe they have. The counselor fidgeted because it's something you've said to them many times, but you haven't taken the action they recommended. That doesn't mean that they think you're a waste of time; they just think you'd be in a better place if you took their suggestion.

Changing others

If only you pushed hard enough or persuaded with the right words, the other person would do exactly what you want and then you'd both be happy. Part of the distortion here is believing that once someone else makes the right changes that would fix everything. The other part is believing that you can change another person.

You might not be happy to get what you think you want, either because that's not what you really want or what you want won't make you happy. Maybe you think that you can be happy once your partner wears the right clothes. But even if you get them to dress differently, they might still not be right for you.

"Shoulding"

It's common to think there is a right way for everyone to act, and they "should" act that way. Including you. So, when you don't do the things you "must" do, such as attain a certain body weight or shape, you'll be upset with yourself. And if someone else "breaks" a rule by acting differently, you'll probably be upset and angry with them.

The reality is not everyone on the planet behaves with the same iron-clad rules and expecting them to only leads to anger and frustration on your part. And if you're using "should" to help motivate yourself towards some kind of ideal behavior, you're setting yourself up to feel guilty and ashamed when you don't do those things you "ought" to do.

Reasoning emotionally

If something feels a certain way, then you might erroneously believe it to be true. For example, you feel like you're a weak person because you weren't able to escape or evade the trauma that happened to you. Since you feel weak, then you believe it must be true that you are weak.

Emotions can be very strong and overrule logical thinking. In fact, logically if you were able to survive the trauma, then you must be strong enough to have done so. Which means you're not truly weak, even though you feel like you are.

Overgeneralizing

With this distortion, people believe that the world is a certain way based on one piece of evidence, or one event. So, if you receive one bad review at work, you may believe that you're really bad at your job, or incompetent in some way.

The issue here is that the situation can become self-fulfilling if you dwell on it for too long or take action (or fail to take action) based on the one event. If you believe that you're bad at your job, then you won't take the steps that your supervisor recommended to improve. You won't take the class you need, or work with your boss to develop an action plan. If you think you're incompetent, you won't take risks that you need to show how competent you really are.

"Heaven's reward"

If you believe that there's a force or energy keeping score, you might think that you'll eventually be rewarded for certain kinds of sacrifices, or by denying yourself certain things. When you make the sacrifices or act in self-denial and then don't get the reward you expected, you might become angry or resentful.

The truth is that life isn't fair. You won't always get what you want, and if you measure every situation in terms of its "fairness" you may end up feeling hopeless when things don't work out the way you believe they "should."

Cognitive distortions and negative self-concept can affect C-PTSD sufferers not only by making you feel badly about yourself, but also interfering with how you interact with others. It gets in the way of your relationships with family and friends, and alters how you behave in public and around others. Fortunately, there are techniques you can use to help you improve your view of yourself.

BUILDING A MORE ACCURATE AND POSITIVE SELF-CONCEPT

The cognitive distortions and negative lens that you view yourself with both involve an error in engaging with reality. The truth is that the complex trauma has led to an inaccurate and destructive perception of yourself. Part of recovery is seeing these distortions for what they are and increasing your ability to see reality for what it is.

Thoughts and emotions are generated by the human brain, but what you think and feel doesn't define who you are. Having the capacity to distance yourself from these activities will help you choose what you want to take action on, instead of reacting as if everything you feel is actually true about the world. Though it's crucial for those with C-PTSD to be able to do this, it's important to anyone's mental health to be able to recognize when to let certain thoughts and emotions go without reacting to them automatically.

Many activities can help you learn to detach from your thoughts, and one that's common is meditation. It'll help you learn to let feelings and thoughts go. There are plenty of ways to meditate, but a good way to start is with a guided meditation. You'll be listening to someone guide you through pleasant imagery or things to focus on, and it's often a lot easier for beginners because having someone else talk helps keep your mind from racing all over the place.

You can find meditations online or by subscribing to an app. If you find a voice that's irritating for whatever reason, try another one. You'll find a lot to choose from, so don't give up if your first try is more annoying than relaxing or you don't like their style of meditation.

Later in this book you'll find some specific exercises that will help you see yourself more accurately. It's critical for you to be able to look at your thoughts objectively, so that you can determine which ones you should pay attention to and which ones should be let go. You are not your thoughts and not your emotions either.

Notice self-critical thoughts

As you go through your day, try to pause whenever you recognize that you're having a negative thought about yourself. For example, if you think "I'm so clumsy" when you drop something, or "I'm so dumb" when someone points out something you think should have been obvious, or "I'm crazy" or whatever thoughts cross your mind that aren't positive about yourself.

Just noticing the thoughts, without judgement, often surprises people when they do this because they have no idea how many times a day they're talking or thinking badly about themselves. Don't feel bad about yourself for feeling bad about yourself either—it's very common!

Acknowledging that you're not speaking well of yourself helps you see that your mental commentary is likely not doing you any favors. In fact, you might conclude that it's no surprise how down on yourself you are, given how often the unconstructive thoughts come up.

Determine how true they are

Look at these thoughts objectively. Everyone drops things from time to time, even those who are trained to catch and hold onto objects. Ask any major league baseball player how often the ball slides right through their mitt!

Likewise, everyone misses what's right in front of their noses sometimes. (Ask any mother whose child can't find what they want in the fridge.) Does missing the obvious really make you dumb? If so, pretty much everyone on the planet is dumb as well.

Think about what evidence you have to support the negative statement you made, as well as what evidence you have against it. Suppose you told yourself that you're dumb because you sent out a document that had grammar mistakes in it. Is that evidence that you're dumb? Or is it evidence that you made errors? Your boss has told you that they rely on your intelligence to get things done, and you can look back on smart choices you've made in the past: evidence against.

We all make mistakes, we all miss what's in front of us, and most of us have done dumb or bad things at least once in our lives. I don't recommend that people go out and get drunk but doing so doesn't make you a bad person. Just because you do something that might not have been such a hot idea, it doesn't mean that you should label yourself negatively over it.

Speak positively to yourself

Many people talk differently to themselves than they would to a friend or loved one. For example, when your friend loses a job, you'll reassure them that any other company would be lucky to have them. Why don't you tell yourself the same thing if it happens to you? Be as kind to yourself as you would be to someone else you love in a similar situation.

When you catch your negative thought, you can try to reframe it right away. For example, if you catch yourself saying "I'm a loser" because you made an error at work, remind yourself that everyone makes mistakes and not being perfect makes you human, not a loser.

Feel embarrassed about dropping something? Tell yourself (or anyone who's listening) that you meant to put that right there.

Write down your good qualities and positive things that you know to be true about yourself. Pull the list out periodically and remind yourself that you do have plenty going for you. You don't have to look at the list only when you're feeling bad. Just give yourself a little boost in the middle of the day. These positive neural pathways will grow stronger as you do.

Reduce shame-bearing opportunities

If there are particular situations that tend to trigger feelings of shame, avoid them if you can. If not, prepare in advance and think about how you can reduce the chances you'll feel ashamed.

For example, suppose you know that your boss is going to call you in because you did something wrong. How could you avoid or lessen the shame you might feel? Maybe by determining how it went wrong and deciding to show the boss that you learned from the mistake. That will demonstrate that you take accountability and also that you understand how to avoid it in the future... all of which is what your boss wants to hear anyway.

Learn to reduce judgments

Holding people, including yourself, up to impossibly high standards is a recipe for failure and shame. If you judge yourself a lot, you probably judge other people as well. And that's a recipe for not having a lot of relationships.

A lot of judgment comes from a place of believing that people know better, and "should" do better, but they're just not doing it. What if you assumed that everyone was doing the best they could at any given moment, including yourself?

None of us can always be at our best, and sometimes you might be running into someone who's not at their best, for reasons that have nothing to do with you. The kind way to act is to assume that they just were overwhelmed. Or that they have different standards and they're meeting their own, which don't happen to be yours.

Ignore the "shoulds"

Thinking that you "should", "ought", or "must" do something is another recipe for failure. It sets you up to feel badly about yourself when you inevitably fall short. Think about why you're not doing something that you feel you should do, or why you're doing something people say you shouldn't.

For example, take the perennial New Year's resolution of "I should lose weight." With that attitude, you won't lose it! Think about why you want to lose weight—maybe you have health issues, maybe you want to look good at a reunion, maybe you just hate buying large-sized clothes because they're not as nice as the smaller sizes.

Now, why haven't you lost the weight? And no judgment! It's not because you're lazy or doomed to be overweight for the rest of your life. Maybe you grew up eating a certain way that was heavy on the processed foods and fat and light on veggies and fruit, and now it's a problem that you're older. Maybe you weigh too much because you've always leaned on food for comfort, and you're extra stressed out at the moment.

Or you always ate a bit more than you really needed, but you exercised it off every day at the gym. Now ask yourself, why aren't you exercising every day at the gym? Maybe you don't have time between getting the kids off to school and yourself to work. Maybe you actually hated working out but did it anyway, and now you have no patience to do things that you dislike. Or you used to go in the mornings before work, which you no longer can because your schedule changed, and the gym isn't open early enough for you to make it to work on time anymore.

Instead of shoulding yourself into making temporary changes that go away as soon as life gets busy or stressful again, think about the choices you can make. You can choose to lose weight to buy cute clothes again, and you'll choose to find a way of eating healthier in order to do so.

Live your own life

A woman who had worked for years with people who were dying asked her patients what their biggest regrets were. And the number one regret that they had was that they hadn't lived a life that was true to themselves.

Everyone has their own ideas about what's worth doing, what they love to do and how they want to spend their time. The people who love you want you to do well in life, but they may have specific ideas as to how you should go about it. Parents and grandparents have ideas that are rooted in the time and culture that they grew up in, which may no longer be true today.

For example, up until very recently many working Americans had one job at a company that they worked at for years and which provided them a pension in retirement. Someone from that background might think it best that you do the same thing, not realizing that the number of companies with pension plans is vanishingly small, and that it's now common and expected to move from job to job.

Your friends may have ideas for you too, as might your colleagues, supervisors, or others. But they're not you, and you're the only one who gets to live your own life. Do what you want to do, even if it's not popular or people think it's unusual (as long as it's legal!)

Change the impact of mistakes

With very few exceptions, modern educational and professional culture is not happy when people make mistakes. Even though errors are inevitable, given that no human is perfect, they're generally looked on as a bad thing and something that should be avoided whenever possible.

However, Silicon Valley and a few other companies have figured out that in order to keep up with the speed of modern technology, they need to try things and have them fail, then figure out what went wrong and improve it for the next round. "Fail fast and iterate" is the motto.

In other words, not only is failure not something to be avoided, it's to be embraced as quickly as possible so that the lessons can be learned, and the next iteration is better. What if you took on Silicon Valley's way of using a mistake, not as a cudgel to beat yourself with, but instead an opportunity to learn? And then take that lesson with you?

LACK OF MEANING

According to DESNOS, in addition to these alterations of thought and self-perception, there are also changes in the system of meaning. This is the difficulty in holding onto a system of faith, or even a belief that justice will eventually be served. Complex trauma can change your outlook on the whole world, including the way that it works or was designed. You might no longer believe that your life has a purpose, or that any life has a purpose

Some with C-PTSD might not believe that there's any real kindness or goodness in the world, that everything is based on selfishness. Or they might lose the hope that they'll ever be forgiven. Some may believe that there's nothing good that can happen to them in this world, because they only exist here to be hurt.

This despair and hopelessness tends to fluctuate over time, so there may be seasons where everything doesn't seem quite so hopeless, mixed in with times of complete despair. Survivors may come to accept what happened to them on a certain level, but have these issues bubble up again when they're ready to go deeper.

Another symptom is questioning the faith or ethics system in which they were raised. This sometimes leads to a belief that the spiritual head is in fact an agent of dark or malevolent forces instead.

Unfortunately, this can lead to a significant inability to make any changes. A complex trauma survivor who no longer believes that life or the world makes any kind of sense ends up in a persistent state of *learned helplessness*. It's what happens when you feel that you're unable to ever escape, and so you stop trying to change your circumstances.

Recovery from the disorder does require you to make some changes in order to help rewire your brain. If you're in a state of learned helplessness, you feel incapable of making choices, acting to support yourself, and making any adjustments that will help you feel better. However, you're not your thoughts and feelings. Just because at the moment you feel unable to do these things doesn't mean that you are actually unable to do them.

CHAPTER SUMMARY

Having a negative self-concept is having a negative view of yourself, one that doesn't match up with reality. Complex trauma brings cognitive distortions, where you think things that aren't necessarily true and lead to a more negative view of yourself and others. However, there are ways that you can learn to improve your relationship with reality and start thinking more constructively.

- Self-concept includes the way you view yourself, your evaluation of your own worth, and your ideal self.
- Having a negative self-concept leads to consequences such as fear of rejection, extreme self-protection, and an inability to understand and take care of your wants and needs.

- Negative self-concept also results in cognitive distortions such as all-or-nothing thinking, catastrophizing, difficulty with relationships, and believing you can read others' minds (usually to your detriment).
- You can build a more positive self-concept by methods such as ignoring "should" statements, noticing your self-critical thoughts and determining whether or not they're true, and reframing mistakes as opportunities to learn.
- The DESNOS criteria also includes a change in the systems of meaning, such that C-PTSD sufferers may no longer see a purpose in life or feel a sense of overwhelming despair and hopelessness.

In the next chapter you will learn about the third factor in a C-PTSD diagnosis which deals with interpersonal issues.

6

DISTURBED INTERPERSONAL RELATIONSHIPS

At this point in the book, you understand how important it was for the survival of humans to have relationships with other humans. Living together helped ward off predators, and by working together groups of people could kill large prey to feed the village or tribe. As a species, we are wired to be sensitive to other people and to enjoy bonding with them.

So much so that the human brain rewards us when we help or give to another person. There are three main neurochemicals that lead to a feeling of happiness, or the "Happiness Trifecta": dopamine, oxytocin, and serotonin (Ritvo, 2014).[1] In addition to the happiness part of the equation, each chemical is responsible for some other activities. You've probably heard of serotonin before, especially if you struggle with depression, because many of the medications that treat the condition work through increasing the availability of serotonin in the brain.

Dopamine is also important in motivation, and you may have heard of oxytocin as the cuddle hormone. When it's released, blood pressure decreases, as does the level of social fear. Trust, empathy, and bonding are all increased when oxytocin is flowing. Giving to other people activates the entire Happiness Trifecta. In other words, relationships are so important to us that our brain releases these three chemicals to encourage us to be happy by bonding more with each other.

That's why disturbed interpersonal relationships are such an issue for anyone who encounters these difficulties. You're missing out on happiness chemicals, and it's distressing for your brain which knows you need to bond with others to survive.

MASLOW'S HIERARCHY OF NEEDS

You may have heard of this concept before, as it's foundational to how science views the personal growth that a person can attain. It helps explain further why being successful in life requires healthy relationships.

Psychologist Abraham Maslow suggested that people are motivated by the need to achieve certain things, and that some needs are more pressing than others (Mcleod, 2020).[2] Imagine the various needs as levels in a pyramid. At the bottom is the largest tier, or the foundation of the most basic survival needs, and at the top is fully achieving your potential as a human being. The original pyramid had five levels, and this has been expanded in some theories, but the basics are the same.

1. Physiological needs (survival)

These are the requirements for functioning as a human being: food, water, rest, shelter, clothing, warmth, and sex. If you're deficient in this level because you're not getting basic needs met, you can't even think about the rest of the growth pyramid.

For example, children who are malnourished don't spend a lot of time learning in school. Their brains can't function properly because they don't have the required fuel. The brain won't want to waste energy on logic and reasoning when other, more important organs need the food instead.

Similarly, if you're constantly seeking shelter from the environment because you don't have a steady place to go, your brain is far more concerned about finding a safe spot than it is about learning subtraction.

Once most of these are taken care of, and they are for most people in developed countries, you can move on to the next level of needs.

2. Safety and security

People like some order and predictability in their environment, which gives them a measure of control and helps them feel safe. Family and society (when both are healthy) can provide this kind of security.

For example, a child who grows up going to school regularly, has a packed lunch or is able to get it at the school cafeteria, and can go to the nurse when they're not feeling well and get something to feel better has order in their lives.

Likewise, an adult who goes off every day to work and comes home to have dinner with the family has a predictable life. They can go to the doctor if they need medical care, send their kids to school, and have the financial stability to buy what they need.

Social stability is another important factor in security. Living in a neighborhood where there's little crime helps people feel safe. And having a police force that catches criminals and a justice system are additional predictors of security.

Someone who's living in a country at war or who is a refugee doesn't experience much of this, and neither do victims of violence and abuse. Having an abuser in the household means that days are unpredictable, because what didn't set them off yesterday could very well set them off today. Living in a region of chaos means that you can't rely on the police or the justice system to capture and deter criminals, who are then free to come after you.

When you've been able to bring a semblance of order and control to your situation, you're then ready to move up to the interpersonal level.

3. Belongingness and love

It's what this chapter is about: the need for healthy relationships with other people. Once someone is fed and clothed and sheltered, and feels reasonably safe in their home, they now turn to the social aspect of life.

Recall that humans who were evicted or shunned from their community in the early days of the species faced death, so having a "tribe" of some sort is built into the human psyche. It doesn't really matter which group, either: any group will do as long as you feel some identification with the others and that you belong.

This is necessary for every person, even those who might consider themselves *introverts* regardless of previous trauma. Introverts need time by themselves to relax and recharge, yet they still require some social interaction and support. Though they may not need as many friends as an *extrovert*, who revels and is energized by spending time with other people.

The need for belongingness consists of a variety of components: friendship, love, affection given and received, intimacy, acceptance, and trust. For someone who is unable to trust others due to the trauma they survived, this level is hard to fulfill. Trust is the basis of bonds with other people, and that in itself is difficult. Not to mention the rest of it, like affection and intimacy.

For those not suffering from a disorder, trust is not hard to come by and they find it easy to accept and be accepted by others. Their default assumption is that others mean well unless they prove otherwise, and relationships aren't held back by suspicions about others.

Once someone has a satisfactory sense of belonging to a group and having relationships, they can move on to the next level.

4. Esteem

Maslow classified this level into two categories: one, the need for external reputation such as status and prestige, and the second of internal esteem from dignity, mastery and independence. For children and teens, the external desire for status and being respected is more important.

As they develop into adults, the internal motivations become stronger. It's less important to achieve a reputation in the field as it is to master it, or to become independent and to achieve your goals.

As you might imagine, C-PTSD sufferers struggle with these as well. People who are abused as children don't feel respected. They have no status since they're the lowest on the totem pole. Their parent might not want to lash out at their spouse, so they lash out at the kids instead where there's less potential blowback. There's no prestige in being hurt or left.

In adulthood, not having been able to reach better status as a child makes it harder to achieve at work. Or even at home. Being able to move up the corporate ladder depends on making key contacts and relationships in the office or in the industry, which are hampered by the lack of healthy interpersonal skills.

On the other hand, those who are able to fulfill themselves internally and externally can make plans to advance. They'll see what they need to obtain to achieve their goals, which may be more schooling or a helpful friendship with a colleague and make those things happen for themselves.

After someone has been able to attain some degree of mastery in their chosen field and have the independence and status that they like, they can then begin to work on the highest and last level in the pyramid.

5. Self-actualization (realization of potential)

In order to reach your full potential, you need to have a solid foundation of self-esteem and compassion. You need to believe not only that you can do what you set out to do, but also that you deserve to be the best version of yourself that there is.

At this point you can focus on your personal growth and fulfillment. You can search out "peak experiences," which are the things that fill you with awe and wonder and where you lose all sense of time in the joy of the experience.

A peak experience occurs when you have a balance between your skill and the expected challenge. It's all-absorbing, and a variety of brain activities occur to facilitate it, which I won't get into in too much detail.

The important thing about the neuroscience behind peak experiences is that you can't be in a hyper-aroused state of threat. You have to be performing at optimal levels, which means your brain can't be consistently scanning for threats.

For example, some people have peak experiences while skiing extremely difficult trails, or bungee-jumping or engaging in similar physical activities. Is there any way that someone who is in fight-or-flight mode would be able to jump off a high bridge attached to some cords? Or decide to get off the ski lift at the top and see the twisting, dangerous trail below?

It's not just dangerous physical activities that can be peak experiences. Some people have them at very large concerts or religious services, where they can be caught up in the joy of all the people surrounding them and the music pumping through their veins. Not great for someone who doesn't trust people, who now is surrounded by hundreds or even thousands of them.

It takes most people a while to reach this level, if they ever do. Not everyone is able to reach their full potential. However, someone with C-PTSD has some things to take care of on the lower levels so they fulfill some more basic needs before they move on to self-actualization.

These five hierarchy levels aren't necessarily rigid, but most of one level must be satisfied before you can be comfortable working on the next level up. Sometimes you might be working on a higher level, and then for whatever reason dip back down into a lower one. However, the basic principle, which is that you need to mostly fulfill one level before you can start work on the next, holds true no matter the situation.

HEALTHY RELATIONSHIPS

Even those without C-PTSD can have difficulties with unhealthy relationships. What does a healthy one look like? It's helpful to know where you're diverging from a healthy place, so that you're aware of the way that it impacts your life and choose to do something differently. There are plenty of examples of dysfunctional relationships, so here's what a healthy one looks like.

It's based on mutual trust, respect, and honesty. (You probably can already see why they're so difficult for a complex trauma survivor, who has understandable issues about trust.) In a healthy partnership, both parties believe that the other has their best interests at heart and doesn't want to hurt them. When you're open and vulnerable to another, you do run the risk of getting hurt, but you understand that's not what they're trying to do.

Both parties respect each other. Obviously, different people have different strengths and weaknesses, but healthy partners believe that they're equals. Neither looks down at the other or feels that they're superior—or inferior. They're two adult humans who have their own minds and bodies, and they respect that each has *autonomy*, or the ability to make choices about their own minds and bodies.

They're honest with each other. If one isn't feeling cherished or respected, they explain this to the other without being confrontational. They don't want conflicts raging out of control, or to allow resentments to grow without telling the other person what's going on. Nor do they want to pretend that everything's fine if it's not. Healthy partners don't sulk or throw temper tantrums or freeze the other person out when they have a problem. Instead, they discuss it to find out if anything went wrong and needs to be fixed.

With all the trust they have in each other, they can be open and honest and communicate well together. This leads to emotional intimacy as they care for each other. In addition, the partners feel safe with each other, because they know the other one isn't going to punish them for no reason. They can share their feelings without concern for being rejected or criticized.

As emotional intimacy builds, so too does the commitment to each other. They want to make the partnership a success, so they're more willing to make compromises that will help keep them together. They are accountable to each other and responsible for whatever household tasks they each end up choosing. In a good partnership, tasks are shared between them so that no one person is shouldering a burden all by themselves.

Maybe most importantly, in a healthy relationship both partners encourage each other to grow and be the best versions of themselves that they can. That means taking risks, which are much easier when you feel safe and cared for, that the other person has your back in case something goes wrong.

Obviously, this is good for romantic relationships, but it can apply to friendships too. Being able to talk to a friend about what's going on in your life and not be worried that they'll reject you or laugh at you is an important part of life. You can have mutual respect and trust for people that you're not especially close to as well. It's the ideal way to relate to friends and family.

You can also extend the idea of healthy relationships to people that you work with. You may not be as close, and you might restrict the trust you have in them to whatever goes on in the office. Respecting your coworkers and supervisors and trusting them is key to having a robust relationship. They might be able to help you in your career, and vice versa. Similarly, you have an equal responsibility for the tasks in your group or department, and everyone communicates well and honestly with each other.

In real life, even people who don't have a disorder don't always have healthy relationships with everyone they know. They might have a dysfunctional family or family member, or colleagues with low levels of emotional intelligence. However, knowing what a healthy relationship looks like gives you something to look forward to. It may also help you determine whether a particular person will be healthy for you, which is important since many C-PTSD sufferers end up with the wrong partners.

WHY HEALTHY INTERPERSONAL RELATIONSHIPS ARE TOUGH ON COMPLEX PTSD PATIENTS

The nature of complex trauma, in addition to the brain's response to it, makes it very hard to form solid bonds with others. The brain is stuck in survival mode, always searching for threats. Which makes every single person you come across a potential danger, and certainly someone you can't trust.

No one can perceive someone as a threat to their very survival and simultaneously trust them with intimate truths about themselves. The protection instinct doesn't diminish, and so your brain is always trying to figure out what the other person's angle is and what they really intend to do. There's no chance for the other person to demonstrate their trustworthiness, and you won't be able to trust them.

Or you may be able to trust them a little bit and have some kind of relationship with them. But as soon as you perceive that they've messed up or abused your trust, you lose even that tiny bit of trust. Unfortunately, since everyone's human, it's likely they'll unintentionally do something to break that trust. A hyper-aroused brain will assume it was done with malicious intent, even though it may have been a completely innocent error.

The very nature of complex trauma makes it likely that the survivor's trust in other people was repeatedly broken and abused. In addition to a brain constantly searching for threats, they have solid evidence that people cannot be trusted.

This might most obviously be the case for those who suffered domestic and/or childhood abuse. In either case someone who was supposed to protect them, either spouse or parent, betrayed that trust over and over again during the time of the abuse. However, refugees and those who grew up in war-torn nations or other areas of chaos have the same issue. Their governments may have betrayed them, or the police that were supposed to protect them, or people in other organizations who repeatedly violated their trust.

Having difficulty regulating emotions is another reason why relationships can be so difficult for someone with the disorder. Whether you tend to lash out in anger, or are constantly extremely worried, or can't seem to get out of your negative moods very easily, partners can find this very difficult to live with. Not knowing what the triggers are for an outburst often makes the partner feel that they have to tiptoe around you, which adds additional stress onto them as well.

In general, there are two developmental issues that are directly impacted by C-PTSD and create problems with having healthy relationships. One of them is self-regulation, which you've already read quite a bit about. The other is attachment, or how people learn to have interpersonal relationships.

People who are able to develop normal interpersonal attachments experienced enough nurturing from their caregivers in childhood that they know other people will stick around. They don't tend to have abandonment issues, because they themselves were not abandoned or neglected when they were young. Children typically blame themselves for things that go wrong (for example, if their parents are getting divorced), but as they grow, they're able to understand that not everything is about them, and therefore, not everything is their fault. They know other people have different thoughts and experiences and that's what causes the actions that they take.

While those who developed a healthy attachment style may occasionally run into people who are not trustworthy, they don't assume that everyone is dangerous until proven otherwise. They can be vulnerable with other people, because in their experience other humans are trustworthy. And if someone else is not trustworthy, they can often see this ahead of time because they can spot the red flags of someone who may be neglectful, abusive, or otherwise not someone to get involved with.

By contrast, someone who survived complex trauma has a very different template for interpersonal interactions. They learned early on that anyone who "loves" (or is supposed to love them, like a parent) will either leave or hurt them, or both.

Not a recipe for being able to trust or rely on others, and dovetails with hypervigilance. If you know someone is going to leave you or hurt you, because in your experience that's all that can happen, then you'll be looking for signs that the person is thinking about leaving or hurting.

When it comes to danger and human evolution, what we as a species learned as we developed that we were better off seeing threats that didn't exist, as opposed to not seeing threats that did exist. If early humans saw grass waving and thought that meant a predator was lying in wait, they'd be able to flee.

If there was something in the grass, then they escaped death. If there wasn't something in the grass, they experienced fight-or-flight prep that ultimately wasn't necessary. It didn't do long-term damage. Acting on a potential threat had no bad consequences: either you survived a predator or some extra stress hormones. (Recall it's only the continuous or too-often release of stress hormones that damages your body, not the one-off, occasional bursts.)

On the other hand, if the early human didn't take the grass waving seriously and there was a predator, they might not survive the encounter. If there was nothing there, they were fine. In other words, not acting in the face of potential danger had potentially deadly consequences. We're the descendants of the ones that survived by taking threats seriously.

In someone who's hyper-aroused, that often means that every little signal is the potential sign of someone who's about to hurt or leave you. Are they wearing a different cologne? Did they look away while you were talking? Did they suddenly start going to the gym? Did they turn down an invitation to lunch because they said they were too busy? Did they take a little too long responding to your work email labeled "urgent"? This is all waving grass to someone with the leave-or-hurt template.

Being able to have (or develop) a supportive relationship is one of the factors in successfully recovering from C-PTSD. Most people who do recover have at least one of these partnerships in their life (Franco, 2017).[3] If you don't currently have one, it's not the end of the world, but it may take you a little longer to heal. At the end of this chapter you'll learn some techniques that will help you navigate the disorder with another person so that they understand what's going on.

SYMPTOMS OF RELATIONSHIP DIFFICULTIES

As you might imagine, there are a number of responses to that earlier, unhealthy template that sufferers of C-PTSD can demonstrate when it comes to relating to other people.

- Find trust hard (as this was already mentioned before, it is not discussed again here)
- Find intimacy hard

You already know how hard it is to trust people, which also makes it difficult to build close bonds with them. Intimacy is the mutual openness, willingness to share and be vulnerable that two people have with each other. It can be sexual as well but doesn't have to be. You can have intimate friendships and be intimate with family members as well.

In fact, there are four kinds of intimacy, all of which can be problematic for a survivor of complex trauma (GoodTherapy, 2019).[4] All of them take some time to develop and don't necessarily happen right away.

1. Experiential

This type of intimacy occurs when people build or strengthen their relationship through leisure activities. For example, if you play in a recreational soccer league, you could share this with your teammates.

2. Emotional

When you feel close enough to another person to share yourself, even when it's not something you're proud of. Someone with body image issues might consider telling their sister about it, knowing that she won't be hurtful about it.

3. Intellectual

Two people can enjoy discussing ideas and opinions with each other, even when they disagree. There's no need to win or compete on whose idea is better; they just enjoy the discussion and learning how the other thinks about the topic.

4. Sexual

This one is the type that many people first think of when they hear the word "intimacy." Not only can people be intimate with each other without sex, they can be sexual with each other without being intimate.

For example, one-night stands are often not so much about the bond between the two partners, but more about the sexual act itself.

In order to allow themselves to be vulnerable, which is an important element of intimacy, people have to feel some measure of security first. Allowing others to see who they really are, both good and bad, is risky. It could lead to rejection, and only those who are comfortable with that possibility can be so open with other people.

Even individuals who don't have a disorder sometimes have a tough time with being vulnerable. But it's particularly problematic for anyone with C-PTSD. They grew up in a world that wasn't safe for them, or have spent years in an unsafe environment. They haven't developed the sense of security that makes vulnerability possible.

Yet everyone wants intimacy of some kind. Complex trauma survivors may seek out relationships and want to build that closeness but pull away as soon as they become uncomfortable. This is puzzling and disappointing to their partners, who don't understand why they're involved in a relationship where they're pulled in, then pushed away repeatedly.

Sexual intimacy is often very challenging for those with C-PTSD, especially those who suffered sexual abuse. There is a lot of shame wrapped up in the act, in addition to any physical damage that may have occurred.

Choose the wrong partner

Many survivors of complex trauma know unhealthy relationships far better than they know healthy ones. They often end up with another abusive partner when it comes to romantic relationships.

For one thing, the survivors find abuse familiar. It's the healthy partners that seem strange or odd, because they have different behavior patterns than someone with C-PTSD is used to. Bad partners (abusive, neglectful, etc.) often display warning signs early on that would drive away anyone with a healthy attachment style. Since trauma survivors haven't been able to develop properly, they don't recognize the red flags that would scare off others.

In addition, as noted above, everyone wants intimacy, even if they don't really know how to go about it because they've never seen it in their own lives. Someone with the disorder may be so desperate to be loved that they're easy prey for an abusive partner. They may not be able to attract a healthy person, so they take what's available.

Or the survivor might be constantly searching for a rescuer. While the specific circumstances of the complex trauma may be long gone, the desire for someone to help them escape may not be.

This could lead to attachment with someone who appears to be a rescuer but is in fact abusive. Alternatively, they might demand that a non-abusive partner be the savior, which is hard on their partner.

May be preoccupied with the personal cause of the trauma

Especially when the trauma is due to abuse or personal violence, the survivor often becomes obsessed with the perpetrator (Richter, 2018).[5] They often see this person as all-powerful or unstoppable. Their own survival depended on their relationship with their tormentor, so they may be unable to let thoughts of the perpetrator go.

Always thinking about someone else creates problems in relationships, particularly romantic ones. Your partner might be upset that you still think about another person, long after that relationship is over.

Create tough living situations for other people

C-PTSD sufferers don't intend to make life hard for their partners, but it usually winds up being the case due to the nature of the trauma. Given that triggers can be unpredictable, even for the survivors, their partners don't know what will set off a scene or emotional outburst, or even total withdrawal.

You learned in Maslow's hierarchy of needs that after the basic needs have been satisfied (food, shelter, clothing) the next level is for safety: predictability and order. Someone living with a trauma survivor loses that sense of predictability in their lives to some extent.

The one with the disorder feels guilty or ashamed when they have an outburst or are otherwise triggered, so they may want to isolate themselves from their partner. Unfortunately, that just makes their partner feel even more rejected.

Even something as simple as a disagreement can make for a truly tense situation if the survivor is triggered and unable to regulate themselves during the discussion. Their partner may be reluctant to bring up any disagreements because they don't want to set the C-PTSD sufferer off. At the same time, they're likely to feel resentment that they can't communicate the way they want.

That resentment can build over time until the partner feels they can no longer be a part of the survivor's life. This only reinforces that early template that people who love you will either hurt you or leave.

IMPROVING YOUR RELATIONSHIPS

While the issues covered above are significant, they're not insurmountable if you're willing to do some work. You'll also need a partner who understands what's going on and is willing to work with you as well. There is hope and you can learn to develop strong bonds with other people.

Have you ever heard the saying that sunlight is the best disinfectant? It comes from a former US Supreme Court justice, Louis Brandeis. He was talking about the benefit of publicity. Transparency, or bringing issues into the bright light of the sun, is the best method of avoiding corruption in public policy (and management). But it's also true for relationships, which require honesty.

One of the best things you can do for potential partners is to be honest about your C-PTSD and the ways that it demonstrates in your actions. There are a number of websites that you can point to (and many referenced in this book) to help your partner understand what it is and how it affects your daily life. There are things that people without the disorder take for granted, and they may not recognize that the reason you don't do the same thing is because of the disorder.

You'll probably still have to explain after a triggering situation what happened. They'll understand it as a function of the disorder, not how you feel about them, if you've previously been open about it. It's important that they know many of your actions aren't personally biased against them but are a reaction to what happened to you earlier in your life.

You can also discuss some of your likely triggers. If you can see a pattern for some of your actions, you can let them know what's likely to cause a reaction. Not only will they understand when it happens, but they can also help you avoid the situation.

For example, suppose one of your triggers is a dark alley. If you let your friends know, they'll try to avoid the bars that open off a dark alley and go into the brighter ones or those with entries on a bright sidewalk instead. Bear in mind that you may have to remind people more than once. This lets you practice not taking things personally and recognizing that other people have a variety of things on their minds.

Another great tactic is to see a therapist or counselor who specializes in C-PTSD. Even someone who loves you and wants you to heal and be well isn't equipped to handle everything that the disorder throws at you. Rather than overwhelming a loved one or friend by asking for help that they just aren't capable of, find someone who understands how to provide that kind of assistance.

A professional won't make you feel bad or guilty about the trauma and how it's impacted your life. They can help you look back to see if you can find any patterns in your triggers. You also may sometimes have unconstructive thoughts about your partner and a therapist is a much better person to discuss those with! They provide objective guidance, and you can be honest with them because you don't have to worry about hurting their feelings.

Therapists are there to help you, specifically. Unless you're in couples counseling (and you can certainly be in both), the counselor wants to help guide you to the best outcome for you, not necessarily the best outcome for your partner.

Anyone who's involved with you, either friends or family or sexually, has mixed motives because they need to take care of themselves as well. They bring their own biases and experiences to the table, which may result in them giving advice that's not helpful or even counterproductive. Not because they're out to get you, but simply because they don't know any better.

A counselor who's experienced with C-PTSD sufferers knows that you probably don't have the knowledge you need to determine who's a healthy partner for you or not. At least not yet. They can help you identify warning signs in potential partners, with no ulterior motive than assisting you in the healing process.

You might have noticed that both of these recommendations entail asking for help, which can be very difficult for complex trauma survivors. You have to trust that the people you're asking will provide it and not use your pain against you. It's also critical to recognize that asking for help does not make you weak.

In fact, asking for help shows strength because you are taking that risk. Though it may seem like a huge risk to you, remember that people love to help others. It's ingrained in the human brain to make us happy by releasing the trifecta of pleasure neurochemicals: serotonin, oxytocin, and dopamine. When you're asking for help, you're actually giving these other people a chance to feel a wash of happiness.

It's not really as one-sided as many people think it is. Yes, you're receiving help. But your helpers are getting something out of it too, even if they don't know it. As you get stronger, you'll also have the opportunity to help others and release the Happiness Trifecta in your own head.

CHAPTER SUMMARY

Difficulty with interpersonal relationships is one of the key markers for C-PTSD. It can make you and the people around you miserable until you start taking steps to counteract it. You can learn techniques to make building bonds with other people easier, which is important because we all need relationships to thrive as people.

- Maslow's hierarchy of needs shows that after satisfying basic necessities like food and shelter and being safe and secure, people are motivated to fulfill themselves through relationships.
- Healthy relationships are based on mutual trust and respect,

and are characterized by the support each gives the other in fulfilling their potential.
- Due to the nature of complex trauma and the way that it impacts survivors, relationships are hard for them to develop and sustain.
- Relationship problems include difficulties with intimacy, trust, choosing the wrong partner, being obsessed with their tormentor, and creating a chaotic environment.
- Explaining to others the nature of the disorder and how you typically express it, as well as finding an experienced therapist, are helpful for improving interpersonal relationships.

In the next chapter you will learn techniques to help you on your road to recovery.

7

RECOVERING AND RECLAIMING YOUR IDENTITY

Healing from complex trauma isn't easy. If it was, you'd already have done so! In the last chapter you learned that asking for help is an excellent way to assist you in the recovery process. There are a variety of psychological treatments (known as *modalities*) that have been shown to help sufferers of C-PTSD that can be prescribed for you, and those are listed at the end of the chapter.

There are also exercises and techniques that you can learn to do yourself. In addition to working with a therapist, you can start counteracting the negative self-perception that you've been carrying around with you. There are known methods for helping you increase your self-esteem, as well as emotional regulation exercises. By working to grow as a person beyond the trauma, you open up whole new worlds for yourself and increase the possibility that you can find intimacy with others in a healthy, nourishing way.

Most of these exercises you'll need to revisit periodically, because one session isn't going to get you to where you want to go. You might feel that you're recovered to some extent, and then discover a new trigger or a new issue. Coming back and reusing these techniques will help you stay healthy and on your path.

There is hope. You don't have to suffer alone. Although right now you may feel completely isolated, there are others who have struggled just as you are. Not only are you not the only person to experience these issues, others have been able to heal from them. As they say, the journey of a thousand miles starts with one step. All you need is the willingness to take a step, and then take a step after that.

EXERCISES FOR BETTER SELF-PERCEPTION AND SELF-ESTEEM

You've learned how critical it is to look at yourself accurately, instead of through the dark lens that you've been using for so long. It may seem difficult, but you can prove to yourself that what you've been telling yourself up until now isn't actually true. In Chapter Five you learned about the mental habits that need to be adjusted in order for you to be more in tune with reality, and here are some activities to perform that will help you along the way.

Evidence that confirms or denies

In this exercise, you'll reflect on each belief that you have about yourself. On a sheet of paper or in a journal, divide the page into three columns. Label the left column "Proves" and the right column "Disproves."

In the middle, write down all the negative beliefs that you have about yourself and the negative self-talk. It might take you more than one session to identify them all, but at the end you want to make sure that you've written down every single one of them.

For each belief or negative statement, think of the evidence that you have that either proves or disproves what's in the middle column. Write them down in the appropriate column.

Suppose one of your beliefs is that you're always afraid. When you think about it, you remember a time in the past when you weren't afraid. You write that down in the right-hand column because it disproves this belief about yourself. Write down as much about this time you weren't afraid as you can recall. What was the situation, what action you took, how you felt, where you were, etc. If you can't remember all the details it's fine, but just write down as much as you can.

This not only helps you see that the belief is incorrect, but helps you remember what it was like not to be afraid. When you write it down, you can always look back on your evidence when the thought or belief comes back.

Repeat this for all your beliefs, and make sure that what you're writing down as evidence in either the Proves or Disproves column is true.

For example, suppose that you write down your belief that your date the previous night doesn't like you. You're tempted to write down the fact that they looked away from you while you were talking as proof. But is it really?

There are many reasons why they might have turned their head, and only one of them is because they don't like you. Unless they specifically said to you that they looked away because they don't like you, it's not proof of anything.

They said they'd like to see you again at the end of the date. Would someone who doesn't like you say that? You'd have to put that in the Disproves column.

Once you complete the exercise, if you've done it truthfully, you will probably have a lot more material in your Disproves column than in your Proves column. If that's not the case, I invite you to take a closer look at everything you considered proof. Is it really, or is it your negative thoughts tinting the facts?

You might have a couple of beliefs where you have more proof than disproof, or you might have none. If you have many though, you'll need to go back and think more objectively about the facts you have in evidence and see whether the proof really is true.

Reframe based on the previous exercise

Once you've finished the previous exercise, you'll see that you have disproved many of the negative statements you tell yourself. This shows you very clearly that what you think really isn't rooted in reality, because the facts are telling you something different.

Use this information to reframe your beliefs into something positive. When a negative statement or thought comes up, reframe it. Many people find it helpful to write down these new statements, so you have them handy when the old thoughts return.

For instance, in the example above you disproved the belief you had that your date's actions meant they didn't like you. You could reframe this in more than one positive way. You could say "Someone can look away from me when I'm speaking and still like me." Or "I don't always have to assume the worst about people." Or "I can look at the big picture and not worry about small circumstances like having a date look away from me."

You can do this for each belief. Suppose you proved to yourself that you're not always afraid, because you recalled times when you weren't afraid. You might say "I won't always be afraid," or "I may be afraid right now, but I won't always be."

It is important that you say things in a positive way but also be honest. If there's a statement that you're having difficulty with, you can always reframe it to something like, "I am working on [thing that's difficult]." For example, "I am working on not taking what other people do personally" or "I'm working on not being afraid all the time." Make sure it's both positive and true.

Over time you'll be able to do this exercise and have fewer negative beliefs, because the positive reframing you did helped require the pathways. And instead of saying "I'm working on not taking everything personally" you can truthfully say, "I don't have to take things personally" or even simply, "I don't take things personally."

Visualize achieving a goal or way you'd like to lead your life

Visualization is surprisingly powerful. When you're suffering from C-PTSD, in some ways your brain is (unintentionally) working against you. But when you can harness it in positive ways, it can help you more than you might think.

One thing that athletic coaches, especially at the elite competitive level, have known for some time is that visualizing the race or competition helps athletes win. For example, if you're a swimmer, your coach would advise you to make a movie in your mind where you feel yourself exploding off the starting block, quickly finding your rhythm, passing your closest competitor, and touching the wall first at the end.

When you visualize in detail, it's a dress rehearsal for what you're actually going to do. Your mind movie activates the same mental pathways that it does when you are actually performing the action (Swart, n.d.)[1]

You don't have to be an athlete to use visualization, as successful people in other areas of life do this as well. You can use it to work through a tricky situation that's coming up or think about how you would like your life to look in recovery, or to reach a certain goal.

For example, suppose you want to have a certain daily routine where you get out of bed, exercise (which is great for you for a variety of reasons), have a nutritious breakfast and some family time before you leave for work at a job that you love. Walk through this all in detail, including what it smells, sounds, tastes, and feels like, not just what it looks like. Feel (or imagine) how relaxed you are after a good night's sleep. Picture yourself putting on your favorite workout clothes that make you feel good.

What kind of exercise do you like? If it's biking, in your mind put on your helmet and start pedaling. If you're pedaling down a pretty forest path, imagine how good the woods smell and what the bird chirping sounds like. Or "hear" your favorite playlist.

Or maybe you prefer a hard mountain bike trail that's rough and rocky and gives you a thrill when you get to the top, just before you start blasting your way back down. Mentally see the obstacles you ride over and feel the wind in your face, the muscle tension in your arms and legs, the snapping of branches.

When your mind arrives back home, imagine sluicing off in the shower or bath and then putting on your favorite clothes for work. Then you get to sit down at the breakfast table with your family and your favorite thing to eat. Smell the eggs frying or the pancakes browning. Listen to the happy chatter of your kids and feel the dog's tail wagging against your leg.

Now you're on your commute to work. What music are you listening to? Where do you want to work—inside at the office, using the company truck to get around from site to site? Imagine a great day at work.

All that sensory detail is helpful for your brain. Many people like to make vision boards that keep these dreams or ideas front and center. You find images or objects that represent what you want and put them on the board where you're constantly reminded of them. You might cut out pictures from magazines or download them online; use objects that you've found, like stones that represent mountain biking; and anything that brings these details to mind.

There's a lot of stimuli out there in the world, so human brains naturally filter a lot of it out. Otherwise, there would be too much detail for the person to function. When you visualize and have a vision board, you're telling your brain what it should pay attention to.

Have you ever noticed that when you decide to buy a certain kind of car that all of a sudden you see that car everywhere you look? Suppose you decide you want to buy a Jeep or something like it for off-roading. All of a sudden, there are so many more Jeeps on the road than you've ever seen before!

It's not because everyone had the same idea as you, all at the same time. It's because you, in effect, told your brain to focus on Jeeps. Now your brain sees a Jeep and brings it to your attention. You just never noticed before because your brain was filtering them out instead.

Use this to your advantage. Tell it to pay attention to a job where you can drive around from site to site and make your own schedule because that's your preferred way of working. You can visualize yourself at such a job, and if you decide to use a vision board, find pictures of happy workers in their trucks. When your brain comes across something related to these images, it will stop filtering it out. You might catch a job listing or find someone who's working in a job like this, because your brain is now attuned to focusing on it.

Make three lists

In addition to reframing your negative beliefs about yourself, it's helpful to make positive lists. When you start off, you might find you don't have a whole lot of positive things to say. But keep adding to it. As you work on the healing process, you'll be able to set aside more negativity and discover more constructive ways to talk to yourself.

1. What you like about yourself

Everything you like needs to be on this list, no matter how silly you think it might be. Maybe, in addition to being kind to animals, you like that you can roll your tongue. Or you can imitate accents. Or you have compassion for others. Or you're good at playing with kids.

Whatever it is that's positive about you, write it down. Make sure you keep a copy of it so you can come back to it periodically. Refer to it when you're feeling particularly disappointed or upset with yourself, so you have a reminder of all your good qualities.

Also, reflect on it periodically through your healing journey. Many people start off feeling like they're weak but reach a point in the process where they're able to recognize how strong they really are, to have made it through. You can add it to the list. As you feel more secure and confident, you can try new things. You may or may not be a success. But you can still be proud of yourself for trying.

2. Your proudest moments in life

Likewise, when you reflect on your life you can find things that you did well or that reflect well on you. Maybe you found a dog lying by the side of the road and you took it to the vet. Making a friend who was having a hard day feel better. Write down as many as you can.

Reflect on this one too. Sometimes when you're feeling worthless or weak come back to the list and remind yourself that you have done worthy things and that you are a worthy person. And as you go through the process, come back to it to write down more things that you're proud of. You might have done things that you forgot about.

Or you've been doing activities during your healing that you can be proud of. Continue to add those to the list.

3. Everything you're thankful for

Take your time with this list. Write down as many as you possibly can, no matter how small it seems right now. Every tiny little thing counts. Once you've written them all down, cut the sheet of paper into strips with one item of gratitude on the strip. Fold them up and put them in a jar or other container.

When you could use a shot of gratitude - which is usually when you're feeling bad - dip into the jar and grab a piece of paper at random. Read your statement. If you need more, pull out more. When you're able to shift into a feeling of gratitude, refold them and put them back in the jar so they're available for next time.

Any time you think of something else to be grateful for, write it down and put it in the jar. Like the other two lists, these will probably grow as you progress along your road to recovery.

It's important to remember that the road isn't usually linear. Most people don't go from suffering C-PTSD symptoms to being recovered in a completely straight line. Instead, for many you make some progress, and then either plateau or retreat a little bit. Then you move forward again, and again there will be a hiccup.

If you move back one step for every two steps forward, you're still making progress. Don't let the interruptions, plateaus, and bumps throw you. They'll happen, but you can keep moving forward anyway.

Help another person

If you've ever been in a 12-step recovery program, you might be familiar with the saying, "If you want self-esteem, perform esteemable acts." Helping other people isn't the only method of creating a truer self-perception that isn't so negative, but it is a good one.

And it doesn't have to be big: you don't have to save someone's life or donate a kidney. You could let someone who's got two small children and a big shopping cart and look of exhaustion go ahead of you in line at the grocery store. You could pay for the person behind you at the coffee shop.

Pick up whatever the person in front of you dropped, particularly if they're elderly or otherwise have a hard time bending down. Give up your seat on the bus to someone who's older or more tired than you. Small acts of helping may be the only things you can do for others at the moment, and they're still good for the person you're helping as well as yourself.

This works in two ways for you, the helper. One is that you get that release of the Happiness Trifecta neurochemicals, so you get pleasure out of the deal. It also helps you affirm to yourself that you are a good, giving person. That you're not as bad as you sometimes tell yourself that you are. The more you help, the better you'll feel about yourself.

And sometimes it's just nice to get out of your own head. Even people without a disorder of some kind like to spend time concentrating on other people so they don't have to think about themselves or worry about anything. They can focus on the other person instead.

Practice self-confident body language

As you become better able to recognize your own positive traits and be less negative in your self-talk, you'll be more confident. Another powerful way to boost your self-confidence is to act like it.

While in many aspects of life it's not possible to "fake it 'til you make it," self-confidence is an outlier in this regard. To some extent, the more you practice acting self-confident, the more self-assured you'll feel. That doesn't mean that you can do a "power pose" for a couple of minutes and suddenly you're ready to take on the world! But it does mean that you can act *as if* you're self-confident and it will have a positive impact.

Earlier in the book we discussed the mind-body connection, and that it goes both ways, not just from mind to body. Smiling even when you don't feel like it tells your brain that you're happy, or at least pleased about something. Even a fake smile can change your mood.

Similarly, taking on self-confident body language tells your mind that you are feeling self-confident. Regularly doing so can help you strengthen that positive pathway in your brain. The good news is that acting as if you're self-confident isn't really all that hard. You don't have to do any strange contortions or stand on one leg or anything physically difficult.

When you think about confidence, who springs to mind? An athlete like Serena Williams or Lionel Messi? Or maybe you're thinking of business leaders, such as Richard Branson or Jeff Bezos. Perhaps you've got a politician in mind, or a friend you know who always seems self-assured.

How do they stand? When they talk to reporters, how do they hold themselves, and where are they looking? When they enter a room, what do they do when they want to introduce themselves to someone? How do they walk around the room?

You can probably picture a lot of that in your head right now. They stand tall with their heads held high. When they speak to people, even reporters, they look directly into the other person's eyes. They smile and nod at what the other person's saying - sometimes even when the reporter's giving them a hard time!

When a confident person walks into a room, they have that same erect stance, and when they see someone they want to talk to, they introduce themselves and give a firm handshake. As they're walking around the room, they plant their feet firmly and move without much hesitation.

Even if you're not feeling particularly (or even at all) confident in yourself, you can still mimic these mannerisms and they'll help you feel more positive. Best of all, you can practice many of these moves wherever you are.

Stand tall when you're in line at the grocery store. Look directly at the cashier when you're ordering food. Not only does the eye contact benefit you, but it helps them feel like less of a robot. Win-win! People respond well to others who appear confident, so you may find that your interactions improve while you're practicing.

With your friends you can practice standing tall and shaking hands, in addition to eye contact and allowing yourself to react to their speech with nods and smiles. Even when you're watching TV at home, practice sitting tall with your head held high and shoulders back instead of hunched or curved.

There are ways to stand to give yourself a temporary confidence boost as well. A well-known "power pose" is to stand tall with your legs spread apart and hands on your hips. This appears aggressive to other people if you do it in front of them, so try to do it when no one's watching. Or in a quiet place just before you do something that triggers anxiety, like a job interview or speaking on stage.

There's a lot of information available elsewhere about body language, but the basics of confidence will help you on your journey to recovery.

Make positive and truthful affirmations

Affirmations, while they may sound a little weird or silly, do have neuroscience backing their use. The more you repeat positive affirmations, the more those constructive neural pathways get strengthened while you sleep.

It's also important that you believe what you're saying. For example, if you're unhappy with your body because it's too thin, you won't believe yourself if you say something like, "My body is the right weight." That type of affirmation doesn't help. Instead, you can change it to something that is true, such as "I am working on my body to achieve a weight I am happy with" or a similar statement.

Affirmations will also work much better if you genuinely think about what you're saying as you make the statements. If you just blast through them without thinking, you're not giving your brain a lot of time to process and really be aware of what you want it to pay attention to. Really think about what each statement means as you say it.

You can give yourself reminders, such as putting them on sticky notes on your mirror or in your phone with an alarm so that you do your affirmations every day. Once daily is good, but twice is even better.

If you're not sure what affirmations to use, you can try this exercise of seven sets, memorizing one per week. After you've practiced consistently for seven weeks, you'll have a healthier view of yourself.

Week one

1. I accept responsibility for myself and for everything I think, say, and do.
2. I choose to stay constructive in my actions.
3. I refuse to talk negatively to and about myself and to accept the negativity others may have towards me.
4. I make choices and accept the results of those choices.
5. I control the expression of my thoughts, ideas, wants, expectations, and perceptions.

Week two

1. I do my own thinking and act accordingly.
2. When I make a mistake or experience defeats or losses, I don't blame anyone else.
3. I enjoy doing my work to the best of my ability and on a consistent basis.
4. I do not attach to thoughts of shame, guilt, or blame.

Week three

1. I accept that problems and obstacles are challenges for my own personal development.
2. I rid myself of shame, guilt, or blame.
3. I don't procrastinate because my goals motivate me.
4. I don't quit.
5. I don't compare myself to anyone else, nor do I let comparisons affect me.

Week four

1. I do my best to develop and maintain a positive image of myself.
2. I am always authentic and true to myself.
3. I don't base who I am on what roles I play in life.
4. I totally and unconditionally accept myself exactly the way I am.

Week five

1. I am confident in my convictions and stand up for them.
2. I rely on myself for support, both financially and morally.
3. I see reality clearly and let go the things I can't change.
4. I don't allow fear of failure or rejection to hold me back.

Week six

1. I don't need anyone else's approval for the way I live my life.
2. I don't let others talk me into things that aren't good for me.
3. I treat myself gently and kindly.
4. I don't overdo it, preferring to avoid excess.

Week seven

1. I stand tall and smile when I greet others.
2. My mistakes teach me lessons I learn.
3. I don't need to impress others with my importance or value.
4. I love being me.

SELF-CARE AS BEST YOU CAN

You've probably had well-meaning people tell you about these acts of self-care in the belief that they would "fix" you. They won't, but they can help you in your quest for trauma recovery. These are ways that you can be kind and compassionate to yourself, as well as giving you the best chance for healing. These are good habits that will help you with physical health, which also supports your mental health.

Sleep

Any form of PTSD, including Complex, usually results in sleep difficulties. But the more you can practice what's known as "good sleep hygiene," the better off you'll be along your journey to recovery.

Standard go to sleep/wake up times

Since sleep for many survivors isn't very deep or healing, they often find themselves sleeping in the morning or during the day. This makes it hard to sleep at night and creates a vicious cycle. Try to stick to a schedule for the entire week and not alter it too much.

If you wake up very tired, you can have a quick nap in the late morning or early afternoon. Keep it quick and early so you can get through the day without compromising your nighttime sleep.

No screens, heavy exercise, heavy food, or heavy alcohol within an hour of bedtime

Modern screens, which means cellphones, tablets, laptops, TVs, etc., emit blue light which tricks your body into thinking it's daylight, so it doesn't release the sleep prep mechanism (melatonin). Give your body a break so it can get ready for sleep naturally.

Heavy food, exercise, and drink within an hour of sleep will prevent you from having the rest that you need. You'll likely be waking up frequently even if you can get to sleep easily.

What can you do in that hour? Spend time with the family, on a favorite hobby, reading, or any combination of these three.

Keep your cell phone in another room

In addition to the blue light the screen emits, most people have notifications and messages beeping and buzzing and flashing lights. These are bad for everyone, not just people with C-PTSD. Keep your phone charger in a different room and leave your phone there overnight.

There's no reason for you to wake up and immediately scroll through social media or check your email. Give yourself time in the morning to do positive things like exercise, meditate, and repeat your affirmations.

Keep the room quiet, dark, and cool

Most people sleep best when their environment is dark, not too warm, and silent. There are a variety of ways that you can achieve all these objectives, according to what you personally find comfortable.

You can buy eye masks, most of which can also be heated up or cooled depending on preference. Some come with soothing scents like lavender. Or you can get room-darkening shades to block out light for the whole room (or both).

Earplugs or sound generators are great ways to shut out noise. Turn down your thermostat in the winter for better sleeping and use a ceiling or other fan in the summer to keep the room cool.

Nutritious food

You don't have to follow a specific diet if you don't want to. You probably already know what's good for you to eat: a balance of fruits and vegetables, lean protein, good fats like avocados, walnuts, olives and their oils, and whole grains. Not too much.

Processed food has a lot of preservatives as well as sugar, fat, and salt which can damage your body. Think of adding healthy, pretty food with vibrant colors like berries instead of what you're removing from your diet (store cookies, fried foods, too much fast food.)

Exercise

It's not so much about what you do as making sure you're consistently doing it. If you haven't been moving at all, make it a goal to walk outside for ten minutes a day to start and work your way up. The guidelines recommend 150 minutes moderate exercise per week for basic health.

It's best not to do one 150-minute session or two 75-minute ones, but to do something more like half an hour five days a week. Brisk walking counts as moderate exercise, so if you can get out the door for half an hour a day and walk briskly, you're all set. Bring the family with you too!

If you really don't think you have a half hour all at once in your day, don't worry, you can break that up into two 15-minute sessions or three 10-minute sessions. And if you don't like walking, do what you like, as long as it's moderate (or harder). Play tennis or basketball, dance, and mix things up so you don't get bored.

Hydration

The body is on average mostly water (60%) and your brain is composed of even more water, about 73%. When you're not getting enough water, your body isn't working optimally. Food that is mostly water, like strawberries and watermelon, counts toward your intake.

Get a reusable water bottle and bring it with you. You can find some that tell you how much to fill up each day and how much you should drink by a certain time if you find that helpful. Reusable water bottles cause less environmental harm than water you pick up in bottles at the store. Start drinking! If you live in a dry climate or at high altitude you may find you need more water.

Mindfulness exercises

Earlier in this book we mentioned that meditation is a good way to get started with mindfulness, and that guided meditations are good for beginners. You can choose any method that works for you. Mindfulness is one of the best ways to develop better emotional regulation (The Wellness Society, n.d.)[2]

Some people don't do well with traditional meditation and that's OK. Exercise itself can be a good way to be mindful. Or you can choose an activity during the day to really experience, like brushing your teeth, washing dishes, or taking a shower.

Key into the sounds, smells, and how it feels in and on your body for the short time that you do these activities. Pay attention only to what you're doing, and when your mind wanders (as it likely will) just bring yourself gently back to the activity.

It's also helpful to combine mindfulness, breathing, and movement. Becoming aware of your body and your breathing sensations helps you feel safe with your body. Instead of being fearful of it, you can learn to approach with curiosity instead. As strange as this may sound, you can actually practice and get better at relaxing.

There are a variety of methods you can try. Some you've probably heard of and others you might not have, but you can find information about all of these online. You might be able to find a teacher of the practice near you, and if not, you can search for online classes.

Yoga

There are many varieties of yoga, and you'll likely find a studio or classes near you. It is common for yoga instructors to touch students to help guide them into the poses or movements correctly. If that's an issue, you can let the instructor know ahead of time. Or stream classes in your home.

The Wellness Society notes that the ending pose for most yoga classes, known as Shavasana, is particularly helpful for helping you learn to relax. In this pose you simply lie on your back with limbs relaxed and eyes closed for a period of time, usually several minutes.

Tae Kwan Do (or Taekwondo)

This Korean martial art is about much more than fighting. If you've seen competitions, you've seen some amazing kicks, as the name is about the discipline of "fists and feet." However, the other element is discipline.

Taekwondo practices unity: body, mind, and life, and dealing with confrontation (USATKD, n.d.)[3] Its practitioners seek harmonious personal development.

Tai Chi (tai chi chuan)

Originally, the Chinese practiced this as a martial art, but now it's used as a form of exercise that employs grace in its movements. Each action flows naturally and smoothly into the next and is accompanied by deep breathing. It's noncompetitive, and like yoga, there's more than one style.

It's low impact and suitable for most people, including older adults.

Qi Gong (chi kung)

This Asian practice is similar to yoga, with many different styles. It also incorporates breathing, posture, and movement. The name refers to skill obtained by practice and breath or energy.

Feldenkrais

This is a method that uses visualization and gentle movement to focus on functionality. It too makes use of awareness (connecting the physical body to what's going on within you) and breathing techniques. The Russian doctor Moshe Feldenkrais developed it to help people live the life they want.

Quit smoking, and quit drinking

There are no health benefits to smoking, and a variety of methods of quitting. If you know cold turkey won't work for you, try using a patch or gum or other way that you can gradually decrease your use.

Even one drink per day has been proven to have a negative impact on health mentally and physically. Any benefits in alcoholic drinks can be found in other substitutes. For example, the antioxidant *resveratrol* is the healthy element in a glass of wine, but you can also get it by eating skin-on red grapes.

PSYCHOLOGICAL TREATMENTS

In addition to the suggestions and exercises above that you can do yourself or practice with friends, loved ones, and/or fellow survivors, there are a number of therapeutic treatments that have been shown to help C-PTSD sufferers begin to live a better life.

Unfortunately, our culture tends to stigmatize people with mental health issues. We don't try to shame someone with a broken foot for getting treatment, and likewise no one who has a mental health condition should be shamed for it either. But people do. However, don't let this hold you back from seeking help.

As noted earlier, the disorder is called "Complex" for a reason. It's not like having the flu, or a broken leg, or even something as relatively "simple" as depression with no other conditions. People don't simply grow out of it. Or get better by eating nutritious food and getting enough sleep, though those things are certainly helpful. There are a variety of symptoms that require treatment in order to heal.

Because of the nature of complex trauma, it's not very likely that you'll be able to heal yourself without some competent therapeutic help. Don't be shy about seeking it out. You'll want to find someone who specializes in C-PTSD (or DESNOS), if you can; otherwise, an expert in PTSD is best.

Finding one is fortunately not as hard as it used to be with the internet, and you can make your search in private if you're concerned about anyone finding out. If you're a veteran, whether or not your complex trauma resulted from your service, check with the Veterans

Administration and their mental health resources. Fortunately, they have a lot of expertise in helping people recover from PTSD and C-PTSD.

If you work for a large company, they may have an EAP or Employee Assistance Program that can help refer you to someone who'll be able to help you. It's possible they'll have someone on staff who's an expert, but more likely they'll help you find someone. You can also search the Internet for therapists and doctors who specialize in C-PTSD and see if you can find one near you. If you're in the US and mental health isn't covered by your insurance, many have sliding scale fees where you pay what you can afford.

Anxiety can be either mentally or physically based. A treatment that's based on reframing your thoughts may not work as well when your anxiety has become so physical that now fear itself is the problem. Once you find someone to help you, they may work with one or more of the following *modalities* or types of treatment.

Cognitive behavioral therapy (CBT)

This method is used with a variety of disorders including anxiety and depression. It involves looking at your thoughts to see if they're true. You learn to stop attaching to your thoughts and to reframe back to reality when negativity strikes. This can be very effective for mental anxiety but may not work as well for anyone who's dealing with the physical type.

Although you do talk about your thoughts with your therapist, you're not typically lying down on a couch and closing your eyes as you might have seen on TV or in the movies. Normally you'll both be sitting across from each other and having more of a conversation.

EMDR

Eye Movement Desensitization and Reprocessing seems to make disturbing thoughts less intense by using eye movement (typically side to side). The eye movements are similar to what our eyes do in REM sleep, which is when we dream and find associations between memories.

Similarly, EMDR can help people get more perspective on their trauma, by moving it to regular memory and relegating it to something that happened in the past instead of now.

Sensorimotor psychotherapy

This modality focuses on the body and what we can learn from physical reactions, so it can be worthwhile for those suffering from physical anxiety. It works with the body as well as the thinking mind and emotions. (Sensorimotor refers to pathways that involve sensory and motor functions, which basically means body movements.)

Pesso-Boyden System Psychomotor (PBSP)

Developed by two dancers, PBSP combines a body and mind approach. You learn exercises that help you learn about your sensorimotor and emotional signals in your own unique body.

Somatic experiencing

Another body-oriented therapy, it helps you make use of your body's own healing systems. While you're tracking feelings, images, and sensations in your body, you'll learn how to get past the emotionally frozen state of overwhelm.

The Comprehensive Resource Model (CRM)

Instead of a phased model, in CRM the work occurs simultaneously. The therapist helps you find that everything you need is within you and teaches you how to ultimately do this on your own.

Internal Family Systems (IFS)

IFS may sound like "family therapy," which many addicts are exposed to in a treatment center, but it's actually quite different. Many people feel that they're made up of different parts and each part has a different role. For example, you might have a version of you as a frightened child, a boss or thinker, someone who gets angry very easily, a people-pleaser, and so on. This therapy helps you integrate all your different parts, because there's a reason each of them is there. You don't need to get rid of any of them, and all of them can work towards your healing.

Tension, Stress and Trauma Release (TRE)

Developed by a doctor who noticed that children in bomb shelters shake like animals when they're scared but adults don't, this method takes the natural inclination to shake as a way to recover. Shaking, or vibrating if you prefer, soothes muscle tension and the nervous system as a whole (The Wellness Society, n.d.)[4]

However, a word of caution here: C-PTSD patients may feel retraumatized if they do too much too soon. Start with a minute or two, two or three times a week. Or better yet, find a certified practitioner by searching online.

If the first therapist that you see doesn't make you feel safe or comfortable with them after a few sessions (it may take you a while to trust them), feel free to search for another. And if a modality isn't working for you after several months and you don't see progress, you can discuss your expectations with the therapist. It does take time, so don't expect to be healed in a few sessions.

If you don't want to tell anyone because you're afraid of the stigma, that's OK. Just don't stop going or doing whatever "homework" your therapist may recommend. Your healing is the most important thing, not what anyone else thinks or says about it.

CHAPTER SUMMARY

While it's not the easiest journey, it is possible for a complex trauma survivor to regain control over their lives and begin to live the way that they prefer, without constant hyperarousal and fear around triggers.

- There are exercises that you can do to improve your self-perception and self-esteem, including positive affirmations, acting in a self-confident way even when you don't feel like

it, and making lists of the things that you like about yourself and have accomplished that you can refer to regularly.
- Practicing self-care in the form of getting enough sleep, eating well, staying hydrated, exercising, etc. won't heal you, but they will make it easier for you on your journey to recovery.
- Complex trauma often requires the help of a therapist to unlock healing, and there are several therapeutic techniques they may use including cognitive behavior therapy, EMDR, and internal family systems.

FINAL WORDS

While Complex Post-Traumatic Stress Disorder is not as well-known as PTSD itself, it has a significant impact on its sufferers. Survivors of complex trauma can go through the recovery process and begin to function more normally. However, they have to address the problem because it won't heal on its own or go away after a period of time.

There are a lot of situations in this book that you might relate to and lots of information, so don't worry if you feel a bit like you're drinking from a firehose. You can always go back and refresh yourself on the topics when questions come up. Healing from complex trauma isn't usually a linear process, where you start at one end and make steady gains every day or week until you reach functionality. You might make big gains and then end up walking them back a bit, before you make another leap.

First you discovered what trauma is: an event that affects the nervous system and prevents it from functioning properly. The brain essentially gets stuck in the fear response and can't return to normal. People respond to trauma in common ways, and PTSD won't be diagnosed unless the person has been suffering the same symptoms for over a month since the incident.

They must be re-experiencing the traumatic event, often as nightmares or flashbacks, and trying to avoid any reminders or triggers of the event, often going out of their way to do so. In addition, the person must be feeling like they're constantly under threat, which can be expressed through an excessive startle response or being constantly on edge.

Usually, trauma happens once and for a discrete period of time. For example, a car crash, a mugging, a sexual assault are all traumas that can lead to PTSD. However, the Complex form is characterized by repeated traumas over a period of time. For example, childhood abuse, domestic abuse, being a refugee, and living in a war-torn or otherwise violent and chaotic environment.

While the World Health Organization classifies it as a separate mental health condition, the US diagnostic tool known as the DSM-V considers it a DESNOS diagnosis - Disorders of Extreme Stress Not Otherwise Specified. As well as the regular PTSD symptoms, someone with the Complex form experiences *affect dysregulation*, or the inability to manage and control their emotions. They also have an extremely negative self-perception and have intense difficulties in their relationships with others.

C-PTSD shows up in people in a variety of ways, including physical symptoms such as pain, digestive disorders. People with the disorder often believe that they're alone in their misery and have feelings of guilt and shame. It's common for additional *comorbid* conditions like substance or sexual addiction to be present as well.

You also learned that the disorder stems from brain processes that have gone awry as a result of the trauma. Ordinarily, when the fight-or-flight reflex is activated, the person's systems return to baseline and the fear response is no longer activated. However, with complex trauma the brain doesn't receive the instructions to "stand down" and continues on as if the person is in immediate physical danger. It's not known yet what exactly causes C-PTSD in some people and not in others with similar experiences, but there are some underlying conditions that make the diagnosis more likely. Mood and personality disorders, anxious temperaments, and lifestyle factors like a lack of support may all contribute.

The book covered the specific symptoms of C-PTSD in detail, including affect dysregulation, avoidance, disturbance in interpersonal relationships, re-experiencing the trauma, and negative self-perception. Finally, in the last chapter you discovered suggestions and steps that you can take to help overcome the negative self-perception and take better care of yourself, as well as a summary of the psychological tools that a therapist can provide.

The most important thing I want you to take from this book is that you are worthy of recovering and that you can do it, as long as you tackle it. As someone who's been affected by C-PTSD, I know what it's like to feel shame about what happened and to be down on yourself for your supposed weakness. I say "supposed" because it takes a lot of strength to survive and keep going!

Even if you're not sure you're worth it right now, try to start your healing journey. It is possible, and you'll eventually get to the point where you can feel worthy of recovery. C-PTSD touches everyone in your life, not just you, and recovery benefits them as well. But primarily it's your journey, and you're the one who will heal and develop so that you can lead the life you want.

You've now got the tools from this book, and you can also seek out help to support you. Take action now so that you can have a life that doesn't revolve around avoiding triggers or upsetting emotional outbursts. Don't close this book and leave it on your shelf, digital or otherwise. Use what's in here to start and stay motivated as you make your way to recovery.

I want to make sure that everyone who could use this book knows it's here for them. If you found this book helpful, please leave a review on Amazon so that it can reach others.

NOTES

INTRODUCTION

1. https://www.therecoveryvillage.com/mental-health/ptsd/related/ptsd-statistics/

1. WHAT IS COMPLEX TRAUMA?

1. https://www.dictionary.com/browse/trauma?s=t
2. https://www.verywellmind.com/common-symptoms-after-a-traumatic-event-2797496
3. https://www.researchgate.net/publication/12554195_Posttraumatic_stress_disorder_The_burden_to_the_individual_and_to_society
4. https://apps.who.int/iris/bitstream/handle/10665/85623/9789241505932_eng.pdf;jsessionid=23D482DC7C709E883922871E785F4161?sequence=1
5. https://www.psychologytoday.com/us/blog/fostering-freedom/202005/revictimization-how-can-keep-happening

2. WHERE DOES C-PTSD COME FROM?

1. https://www.verywellmind.com/what-is-the-fight-or-flight-response-2795194
2. https://bigthink.com/experts-corner/decisions-are-emotional-not-logical-the-neuroscience-behind-decision-making
3. https://www.psychologytoday.com/us/blog/in-the-body/201910/when-trauma-gets-stuck-in-the-body
4. https://www.ncbi.nlm.nih.gov/pmc/articles/PMC2816923/
5. https://www.ncbi.nlm.nih.gov/pmc/articles/PMC4263906/
6. Ibid.
7. https://www.ncbi.nlm.nih.gov/pmc/articles/PMC3614697/
8. Ibid.
9. https://eating-disorders.org.uk/information/why-people-get-eating-disorders/

10. https://www.verywellmind.com/ptsd-causes-and-risk-factors-2797397

3. SYMPTOMS OF PTSD

1. https://www.talkspace.com/blog/happens-brain-ptsd-flashback-2/
2. https://www.ptsd.va.gov/understand/related/nightmares.asp
3. https://www.psychologytoday.com/us/blog/the-aftermath-trauma/201407/what-dreams-may-come-treating-the-nightmares-ptsd
4. https://www.whoop.com/thelocker/stages-of-sleep-cycles/
5. https://www.sciencedaily.com/releases/2017/11/171103085308.htm
6. https://www.bbc.com/future/article/20140728-why-is-all-the-news-bad
7. https://depts.washington.edu/psyclerk/glossary.html
8. https://www.militarytimes.com/pay-benefits/military-benefits/health-care/2015/03/30/depression-or-ptsd-can-cause-irritability/
9. https://www.verywellmind.com/sleep-problems-when-you-have-ptsd-2797478
10. CRF: corticotropin-releasing factor

4. AFFECT DYSREGULATION

1. https://psychcentral.com/blog/what-is-affect-or-emotion-dysregulation
2. https://traumaticstressinstitute.org/wp-content/files_mf/1276631745ShameandAttachment.pdf
3. https://www.nationaleatingdisorders.org/blog/eating-disorders-and-complex-post-traumatic-stress-disorder
4. https://www.ncbi.nlm.nih.gov/pmc/articles/PMC5902809/
5. https://www.goodtherapy.org/learn-about-therapy/issues/aggression-violence

5. NEGATIVE SELF-CONCEPT

1. https://www.simplypsychology.org/self-concept.html
2. Ibid.

6. DISTURBED INTERPERSONAL RELATIONSHIPS

1. https://www.psychologytoday.com/us/blog/vitality/201404/the-neuroscience-giving
2. https://www.simplypsychology.org/maslow.html
3. https://psychcentral.com/lib/c-ptsd-and-interpersonal-relationships
4. https://www.goodtherapy.org/blog/psychpedia/intimacy
5. https://www.brightquest.com/blog/complex-ptsd-and-romantic-relationships-healing-trauma-together-through-treatment/

7. RECOVERING AND RECLAIMING YOUR IDENTITY

1. https://www.fastcompany.com/90346545/this-is-a-visualization-exercise-that-actually-works-according-to-neuroscience
2. https://thewellnesssociety.org/healing-cptsd-the-ultimate-online-guide/
3. https://www.teamusa.org/usa-taekwondo/v2-getting-started-in-taekwondo/what-is-taekwondo
4. https://thewellnesssociety.org/healing-cptsd-the-ultimate-online-guide/

Made in the USA
Monee, IL
16 May 2023